The rough guide to

GREECE

=The=
rough
guides

Other available rough guides include
**YUGOSLAVIA, SPAIN, PORTUGAL, MOROCCO, TUNISIA,
AMSTERDAM & HOLLAND, MEXICO** and **PERU**.

Forthcoming:

**CRETE, FRANCE, EASTERN EUROPE, ISRAEL,
KENYA, CHINA, NEW YORK, PARIS** and
FLORENCE, TUSCANY & UMBRIA

Series Editor

MARK ELLINGHAM

The rough guide to

GREECE

Second edition completely revised and updated
Written and researched by

MARK ELLINGHAM, NATANIA JANSZ AND JOHN FISHER

With additional research and accounts by
Sarah Peel, Richard Hartle, Charlie Hebbert,
Graham Kenyon, Stephen Lees and Marc Dubin

Edited by
MARK ELLINGHAM

Routledge & Kegan Paul
London, Boston, Melbourne and Henley

Thanks for help, information and encouragement
on the first edition to Barbara Ellingham, Johnny
Sanderson (of 'Eclipse'), Jon and Jan Burt,
Rachel Priestman, Elli Georgiadou, Laura
Longrigg, Alasdair Palmer, Janis McKay, Mireille
Muller and Litza Jansz.

For this new revised edition Marc Dubin and
Stephen Lees have both contributed immense
amounts of knowledge; but above all we're really
grateful to the dozens of ˙**readers** who have sent
us new information, suggestions and corrections
– particularly, for some enlightening and detailed
accounts, Christine Calahan, Ron Murray, Anne
Dutech, Christopher Clarke and Andrew
Trumpington.

Keep 'em coming!

First published in 1982
second revised edition 1984, reprinted with further revisions 1985
by Routledge & Kegan Paul plc
14 Leicester Square, London WC2H 7PH
9 Park Street, Boston, Mass. 02108, USA
464 St Kilda Road, Melbourne,
Victoria 3004, Australia, and
Broadway House, Newtown Road,
Henley-on-Thames, Oxon RG9 1EN
Printed in Great Britain by
Cox & Wyman Ltd, Reading

Library of Congress Cataloging in Publication Data

Ellingham, Mark
The Rough Guide to Greece
Includes index.
1. Greece – Description and travel – 1981 – 1 – Guidebooks.
I. Jansz, Natania. II. Fisher, John. III. Title.
DF716.E44   914.95'0476   82–5321

ISBN 0–7102–0311–X

FREE MAPS AND INFORMATION

This book includes plans of Athens, Piraeus, Thessaloniki and other places where we think you'll need one. To keep the price down though we've tended to avoid duplicating maps which you can pick up for free from the **National Tourist Organisation of Greece** (NTOG, or 'EOT' in its Greek acronym). These include excellent cityplans of Volos, Kavala, Kerkira and Iraklion, and detailed maps of the ancient sites at Delphi and Olympia. Also available (but you have to ask) is a very well produced pamphlet of seven maps covering each region of Greece and the islands; this isn't as up to date as the Michelin map (best of the commercial ones) but it's adequate for most purposes.

All of these maps/plans can be picked up in the **NTOG offices** around Greece (in Athens the most central one is inside the National Bank in Sintagma Square) but supplies run out in midsummer and you'll do best to get them before you set out. There are NTOG offices in most major capitals; below are the principal addresses:

LONDON   195–197 Regent Street, W1 (734 5997).
NEW YORK   645 Fifth Avenue, Olympic Tower (421 5777).
LOS ANGELES   611 West Sixth Street (626 6696).
CHICAGO   168 North Michigan Avenue (728 1084).
MONTREAL   1223 de la Montagne (871 1535).
SYDNEY   51–57 Pitt Street (241 1663).
AMSTERDAM   Leidsestraat 13 (254 2123).
STOCKHOLM   Grev Turegatan 2, Box 5298, 10246 (211 113).

You'll find NTOG offices at all the main Greek towns and frontier posts, including Athens airport. Elsewhere in the country the local 'Tourist Police' double up as an information service – and in some towns they're even responsible for letting out rooms.

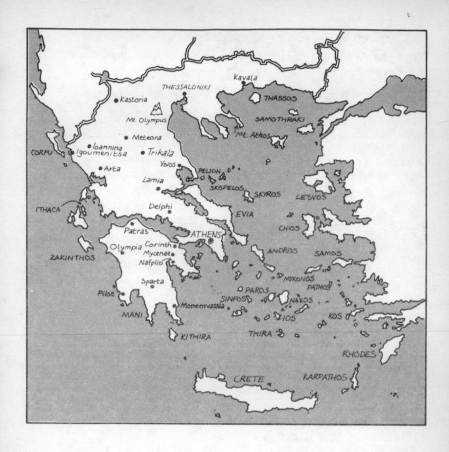

CONTENTS

Part one BASICS
1

Cost and time of year / Getting there / Rod tape and visas / Sleeping / Eating and drinking / Getting about / Sexual harassment / Feminismos / Health and insurance / Money / Phones, mail and poste restante / Sites and museums / Public holidays / Festivals / Culture / Finding work / Greek police and trouble / Other things /Greek terms: a glossary.

Part two MAINLAND
23

Part three THE ISLANDS
159

Part four CONTEXTS
273

This edition still dedicated to
allagi and a nuclear-free Greece,
with the removal of all
foreign military bases.

Part one
BASICS

CREEK
- TRAINS -

COST AND TIME OF YEAR

Greece is no longer a *really* cheap country – the days of four people renting a house for £10 a week are gone, even on the most remote islands, and EEC membership (since 1980) has brought the familiar pattern of spiralling food prices. Still, it remains a remarkably inexpensive place to stay in comparison with either Britain, the United States or Australia, and if you're willing to cut a few corners you can get by on very, very little. Needs are simple.

If you camp, hitch most of your transport and buy some of your own food in the shops it should be possible to manage on £4–£6 a day: whilst on £8–£12 a day you could actually be living very well. **Ferries** to the islands – the main extra expense – are still reasonable. A deck class ticket from Athens (Piraeus) to Chania on Crete will put you back under £8 for less than that there are dozens of other accessible islands. **Buses** and **trains** – the latter slightly cheaper – are also both extensive and cheap. Athens to Thessaloniki, probably the longest single journey you'd think of making, is only around £6 one way. A **room** for two, on most islands, haggles down to around £5 a night; **campsites** a little more than £1 a person. Or, like hundreds of other travellers, you can camp on your own near the beaches for free. A solid **taverna meal** even with considerable quantities of wine should rarely work out above £3 a head. It's with

these kind of limited budgets that the Rough Guide has been researched and written: with luck it'll help you stay in Greece a little longer as well as to reach some of the more offbeat parts of the country.

The best **time to come** is either late spring (April–mid-June) or autumn (September–October): spring best of all when the countryside's covered in a wealth of wild flowers and green unimaginable three months later. Most tourists come in July and August which are also the hottest months – Athens at this time of year is unbearably hot and stiflingly full, as are the boats and buses on all the main tourist routes. Also in August the Meltemi, or sirocco, wind blows across Crete and the Cyclades; although cooling it can become unpleasant, especially on Crete where it is often remorseless.

If you can only come in July or August you'll find Crete, Rhodes, Corfu and the more popular islands and resorts packed – you'd do better to try less well known islands (like Nissiros or Skyros, for example) and the cooler, less visited parts of the mainland (perhaps exploring western Greece instead of the Peloponnese). Where places differ radically in feel or climate depending on time of year the later sections point this out.

It's warm enough to swim (and to sleep out) in all but the most northerly or mountainous regions from May till

Average Temperatures (°C)

ATHENS	9.3	10.0	14.4	15.5	20.2	24.7	27.5	27.5	24.6	18.8	14.9	11.1
CORFU	10.0	10.4	12.1	15.3	19.6	24.0	26.7	26.6	22.9	18.8	15.0	11.7
CRETE	11.9	12.2	13.5	16.4	20.4	24.7	26.9	26.7	23.6	20.0	16.9	13.6
IOANNINA	5.2	6.3	9.0	13.0	17.5	22.2	25.5	25.0	20.6	15.3	10.4	6.7
KALAMATA	11.3	11.6	13.1	16.2	20.0	24.3	27.1	27.1	24.1	20.0	16.2	12.8
KAVALA	5.0	6.2	8.8	13.7	18.6	22.9	25.7	25.4	21.5	16.2	11.3	6.6
LESVOS	9.5	10.4	11.6	15.7	19.9	24.3	27.0	26.6	23.0	18.7	14.6	11.8
PAROS	11.5	12.0	13.2	16.4	20.2	24.0	25.6	25.6	22.9	19.4	16.7	13.7
RHODES	11.6	12.0	13.3	16.6	20.6	25.0	27.2	27.6	24.9	20.4	16.4	13.2
SAMOS	10.9	11.2	12.8	16.3	20.4	24.4	26.5	26.4	23.8	19.7	16.1	12.8
SKYROS	9.9	10.3	11.4	15.0	19.4	23.5	25.6	25.3	22.0	18.5	15.0	11.6
THASSOS	6.2	6.9	9.1	14.1	19.1	23.6	26.3	26.2	21.8	16.6	12.4	8.7
THESSALONIKI	5.0	6.5	9.4	14.4	19.9	24.2	26.6	26.3	21.7	16.0	11.5	7.1
ZAKINTHOS	11.4	11.5	13.2	16.0	19.8	24.0	27.8	27.1	24.2	20.2	16.5	13.1

To convert to **Farenheit**: Multiply by 9, divide by 5 and add 32. As a quick reference 6°C is 43°F, 12° – 54°, 20° – 68° and 25° – 77°.
Note, though, that these are all *average* temperature: Crete can hit the 30s (90–105°F) at midday in midsummer, Ioannina can literally freeze at night in early January.

October. In the hottest parts like Crete, Rhodes and the Dodecanese you can add to that March, April and early November — but even here it can get very cold in December or January whilst February, for most of the country, is a dismal month of wind and rain. Elsewhere in Greece March and April are also uncertain with warm, sunny days regularly interspersed with cold, windy weather.

Two other factors need to be considered with out of season travel: inter-island **ferry services** and closing **rooms**. Greek waters are none too predictable in either early spring or late autumn and intermittent storms can play havoc with boat schedules. Ferries (especially the smaller ones serving more remote islands) simply stop running at the first sign of bad weather: so be prepared to accept the fates. Services anyway are severely reduced outside the tourist season and in winter they reach an absolute nadir — islands served daily in summer may be reduced to a single weekly boat. Closing *rooms* are less of an off-season problem but can create extra expense. There's a general rule that privately let rooms (usually the cheapest island lodging) close down from November until the following Easter, leaving you dependent on the small hotels that stay open. Usually at least one will be happy to see any kind of winter guest and drop their normal rates but there will be times when you're stuck paying over the odds.

GETTING THERE

Flights from Britain

If you're planning to stay less than a month **charter flights** can actually be the cheapest form of travel to Greece; and sometimes they can even prove economic if you just use the outward flight — the more so if you manage to sell your return half in Athens (a practice that's officially illegal but much in evidence on the notice boards of youth and student hostels). Any number of travel agents have cheap, last-minute offers: for London flights you'll find the best selection of ads in the magazines *Time Out* and *LAM*, elsewhere check the travel pages at the back of the *Sunday Times*. Obviously the more flexible you can be on dates the better your chances of a rock-bottom deal: ring as many agents as you have patience for and aim at a return flight for around £75-£110. Just occasionally — if you're prepared to take a 'leaving tomorrow: 2 am, Luton' flight — you might even find something for half that figure.

One word of warning, however, about charter tickets: they must meet the peculiar conditions of Greek aviation law. This specifies that a ticket must be for no less than three days and no more than four weeks and must be accompanied by an accommodation voucher for the duration of your stay: check that your ticket satisfies these conditions or you could be refused entry. In practice the 'accommodation voucher' has become a formality — it has to name an existing hotel but you're not expected to use it (and probably won't be able to if you try).

Scheduled flights offer much more flexibility and there are occasionally some very good offers — especially for students. Olympic Airways have useful deals out of season, and Balkan and Kenyan Airways regularly offer cheap flights to anyone under 26.

Most frequent flights from London, and usually the cheapest, are of course to Athens, but you can also fly direct to Crete, Rhodes, Kos, Corfu and Salonika, and there are connecting flights (with Olympic) to Skiathos, Mykonos, Thira and numerous other destinations.

Flights from the USA and Australia

There are few direct flights to Athens from America's Pacific coast and those that there are fill way in advance. If you want to fly direct your best bet is likely to be from **New York** — quite a number of charters appear in the Sunday travel section of the *New York Times*.

On the whole, though, you'd be wise to accept the fact that bargain flights from the USA to Greece are not going to come your way and start by taking a standby to London. Other possible options, depending on what's currently on offer, are budget flights to Rome, Belgrade or Istanbul: all within easy train-ride distance of Hellas.

Australians, due to the number of Greeks who've adopted the country, may have better luck. There are affordable flights most weeks from both Sidney and Melbourne. Long-term travellers, however, are going first to want to cover some of the ground in between. This works out well: Athens is a prime destination on cheap flights from India, Sri Lanka, Nepal and Thailand. Aeroflot, Iraqi Air and Syria Air are among the lowest Asia–Greece operators: though US passport holders may find complications on the last two and they almost always turn into elaborate relay-flights! Australians transiting in London, incidentally, should be sure to check out the free weekly listings magazine *LAM* (London's Australasian Mag), a good source of both flights information and work ads.

Rail

If you're under 26, the cheapest return train ticket to Greece is an **Interail** Pass (around £120 from British Rail or any travel agent), valid for a month's free travel on all European railways. It's a very good deal if you're planning to visit several countries, but in Greece itself you won't get much mileage out of it since the railway network is slow and limited.

Alternatively, and again if you're under 26, you could get a **Eurotrain** or **Transalpino** ticket. These are slightly more expensive but they do allow you two months validity, and as many stops as you like along the way. Details and tickets are available from *USIT-Eurotrain* (London Student Travel, 52 Grosvenor Gardens, SW1, 01–730 8111; and other offices throughout Britain and Ireland) and *Transalpino* (Head office at 71–75 Buckingham Palace Road, London SW1, 01–834 9656; or from any travel agent). Standard rail tickets cost about 25 per cent more.

There are two basic routes to Athens, both of which take around three and a half days with the minimum of stops on the way. The cheaper one is London–Ostend–Munich–Belgrade–Athens but the last leg of this journey, through Yugoslavia, is usually pretty dreadful – crowded, hot and interminable. An alternative is to pay the additional £16 return and travel down through France and Italy, crossing over to Greece on one of the Italy–Greece ferries – it's well worth the extra money.

Coach

Unless you're lucky enough to get a rock-bottom flight, coaches are going to be your cheapest form of transport between London and Athens. Again you'll find the ads in the back of *Time Out* and the *Sunday Times* – but don't necessarily take the cheapest unless you've heard something about it, there've been a string of accidents in recent years with operators flouting the terms of their licence. The **Miracle Bus Company** (408 Strand, London WC2; tel. 01 379 6055) seem quite organised; **Supabus**, operated by National Bus and other international companies, are the most official and reliable though considerably more expensive.

The journey itself takes 3½ days with stops of about 20 minutes every five or six hours. You'll probably spend the first few days in Greece recovering from the ordeal but a bus will at least get you there for £35–£40 one way. Copious supplies of food and drink are advised – and no illegal substances, customs checks are often thorough.

Hitching or driving

It's about 1,900 miles from London to Athens and there are two routes you can take – overland via Yugoslavia, or down through Italy and across to Greece on the Brindisi ferries. There are arguments for both if you're hitching, but either way is liable to take a full week. On the whole it's better to set out from Ostend or the Hook of Holland – thereby bypassing French indifference to hikers.

The Yugoslavian route is a major European travel vein and if you're lucky you could get a ride from Ostend all the way to Greece. On the other hand, Yugoslavia is a bad place in which to run out of lifts: it has two main highways – the coast road which is beautiful but very slow, and the central route through Zagreb and Beograd which is fast, dull and accurately nicknamed 'the death road' for the number of heavy lorries which thunder down it. The drive through Italy, while perhaps slower, is rather more pleasant and Italian trains are cheap if you want a break from the road. Your main expense will be . . .

Italy–Greece Ferries

Regular ferries run from **Brindisi** in southern Italy to **Patras** (at the tip of the Peloponnese) or **Igoumenitsa** (the port for Epirus in western Greece); both sail via the island of **Corfu**, on which you can stop over at no extra charge if you get this specified on your ticket. It takes about 9 hrs from Brindisi to Corfu and from there it's 2 hrs more to Igoumenitsa, 10 hrs to Patras. The cost at peak season is around £27 to Corfu/Igoumenitsa or £32 to Patras though students can get a 20 per cent reduction on most of the lines. Small cars are charged about £30 and £32 respectively, motorbikes £18. Schedules of the various operators can be picked up in London at the Italian State Tourist Office (201 Regent Street, W1; tel. 01 439 2311); these also list local agents and if you're taking a car over in midseason it would be wise to book in advance.

Brindisi is a stridently unattractive town – and since almost all the ferries leave between 9 pm and 11 pm there's no great reason to get there too early in the day. Hustlers who greet you in the train station with the information that 'all boats except x lines are full' are likely to be a little over-alarmist: take your time and look around. In fact most lines charge about the same; the only one substantially cheaper is '**R-Line**', who run from April–October only from Otranto, 70 km downcoast; there's a microbus shuttle service from Brindisi which may be included in your fare. R-Line tickets are sold by a small agency 60 yards in front and to the left of the Brindisi train station.

One other marginally cheaper option is **Minoan Lines** ferry from **Ancona** which calls at both Igoumenitsa and Patras. This, however, runs just twice a week (currently Weds and Sats from Ancona; Mons and Thurs from Patras) so definitely book if you're taking a car across. Offices are in Athens at Leof. Vass. Konstantinou 2, and in Ancona at 4 Via XXIX Settembre; or tickets can be reserved by travel agents. Ferries also run to Corfu/Patras several times a week from Bari and once-weekly from Venice but these both work out much more expensive and if you find yourself this far up the Italian boot – or you're already in Yugoslavia – you might just as well take one of the **Jadrolinija Ferries** from Zadar or Rijeka down the Dalmatian coast to Corfu. These run once or twice a week – and are a much more interesting ride.

Most travellers tend to buy tickets from Brindisi the whole way through to **Patras** – admittedly a good bargain and useful starting point for getting to Olympia (connected by bus and train) and the great Peloponnesian sites. **Igoumenitsa**, however, is well worth considering. Although nothing much in itself, it's an excellent starting point for exploring western and central Greece. The route from here through the Pindus Mountains to Kalambaka and the Meteora is one of the most spectacular and beautiful in all Greece.

RED TAPE AND VISAS

British, Australian, New Zealand, Canadian and American nationals don't need visas for entry to Greece and can stay for up to three months. Canadians, Americans and those on Temporary British Passports will need visas to travel through Yugoslavia but these can be routinely obtained at frontier posts.

If you want to stay longer than three months you must apply for an extension to the Aliens Bureau in Athens (Halkondhili 9, off Kaningos Square; open 8 a.m.–1 p.m.) or, if you're away from the

capital, you can apply in person to the local police. It is advisable to apply a couple of weeks before your time runs out and also to keep all the pink bank slips confirming that you have changed foreign currency and can support yourself in Greece without working. It's also possible, although not strictly legal, to get round this law by leaving Greece for a couple of days every three months – thus bypassing the bureaucracy and living in the country for as long as you like on an ordinary visitor's stay.

SLEEPING

Hotels, hostels, rooms and roofspace
Hotels are categorised by the tourist police from 'Luxury' down to 'E' class and all except the top category have to keep within set price limits. Each room

must have its cost displayed on the door so there's no chance of being ripped off – though bear in mind that all charges are subject to local tax. 'D' and 'E' class hotels are usually very reasonable (costing around £4–£7 for a double room, £3–£5 for a single) although, since the categories depend partly on location, those in Athens are well below par. If you want a roof over your head travelling about the mainland you're generally going to have to depend on these small hotels.

On the islands – and to some extent elsewhere – the places to go for are '**rooms**' (*dhomatia*), which once again are officially controlled and divided into three classes ('A' down to 'C'). These are usually a fair deal cheaper, spotlessly clean and much more congenial. These days the bulk of them are in new purpose-built blocks but some are still let out in people's homes – where you'll often be treated with disarming hospitality. How do you find them? On the islands, as often as not, they find you: owners descending on ferry arrivals just as soon as they dock. Outside the port-villages they'll usually be prominently advertised in at least two languages – usually English and German – or you can ask at the local taverna, there'll usually be someone who will escort you to a place. Just occasionally, though, you come on an incredibly officiously-run system where all rooms are let out by (and only by) the tourist police: this in itself *can* be useful but there are times and places where they'll refuse to let out any *dhomatia* until all the hotels are full, an infuriating business. In **winter** – designated to begin 1 November and close either just before or just after Easter – 'rooms' are closed pretty much across the board to keep the hotels in business. There's no point in traipsing about hoping to find exceptions – most 'rooms' owners obey the system very strictly and if they don't they'll find you themselves and, watching out for hotel rivals, guide you back to their place!

Greece is not exactly packed with **youth hostels** (*ksenon neotitos*) but those that there are tend to be fairly easy-going affairs: slightly run-down and a far cry from the harsh institutions you find in England or Germany. Very few of them ever ask for a youth hostel card and if they do you can usually buy one on the spot – or maybe just pay a little extra for your bed. Charges are around £1.50 (200 drx) a night. The only annoying factor is a curfew, most often around 11.30–12 p.m. but occasionally as early as 10 p.m. but this is usually offset by the company of fellow travellers – the

hostels simply turning into a kind of members-club. They can be a good source of up-to-date information and are sometimes handy for finding work, farmers marching down to the rural ones at harvest time to pick up casual labour. Hostels on the mainland are at Athens (3), Nafplio, Mycenae, Olympia, Patras, Delphi, Litohoron (Mt Olympus) and Thessaloniki. On the islands you'll find them only on Corfu (2), Thira and Crete (where there are 7: at Iraklion, Mallia, Ierapetra, Rethimnon, Chania, Sitia and Mirthios).

In Athens there are also cheap dormitory-style '**Student Houses**', hostels which despite their name are in no way limited to students. These – and sometimes rural/island *tavernas* – will also often let you '**roofspace**', usually providing a mattress for you to lay a sleeping bag down on. If any place seems full it's worth asking about this, it can be a cheap and preferably uncramped alternative.

Houses or **flats** can also sometimes be rented by the week or month: well worth considering if you've two or three people to share costs and want to drop roots on an island for a while. Find a place you want to stay, get yourself known around the village and ask about: you might still pick up some fairly wonderful deals.

Greek **monasteries** have a tradition of putting up travellers (of the correct respective sex) but this was abused through the late 1960s–early 1970s and has sadly become much less frequent. It is still customary practice in remote areas – and, for men, on Mount Athos – but you should always ask locally before heading out to one for the night. Dress modestly – shorts are total anathema – and try to arrive early evening, not later than 8 p.m.

Camping: offsite and on
'**Freelance camping**' – outside authorised campsites – is such an accepted part of Greek travel that few people realise it's officially forbidden. There's been a law, though, since 1977 and once in a while it gets enforced – which simply means you should exercise a reasonable degree of sensitivity and discretion. Obviously the police crack down on people camping rough (and littering) on popular mainstream tourist beaches, especially when a large community of

campers is developing, but elsewhere nobody is really bothered. It's actually warm enough to sleep out in just a sleeping bag from May until early September so you don't even need to drag round a tent. A waterproof bag (a 'Bivibag' available from camping shops) or groundsheet is, however, useful to keep out the late summer damp: so too is a foampad, which lets you sleep in relative comfort almost anywhere. You will always need a sleeping bag since even in midsummer the nights get cool but this can be as lightweight as you can find; ultra-light 'Moonbags' (around £10 from camping shops) are quite adequate for Greece.

Official campsites range from ramshackle compounds on the islands to highly organised – and rather soulless – NTOG affairs. Cheap, casual places can be worth using for convenience sake, rarely costing much above £1 a night per person; at the larger sites, though, it's not impossible for two of you and one tent (all separately charged) to come to the price of a basic room.

As a general rule you don't have to worry about leaving tents or **baggage** unattended; the Greeks are one of the most honest races in Europe. The main risk, sadly, comes from other campers and every year a few sleeping bags seem to go this way: you might find it useful to camp close by a *taverna*, if you eat there regularly they'll often keep your pack and let you take showers, etc.

Obviously if you're going to Greece as part of a longer trip you'll need a rucksack but if you're only travelling for a month or so it's worth thinking about using one of the light nylon holdall bags that have been flooding the shops for the last few years; they're large enough to take a 'Moonbag' and adequate clothes. I've found they are less restrictive, much easier to take on buses (rucksacks often have to be tied on to the roof), far less of a problem when hitching, and also create a surprisingly useful aura of respectability – packs often lead to unfortunate assumptions from people and authority ('you have little money and we don't want you . . .') which it's good to avoid.

EATING AND DRINKING

You can get a meal at either an *estiatorio*, a *taverna* or a *psistaria*. Distinctions between the first two are blurred but *tavernas* tend to be cheaper and simpler, perhaps more 'Greek'. *Psistarias* are restaurants that specialise in fresh prepared plates – predominantly grilled meat but often good vegetables too. They're always worth looking out for, as are *tis ores* (grill-to-order) *tavernas*; both are often quite cheap since you're not paying for the oven to stay on heating one or two pans of food.

Often at *tavernas* and *estiatoria* there are no menus and you're taken into the kitchen to inspect what's on offer. This is a good time to fix on prices, too, since they always seem to turn out higher if you wait until after you've eaten. In more touristic places there'll be a menu in Greek and English – a sure sign that you're in the wrong eatery! – in which case you'll be paying the right hand (higher) set of prices plus an ingenious selection of taxes to suit all occasions (holidays, Easter, Sundays, etc.): budget on such extras.

A typical Greek **meal** consists of a starter and main course (only the tourist restaurants serve sweets though some have fresh yoghourt) and these will often be served at the same time – if you want the main course later don't order it for a while! The main course of meat or fish comes on its own except for maybe a piece of lemon or half a dozen chips; salads and vegetables are served as separate dishes and usually shared. Vegetable dishes (often cooked in a tomato sauce) can be very good in themselves and if you order a few of these between several people they can make a satisfying meal for well under £1 each. Some of them, like the tomatoes, peppers or aubergines stuffed with rice and mince (*yemistés*) are basically a main course. And if you're really pushed for money you can always fall back on pastas – macaroni pie (*makarónia*) and spaghetti are usually available – or, better by far, bean soup which is really filling and can be delicious.

Wine (*krasi*) is usually *retsina* and served from the barrel in quarter, half or kilo metal jars; this resinated wine is an acquired taste but once you have it you'll start finding some local varieties are extremely good. Actual bottled wine is always more expensive and with retsina it's usually not so good. If you ask for unresinated wine (*aretsinoto*) you're likely to be offered either *Demestica* or *Amalia*; the latter is much the best but a far superior wine is *Boutari*, from the region of Naoussa in Macedonia. Retsina should never really be drunk outside Greece (you need the climate and, above all, an abundant barrel) but if you

Soups, dips, salads and vegetables

Avgolómono	Egg-lemon soup	Dolmádhes	Stuffed vine/cabbage leaves
Fakés	Lentil soup		
Fasoláda	Bean soup	Piperiés	Peppers
Táramasalata	Fish roe pate	Domátes	Tomatoes
Tsatsíki	Yoghourt/cucumber dip	Fasolákia	String beans
Melitzánasalata	Eggplant dip	Anginária	Artichokes (spring)
Horiátiki	'Greek' salad (with olives, feta, etc.)	Gigántes	Broad beans
		Melitzánes	Eggplant (often fried)
Hórta	Spring greens	Kolokithákia	Zucchini/marrows
Rizospanáki	Rice-spinach mix	Maróuli	Shredded lettuce

Meat and meat-based dishes

Moussáka	Eggplant/mince dish	Keftédhes	Meatballs in sauce
Stifádho	Meat/tomato stew	Biftéki	Burgers
Pastítsio	Noodles and meat	Kotópoulo	Chicken
Paidhákia	Lamb chops	Kokorétsi	Liver/offal kebab
Brizóla	Pork chop	Kohlióudhes	Garden snails

Fish and seafood

Ktapódhi	Octopus	Barbóuni	Mullet
Kalamária/ Soúpiez	Squid	Gópes	A cheap fish!
Kalamarákia	Baby squid	Péstrofa	Trout
Glóssa	Sole	Psária	Any fish

Sweets and fruit

Baklává	Honey/nuts pastry	Fraóules	Strawberries
Kataífi	Honey/nuts shreddie	Míla	Apples
Rizógalo	Rice pudding	Portokália	Oranges
Galaktobóuriko	Custard pie	Stafília	Grapes
Pagotá	Ice cream	Sika	(Dried) Figs
Fistíkia	Pistachio nuts	Kasséri	Hard cheese
Pastéli	Sesame bar	Týri	Any cheese

Basics and drinks

Neró	Water	Boukáli	Bottle
Psomí	Bread	Potíri	Glass
Sitaréno psomí	Wholemeal bread	Me to kjlo	House wine
Aláti	Salt	Mávro/Áspro	Red/White
Méli	Honey	Bíra	Beer
Avghes	Eggs	Tsai	Tea
(Horís) ladhi	(Without) oil	Gálakakáo	Choco-milk
Katálogo/lísta	Menu	Portokaláta	Orangeade
To logaríasmo	The bill	Stiniyássas!	Cheers
		Mas leépa . . .	We're missing . . .

want a really good wine to take back get a bottle of *Special Reserve Boutari* – they come in numbered bottles and are sold in the duty free shops for about £2.50.

For ordinary drinking you go to a **kafeneion** – simple places filled with old men arguing and playing *tavli* (backgammon). They start the day selling coffee (*kafé*) until this is gradually replaced by *ouzo* (an aniseed-flavoured spirit, drunk neat or mixed with water) and, later still, brandy (which is usually *Metaxa* or *Botrys* and graded with 3, 5 or 7 stars). Coffee is 'Greek' (like Turkish coffee) and is usually very sweet – if you want less sugar ask for *metrio* and if none at all *sketto*; ordinary coffee is also available now in most of Greece – ask for 'Nescafé', which is what it generally is. Ouzo is often served with small snacks (*mezes*), perhaps to dilute its strength. Incidentally one of the best ways to idle away hours at a *kafeneion* is to play *tavli* – the Greeks are addicts for the game and most places will lend you a set if you ask; occasionally there's a small charge.

For breakfast you can usually persuade a *taverna* to serve you some bread and jam or maybe an omelette but it's far more enjoyable, if you're in a place of any size, to go along to a **zakoroplásteia**, or patisserie, where you can get a delicious range of cakes and pastries. They are usually inexpensive and make a magnificent feast washed down with coffee and water or lemonade. My own favourite are *loukoumadhes*, light puffs of dough sprink'ed with cinnamon.

You can save money if you buy some of your **own food** for meals – bread,

cheese, salami, olives and tomatoes are always easy to buy. Remember that Greek cheese isn't all *feta* (strong white goat's cheese) and, if you ask, there are some remarkably tasty local varieties. Picnic meals can also be enlivened by trying some of the tinned foods around – ranging from stuffed vineleaves (*dolmadhes*) to baby squid (*kalamarákia*). There's cheap fruit about throughout the summer amongst which *karpoussi* (water melons) are often good value – they are frequently sold from the back of a van by itinerant *manave* travelling around country regions. Don't forget, also, that Greece is the home of the pistachio nut and that in late summer there are figs and cactus fruit around.

Almost anywhere in Greece it's possible to get *souvlaki* – small kebabs served with a hunk of bread; add a salad and you've got a fair-sized lunch. Other **snacks** you'll find in towns include pies filled with feta cheese (*tiropita*), with spinach (*spanakopita*) and sometimes sausage (*louhanikapita*). These, along with the doner-kebab type *pita-souvlaki* (far superior to any you'll find outside Greece), are all cheap, useful substitutes for a meal. Snacks are best and most varied in Athens; elsewhere, bus or train stations are often good territory – but around them, not inside where the food is usually poor and overpriced.

On p. 9, as a general guide, is a list of *food and dishes*: it must be stressed, though, that this is in no way comprehensive and you'll always do best by following local preferences. On no account leave Greece without sampling vast quantities of yoghourt (*yiaourti*), beyond a doubt the finest in the world.

GETTING ABOUT

Buses and trains

Buses are really the standard form of transport in Greece – you can go virtually everywhere on them and, since everybody seems to get on, they're the most interesting way to travel. The main routes are served by good air-conditioned buses which are invariably faster than the trains whilst, off the major roads, local buses serve nearly every town or village. On the more out of the way routes don't expect buses to run throughout the day – small villages are

often connected only by school or market buses which go early in the morning and return around midday.

A few major routes are served by buses operated by OSE, the State Railway Organisation, and these always leave from the railway stations. Most, however, are privately run by a syndicate of companies known as KTEL; remember that even in modest-sized towns there can be four or five companies operating different services – so always ask for the bus station that serves a specific location as the independent bus terminals are spread throughout the town.

The Greek **railway** network is neither extensive nor efficient and you're unlikely to get a seat on any of the main routes in or out of season; it is, however, marginally cheaper than going by bus. Obviously if you've got either Eurail or Interail passes you'll want to make use of them as much as possible but don't feel tied to train travel – buses are cheap enough radically to expand your route beyond a rather dull circuit (inevitably so since the mountainous and more beautiful parts of Greece pose obvious difficulties for railway lines). One terrific exception to this is the narrow-gauge Kalavrita railway – see p. 89.) You'll find that you have to pay a small surcharge for express trains but this is well worth doing – they knock hours off a journey and often have four carriages instead of three.

Hitching

Hitching is fine in Greece as long as you're not too bothered by time: lifts are fairly frequent but tend to be short. Most important it's also one of the safer countries for women travellers, though as ever you find a great deal of confidence in numbers (see also the following section).

Still it can be done and may even prove the quickest form of travel if you want to take an unusual route which would otherwise involve a string of bus connections. At its best it's a wonderful way to get to know the country – there's no finer way to take in the Peloponnese than from the back of a truck which looks converted from a lawnmower – and a useful means of picking up some Greek. Whilst you'll often get lifts from Greeks eager to display or practise their English there'll be as many where to communicate you're forced to try the language. As it can be all too easy to stay in Greece without picking up more than restaurant talk, this is one way of breaking out!

If you're a believer in hitching-signs, master the alphabet and write them in Greek: this can create immediate goodwill and curiosity.

Driving and car hire

Cars have obvious advantages for getting to the more inaccessible parts of mainland Greece but if you're thinking of **renting** one bear in mind that this is probably the most expensive country in Europe to do so – upwards of £110 a week before you begin to think about petrol. It's also a deceptively easy way to cut yourself off from the country and people, turning your entire travels into Michelin-style sights and stops.

If you do try it you'll need International Third Party Insurance (Green Card) whether you're driving your own car or hiring one. The cover given by some rental companies isn't comprehensive so check the small print pretty scrupulously. When **driving** remember that Greece has the highest accident rate in Europe after Portugal and that many of the roads, particularly if you're unfamiliar with them, are quite perilous. Tarmac can turn into a dirt track without warning on the smaller routes and railway crossings are very rarely guarded. If you are involved in any kind of accident it's an offence to drive away and you can be held at a police station for up to 24 hrs. Often the talk will be out of all proportion to the incident – but if it is serious ring your consul immediately in order to get a lawyer, you have this right. Don't make a statement to anyone who doesn't speak – and write – very good English.

Tourists with AA or similar membership are given free **road assistance** from ELPA, the Greek equivalent, who run breakdown services centred on Athens, Patras, Larissa and Thessaloniki. Their 'guidance service' number is 174. In an **emergency** ring the tourist police on 104, anywhere in the country.

Motorbikes, mopeds and bicycles

These are available for hire on many of the islands and in a few of the popular mainland resorts. Mopeds cost upwards of £4 a day and bicycles around £1.50 but out of peak season these prices can be reduced by concerted bargaining. **Mopeds** are perfect for the islands since on most you literally can get everywhere – make sure you check them thoroughly before riding off, however, since many are only cosmetically repaired and if you break down it's your responsibility to return the machine. It's also worth taking the phone number of whoever hires them to you in case they do give out miles from anywhere. There are a steady number of accidents each year so you really should take care; it's very easy to come to grief on a dirt track and in addition to your own injuries you're likely to be charged a criminally high price for any repairs needed for the bike.

Sometimes it's possible to hire motor-bikes too, but you're usually required to show some kind of provisional licence; they cost upwards of £7 a day.

Few people seem to **cycle** in Greece but it isn't actually such hard going as you might imagine – I've met a number of people who have cycled enjoyably and extensively in what I'd have considered quite unsuitably mountainous areas. It's worth considering taking your bike down to Greece by train and setting out. You should be able to take it for free on most of the ferries, or alternatively you can hire a bone-breaking old model on many of the larger islands.

Ferries and flights

For information on **island ferries** see the introduction printed at the beginning of the island section (page 161) and the travel details at the end of each chapter. On the **mainland** the only boats you might want to use are those round the coast of the eastern Peloponnese: from Athens and the Saronic islands down to Monemvassia. Details of these are given on page 90.

One general point does seem worth stressing here, though. *Never* buy tickets far in advance for inter-island ferries. These are totally unchangeable, limiting you to one particular boat at one particular time – if it doesn't turn up and/or you change your plans you're stuck. Only on about three days of the year – last day of Easter, 25 March and 15 August – do ferries ever leave completely full. And despite what an island travel agent might tell you, you can always buy a ticket on board.

Olympic Airways operate all domestic **flights** within Greece and you can pick up a schedule from almost any NTOG office. Prices usually work out around two and a half times the cost of an equivalent bus or ferry journey but on a few long island hauls (Athens to Lesvos or Karpathos for example) you might consider this time well bought. In contrast to the ferries Olympic's island-flights are often full in midseason: if you have a tight schedule, and above all if the weather's looking uncertain for ferries, book well in advance.

Hiking

Locally produced island **maps** should always be read with a certain irony. The only really reliable ordnance-type maps are the 1:250,000 sheets available from the Athens Statistical Service at Likourgou 14 (one block from Omonia Square). Take your passport along if you want to buy any – and start learning the alphabet, all place names are printed only in Greek.

Intent hikers might also be interested in Marc Dubin's book 'Back-packer's Greece', detailed in the books section in Part Four.

SEXUAL HARASSMENT

Many women travel about Greece on their own without feeling intimidated nor constantly harassed – but some undoubtedly are. This has little to do with the way we each look or behave, and only indirectly relates to the way Greek women themselves are treated. What is important is that different assumptions are made about you as a foreign woman depending on where you are.

In most of the **rural areas** – which are still essentially Greek – you'll be treated first and foremost as a *xenos*, a word which means both stranger and guest, in much the same way as a foreign man. You can sit and drink ouzo in the exclusively male *kafeneia* (there's often nowhere else) without always suspecting the hospitality and friendliness that's offered.

In the *large resorts* and in *cities* where tourism has for a long time determined the local culture – parts of Crete, Rhodes (notoriously), most of the Argo-Saronics, and of course Athens – things are very different. Here you get foisted with the myths and fantasies of the 'liberated' and 'available' woman: not perhaps to the extent of other Mediterranean countries but it is oppressive and without a good control of the language can be hard to deal with. Words worth remembering for an unambiguous response are *stamata* (stop it) and *fiyeteh* (go away).

It takes no more confidence to **hitch** than in Britain or the States though on long rides the language barrier can add to the strain. In some remote areas and islands, with just a daily bus, there really isn't that much choice, but here the vil-

lagers themselves often hitch local farm trucks and the lifts anyway tend to be short. *Afistemeh* means 'let me off'.

FEMINISMOS

Full franchise, a vote for all women, wasn't achieved in Greece until 1956, and up to two years ago adultery was still a punishable offence with cases regularly brought to court. The Greek Women's Movement has a long tradition but in recent years it has conspicuously emerged, with an impact that is beginning to spread outside the main cities. Sexual equality was one of the election issues that brought PASOK to power in 1981 and though commitment to radical change will take time to assess they seem to be making political space for the issues.

As a first move the socialist government has set up a Committee on Women's Rights to reform family law and to improve child care and family planning facilities, with an administrative body (the Council of Equality) to respond to discrimination. There is currently no sex education in schools and contraception is not available as part of the skeletal Greek public health service. Women have had to rely on abortions: illegal, dangerous and expensive but they run to an estimated 350,000 a year.

Other women's groups, which have mushroomed under the changing political climate, concentrate on setting up advice and support networks, and agitating in the workplace, within the unions and for changes in media representation. None of this is easy in a country as polarised as Greece. There are still isolated rural areas where women are defined by traditions which deny them either property rights or access to an independent living. For these women even to sit in a *kafeneion* would itself be a political act.

If you're interested in making contact, groups' addresses include:

The Multinational Women's Liberation Group of Athens Produces an English language newsletter, *OUT*, and meets every Wednesday at 8.30 p.m. at THE WOMAN'S HOUSE (Romanou Melodou 4, Lykavitos, Athens; tel. 281 4823). This building, which operates a bar on Tuesday and Thursday nights (and where the Autonomous Group of Gay Women also meet), isn't labelled: it's on the side road off Dafnomili Street, the second building on the right, up two flights of stairs. Most groups here and around the country suspend their activities through the month of August.

Greek Women's Liberation Movement Tsimiski 39, Athens.

Massalias The Athens feminist bookshop at Sina 38.

Shic Piano bar/feminist meeting place at Layamarguerita 5, Thessaloniki.

Federation of Greek Women (Omospondia Gynaekon Elladas) Focuses on women at work, unequal pay and job discrimination; active in organising Women's Peace Movement. Many branches include Akademias 52, Athens (tel. 361 5565).

Movement of Democratic Women (Kinisi Demokratikon Gynaekon) Interested in family law and sexual liberation. Athens branch at Genadiou 5 (tel. 363 0661).

Union of Greek Women (Enosis Gynaekon Elladas) Emphasis on problems of peasant women and Mediterannean women in general and responsible for forming the Council of Equality. Branches in all the major towns – in Athens at Enianon 8 (tel. 823 4937).

HEALTH AND INSURANCE

There are no required **innoculations** for Greece, though like all southern countries it's wise to have an up to date typhoid–cholera booster – and essential if you plan to travel onwards to Turkey or Egypt.

If you do need medical care you're going to have to pay quite heavily for it – so **travel insurance** is a sound investment. You can get comprehensive cover (which includes loss/theft of baggage) for around £10 a month from most

British banks or travel agents. If you need to claim be sure to keep all receipts, including those from the pharmacy. For claims on stolen items you need to get the loss registered at the local police station. This can be a tricky business as many officials simply won't accept that anything could be stolen on their patch, or at least don't want to take responsibility for it; be persistent — I heard of someone losing a camera on Crete and finally, four islands later, getting the theft registered for Kos!

For serious **medical attention** ring either the tourist police (104) or your own consulate: one or other of these should be able to recommend an English-speaking doctor or hospital. If you are in Athens you'll also find adverts for private doctors, dentists and gynaecologists in the English-language daily *Athens News*. With **minor complaints** you'll just need a *farmakia* (chemist). Greek pharmacists are highly trained and dispense a number of medicines which in Britain could only be prescribed by a doctor. In the larger towns there'll usually be one who speaks good English.

British and other EEC nationals are officially entitled to **free medical care** in Greece — but this means admittance to only the lowest grade of state hospital. Treatment should be fine but nursing will be virtually non-existent; Greek families take in food and bedding for relatives so as a tourist you'll find difficulties. Rather better are the ordinary state out-patient clinics attached to most hospitals — these operate on a first come-first served basis so go early, usual hours are 8 a.m.–noon. To qualify for any free treatment you'll need to produce Form E111, available from any DHSS office: without this out-patient clinics make a small charge.

Homeopathic drugs can be obtained in Athens at the Marinopoulis pharmacy in Kanari Street (Kolonaki district); they will also be able to give you the address of a homeopathic doctor.

MONEY

Travellers' cheques are accepted at all Greek banks and when they're closed at quite a number of hotels, agencies and tourist shops. On the islands though you should plan to have a fair amount of currency to hand: there are often only banks in the main port or town and on the most remote you won't find any at all.

One useful solution — and on big resort islands a considerable timesaver — is a post office **giro account**. Almost any post office will be able to draw money out for you and you'll bypass the bank cheque queues.

Banks are normally open from 8 a.m.–2 p.m. Monday–Friday; occasionally for an hour in the evening also. Bigger branches in Athens (like the National Bank in Sintagma Square) stay open until 8 p.m. for currency exchange. If you have a VISA card make for a branch of the Emboriki Trapeza (Commercial Bank); branches of the Ethniki Trapeze (National Bank) handle Mastercard advances and are also the best bet for getting money cabled out to you — there is one in every town. **American Express** have offices in Athens (Sintagma square/corner of Ermou), Thessaloniki (Venizelou 10), Corfu Town (Capodistria 42 Kerkyra), Rhodos Town (Vass. Sofias 41) and Iraklion, Crete (Augostou 25).

PHONES, MAIL AND POSTE RESTANTE

Local phone calls are very cheap and can be made from either telephone boxes or *periptero*, the miscellaneous provisions kiosks that you find in all Greek towns. At boxes you pick up the receiver, put the money in and dial; at *periptero* you ask for the phone and pay once you've made a call — most have a meter. **International calls** can also be made from the orange-coloured kiosks but you'll usually find it easier to go through the local OTE ('oteh') telephone office. These generally keep hours from around 6 a.m.–midnight and in the bigger cities there'll be at least one OTE branch open 24 hrs a day. To call Britain dial 0044 and then the number you want with its usual town code minus the initial '0'. You should pause between dialling the international and town codes: if you don't get a fast bleeping tone (all lines engaged) then go ahead.

Air mail **letters** take around 5–8 days to Europe, 8–10 to the States or Australia; postcards are a little slower and a couple of drachmas cheaper. You can buy stamps at *peripteros* (plus 10 per cent commission) or post offices (*tahidhromío*; open 7.30 a.m.–8 p.m.). Mail can be sent to you **poste restante** at any post office in Greece – just have it addressed 'Central Post Office . . .' and any fair-sized town. With islands always use the main town-capital; in Athens the most convenient and officially the main office is at Eolou 100, just off Omonia Square. If you use their cheques you can also have mail sent to American Express: see 'Money', above, for addresses of their offices.

SITES AND MUSEUMS

All the major ancient sites are now fenced off and, like museums, charge admission. This ranges from around 25–150 drx but with a **student** or FIYTO youth card (see p. 20) you can get up to 75 per cent reductions. Current students of archaeology, classics or history of art can also get a completely free admission permit by writing (well in advance) to the Ministry of Science and Culture (Museums Section), Aristídou 14, Athens. On **Sundays** – and at some sites Thursday, too – admission is free for all.

Opening hours vary from site to site so we've detailed individual times in the text of the guide: these are all summer hours, which operate from around April to the end of September. In winter most of the major sites open 9 a.m.–4 p.m. (weekdays) and 10 a.m.–4 p.m. (Sundays), the smaller ones from 10 a.m.–4 p.m. and 10 a.m.–2.30 p.m. Bear in mind also that the majority of smaller and provincial sites and museums close in summer for a long lunch and sometimes, due to staffing problems, don't open again until the next morning. This is a widespread problem at the moment with even sites like Knossos on Crete shutting down at 2.30 p.m. or so.

Some museums won't allow entry if you're wearing shorts and this is also, of course, the case for visiting **monasteries**. Most monasteries, additionally, require women to cover their arms and many (including those of the Meteora) also to wear skirts. With a few exceptions – most obviously the Mount Athos peninsula – monasteries allow both men and women to visit their chapels (*katholikon*) and perhaps a couple of other buildings. Many these days, however, have imposed visiting hours – usually from around 8 a.m.–noon and 4 p.m.–6 p.m.

PUBLIC HOLIDAYS

Museums, banks, post offices and tourist offices all close down for a vast range of public holidays and festivals: archaeological sites tend to close too, or just open for a couple of hours in the morning. Keep note of the following which can blow the best-laid plans: 1 January; 25 March; Good Friday and Easter Sunday (according to the Orthodox calendar, see below); 1 May; 15 August; 28 October; and 25 December. On top of these there are also local festival-holidays, the most important of which are mentioned in the text of the guide.

FESTIVALS

Many of the big Greek popular festivals have a religious base so they're observed in accordance with the Orthodox Calendar: this means that **Easter**, for example, can be one, four or five weeks later than we celebrate it. It is also by far the most important festival of the Greek year – infinitely more so than Christmas – and taken much more seriously than anywhere in the west; from Wednesday of Holy Week, the whole radio and TV networks are given over solely to religious programmes until the following Monday. It is an excellent time to be in Greece, both for the beautiful and moving religious ceremonies and for the days of feasting and celebration which follow. The mountainous island of Hydra with its 360 churches and monasteries is the prime Easter resort but unless you're organised well in advance you have no hope of finding accommodation there. Probably the best plan is to make for a medium-sized village where, on the whole, you'll be accepted into the community's celebration.

The first great ceremony takes place on **Good Friday** evening as the Descent from the Cross is lamented in church. At dusk the *Epitafion*, Christ's funeral bier, leaves the sanctuary and is paraded solemnly through the streets; in many places, Crete especially, this is accompanied by the burning of effigies of Judas Iscariot.

Late **Saturday** evening sees the climax in a majestic *Anestisi* mass to celebrate Christ's triumphant return. At the stroke of midnight all lights in each crowded church are extinguished and the congregation plunged into the darkness which envelopes Christ as He passes through the underworld. Then there's a faint glimmer of light behind the altar screen before the priest appears, holding aloft a lighted taper and chanting 'Avto to fos . . .', (This is the Light of the World). Stepping down to the level of the parishioners he touches his flame to the unlit candle of the nearest worshipper – intoning 'Devthe, levethe fos' (Come, take the light) to be greeted by the response 'Hristos Anesti' (Christ is risen). And so it goes round, this affirmation of the miracle, until the entire church is ablaze with burning candles.

Even solidly rational atheists are likely to find this somewhat moving: the traditional greeting, as firecrackers explode all around you in the streets, is 'Hronia Polla' (Many Years).

Other important festivals include:

Pre-Lenten carnivals These span three weeks, climaxing over the seventh weekend before Easter. Patras Carnival, with a chariot parade, is the most famous. More interesting are the *boules* or masques, which take place around Macedonia (particularly at Naoussa) and on Skyros. Athenians traditionally celebrate by going round hitting each other on the head with plastic hammers; a source of real street-gang brawls a few years back!

Independence Day (25 March) Parades and dancing to celebrate the beginning of the revolt against Turkish rule in 1821. Major festivities on Tinos island and at Olimpos on Karpathos, among many others.

Agios Georgios (23 April) St George is patron of shepherds so there are big rural celebrations: Arachova, near Delphi, has dancing and feasting.

May Day The great urban holiday – most people make for the countryside.

Agios Ioannis (24 June) St John the Baptist's feast – a thinly disguised summer solstice with giant bonfires in the streets.

Profitis Ilias (20 July) Festivals in honour of the Prophet Elijah, displacer of Apollo on Greek peaks, take place in mountain areas. The most famous is at Mount Taygetus, near Sparti.

Assumption of the Virgin (15 August) Great pilgrimage to Tinos and widespread festivals, particularly on Paros and around the Cyclades.

Ohi Day (28 October) Lively national holiday celebrating the cable – 'Ohi', or 'No' – replying to Mussolini's invasion ultimatum of 1940.

On top of all these there are literally scores of local festivals, or **panayiria**, celebrating the patron saint of the village church: and with some 330-odd possible name saints' days you're unlikely to travel round Greece for long without stumbling on something! A good source of information if you want to deliberately coincide is the monthly *Athenian* magazine which has listings and some background on forthcoming events.

CULTURE

Big summer event is the **Athens Festival** (June to September), a wide range of performances which include modern and ancient theatre, ballet, opera, jazz and classical music. For most people the highlights are the open-air performances of classical drama in the ancient theatres of Epidavros and Athens's Herod Atticus. Those at Epidavros take place at weekends (there are special coaches from Athens); at Herod Atticus they are usually spread through the week. There's also a kind of **fringe festival** with some rock, jazz and experimental dance groups at another (modern) open air theatre on Likavitos hill.

Details and tickets for both festivals can be obtained from one of two Athens Festival offices – at Stadiou 4 (near Omonia Square) or Voukourestiou 1. It's worth calling in very soon after you arrive in Greece since the more prestigious events often sell out.

You might also pick up an annual leaflet published by the NTOG called 'Greek Festivals' which includes details of other **local festivals** of music, drama and dance. Amongst these are sporadic performances of classical plays in the ancient theatres of Thassos, Dodona and Philippi.

Ordinary **indoor theatre** gets suspended through the summer months but from around September through to May there's a lot of activity: Athens alone has some 45 theatres, quite a number of them run by women's groups. **Cinemas** are cheap and show a large proportion of American and British movies, often undubbed with Greek subtitles and in summer these too move outside and on to a whole new level. I once caught an open-air showing of Kirk Douglas in *The Odyssey* on Ithaca, quite amazing experience!

For **more details** on theatre, jazz, rock and dance events, see the Athens section.

FINDING WORK

Temporary

Short-term work in Greece is always on an unofficial basis and for this reason it will generally be where you can't be seen by the police or you're badly paid – or, more often, both.

Casual work in **bars or restaurants** around the main tourist resorts is one of the best bets – though very much more so for women than for men. If you're waiting/serving most of your wages will probably have to come from tips but you may well be able to get a deal which includes free food and lodging; evening-only hours can be a good do leaving a lot of freedom. The main drawback may be the machismo and/or chauvinist attitudes of your employer. (Adverts in the *Athens News* for 'girl bar staff' are probably best avoided. The work tends to be drinking rather than serving – with a commission on whatever you sell; a fairly desperate business.) Corfu, with its big British slant, is usually the most rewarding place to look for bar work, if perhaps less of an attraction for living. Men ought to aim their sights low and be moderately pleased with washing-up. Start looking, if you can, around April–May: you'll get better rates if you're taken on for a season.

On a similar level you might be able to get a job touting/selling for **tourist shops** on Corfu, Rhodes or Crete, or if you've got the expertise helping to supervise one of the **windsurfing** 'schools' springing up all around the coast. **Yacht marinas** can also prove good hunting-

grounds though less for the romantic business of crewing (still a possibility if you've got the charm and arrogance) than scrubbing down and repainting. With this in mind your best possibilities are likely to be on Corfu or Crete; the Zea Marina at Piraeus is actually the biggest but non-Greek owners don't tend to rest up there for long.

For a full season's work in Greece relatively slim credentials might also get you a job as a **tour-group courier**. Some firms are willing to take on people waiting to go to university or, more promisingly, having just finished. Nominal pay will be appalling but you'll get a place to live in Athens when not touring and you can make a lot of money in tips from grateful 'clients'. Scour the brochures as early in the year as possible and turn up at companies' British offices.

Outside the tourist season there can be **building/painting/signpainting** work preparing for the influx: ask around at Easter-time. This aside you'll probably be down to **harvesting/agricultural** jobs – invariably low-paid and often still more so for women whom some Greeks feel they can pay a lower rate. Youth hostels tend to be about the best source of this work since farmers will often turn up to get as much labour as they can find. Crete is where most travellers descend since it has the longest and widest range of harvests (potatoes – end of May; grapes – late summer; olives – end of October; pickling/processing – winter in Ierepetra and Agia Galini). Elsewhere you might have less variety but less competition: the Peloponnese has a big olive crop and in the Argos-Nafplio-Tolo area there's a major orange season in early November, slightly better paid than usual; the grape harvest on the Ionian islands might also be worth trying. Talk to as many travellers as you can – something is usually being picked somewhere.

Long-term

The only long-term jobs you're likely to get in Greece are teaching English in a language school (*frontistirion*) or with a family as an au-pair.

Language schools – *frontistiria* in the plural – are expanding fast throughout Greece and English is the most popularly required tongue. To get a job in one you don't necessarily need a TEFL (Teaching English as a Foreign Language) certificate, nor do you need to speak Greek – though both are obviously a help. You will, however, find work much easier to come by if you've got a degree certificate: take it with you, along with any other impressive documents you can muster, if you plan to go to Greece first and find work once you're there.

Obviously, the simplest way to get a teaching job is to apply before leaving. There are adverts – particularly from August to October – in the *Guardian*'s Tuesday Education Supplement and in the *Times Educational Supplement* published weekly. This way you should get one-way air fare paid, accommodation and a salary of £35–£50 a week – enough to live on in Greece since you pay no tax for the first year you work. The other big advantage of arranging work from England is that the red tape of work permits and teaching licences will be cleared up for you before you set off.

If you're already in Greece and want teaching work it looks difficult on paper since you do officially need a licence (a complicated procedure). In practice, however, this is very loosely enforced and if you're around at the right time (try at the end of August) you're likely to find a place. The best technique for finding a teaching post is to approach *frontistiria* directly – dozens are listed in any phonebook; many are jointly owned and will send you elsewhere if they don't have a vacancy.

Teaching is, however, essentially a winter exercise – the schools close down from the end of May until mid-September, operating only a few special courses in June and July. It's general practice to supplement your income by giving private lessons and for this the going rate is around £4–£6 an hour. Many teachers finance themselves exclusively on private lessons and, although you still officially need a teaching permit for this, few people experience any problems over it. The British Council in Athens will put you in touch with people who want lessons and you can also advertise in the *Athens News*.

The popularity and scale of private English teaching also means that English-speaking women are heavily in demand as **au-pairs**. As ever positions tend to be exploitative and low-paid but if you can use them to your own ends – living reasonably well and learning Greek – there can be mutual benefits. It's unwise to arrange anything until you're in Greece, so you can at least meet and talk terms with your prospective family, and in Athens you should find little difficulty fixing something up. Posts are advertised regularly in the daily *Athens News* and there are quite a number of specialist agencies. These include:
International Staff (Th. N. Cammenos), Botasi 12.
Miterna, Ermou 28.
Working Holidays, Nikis 11.
Greek YWCA (XEN), Amerikis 11.

GREEK POLICE AND TROUBLE

It's ten years now since the Colonels went out and Greece ceased to be a **police** state though, as everywhere, there are still a few mean characters around. Unlike the Spanish, however, your average Greek policeman is not likely to have too much of a power complex . . . and you'll generally need to do something pretty insensitive to risk arrest. You can, nevertheless, be booked for nude bathing or sunbathing, for camping outside an authorised site and (a major crime in the Greek book) for taking or possessing hash or any other drug.

Nude bathing is, currently, legal on only a very few Greek beaches – some on Mykonos, for example – so you should always exercise considerable sensitivity to local feeling and the kind of place you're in. If a beach has become fairly established for nudity, or is well secluded, it's highly unlikely that the police are going to come charging in. Where they do get bothered is if they feel a place is turning into a 'hippy beach' or nudity getting too overt on mainstream tourist stretches. But there are no hard and fast rules: it all depends on the local cops. Most times the only action would be a warning but you can officially be arrested straight off – facing as much as three days in jail and an £80 fine.

Very similar guidelines exist for **camping rough** – though you're even more unlikely to incur anything more than a warning to move on. If you don't and the

same policeman returns and recognises you things could be different but I've never heard of anyone actually being charged.

Drug offences, as stressed earlier, are a serious Greek matter. The maximum penalty for 'causing the use of drugs by someone under 18', for ox ample, is life imprisonment and a 10 million drachma fine. Theory is by no means practice but foreigners caught in possession of quite small amounts of hash do get jail sentences of up to a year – much, much more if there's any suggestion they're supplying others. Beware.

If you do get arrested for any offence you have an automatic right to contact your country's **consul** who will arrange a lawyer for your defence. Beyond this though, there is little they can – and in the case of minor drug charges, will – do. For addresses of consulates see the listings for Athens (p. 48) and Thessaloniki (p. 141).

OTHER THINGS

ADDRESSES in Greek are usually written with just the streetname followed by the number (as: Nikis 11); numbers outside the city centres usually represent a whole streetblock so you may get an individual building number added in brackets. *Odos* means street; *Leoforos*, avenue; *Plateia*, square. Odos Vironos incidentally, which you'll come upon in almost any Greek town, celebrates Lord Byron, the well-known Greek nationalist, hero and poet.

BARGAINING isn't a regular feature of life though you'll find it possible with 'rooms' and some off-season hotels. A nice line is always to offer to use your sleeping-bag, saving the washing of sheets . . .

CASH Greek currency is drachmas (drx), currently about 130 of them to the £1.

CONSULATES See listings for Athens (p. 48) and Thessaloniki (p. 141).

CONTRACEPTIVES Durex are available from city kiosks or *farmakias*; the pill too can be obtained from a *farmakia* – you shouldn't need a prescription.

EMERGENCIES Phone 166 for hospital cases; 171 for the tourist police.

GAY LIFE is centred on Mykonos, still

the most popular European gay resort after Ibiza in Spain; lesser action on Rhodes and Ios and (for women only) to a small but growing extent on Lesbos. Homosexuality is legal over the age of 17 and (generally, male) *bi*sexuality quite widely accepted. See also Athens listings.

HAYFEVER sufferers should be prepared for the season starting a couple of months earlier than in Britain: highest pollen counts are in May and June.

JELLYFISH Beware the hazards of the deep – jellyfish and sea urchins. The worst jellyfish is the small brown Medusa, often blown ashore by the Meltemi winds in August, but it won't incapacitate you. Sea urchins are a year-round hazard on rocky coasts. If you get spiked by one, liberal doses of olive-oil help relieve the pain and loosen the spike. Olive oil (*ladhi*) also gets beach tar off clothes.

LAUNDRIES (*plintiria*) are rare except for the expensive service kind. Ask rooms owners for the laundry trough: they often freak out if you use basins, Greek plumbing being what it is.

MAGAZINES & PAPERS *The Athenian*, an English-language monthly, is sold in

Athens and major resorts – well worth a look for its cultural/festival listings, updates on Greek life/politics and occasionally excellent articles. A daily paper, the *Athens News* is also produced: its main virtue is Greek and world news for less than a third the price of imported British newspapers though it does also feature an interesting summary of the (very diverse) Greek press from the previous day.

MOSQUITOES (*mouquitas*) aren't often a problem, particularly if you sleep right by the sea; *fidhakia* incense coils are sold in bad areas (notoriously, the pine-covered Halkidiki).

ODD ESSENTIALS An alarm clock helps out with early ferries and market-buses; flashlights are useful if you're camping; various people also write to us recommending 'universal plugs' – so if you want one, take it!

PERIPTERO are kiosks and they sell virtually everything.

RADIO You can pick up the BBC World Service on various short-wave frequencies through the day – the main ones being 15.07 and 12.09 mhz. There's also news in English on the Greek National Station (412m MW) at 7.30 a.m. each day, or headlines on the TV at 6 p.m. (often followed by the most unlikely British and American imports, many of them positively bizarre with Greek subtitles).

SHOP HOURS *Farmakias* and general stores open Mon., Wed., Sat. 8 a.m.–3 p.m.; Tues., Thurs., Fri. 8 a.m.–2 p.m. and 5 p.m.–8.30 p.m. In summer *farmakias* close Saturdays but there should be a note on the door directing you to one that stays open.

SKIING is just developing in Greece. You have three main options – Parnassus (above Arachova/Delphi), Pindus (Metsovo) or Vermion (Naoussa/Seli). Details from the NTOG or Hellenic Alpine Club (Pl. Kapnikarea 2, Athens).

STUDENT CARDS give reductions on museum and ruin admissions and some flights. A FIYTO youth card is almost as effective – anyone under 26 can buy one (for £1.50) from WST, 37 Store Street, London WC1. In Athens student cards are issued at Fillelinon 11 but you'll need a valid-looking letter.

TAMPAX are sold at *farmakias* and some kiosks.

TIME Greek summertime is GMT plus three hours.

TOURIST POLICE Phone 171 for information and help.

WATER is safe (and tastes wonderful) pretty much everywhere in Greece; on many islands, however, there are summer shortages and the supply is switched off in the evening.

WINE FESTIVALS take place each evening through the summer at Dafni (Athens). Alexandroupoli and Rhodes – and for a small admission charge you get unlimited tasting. See these respective towns in the guide for details.

GREEK TERMS: A GLOSSARY

ACROPOLIS ancient, fortified hilltop.

AGIOS/AGIA saints (m/f), common placename prefix (abbrev. Ag. or Ay.).

AGORA market and meeting-place of an ancient city.

AMPHORA tall, narrow-headed jar for oil or wine.

APSE domed recess at the altar end of a church.

ARCHAIC PERIOD late Iron Age from around 750 BC to the start of the Classical Period in the C5th BC; also known as the HELLENISTIC civilisation.

ARGOLID north-east Peloponnese, around Argos, Mycenae and Corinth.

ATRIUM central altar-court of a Roman house.

BASILICA colonnaded 'hall-type' church.

BYZANTINE EMPIRE created by the division of the Roman Empire in AD 395, this was the eastern half, ruled from Byzantium or Constantinople (the modern Istanbul). In Greece Byzantine culture peaked twice: in the C11th (at Daphni, Ossios Loukas, Mt Athos, Thessaloniki, etc.) and again at Mistra in the early C15th. Constantinople fell to the Ottoman Turks in 1453; Mistra seven years later. See Thessaloniki for a broad outline of Byzantine church architecture.

CHORA (or **HORA**) main island town, often also known by the name of the island; literally it means 'the place'.

CLASSICAL PERIOD essentially from the end of the Persian Wars in the C5th BC to the unification of Greece under Philip II of Macedon (338 BC).

DIMARHEIO town hall (modern usage).

DORIC early, pure order of temple architecture; Doric columns are slightly pinched, their capitals simple and decoration limited to the frieze and pediment.

FRIEZE band of sculptures on a temple. Doric friezes consist of tableaus of figures (METOPES) interspersed with grooved panels (TRIGLYPHS); Ionic ones have continuous bands of figures.

FROURIO medieval castle.

GEOMETRIC PERIOD post-Mycenaean Iron Age named from the style of its pottery; beginnings are in the early C11th BC with the arrival of Dorian peoples – by the C8th BC, with the development of representational art, it becomes known as the ARCHAIC or HELLENISTIC period.

HELLADIC CIVILISATION Bronze Age culture of the Greek mainland (correspondent with the CYCLADIC culture of the islands) stretching from around 2500–1100 BC. MYCENAEAN civilisation developed in the late Helladic period.

HELLENISTIC PERIOD the last and most unified Greek empire – created by Philip II and Alexander the Great in the C4th BC and finally collapsing with the fall of Corinth to the Romans in 146 BC.

ICONOSTASIS Screen blocking off altar-sanctuary from nave.

IONIC elaborate, decorative development of the Doric order; Ionic temple columns are slimmer with deeper 'fluted' edges, spiral-shaped capitals and ornamental bases. CORINTHIAN capitals are a still more decorative development.

KAFENEION coffeehouse and centre of any small town or village, for which it is also quite likely to serve as the bus station.

KASTRO medieval castle or any fortified hill.

KATHOLIKON monastery chapel.

KOUROS, KORAI sculpted, motionless figures of the Archaic period – *kouros* are young male nudes, *korai* clothed maidens.

KKE acronym for the Greek Communist Party (now split in two groups: the Moscow-aligned Exoterikou, and the smaller national Esoterikou).

KTEL acronym for all bus companies, also the usual word for bus station.

MELTEMI north-east wind that blows across the Aegean in summer; its force is gauged in terms of what it knocks over – 'tableweather', 'chairweather', etc!

METOPE see **FRIEZE**.

MINOAN Bronze Age civilisation of Crete, from around 2500–1400 BC.

MONI, or **PANAGIA** monastery.

MOREA medieval name for the Peloponnese.

MYCENAEAN late-Helladic (and Homeric) civilisation, centred on Mycenae and the Argolid; broadly 1700–1100 BC.

NARTHEX vestibule, or entrance hall, of a church.

ND (NΔ) acronym for the Greek Conservative, Nea Demokratia, party.

NEA new.

NEOLITHIC the first settlement periods – Early (c. 6000 BC), Middle (c. 5000 BC) and Late (c. 3000 BC).

OTE acronym for phone company.

PALEA old.

PASOK (ΠΑΣΟΚ) acronym for the Pan-Hellenic Socialist Party led by Andreas Papandreou; and in government since October 1981.

PANTOKRATOR literally 'the Almighty', a stern figure of God the Father frescoed or in mosaic on the dome of most Byzantine churches.

PEDIMENT triangular, sculpted space below the roof of a temple.

PLATEIA square or plaza; **KENTRIKI PLATEIA** is main square.

PROPYLAIA entrance gates to an ancient sanctuary, agora or major building.

SQUINCHES arches across the corner of a church supporting the dome or cupola.

STELE tombstone.

STOA portico in an ancient marketplace for discussion and debate.

TEMENOS sanctuary, or sacred temple enclosure.

THOLOS conical, beehive-type building or tomb.

TRIGLYPH see **FRIEZE**.

Part two
MAINLAND

THE NORTH: MACEDONIA AND THRACE

CENTRAL AND WESTERN GREECE

P

THE PELOPONNESE

ATHENS AND AROUND

Chapter one
ATHENS AND AROUND

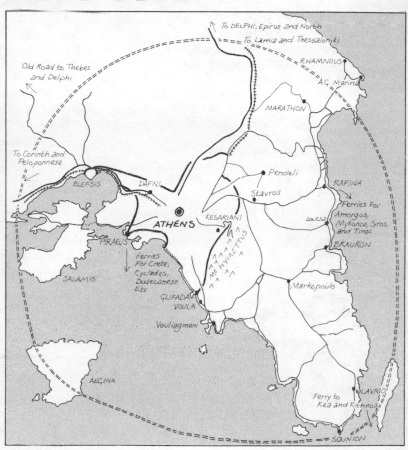

ATHENS

For most of the 3 million-odd tourists who pass through each year, Athens means two frantic days – seeing the Acropolis, spending a morning at the immense and wonderful National Archaeological Museum and an evening on the slopes of Plaka . . . then getting out as soon as possible, disappointed so much was so modern, and horrified by the sheer number of manic fume-heavy cars sweeping anarchically about the streets.

Obviously there's a certain truth in this impression but it's an accusation that could be levelled against most European capitals; Athens is somehow expected to be different because it was a great city 2,500 years ago. Today, with a population counting for nearly one-third of the Greek nation, it's many very different things – few of which are going to key with visions of picturesque provincial ruins. Once you accept this you can start tuning in, instead, to the really extraordinary feel of the place – its hectic neon-bright buzz mixed with an easy-going almost rural spirit. You'll find, too, that the Acropolis – supreme monument though it is – is only the most obvious of Athens's attractions; there's a city here, also, with nifty jazz-clubs, shadow puppet theatres, Byzantine churches, open-air movies . . . and much more besides.

That said, it is the 'Golden Age' of C5th, Periclean Athens which stands out in the city's history – and whose echoes still, to a considerable extent, reverberate, not just in the tangible legacy of monuments but in the very choice of Athens as capital of the modern state of Greece.

Almost from the moment of its greatness Athenian power had begun to decline. Torn apart by the Peloponnesian War (432–404 BC) it had recovered politically for less than a century before Philip II's momentous victory at Chaeroneia established Macedonian control throughout the lands of Greece. Culturally and intellectually, however, it was to remain a force for nearly a millennium, exerting considerable influence over the Roman world. The Emperor Hadrian lived frequently in the city and it was the obvious place of study for both Cicero and Horace. Decline came only with the rising forces of Christianity and, yet more drastically, with the division of the Holy Roman Empire in 395 AD. Constantine, first of the Eastern (or Byzantine) Emperors, established a new capital and focus at Byzantium (Constantinople) and Greece almost at a stroke became a relatively provincial backwater. Athens, deprived of any spiritual or symbolic hold over east or west, faded rapidly. After the piratical Fourth Crusade it was seized as part of the medieval Frankish kingdom and finally, in 1456, was annexed to the Turkish Ottoman Empire. In neither did it have any significant role – an inevitable fate, perhaps, for the importance of Athens was all too closely linked to that of Greece, as an entity and a free, independent state.

When eventual liberation had been wrested from the Turks, however, Athens was not the original choice of capital; the first Greek government met at Nafplio in the Peloponnese. It was only in 1834 – after the accession (and western foisting upon Greece) of the Bavarian King Otho – that the court transferred to Athens. Its claims by this time were purely symbolic. Under Turkish occupation the city, a democracy of 250,000 in classical times, had shrunk to a ramshackle village of a few hundred dwellings clustered at the foot of the Acropolis: the area known today as Plaka. When Byron had first visited in 1809 there was not even an inn – whilst Piraeus, ancient and modern port of Athens, was a mere fishing hamlet of under 1000 people.

All this is difficult to imagine when confronted by modern Athens, yet the transformation is in fact almost entirely the product of this century and above all of the last three decades. In 1830, Otho, first King of Greece, had brought architects with him from Germany and it was their modest neo-classical grid that the C19th city developed. Piraeus, meanwhile, grew into a port again, though its activities continued to be dwarfed by the main Greek shipping centres on the islands of Siros and Hydra. The sudden expansion – to the present population of over 3 million – came in two waves: the first with the disastrous exchange of Greek and Turkish subjects in 1922–3, the second in the economic upsurge of the 1950s and 1960s which brought enormous depopulation of the villages for the city suburbs. This second wave, largely stripped of economic advance, is still happening and the cityscape has radically changed – an unchecked mass of concrete apartment blocks and incredibly pollutant factories swamping the whole area around Athens, Piraeus and Elefsis (Elefsina).

Today the city is in something of a crisis. With around half the country's industry and over two-thirds of its motor vehicles crammed into Greater Athens it currently has the worst pollution in the world after Tokyo. A sulphurous cloud, *to nefos*, makes increasingly regular appearances, trapped by the circle of hills around the city, and there is a very real threat to public health. Even the Parthenon marble is being eaten away by the ensuing acid rain.

Fierce debate ranges over principal causes of the *nefos* – blame heavy industry or the ragged exhausts of Athenian traffic – but it is now undeniably the major local issue. For years pollution had been disregarded in the face of industrial and commercial factors ('Show me someone who has died from the *nefos*', a Conservative spokesman demanded when 100,000 Athenians took to the streets in protest) but with the change to a socialist government there have been some signs that the problem is being faced. Through last year's summer months the whole city centre was closed to private cars and in Greater Athens systems of alternate days for odd/even number plates were introduced. But despite these measures, and the closure of some of the worst offending factories, there's no real sign of improvement. Perhaps the only genuine solution will come with long-term de-urbanisation plans – though for the moment there are few Greeks who want to return to the villages.

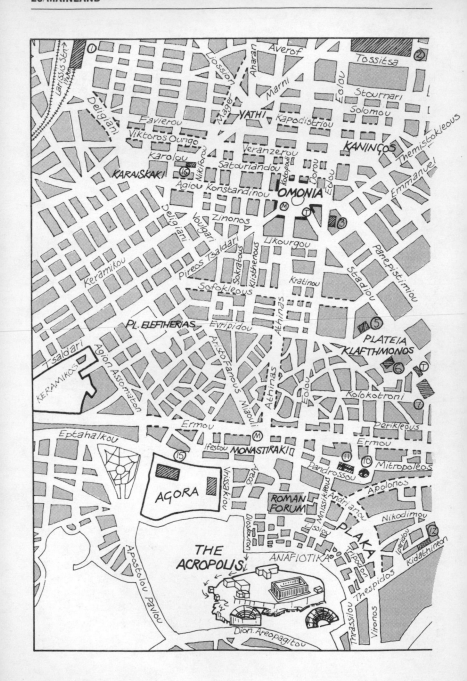

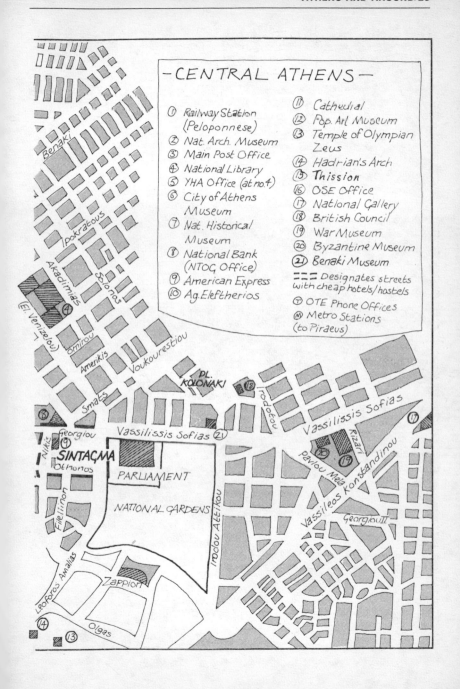

—CENTRAL ATHENS—

① Railway Station (Peloponnese)
② Nat. Arch. Museum
③ Main Post Office
④ National Library
⑤ YHA Office (at no.4)
⑥ City of Athens Museum
⑦ Nat. Historical Museum
⑧ National Bank (NTOG Office)
⑨ American Express
⑩ Ag. Eleftherios

⑪ Cathedral
⑫ Pop. Art Museum
⑬ Temple of Olympian Zeus
⑭ Hadrian's Arch
⑮ **Thission**
⑯ OSE Office
⑰ National Gallery
⑱ British Council
⑲ War Museum
⑳ Byzantine Museum
㉑ Benaki Museum
≡≡≡ Designates streets with cheap hotels/hostels
Ⓣ OTE Phone Offices
Ⓜ Metro Stations (to Piraeus)

GETTING AROUND AND FINDING A PLACE TO STAY

Other than when you arrive at, or leave, Athens there are few times you'll
need to venture beyond walking distance of the centre of the city. On the
area printed on our plan you'll find most of the ancient sites, the museums, entertainments, hotels, hostels and scores of places to eat and
drink. For a slightly broader map (stretching to the PanAthenaikos Football ground) just get hold of the free NTOG pamphlet 'Athens-Attica' –
either in advance, or on arrival at the airport or from the **NTOG Information Desk** inside the National Bank of Greece on the corner of Sintagma Square.

Sintagma (also known as 'Constitution Square') is the principal square
and reference point of central Athens: it's flanked by the parliament
building (formerly the Royal Palace), luxury hotels, foreign banks and
airline offices. The other main square is **Omonia**, roughly the Athenian
equivalent of Piccadilly Circus or Times Square. Work out your bearings
by these two and you should never get lost – anyone will point you in
their direction at the sound of the names.

Additional aids to orientation are the city's two great hills: the **Acropolis** (south of Omonia) and **Likavitos**, a slightly higher landmark, topped
with a Byzantine chapel, to the east of **Stadiou**, the street connecting
Sintagma with Omonia.

Athens has two **airports**. Olympic Airways flights arrive at the West
Airport, from outside which a no. 133 bus runs to the Olympic office on
Sintagma square. All other airlines use the East Airport, with a direct
yellow shuttlebus service to Amalias Street, just off Sintagma. (Both buses
run every 20 mins – 6 a.m.–11.30 p.m. for Olympic, 6 a.m.–2 a.m. for
the other; outside these hours you'll need a taxi – fix a price first, £5
maximum, or it could be very expensive.) The **train stations** are strung
out along Deligiani Street, at the top left-hand corner of our plan: they
have two distinct parts, the first for the Peloponnese, the other (100
metres further up) for northern Greece and international connections.
Both are a short walk from Omonia, or you could take a no. 1 bus to
Sintagma. For details of **buses out** of Athens see the 'Travel Details' on
page 53; if you want to get straight out to **Piraeus** (for ferries to the
islands) you can get a bus direct from the East Airport, otherwise get on
the metro at the corner of Omonia Square.

The NTOG Information Desk in Sintagma book **rooms** for anyone in
'A', 'B' or 'C' class hotels but they don't deal with 'D's and 'E's nor with
hostels; the best they'll do – if you're having real problems – is let you
copy down some phone numbers from the official lists. Generally, though,
it isn't too difficult to find a fairly **cheap bed** – you just have to keep
asking at the innumerable run-down looking hotels and hostels crammed
into two or three central regions of the city. The main point to remember

is that they differ far more in quality than in price, so it's worth a fair bit of hunting around. In peak season, though, and particularly if you arrive late, take the first reasonable offer and head out early next morning if you want a better alternative. To aid your wanderings we've indicated all the streets with a heavy concentration of cheap hotels by a heavy dotted line on the city-plan.

Oddly enough, **SINTAGMA** is probably the best area to start looking – not in the square itself, of course, but in the web of streets behind, leading through Plaka towards the Acropolis. Here you'll find the highest concentration of 'student hostels', dormitory-style places with six or eight beds to a room and quite often roofspace on top. They're a lot more central and congenial than the official youth hostels and don't have factors like YHA cards and curfews to consider either. Only problem is, there's a very quick turnover. But here's a current rundown, working down from Sintagma:

> *George's Guest House*, Nikis 46; 322 9657. (Very cheap, central and probably the best of the really basic).
> *Alfred's*, Fillelinon 18; 322 4193.
> *Hostel Thisseion*, Thisseos 10.
> *Student Inn*, Kidathineion 18; 324 4808 (smaller, plusher rooms including some doubles – good value).
> *Joseph's House*, Markou Moussouri 13; 923 1204.
> *George's Inn*, Markou Moussouri 33; 322 9267. (This street is just off our plan, by the stadium beneath the National Gardens).

For single/double/triple rooms in this area you could start by trying the *Faedra Hotel* (Herofondos 16, corner of Adrianou; 323 8461 – roofspace too), *Hotel Kimon* (Apolonos 27; 323 5223) or one of the places along Ermou street – *Hermion* at 66c (321 2753), Anatoli at 69 (321 3057) or *Nea Epirus* at 90 (321 0426). Slightly more expensive, but good, places in Plaka include *Hotel Kekropa* (Tsangari 13; 322 3080) and *Kouros* (Kodrou 11; 322 7431). Alternatively there's another area with several cheapish youth oriented hotels **around Plateia Viktorias** – off to the north of our map just beyond the National Archaeological Museum. Try *Joy's Hotel* (Akharnon 74 at Feron; 823 1012), the *Athens Connection Hostel* (Ioulianou 20 at Patission; 822 4592) or the more basic *Hotel Feron* (Feron 43).

On the whole, though, the best bet for a cheap, individual room lies in the streets heading off around **OMONIA**. Each of those dotted on our map (particularly **Veranzerou** and **Satovriandou**, towards the train station) should turn up something, but for my money the most convenient locations are a grid of streets running vertically down from Omonia – Menandrou, Sokratous, Athinas and Eolou, and (intersecting them) Sofokleous. Be warned that, though not at all heavy, these streets have something of a reputation as a red light district — what follows are some of the better possibilities:

Menandrou *Neon Lido* (No. 31; 522 1849); *Thessaloniki* (no. 42; 524 5158).

Sokratous *Balkania* (no. 12; 522 7581).

Athinas *Menelaon* (No. 4; 321 2718); *Zakinthos* (no. 22; 324 6783); *Cecil* (no. 39; 321 7079; *Estia* (corner Athinas/Armodiou 12).

Eolou *Hotel Ideal* (no. 39; 321 3195) and *Tempi* (no. 29; 321 3175), both slightly pricey but recommended.

Sofokleous *Parnassos* (no. 27; 321 1551); *Maxim* (no. 27e; 321 1589); Serreon (no. 32; 523 2606).

If you want to phone any of these hotels you'll virtually always be able to speak in English: use one of the phones at any 'provisions-kiosk', they're all over the city — you don't need to find exact coins and a phone booth.

The three official **youth hostels** in Athens are all a little way out from the centre — and they're not too hot when you actually get there. For devotees, though, their addresses are:

Hostel No. 1, Kipselis 57; 822 5860. (10 mins by trolley bus 2 to 'Kipseli' from right outside the National Archaeological Museum.)

Hostel No. 2, Leoforos Alexandras 87; 646 3669. (10 mins by bus 10 from Panepistimiou Street, parallel to Stadiou.)

Hostel No. 4, Patission 97/Hamilton 3; 822 0328. (The easiest to get to — a 400-metre walk past the National Archaeological Museum on Patission Street.)

Hostel No. 3 has closed.

If you're heading for a youth hostel during office hours you could save fruitless walking by dropping in to the **Greek Youth Hostel Office** at Dragatsaniou 4 (off Stadiou, halfway between Sintagma and Omonia). They can phone to reserve a place for you and point directions to a bus stop. Much better placed, though, are the Greek equivalents of the YWCA/YMCA: XEN (Amerikis 11; tel. 362 6970) and XAN (Omirou 28; tel. 362 4291) respectively. Both streets are just a couple of blocks down Stadiou, leading out towards Likavitos hill. XEN (the women's hostel) also operate a cheap self-service restaurant, a small library and run Greek classes.

Camping out rough in Athens would not be a good idea, although if you have a railway ticket it's possible to get a half-night's sleep at the station without too much trouble. The nearest official **campsite** to Athens is at Dafni (11 km from the centre), clearly signposted on the left of the road next to the Monastery and Wine Festival grounds. To get there take bus no. 282 from Plateia Eleftherias (halfway between Omonia and

Keramikos); the journey takes about 20 mins and like all city transport it's extremely cheap. If you're driving head down towards Keramikos and take Iera Odos, which later becomes the main highway to Dafni and Elefsis.

Finding a flat in Central Athens, if you decide to stay and work, is currently not too difficult since the *nefos* has been forcing people out in droves to the higher-lying suburbs. Most days there'll be adverts in the English-language *Athens News* but really the best way to find a place is just by going on to the streets and looking. What you're looking for are signs, usually red on white, announcing 'Enoikiazetai' (To Let): they'll be stuck on doors, walls, windows or lamp posts. Average prices are fairly low at present – around £75 a month for a two-room flat – but on top of the rent you nearly always have to pay *kinohrista*, an all-encompassing term for services, lighting, heating and sometimes cleaning, too. Kolonaki is the smart quarter: if you're looking for something fairly cheap try Pangrati (behind the stadium) or Koukaki (around the base of the Filipapou hill).

And if you are planning to live in Athens try and get a copy of *Athens Inside Out* by one Antoinette Moses (published by Estefthiadis). It's a Time-Out style guide, now some six years out of date, but still trusty for most purposes and an incredible source of knowledge for everything from sound systems to nursery schools.

THE ACROPOLIS AND THE ANCIENT SITES

The Acropolis (Open weekdays 8.00–7.45, Sundays 10–4; Museum closed Tuesday mornings)
The Acropolis is one of the earliest settlements in Greece – its obvious strategic advantages (natural springs and a large flat limestone top 300 feet above the Attic plain) drew a Neolithic community to its slopes around 5000 BC. In Mycenaean times it was fortified with cyclopean walls enclosing a royal palace, and, more importantly, the worship of Athena was introduced. Both city and goddess were integrated by the Dorians and, with the union of Attic towns and villages in the ninth century, the Acropolis became the nucleus of the first Greek city state. It was re-established as a fortified residence under the tyrants of the seventh and sixth centuries BC but when the last Peisistratid tyrant was overthrown (in 510 BC) the Delphic Oracle ordered that it should remain unoccupied – the sole province of the gods.

It is in this context that the monuments visible today were built. Of the Mycenaean walls and the earlier temples and sanctuaries only sparse traces remain, for they were razed to the ground when the Persians sacked Athens in 480 BC. For some years they were left in ruins as a reminder of the Persian action but after that threat had been overcome (notably at

Plateia in 479 and Eurymedon in 468) the walls were rebuilt and plans drawn up to construct new temples worthy of the city's cultural and political supremacy.

Athens had naturally assumed the leadership of the Delian League (a naval confederacy, set up in 478, of virtually all the maritime cities of the Aegean) and by the mid-fifth century this had become all except in name an Athenian Empire – states paying annual money tribute to Athens, whence in 454 the Treasury was moved. Six years later Pericles made a peace treaty with the Persians and despite protests from other members of the league, and from within Athens itself, instigated his magnificent and enormously expensive rebuilding plan. The work, under the general direction of Pheidias, was completed in an incredibly short time (the Parthenon was finished within ten years), 'every architect', as Plutarch wrote, 'striving to surpass the magnificence of the design with the elegance of the execution'. Pericles had intended the design to serve as a 'School for Hellas' and in fact it survived unaltered – save for some modest Roman embellishments – for close on a thousand years until, in the reign of the Emperor Justinian, the temples were converted to Christian use.

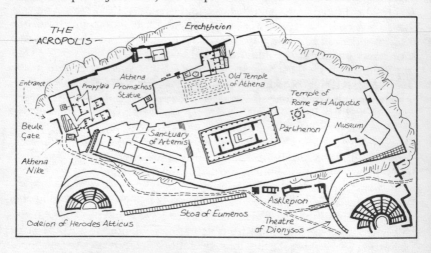

In later years the classical structures underwent a number of uses and indeed were almost obscured by medieval embellishments and additions; fifteenth-century Italian princes held court in the Propylaia, for example, and the Erechtheum became a harem for the Turkish garrison commander. An imperial diplomat, Hugo Favoli, described the Acropolis in 1563 as 'looming beneath a swarm of glittering golden crescents', whilst a minaret rose from the Parthenon itself. But these scenes survive only in the prints and sketches of that period, for when the Greeks took the Acropolis in 1833 work was immediately begun on clearing the Turkish village and the Frankish fortifications – a Greek Regent lamenting in vain that 'the archaeologists would destroy all the picturesque additions of the middle ages in their zeal to lay bare the ancient momuments'.

Today, as throughout its history, the Acropolis offers but one approach – from a terrace above the Agora. Here in classical times the Panathenaic Way extended along a steep ramp to the massive Periclean Propylaia; the modern path makes a more gradual, zigzagging ascent through an arched Roman entrance (the **Beule Gate**) added in the third century AD.

The Propylaia ('monumental entrance') was constructed by Mnesicles upon completion of the Parthenon (437 BC) and its axis and proportions align to balance the temple. It rivalled the Parthenon, too, in grandeur and architectural achievement, for it was built entirely of the same Pentelic marble (most unusual in a gateway) and, in order to offset the difficulties of a sloping site, it combined for the first time standard Doric columns with the taller and more delicate Ionic order. To the left of the Central Hall (which before Venetian bombardment in the seventeenth century supported a great coffered roof, painted blue and gilded with stars) the Pinakotheke exhibited paintings of Homeric subjects by Polygnotus – executed in the mid-fifth century, they were described 600 years later by Pausanias. There was to have been a similar wingroom to the right but Mnesicles' design trespassed on ground sacred to the Goddess of Victory and had to be adapted as a waiting room for her shrine. This, the simple and elegant **Temple of Athena Nike**, was begun late in the rebuilding scheme (probably due to conflict over the extent of the Propylaia's south wing) and stands on a precipitous platform overlooking Piraeus and the Saronic Gulf. Pausanias recounts that it was from this bastion King Aegeus – watching for the return from Crete of his son Theseus – threw himself to his death; Theseus, having slain the Minotaur, had forgotten his promise to change his black sails for white. The Temple's frieze, with more attention to realism and triumph, depicts the Athenians' victory at Plateia. Amazingly the whole building was reconstructed from its original fragments in the nineteenth century, having been demolished by the Turks as material for a gun emplacement; recovered also were the reliefs from its parapet – amongst them 'Victory Adjusting Her Sandal', the most beautiful exhibit in the Acropolis museum.

In front of this small temple stood the **Sanctuary of Brauronian Artemis**, its precinct dominated by a colossal bronze representation of the Wooden Horse of Troy. The sanctuary's function, however, is today obscure and only scant remains of its foundations can be seen. More noticeable is a stretch of **Mycenaean wall** (running parallel to the Propylaia) which was incorporated into the classical design.

From the Propylaia the Acropolis is dominated by the Parthenon – set on the highest ground some 40 feet above – but in classical times only its pediment could be seen through the intervening mass of statues and buildings. The ancient focus was the famous 30 foot bronze of Athena Promachos ('the champion'); created by Pheidias as a symbol of the Athenians' defiance of Persia, its spear and helmet were visible to sailors approaching from Sounion. The **Panathenaic Way** was channelled to its right and the Parthenon entered from the far end; following this route you can make out grooves cut for footholds in the rock and, to either side, cuttings for the rows of statues and offerings.

The **Parthenon**, the first great building of the Periclean scheme, was designed by Ictinus and utilises all the refinements available to the Doric order of architecture to achieve an extraordinary and unequalled harmony. Its proportions, for instance, maintain a universal 9:4 ratio – not only in the calculations of length:width, or width:height, but in such relationships as the distances between the columns and their diameter. Additionally, every distraction of optical illusion is corrected – all the lines that appear straight are in fact slightly curved – by meticulous mathematics and craftsmanship. The columns (themselves swelled slightly to avoid seeming concave) are slanted inwards by 2½ inches whilst each of the steps along the sides of the temple rise just 4 ⁵/₆ of an inch over a length of 228 feet.

Built on the site of earlier archaic temples, the Parthenon was designed as a new sanctuary for Athena and a house for her cult image, a gold and ivory statue by Pheidias – one of the Seven Ancient Wonders. But it never rivalled the Erechtheion in sanctity and its role was more that of treasury and artistic showcase. Originally its columns were painted and it was decorated by the finest frieze and pedimental sculpture of the classical age – depicting the Panathenaic Procession, the Birth of Athena and the struggles of Greeks to overcome Giants, Amazons and Centaurs. Of these, the best surviving examples are in the British Museum (where they were taken by Lord Elgin in 1801) but the greatest part of the pediments were destroyed, alongside the central columns and the cella, on 26 September 1687 – on which day a Venetian shell landed directly on gunpowder stored within the temple, causing a fire to rage on the Acropolis for 48 hours. Some idea of the sculpture (and particularly of its colouring) can be gained from fragments exhibited in the **Acropolis Museum**, to the east of the Parthenon. The actual name 'Parthenon', incidentally, means 'virgins' chamber' and initially referred only to a room at the west end of the temple occupied by the Priestesses of Athena.

To the north of the Parthenon, beyond the foundations of the Old Temple of Athena, stands the **Erectheion** built at the end of the fifth century on ancient sanctuaries which in turn were predated by a Mycenaean palace. Here, in symbolic reconciliation, were worshipped both Athena and Poseidon-Erechtheus – on the spot where, according to myth, they had contested possession of the Acropolis. The myth (which probably recalls the integration of the Mycenaeans with earlier pre-Hellenic settlers) tells how Athena created an olive tree in response to Poseidon's flow of sea-water ('Erechtheus' in ancient Greek) and was deemed victor by the gods. Pausanias wrote of seeing both olive tree and sea water in the temple – adding that 'the extraordinary thing about this well is that when the wind blows south a sound of waves comes from it' – but today, as with all the buildings on the Acropolis, entrance is no longer permitted. Still, its elegant Ionic porticos all repay close attention – particularly the North, with its fine decorated doorway and frieze of blue Elefsinian marble, and the South, where the six famous Caryatid women hold aloft the entablature. All, sadly, are now replacements – the originals having been removed for safety to the Parthenon Museum.

The Ancient Agora (Open weekdays 8–8, Sundays 10–4.15; closed Tuesdays)

Below the entrance to the Acropolis rock-hewn stairs ascend the low hill of the **Areopagus** where, in the early Classical period, cases of homicide were heard by a supreme court. It is scored by cuttings although nothing is actually left standing. Another low hill to the left (directly facing the Propylaia) is the **Pnyx**, assembly place of the citizens, whilst further still rises the **Hill of the Muses**, ostentatiously, and irrelevantly, topped by the funeral monument of Philoppapos, a Roman Consul of the second century AD.

Close by the Areopagus a path leads down into the **AGORA**, administrative centre and marketplace of the classical city; its ruins (which can also be entered from Adrianou in Plaka) are extensive but confusing – dating from various stages of building between the sixth century BC and the fifth century AD. The best plan is to head straight for the **Museum**, housed in the totally reconstructed Stoa of Attalos; here you can get some measure of the original buildings and also find your bearings from plans of the site displayed within. The Stoa (originally one of many in the Agora) was the meeting place of citizens, merchants and philosophers; its porticoes would have been lined with shops and fronted by statues. Recently, on the periphery of the Agora, the foundations of a similar building have been discovered; this, the famous Painted Stoa, was where Zeno expounded his Stoic Philosophy.

Bounding the Agora to the west is the Periclean **Temple of Hephaistos** or Thission, the best preserved though perhaps least admired of all Doric temples – conspicuously lacking in the curvature and 'lightness' of the Parthenon's design. Its remaining metopes depict the labours of Hercules and the exploits of Theseus; its barrel-vaulted roof dates from a fifth-century conversion into the Church of St George.

The South Slope of the Acropolis (Open weekdays 8–7, closed Sundays)

Built into the south slope of the Acropolis hill is the **Theatre of Dionysus**, stage for the first performances of plays by Aeschylus, Sophocles and Euripides. Its ruins are impressive; they are entered from the street behind – Dionissiou Areopagitou. Rebuilt in the fourth century BC to seat some 17,000 spectators at the annual festival of tragic drama, 25 of the theatre's 64 tiers of seats survive. Most notable are the great marble thrones in the front row – each of which is inscribed with the name of an official of the Festival or of an important priest; in the centre sat the Priest of Dionysus and on his right the representative of the Delphic Oracle. At the rear of the stage, along the Roman bema (or rostrum) are reliefs of Dionysus flanked by squatting Sileni.

To the west of the theatre extend the ruins of the **Asklepion** – a sanctuary devoted to the healing god and centred upon a sacred spring; the cure was probably incorporated here by the Byzantine Church of Saints Comas and Damian, of which there are prominent remains. Nearer to the road are the foundations of the Roman Stoa of Eumenes which extended to the **Odeion of Herod Atticus**, built by Herod in 160 AD as a commemorative monument to his wife. It has been heavily restored for performances of ancient drama (and music events) in the modern Athens Festival.

Keramikos (Open daily 9–3; museum closed Tuesdays)

Entered at Ermou 148 the Keramikos excavations are amongst the most fascinating in Athens. A short distance below the site's **Museum** (which contains an extremely thorough display of grave goods from the site – illuminating burials from Mycenaean to Roman times) is the **Street of Tombs** – a C4th BC Funerary Avenue that has been excavated and reconstructed over a distance of about 100 yards. All the main types of funerary monument are to be seen here (a few are replicas but most are original), from the huge marble bull erected for Dionysios of Kollytos to simple carved stelai for children. At its end the street joins a well preserved section of the Sacred Way spanned by the **Sacred Gate**. North of this are the enormous foundations of the Pompeion (used to store apparatus for festivals and processions) and, just beyond, the **Dipylon Gate** the main entrance to the city guarding the road to Piraeus.

The Roman Forum and the Tower of the Winds (Open daily 10–4.30)

The Forum, an irregular-shaped open space to the west of Plaka, is distinguished above all by the **Tower of the Winds** – a beautiful octagonal structure adorned on each face with a relief of its respective wind. It was designed in the first century BC by Andronikos of Kyrrhos, a Syrian astronomer, and served as a sundial, weather vane and water clock – the latter utilising a steady stream from one of the Acropolis springs. At the far end of the site (stretching between Areos and Eolou and entered from the corner of Monastiraki square) stand the surviving walls of **Hadrian's Library** – once an enormous building enclosing a cloistered court of a hundred columns. The converted mosques and old houses nearby, too, are beautiful and resonant of past ages. This is one of the few areas of Athens where you can imagine you're still in the sleepy town of the nineteenth century.

Hadrian's Arch and the Temple of Olympian Zeus (Open weekdays 9– 3.15, Sundays 10–2)
On what is now one of the most hazardous road junctions in Athens (where Leof. Amalias joins Leof. Singrou) stands **Hadrian's Arch**, erected by the Emperor to mark the extremity of the classical city and the beginning of his own; on the near side its frieze is inscribed 'This is Athens, the Ancient City of Theseus', and on the other 'This is the City of Hadrian and not of Theseus'. Directly behind, the colossal pillars of the **Temple of Olympian Zeus** make some account of this show of arrogance. The largest temple in Greece (and, according to Livy, 'the only temple on earth to do justice to the god') it was dedicated by Hadrian in 131 AD – some 700 years after Peisistratos had laid its foundations. Sixteen of the original 104 Pentelic marble pillars remain erect whilst the column drums of another (which fell in 1852) litter the ground. In the middle ages a stylite made his hermitage on the architrave.

THE MUSEUMS

Pre-eminent, of course, is the **National Archaeological Museum**, the most exciting collection of ancient Greek art anywhere in the world. It includes Schliemann's gold finds from Mycenae, superb Cycladic figurines and, upstairs, the incredible Minoan frescoes and household furniture found at Akrotiri on the island of Thira. Although today it no longer receives the pick of new finds (regional museums have the first option) there are also examples here from virtually every period and development of ancient art and sculpture – among them an outstandingly comprehensive collection of Attican 'black' pottery. Go early – and try and give it at least two separate visits. Open Tues.–Sat. 9–7 p.m.; Suns 9–2; 150 drx admission or 50 drx with student card, free on Sundays. In the south wing, entered separately from Tossitsa street, is the extensive **Numismatic Collection** (same hours).

But the museums of Athens by no means finish here. Not to be missed – as it is by ninety per cent of tourists – is the **Benaki Museum** (Koumbari 1, 200 m from Sintagma), a private collection given to the state and literally like a one-man British Museum. Constantly surprising and fascinating, the exhibits range through Chinese ceramics, Mycenaean jewellery, Greek costumes and folk artefacts, Byronia, even a reconstructed moslem palace reception hall. Well labelled and imaginatively displayed, they (and the excellent temporary exhibitions) demand a good few hours. Open Tues.–Sun. 8.30–2; 70 drx admission, free Suns.

Other Athens museums – all of more than specialist interest – include:

Byzantine Museum (Vas. Sofias 22: 250 m beyond the Benaki)   Housed in a peaceful, courtyarded villa and devoted exclusively to Byzantine art and sculpture. Most exhibits are ikons and labelled only in Greek but two rooms reconstructed as basilicas of the fifth and eleventh centuries are quite compelling. Best visited once you've become interested by Mistra, Dafni or Ossios Loukas. Open Tues.–Sat. 9–3; Sun. 9–2; 100 drx admission, free Suns.

War Museum (200 m further down Vas. Sofias)   The only 'cultural' endowment of the 1967–74 junta and of surprising interest – though as it approaches modern times the slant towards military glorification becomes overt and disturbing. However, Greek warfare from Mycenaean times is ably traced with the aid of models, maps and other artefacts. Open Tues.–Sun. 8–2.30; free.

Popular Art Museum (Kidathineion 17, Plaka)   Both free and excellent: an array of (mainly C18th/19th) weaving, pottery and embroidery which reveals the sophistication – and also the strong Eastern influence – of traditional Greek arts. Also outstanding are the vigorous wall paintings by Theophilos, a C19th Primitive artist from Lesvos, exhibited in one room. Open Tue–Sun 10–2.

National Historical Museum (Kolokotroni Square, off Stadiou)   Deals mainly with Byzantine and medieval Greek history but with a strong section on the War of Independence; Byron's sword and helmet are among the exhibits. Open Tues.–Fri. 9–2; Sat./Sun. 9–1; 50 drx admission, free Thurs.

City of Athens Museum (Klafthmonos Square, also off Stadiou)   Housed in the original Royal Palace, residence of King Otho in the 1830s, impeccably renovated to the period. Exhibits are few but extremely high quality, including an interesting model of the city in 1842. Open Mon., Wed., Fri. 9–1.30; 100 drx is pricey, but free on Weds.

Jewish Museum (Amalias 36, above French Consulate) Art and artefacts from the very ancient Jewish communities scattered about Greece. Open 9–1 daily except Saturday.

National Gallery of Art (Vas. Konstantinou 50)   Disappointing in its core-collection of C16th–20th Greek art but often worth a visit for its excellent temporary exhibitions. Open Tues.–Sat. 9–4; Sun. 10–2; free.

OTHER PLACES: PLAKA, THE FLEA MARKET AND LIKAVITOS

Plaka, fanning outwards from the north slope of the Acropolis, is all that remains of the old C19th city. Long the centre of Athenian nightlife, its streets are virtually deserted by day – a good place to wander. A maze of narrow alleys and winding stairways, it is built largely on the old Turkish plan though at its highest level, the area known as **Anafiotika,** the design is more Cycladic. These whitewashed, cubist houses were built by islanders from Anafi employed in the early construction of Athens; unable to afford land, they took advantage of a law which allowed dwellings to be erected on the slope. Lower down, the streets are distinguished by an occasional mansion or Byzantine church (the finest is the tiny Agios Eleftherios, made entirely from re-used ancient blocks) and, towards Hadrian's Arch, by the elegant **Choregic Monument of Lysikrates.** Erected in 334 BC to commemorate victory in a choric festival, this was incorporated into the library of a French Capuchin Convent; here Byron stayed and used the monument as a study to write *Childe Harold.*

At the opposite end of Plaka, in the streets grouped round Monastiraki Square (notably Ifestou and Pandrossou), is the Athens **Flea Market;** there are shops and stalls here throughout the week but the Flea Market proper takes place on Sunday mornings when all kinds of junk is spread out on the ground. The least touristic – indeed almost exclusively Greek-junk part – is on and around Abysinnias Square: ask directions at Monastiraki, it's not marked on any of the maps.

Likavitos the highest hill in Athens is also one of the few green areas – as much of an attraction in its quiet pine-covered slopes as in the views from its summit of the city and Acropolis. There are numerous paths up the south slope, or at the end of Ploutarhou you can take a tunnelled cable railway.

Respite from sun and traffic is also provided by the **National Gardens** behind Sintagma. There are peacocks and ponds and on summer evenings an outdoor cinema operates beside the Zapio Exhibition Hall.

EATING AND DRINKING

Despite some really over-the-top commercialism, the **Plaka** – crammed with *tavernas,* discos and bouzouki bars – still seems the inevitable place to end up an evening. Once it was the natural place to eat, too, but over the last decade many of the *tavernas* have warped into tourist traps – their food a travesty of traditional fare and their prices a wry joke. If you're going to have a meal here – rather than moving up later to drink and eat snacks – you now have to be pretty selective. Here are a few suggestions, starting at the very cheapest of the cheap:

Kea, Panos 6; *Ta Kalamia* (next door). Panos Street is just off the Roman Forum: these two tavernas both have good food at ordinary Greek prices.

Kostas, Adrianou 16. Best *souvlaki* shop in Plaka bar none, and a couple of tables outside if you want to sit and take the business seriously: head for the Monument of Lysikrates, Kostas is just off the square.

To Fanganhiko, Adrianou 81. Reasonable oven-food taverna.

Eden Flessa 3 (off Adrianou). Excellent vegetarian restaurant – a rarity in Greece – with lowish prices. Highly recommended.

Damigos, corner of Adrianou/Kidatheneion. Quality basement *taverna*, and real value for what it is.

Psarra, corner of Erehtheos/Erotokritou. Solid *taverna* food and locally-famed swordfish *souvlakis*.

Piccolino, Moni Asteriou (between Kidathineion and Hatzimichali). Lively outdoor place, *taverna* food and pizzas. Slightly pricey.

The Cellar, corner of Kidathineion/Moni Asteriou. Again, not exactly cheap but Athenian *taverna* fare at its best; good retsina, too.

O Platonos, Diogenous 4. Possibly the oldest *taverna* in Plaka: an attractive garden-courtyard place, though by no means a bargain find.

If your money's really tight, however, it's quite possible to survive (and indeed eat very well) in Athens on **takeaway snacks** – small *souvlakis*, cheese and spinach pies and other pastries, supplemented by cheap fruit and nuts from the market in Euripidou (a street running between Athinas and Plateia Eleftherias). Snacks are available everywhere – for *tiropitas* try one of the stalls in Sokratous, just off Omonia. On the other hand if you can afford to try a really quality Greek (or foreign) **restaurant** get hold of a copy of the *Athenian* magazine and check out some of the recommendations in its centre section; count on £5 a head and upwards.

Breakfast in Athens is always going to be cheapest eaten standing next to a pastry stall then moving elsewhere for some yoghourt, fruit or coffee. For all of these functions Omonia Square is probably as good a place as any – try the *Bretannia*, open all hours of the day. If you have sustaining visions of a straight eggs/bacon breakfast cafe try either the *Titania Coffee Shop* (Panepistimiou 52: parallel, one block out, to Stadiou) or *American Coffee Shop* (Karageorgi Square, just off Sintagma – to the left, looking at a map).

Drinking in Plaka just pick any *taverna* and check prices before you start out: if you're near the steps winding towards the Acropolis it could turn out an expensive business, otherwise most places are quite reasonable if you stick to ouzo or retsina. Actual **bars** in Athens tend to be totally American–European affairs – and, being an un-Greek and rather chic kind of scene, fairly expensive. The best, by a very long way, is *Larry's* at Likavitos 20 (Kolonaki district; closed Suns.) which serves quite remarkable – and not enormously pricey – cocktails.

For a night of **really excessive drinking** there's also the Dafni Wine Festival, open every evening from the 2nd week of July through to the 1st week of September. You pay around 250 drx admission – for which you receive a goblet re-fillable with as many different wines as you can handle. Most are pretty rough numbers but you tend to have a good time. The food, incidentally is neither free nor cheap nor especially appetising so eat before you go. The site is next to Dafni Campsite – a 20 mins bus ride from Plateia Eleftherias (just off Pireos Street, between Omonia and Keramikos); no. 282 and others leave every quarter of an hour and return throughout the evening.

On a more subdued – and fairly expensive – level you might also be interested in trying one of the fast-disappearing **ouzeris**, a kind of Athenian equivalent of 1920s cafe society/beerhouses. The two oldest and most elegant are in Panepistimiou Street (parallel to Stadiou): *Apotsos*, founded in 1900, at no. 10 (in the arcade), and *Orfanides*, haunt of generations of politicians and intellectuals, at no. 7.

MUSIC: ROCK, JAZZ AND DISCOS

Greek **rock music** is thin on the ground but there are gigs most weeks if you want to check out local bands: call in at the *Pop 11* record shop at Skoufa 15 (Kolonaki) and ask what's happening, someone will probably speak English, besides which just about every Athens music event is advertised here. One easy-to-find club where there are live bands most nights is *Tiffany's* at Adrianou 134 (Plaka) but don't expect anything too original.

Jazz, in contrast, is thriving and there's a really excellent small scene centred on two clubs: *Tzaz* in Rangava Square (off Thespidos Street in Plaka: difficult to find, up some steps) and *The Half Note* at Michalokopoulou 56 (Llissia district, on the far side of Kolonaki). If you're seriously interested you might pick up a copy of *Tzaz* magazine from the above-mentioned Pop 11.

Most Athens **discos** tend to be under-inspired and over-priced, with a one-drink admission from 400 drx up. Among the more promising are *Disco 14* (Kolonaki square), *Mad Club* (Lissiou, Plaka; if it lasts another season) and *Paramount* (Soutsou, Kolonaki). Predominantly gay discos include *Jacare* (Tholou 13, Plaka) and *Why Not?* (Hill 3, Plaka). Among the basically **gay bars** are *Rocambole* (Epicharmou 1, Plaka), *Vagelis* (Tholou 9, Plaka) and *Yannis* (Tholou 18, Plaka). Most of these are pretty exclusively male – as with the bulk of the Greek gay scene: *Sirius* in Kolonaki (Haritos 43) is one of the few bars with a sizeable lesbian patronage and even this closes down for most of July–August. For gay group contacts see the listings section a couple of pages on.

MUSIC: BOITES AND TAVERNAS

On an August night in Plaka, Athens reaches an annual musical low. Walls of overamplified bouzouki music crash into each other from across the lanes – and even if you hear sounds you like it ends up costing 500–600 drx for admission and a first thin drink. Ain't always so: the problem is just that most travellers turn up in Athens in the midsummer months. And from late Easter through to September virtually all the real music places close down and their musicians head out for the countryside and islands.

Probably the most exciting summer events will, therefore, be part of the **Athens Festival** – get a programme from the Festival Office (see next section) for concerts at the small theatre on Likavitos. You might even be lucky enough to catch a performance by Mikis Theodorakis, Communist Party MP and most brilliant of the composers to emerge from the radical 'Neo-Kyma' (new wave) boites of the 1960s.

The boites – music clubs featuring a mixture of left-wing songs (often from the Civil War, or settings of poets like Ritsos), satirical theatre and *rebetika* (the old urban blues) – have themselves had quite a strong revival over the past couple of years, after degenerating through the 1970s into glossy mainstream nightclubs. Unfortunately literally all the authentic ones close down each summer – and more often than not they open up again in a different form at a different place. Tholou Street in Plaka, however, looks as fixed a venue as one can find – last season hosting the three best old-style boites in Athens, *Apanemia* at no. 4, *Esperides* at 6 and *Sousouro* at 17. For up-to-date information again try asking at Pop 11 (Skoufa 11, Kolonaki) or check out listings in the *Athenian*.

A completely different form of Greek music is provided by the **tavernas and kentros** featuring *Dhimotiki*, regional folk music kept alive in the capital by village and island communities who've moved into the suburbs. These too have their summer tourist-corruptions in Plaka but a few authentic places usually stay open. Try O *Pontos* at the corner of Ahileos/Terpsitheas (500 m west of Omonia), *Kortsopon* (Pireos 68: beyond Keramikos), or *To Arkadi* (Thivon 50; opposite the PanAthenaikos football ground). Through autumn and winter your choice goes up dramatically – to include many of the places in Plaka and Cretan tavernas all over the city. Listings are often printed at some stage of the season in the *Athenian*: or you could always ask hotel/tourist office people for addresses, stressing that you're not after a tourist folklore evening!

THEATRE, DANCE AND CULTURE

All major summer events are part of the **Athens Festival** – and the sooner you get details and tickets the better, since they're often sold out on the day. Both can be obtained from the Festival Box Offices at Stadiou 4 or Voukourestiou 1 (in the Arcade). Programmes of the main drama/music performances are also available in advance from NTOG offices – though they don't handle tickets or booking.

The main part of the festival consists of classical drama and music performances in the ancient Herod Atticus theatre, on the south slope of the Acropolis, and on weekends at the theatre of Epidavros in the Peloponnese. There's also, however, a small **fringe festival** with some jazz, rock and dance groups: most of whom perform at the open air theatre on Likavitos Hill.

There are cheap tickets and student reductions for most of these shows – the main problem, as stressed, being that they sell out quickly, particularly for ancient drama at Herod Atticus; Epidavros has rather larger capacity. If this happens don't necessarily give up: at Herod Atticus the young and ticketless are often admitted a few minutes before the start to sit on the wall at the back. It's worth hanging about; the entrance is on Dionissiou Areopagus.

Despite its somewhat institutionalised set-up and name, the **Dora Stratou Ethnic Dance Company** is also well worth an evening. They perform each night in summer (usually 10.15) at the open-air theatre on Philopappou hill – 10 mins walk west of the Acropolis, follow the signs. Gathered on a single stage are instruments and pieces that you'd stumble upon only by chance in several months trekking about rural Greece.

Cinemas are dirt cheap in Athens and all show a large proportion of British and American films – usually undubbed with Greek subtitles. In the summer their big pull is in moving outside, often on to really extraordinary sites. Screenings start around 6, 8 and 10 and are listed in the daily *Athens News*.

In pre-movie days one of the most popular Greek entertainments was **shadow puppetry** but today only two of these 'Karaghiosis' theatres survive. One is at Pirgos in the Peloponnese, the other in Plaka; directly behind the Monument of Lysikrates. Performances start at around 8 pm and you don't have to be a kid nor to understand Greek to appreciate the epic struggles before you – Karaghiosis, archetypal Greek, in his deceptions and defeat of the Turk, his support of Alexander the Great . . . whatever the puppeteer decides on.

Out of season you can get a run-down on Greek **theatre** – an extremely active scene, if over-dominated by sit-coms – in the *Athenian*. For English-language events the best places to check out are the foreign cultural institutes – most of whom put on free concerts, films, lectures and exhibitions in an attempt to legitimise their culture before a grateful Greek nation. The big two are the **British Council** (Plateia Kolonaki 17) and the **Hellenic American Union** (Massalias 22). Both of these also have libraries, open through the year with free access, where you can go and read newspapers and periodicals; in summer they open only on weekday mornings.

CONSUMING BUSINESS

Airlines Olympic's main office is at Othonos 6 (on Sintagma); others are grouped in the streets around.

American Express Poste restante/cheques from the main branch at the corner of Sintagma Square and Ermou Street. Open weekdays 8.30–5.30, Saturdays 8.30–1.30.

Banks National Bank in Sintagma stays open for exchange Mon.–Fri. 8 am–8 pm, Sat.–Sun. 8 am–2 pm. Other banks, keeping normal hours of 8 am–2 pm Mon.–Fri. only, include the Commercial Bank (Sofokleos 11), Barclays (Voukourestiou 15), Citibank (Othonos 8) and, in Piraeus, National Westminster (Filonos 137) and William & Glyn's (Akti Miaouli 61).

Beaches Sounion – with its Temple to Poseidon – is the most popular day trip to a beach. Closest, relatively unpolluted escapes are to Vouliagmeni and Varkiza (both 30 km out): both are NTOG pay-beaches, to get there take the bus from a signposted stop on Olgas Avenue on the south side of the National Gardens.

Books Compendium (Nikis 33; off Sintagma) are much the best for English-language ones, including books on Greece. For second-hand try Vassiotis (Ifestou 24, Monastiraki) but you'll probably do better changing with fellow travellers.

Camping gear Try the shops round Plateia Abyssinias, just south of Ermou Street in the 'Greek' part of the Flea Market.

Car rental Three firms in Leoforos Singrou are Hertz (at no. 12), Thrifty (24) and Autorent (118). The latter two give student discounts.

Car repairs and tyres Good for VW vans is Stamatis Papageorgiou, Leof Singrou 216. Others supposed to be reliable include – Mavtis, Leof. Singrou 8 (Citroens); Leonidas Fragos, Minos 21, Kinosarghos, off Leof. Vouiliaghmenis 104 (Fiats and Simcas); Thisseos 7 (Renaults) and Thisseos 226 (Minis). Tyre shops are grouped between 60–80 Tritis Septemvriou.

Dentists Free treatment at the Dentistry School (Odhondiatriko Skolio, Thivon/Levadhias). If you're insured for private fees check the ads in the *Athens News* or ask your embassy for addresses.

ELPA (road assistance) Help and information given free to foreign motorists at Messogion 2. For Emergency Assistance dial 104.

Emergencies Phone the tourist police on 171. If you can travel safely don't wait for an ambulance – get a taxi straight to the hospital address that they give you.

Ferry tickets For Piraeus boats buy at the Piraeus waterfront; for Rafina at Rafina. Combined bus/ferry tickets for the Sporades are sold by Alkyon Tours (Akademias 98: parallel to Stadiou) but see p. 251 first for more on this. Info and tickets for international ferries from George Papazoglou in the arcade at Stadiou 41. The NTOG office can give details of most sailings though their lists don't tend to work out exactly right.

Gay groups The Autonomous Group of Gay Women meet weekly at the Woman's House (see below). 'AMPHI', the Greek Gay Lib Movement, have an office at Zalogou 6 (Mon.–Fri. 6–11 pm) and produce a regular magazine. For gay bars see the 'Music' (!) section above.

Health food Most provisions from Propolis (Fidiou 3: parallel to Panapistimiou, 100 m from Omonia), who also run the Ideal Restaurant at Panapestimiou 46.

Hiking information Limited assistance from the Hellenic Alpine Club (Karageorgis Servias 7). Ordnance survey-type maps from the Athens Statistical Service (Likourgou 14: one block from Omonia).

Hospital clinics For general problems try the Hellenic Red Cross (Tritis Septemvriou/Kapodistriou); for skin and V.D. the Andreas Syngrou Hospital (Draghoumi 5; Mon., Wed., Fri. mornings); for inoculations at a nominal charge IKA Station (Leof. Alexandrhas/Leof. Kifissias – by the Panathenaikos football ground; weekdays 8 am–noon). The Woman's House (see below) have addresses of English-speaking gynaecologists.

Kiosks Remember that Athenian kiosks (*periptero*) stock virtually everything not on this list, from soap to plastic crucifixes.

Laundry Most places do it for you and charge heavily; there's a real live coin-op, though, at Angela Yerondou 10, off Plaka Square, and DIY facilities in some of the hostels.

Opticians Quick repairs at Paraskeropoulos (Stadiou 4).

Peace movement Contact the International Group for Nuclear Disarmament, tel. 895 8349 or 252 9846. Meetings are currently held at the AKE (Non-aligned Peace Movement) offices at Solonos 74; they should be advertised in the *Athens News* and the *Athenian*.

Pharmacies (farmakia) Most pharmacists speak English. The Marinopoulos branches (in Patission and Panapistimiou streets) are particularly good and also sell homeopathic remedies.

Phones You can phone locally from *periptero*; internationally from orange-topped phone-kiosks or the OTE offices – two of which, at Stadiou 65 and Patission/28 Oktovriou, are open 24 hrs.

Poste restante Main post office for Athens mail is at Eolou 100, just off Omonia square (open 7.30 am–8.30 pm).

Railway and coach tickets Info and tickets from the OSE (railway) office at Sina 6 (behind the National Library/University). Times of KTEL buses from the Tourist Office. See also 'Travel Details' at the end of this chapter.

Sandals Best in Athens are hammered out with poems by one Stavros Melissinos, the 'poet-sandalmaker' of Pandrossou street in Plaka. He's still at no. 89 – as when John Lennon sought him out to buy a pair and talk about his wine-dense poetry.

Travel firms Most are in and around Fillelinon and Nikis streets, off Sintagma: wherever you're headed take a full look round, 'Egnatia' at Fillelinon 7 often have good deals. Transalpino have an office at Nikis 28 but don't buy tickets for journeys through Italy – they're cheaper when you get there.

Women's movement Most accessible of the women's groups is the Multinational Liberation Group of Athens: they meet Wednesdays at 8.30 pm at THE WOMAN'S HOUSE, co-ordinating centre for most Athens feminism, at Romanou Melodou 4, Likavitos district (tel. 281 4823). See also 'Feminismos' in the Basics chapter (p. 13).

OFFICIAL BUSINESS

Mount Athos Permits Start off (see p. 149) at the Ministry of Foreign Affairs, Zalakosta 2 (off Vas. Sofias: 50 m from Sintagma); Mon.–Fri. 8–2.

Work/Residence Permits Ministry of Foreign Affairs, Halkondili 9, Pl. Kaningos; Mon.–Fri. 8–1 but go early or you won't get seen.

Tourist police Head Office at Leof. Singrou 7 (round behind the Acropolis). Phone – from anywhere – 171.

NTOG Main office, for special enquiries, is at Amerikis 2b. For most business use the information office inside the National Bank in Sintagma Square.

Embassies/consulates BRITAIN, Ploutarhou 1, Kolonaki (736 211); USA, Vas. Sofias 91 (712 951); IRELAND, Vas. Konstantinou 7 (732 771); CANADA, Ioannou Gennadiou 4 (739 511); NETHERLANDS, Vas Konstantinou 7 (739 701); AUSTRALIA, Messogion 15 (360 4611); NEW ZEALAND, An. Tosha 15, Ambelokopi (641 0311); SWEDEN, Vas. Konstantinou 7 (724 504); DENMARK, Pl. Kolonaki 15 (713 012); NORWAY, Vas. Konstantinou 7 (746 173).

Visa sections EGYPT, Zalakosta 1 (Mon.–Fri. 8–12); ISRAEL, Marathonodhromon 1, Palea Psychiko (Tues.–Fri. 10–12); TURKEY, Vas. Georgiou 8 (Mon.–Fri. 8.30–12); HUNGARY, Kalvou 10 (Mon., Wed., Fri. 10–12); BULGARIA, Akadimias 12 (Mon., Wed., Fri., Sat. 10–12); YUGOSLAVIA, Evrou 25, Mon.–Fri. 9–11.30); INDIA, Merlin 10 (Mon.–Fri. 10–12).

PIRAEUS

The easiest way to get to Piraeus is on the **metro** – there are stops in Omonia and Monastiraki squares and the journey takes about 25 minutes. Piraeus is the last stop on the line; trains run from 5.30 am–midnight and there's one standard price for all journeys – just buy a ticket and get on. The **Green Bus** from Sintagma (Fillelinon) also goes to Piraeus; frequently in the day, hourly at night from 1 am–5 am.

The streets around the metro station are full of **shipping agents** selling tickets to the Greek islands and to numerous foreign ports; although you can get tickets in advance in Athens it's quite usual practice just to turn up and see what's going. There are two main points you should remember – first, that most boats leave early in the morning (night boats to Crete being a notable exception), second, that each agent acts for a few particular boats and will tell you only about these. Prices for all domestic boat journeys are standardised but the boats (and the routes they take) vary greatly so ask around. (See also 'Introduction to the Islands', p. 161.)

All the ferries and also the hydrofoil to Aegina leave from the Main Harbour (right opposite the metro); the other hydrofoils leave from the Zea Marina, about 10 mins walk away. The last harbour (about 10 mins

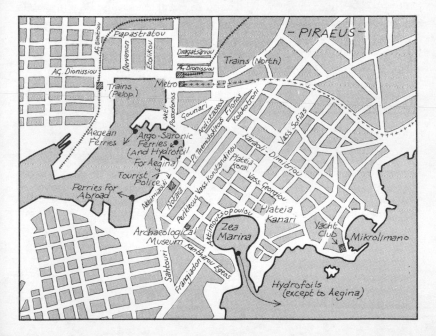

further still) is Mikrolimano – a picturesque yacht marina flanked by fine but expensive fish tavernas. If you want to try hitching a luxury lift this is the place.

Apart from its function as a port (and it's one of the busiest in the Mediterranean) Piraeus doesn't have a lot to hold you. Its ancient walls are largely destroyed or obscured by industrial wasteland and drab suburbs but, if you've a few hours to fill, the **Archaeological Museum** (Filellinon 38) is worth a visit; it contains superb bronzes of Artemis and Athena displayed until recently in the National Museum.

AROUND ATHENS

DAFNI AND KESARIANI MONASTERIES

Just 9 km west of Athens, the **Monastery of Dafni** is one of the classic buildings of Byzantine art. Its design, like Ossios Loukas on the road to Delphi, is a perfect example of the 'Greek Cross-Octagon-plan' and its mosaics are regarded as amongst the great masterpieces of the Middle Ages.

Built in the C11th it replaced a C5th predecessor, built in turn over the ruins of an ancient sanctuary of Apollo; hence deriving its name from the laurels, 'daphnae', sacred to the god. Both the church and the Justinian fortifications which enclose it incorporate reused blocks from the sanctuary. Inside, the mosaics are remarkable in their completeness and power – offering a firm idea of Byzantine iconology. There are scenes from the life of Christ and the Virgin, Saints, Archangels and Prophets, but above all there is a complete mosaic on the dome – the stern image of the Pantokrator, Almighty God. Lit by the sixteen windows of the drum and set against a background of gold, Christ directs a tremendous and piercing gaze upon you, His finger poised ominously on the book of Judgment. It is, simply, the most striking and memorable Byzantine image that survives in Greece.

Dafni can be reached in 20 mins from central Athens (bus 282 from Plateia Eleftherias) but check first with the NTOG that it is open. In the February 1981 earthquake it suffered very severe structural damage and at the time of writing, three years on, restoration is still in progress.

If you do find the monastery closed – or if it spurs your interest in things Byzantine – Ossios Loukas is the obvious substitute/next step. It's best visited en route to Delphi, though, and for a day's escape from Athens you might try instead the **Kesariani Monastery**, contemporary with Dafni, on the slopes of Mount Hymettus. Architecturally it's far more modest, and its frescoes are mainly C17th–18th but it's at least outside the smog-zone of Greater Athens – a popular picnic trip for Athenians, particularly on May Day. Citybus 224 takes you close by, leaving frequently from Akadimias Street.

ELEFSIS (Open weekdays 9–3.30, Sundays 10–4.30; closed Tuesday)

From Dafni the buses continue (in about 20 minutes) to Elefsina – virtually landlocked by the island of Salamis and horribly industrialised. Here, in the most depressing setting in Greece, is the very ancient site of the Mysteries of Elefsis. The extensive, but confusing, excavations are clearly indicated to the left of the modern highway.

A cult of Demeter (Ceres, the Goddess of Corn) evolved at Elefsis in the Mycenaean Age – perhaps as early as 1500 BC. By classical times a highly sophisticated annual festival had grown up around it and pilgrims from all over the Greek world came to witness the proceedings. They gathered outside the Propylaia in Athens and after various obscure rites, including mass bathing and purification in Phaleron Bay, proceeded to Elefsis where, in the windowless Hall of Initiation, they watched the Priests of Demeter exhibit 'the Holy Things' and speak 'the Unutterable Words'. It is believed that the Mystery was a kind of fertility play – developed from the myth of Persephone (daughter of Demeter) who annually descended into, and was resurrected from the underworld. Although the proceedings lasted until the C4th AD, and for much of that period were witnessed by some 30,000 annual initiates, nothing of their content (which was secret on pain of death) was ever recorded. Many, however, testified to the profound effect of the experience, Pindar writing that 'he who has seen the holy things and goes in death beneath the earth is happy; for he knows life's end and he knows the new divine beginning'.

Principal among the ruins is the **Telesterion** (the Hall of Initiation), although it's difficult to visualise with parts of seven different structures having been excavated. Best make first for the **Museum**, to the left, which includes models of the site at various stages in its history.

THE TEMPLE OF POSEIDON AT SOUNION (Open daily 11 am–sunset; closed Tuesdays)

Cape Sounion, the tip of the Attic Peninsula, is easily accessible from Athens; buses run on the half hour from Mavromateon Street (100 m up from the National Museum) and the journey takes under 2 hours. The **Temple of Poseidon** occupies a majestic position on the point itself, overlooking the Aegean and affording views of Kea, Kithnos and the distant Serifos. It was built in the time of Pericles, between 444–441 BC, and to the north are remains of the Propylaia which gave entrance to the sanctuary.

Byron visited Sounion often and is said to have carved his name on one of the Doric pillars – an unfortunate precedent; later he immortalised it in *Don Juan*:

> Place me on Sunium's marbled steep,
>> Where nothing, save the waves and I,
> May hear our mutual murmurs sweep;
>> There, swan-like, let me sing and die:
> A land of slaves shall ne'er be mine —
>> Dash down yon cup of Samian wine!

Sadly the solitude is long gone and the place is packed in summer with coach trips; still, it *is* very beautiful and there's a sandy beach nearby.

There are beaches, in fact, the whole way down the coast to Sounion but – unless you've a car to pick your spot – they're not really worth the effort; virtually all are highly developed with expensive hotels and admission charges – though at both **Sounion** and **Voula**, if you don't feel like returning to Athens, there are campsites. Camping rough on this stretch of coast is not really feasible.

MARATHON, RHAMNOUS AND BRAURON

At **MARATHON** (42 km from Athens; buses hourly from Mavromateon Street) is the **Burial Mound**, 30 feet high and 200 yards round, raised over the 192 Athenians who died in the city's famous victory over the Persians in 490 BC. It's a strangely unimpressive monument – of interest really, only if you want to pay homage. The **Museum**, about 1 km to the west, displays vases excavated from the graves and Neolithic pottery from a local cave of Pan.

More worthwhile (though very difficult to reach without a car) are the ruins of **RHAMNOUS**, 17 km north from Marathon village, in a beautiful and totally isolated setting above the sea. Amongst the scattered and overgrown remains is a Doric **Temple of Nemesis**, goddess of happiness and misery; Pausanias records that the Persians (who landed nearby) incurred her wrath by carrying off a marble block – upon which they intended to commemorate their conquest of Athens.

BRAURON, half way between Marathon and Sounion, is one of the best minor sites in Attica. Here, the **Sanctuary of Artemis** lies in a marshy valley at the base of a low hill (noticeable by a Byzantine chapel on its summit). At a quadrennial festival, young children dressed as bears enacted a mysterious ritual connected with the goddess and childbirth. The arcade where these young priestesses lived ('The Stoa of the Bears') has been restored and there are remains also of a shrine known in the fifth century BC as the 'Tomb of Iphigenia', who legendarily introduced the cult to Brauron. The **Museum** (closed Tuesdays) includes vases of olive wood, found preserved in mud, which are unique in Greece. The ruins are close to the modern village of **VRAONA** – 6 km north of **MARKOPOULOS** (to which there are buses from Mavromateon Street); they are rarely visited.

ATHENS: TRAVEL DETAILS

THE AIRPORTS Olympic Airways flights leave from the **West Airport** – no. 133 bus from Sintagma (opposite the Olympic office) from 06.00–23.30 hours, every 20 minutes, journey takes 20 minutes. All other airlines use the **East Airport** – direct yellow shuttle bus from 4 Amalias (off Sintagma) from 06.00–00.20, every 20 minutes, journey takes 25 minutes. Taxis to either airport should cost around £4–£5 from Central Athens but make sure they switch their meters on (a legal requirement) as many try and cheat tourists, especially at night. If you're making straight for the islands there's also a bus from the East Airport direct to Piraeus.

THE RAILWAY STATIONS Trains for Corinth and the Peloponnese leave from the **Peloponnesian Station**, those for northern Greece from **Stathmos Larissis**; both are west of Omonia off Deligiani. Information and tickets for both – and for many **long distance buses** – from OSE Office, Karolou 1. The OSE buses leave from their relevant railway station.

KTEL BUSES Buses for destinations in **Attica** leave from **Mavromateon Street** (100 m above the National Archaeological Museum, at the junction with Leof. Alexandras). All those for the Peloponnese and most for western and northern Greece leave from **100, Kifissou Street**; to reach this terminal take the no. 051 bus from the corner of Vilara and Menandrou Streets (near Omonia).

Buses for Delphi, Ossios Loukas, Trikkala, Volos, Thebes, Levadia, Larissa, Lamia, Chalkis and most other destinations in Central Greece leave from **260, Liossion Street**; to reach this take bus no. 025 at the Amalias entrance to the National Gardens (by Sintagma) or the metro from Omonia/Monastiraki to the Agios Nikolaos stop (about 100 m down the road). Information and times can be obtained from the NTOG Office inside the National Bank of Greece in Sintagma. (NB – The Kifissou Station is a 25-minute bus ride from the centre – it's the very last stop.)

HITCHING To **Corinth and the Peloponnese/Patras**: bus to Dafni, Motorway starts at junction of Leof. Athinon and Iera Odos. To **Lamia and the north**: bus to Nea Kifissia, National Road starts there. To **Thebes and Delphi** (old road): bus to Elefsina.

THE FERRIES Piraeus (reached from central Athens by metro, or directly from the airport) has ferries to Crete, the Cyclades, Dodecanese and north-east Aegean islands in addition to many international routes (to Cyprus, Haifa and Alexandria, for instance). There are also ferries from **Lavrio** to Kea and Kithnos; and from **Rafina** to Amorgos, Andros, Mykonos, Siros and Tinos. See the Travel Details at the end of each island section for more details. Rafina and Lavrio are both well connected by bus with Athens.

Chaptertwo
THE PELOPONNESE

Hitching through the Peloponnese for the first time I kept being warned: 'It's a special part of Greece', people would say, 'and you shouldn't hurry through it.' This is good advice. The region has a strictly defined tourist route which plods through the main ruins and hovers around a few escalating resorts, but outside this narrow circuit it is still completely unspoilt, beautiful, remote and often wild. If you have the time to fit in with erratic bus schedules — or better still to hitch along minor roads, being dropped at villages along the way — you'll find a land that pays back almost in direct ratio to the effort you put in.

The usual approach from Athens is through Corinth into the region known as the **Argolid**; buses and trains run this way at least every hour. This is the area of Greece richest in ancient sites – with Agamemnon's fortress at Mycenae, the great theatre of Epidavros, and lesser sites at Corinth, Tiryns and Nafplio all within an hour's journey of each other. Inevitably it's extremely popular and in peak season the sites can lose a little magic under the shadow of constant tourist coaches. But, this accepted, you shouldn't even consider missing it out. The secret is just to go on, to head down south into **Lakonia** – a strange, arid, rocky country with much better beaches and some quite extraordinary medieval ruins, pre-eminently at Mistra and Monemvassia. Most tourists, having gazed upon Mycenae, cut straight across the peninsula to **Olympia**, a target you can quite happily take weeks in reaching.

A dramatic and alternative beginning is to take the weekly boat, or in summer daily hydrofoil, from Piraeus to **Monemvassia**, at the south-eastern foot of the Peloponnese. Or, taking things slower, you can edge your way around the **Argo-Saronic** islands of Aegina, Poros, Hydra and Spetses, each well connected with the Peloponnesian mainland. **Leaving** the Peloponnese your options, too, are varied. There are boats from Neapolis (and irregularly from Githio and Monemvassia) to the island of Kithira and thence onwards to Kasteli on Crete; at Killini, under 2 hrs from Olympia, there are ferries to Zakinthos; and from Patras to Corfu, Ithaca, Kefalonia, Italy and Yugoslavia. If you're making for Delphi, or the west and north, there's also a very useful ten-minute ferry link from Rio (just above Patras) to AntiRio on the opposite edge of the gulf.

THE ARGOLID

CORINTH (Ancient site open weekdays 9–6.30; Suns and hols 9.30–5.00)

The modern town of Corinth, **KORINTHOS**, is grim and characterless – levelled by an earthquake in 1928, it again felt the brunt of the quake last year. The only reason to stop off here is to visit the notorious ancient city, now partially occupied by a village, about 6 km to the south. Buses there (marked 'Arhea Korinthos') go on the hour, every hour, from the station at the corner of Koliatsou and Ermou streets in the centre of town. There are hourly buses back to Corinth, on the half hour, from the ancient site.

The ruins of **ANCIENT CORINTH** lie at the base of an imposing acropolis; ramshackle and overgrown they only begin to suggest the majesty of this once supremely wealthy city. The area was inhabited almost continuously from the early Bronze Age due to its geographical importance as a gateway to the Peloponnese from the rest of Greece and as a link between east and west Europe. At its peak around the 6th and 7th centuries BC it rose to become the chief commercial city of all Greece, its two harbours, on either side of the Isthmus, packed with Phoenician, Syrian, Egyptian and, later, Roman ships. The magnificence of its wealth was obviously matched by its pleasures for Corinth, since these early centuries, was notorious for luxury. A temple to Aphrodite, served by over 1,000 sacred prostitutes, once stood at the top of the acropolis and the phrase 'Corinthian girl' came to be synonimous with 'whore'. In Roman times St Paul attempted to reform their ways but was met only by rioting in response; trials recorded in the 'Letters to the Corinthians'.

It is in fact the remains of the Roman city, refounded on an imperial scale by Julius Caesar in 44 BC, that are visible today. From the classical Greek era only seven austere Doric columns of the Temple of Apollo remain, set slightly above the agora as if in quiet defiance of the destruction vented upon the rest of the city when the Achaean league collapsed in 146 BC. The Roman city, once inhabited by 300,000 people, was originally encircled by some eleven miles of wall. It was approached from the sea along the Lechaion road – 40 feet wide, drained, and paved in marble. This remained in use for centuries and an excavated section still leads into the site (from what is now the exit gate). At its end steps ascend into the old market place and to an extraordinary construction – the Fountain of Pereine. This was one of two natural springs in Corinth (the other, astonishingly, was on the acropolis) and its cool water was elaborately channelled into a fountain and pool in the courtyard. The magnificently designed fountain-house was, like the one at Olympia (and also the theatre carved into the side of the Athens Acropolis), the gift of the wealthy Athenian and friend of the Emperor Hadrian, Herod Atticus; its waters still flow through the underground cisterns and supply the modern village.

ACROCORINTH, towering 1,885 feet above, is an amazing mass of rock – still largely encircled by a mile and a half of wall; if you don't get a lift it's an hour and a half's walk to the summit. The ancient brothel stands no longer – replaced in turn by a church, watchtower, mosque and Venetian belvedere (for despite its apparently impregnable position AcroCorinth was taken by successive waves of invaders). It's a fantastic place to wander around, a jumble of ruined chapels and houses set amidst seemingly endless strings of battlements – fortified by Greeks, Romans, Byzantines, Franks, Crusaders, Venetians and Turks. The enormity of the site, some 60 acres, is matched only by Monemvassia and, looking down over the Saronic and Corinthian gulfs, one really senses the importance of its position – the cause of sporadic battles over nearly 2000 years of history, the last in 1828 when it became a vital strategic point in the War of Independence.

Among the fortress ruins you notice the predominance of Turkish building – houses, minarets, even parts of a bath-house. This is unusual in Greece, for in any less isolated place all evidence of Turkish occupation would have been physically removed or at least heavily defaced. Here, halfway up the hill, you can see a compromise point in this process – the still functioning 'Fountain of Hadji Mustafa', Christianised by the addition of great carved crosses.

Old Corinth, to an even greater extent than most Greek sites, becomes deserted when the gates are locked on the ruins. Very few people stay in the village, although there are a handful of **rooms** to rent and possibilities of camping (try the enclosed football ground). It's probably better, however, to move on by bus or train to **MIKINE** (Mycenae), only half an hour's journey. Neither modern **KORINTHOS** nor its industrial-set beach campsites are likely to take any great hold on you: though if you're stuck there are cheapish rooms in town along the waterfront.

MYCENAE (MIKINE) (open weekdays 9–5; Suns and hols 10–5)

Tucked into a fold of the hills just off the road from Corinth to Argos is Agamemnon's citadel, 'well-built Mycenae, rich in gold'. Nowhere in Greece does the place better fit the legend. It was uncovered in 1874 by the German archaeologist Heinrich Schliemann (who also found the site of Troy), impelled by his single-minded belief that there was a factual basis to Homer's epics; his finds of brilliantly-crafted gold and sophisticated tomb-architecture bore out the accuracy of the poet's epithets.

The modern village of **MIKINE** is 2 km from the Argos road and the railway station, along a beautiful, straight road lined with eucalyptus trees through which glimpses of the citadel appear, flanked by the twin mountains of Zara and Elias. The 'Restaurant Iphigeneia', halfway up the single street, doubles up as a **youth hostel** (with plenty of roofspace); there are also a number of **rooms** and, for a few drachmas less, '**Camping Mycenae**'. Towards the fortress, which is a further 2 km up the hill, is the old house used by Schliemann, now the 'Belle Helene Hotel'; it's worth wandering in, on your way, to see the signatures of former visitors displayed on the walls – what, for instance, did Virginia Woolf reflect as she climbed the last stretch towards the Lion Gate?

The region around **MYCENAE** was occupied from Neolithic times (around 3000 BC) but it is a period about 1,000 years later (the 'Mycenaean Civilisation' which was pre-eminent in southern Greece from c. 1550–c. 1200 BC) that produced the buildings of a fortress, and town, whose ruins Schliemann found. The area is also dotted with 'tholos tombs' looted by modern times, and the finest of these is entered across the road from the main fortress site. Known as the **Treasury of Atreus** (or the 'Tomb of Agamemnon' which is, just, historically feasible) it is an impressive monument to Mycenaean building skills – an extraordinary feat of construction designed like a 'beehive' without the use of mortar. It is entered through a majestic 40-foot corridor with a great lintel above its chamber doorway – formed by two vast slabs of stone, one of which, a staggering 27 feet in length, is estimated to weigh 118 tons.

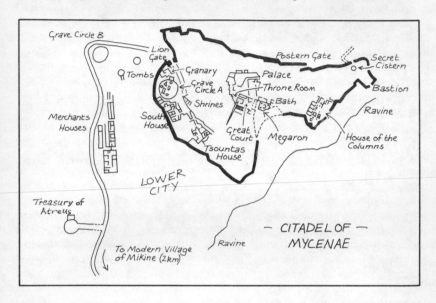

The entrance to the **Citadel** through the famous 'Lion Gate' is equally awesome. Huge sloping gateposts bolster the walls (termed 'Cyclopean' by the ancients in bewildered explanation of their construction) and above them a graceful carved relief stands out in confident assertion of its powerful and advanced domain. The motif of a pillar supported by two muscular lions was probably the royal symbol of the Mycenaean House, for a seal found on the site depicts a similar device.

Inside the walls to the right is the **grave circle** excavated by Schliemann and which he believed to contain the bodies of Agamemnon and his followers – murdered by Clytemnestra and her lover Aegisthus on their triumphant return from Troy. Opening one of the graves he found a tightly fitting and magnificent gold mask which had preserved the actual flesh of a Mycenaean noble; 'I have gazed upon the face of Agamemnon', he exclaimed in an excited cable to his fellow countryman Otho, then King of Greece. For a time it seemed that Homer's tale had received documentary evidence but in fact the burials date from some centuries *before* the estimated date of the Trojan war.

Schliemann, once again mistaken – his genius for discovery was never matched by any great skill as a historian – took the extensive 'South House', beyond the grave circle, to be the Palace of Agamemnon. In fact the **Royal Palace** was later discovered on the summit of the acropolis – a far more impressive building complex; although the ruins are only at basement level the different rooms are not hard to make out. It was probably rebuilt around 1300 BC (along with the Lion Gate and the citadel's fortifications) and is centred around a great court. On the south side a staircase would have led via an anteroom to the big rectangular throne room and on the east a double porch gave access to the Megaron with its traditional circular hearth. The small rooms to the north are believed to have been royal apartments and in one of them the remains of a red stuccoed bath have led to its fanciful identification as the very spot of Agamemnon's murder.

Walking around the citadel it's quite easy to lose the trudging masses from the tour buses, to sit by the walls and feel the timelessness of the place. The sound of bells, from a herd of goats scratching about the mountains, echoes down yet there *is* something terrible and sinister about these great limestone walls; the decline of the Mycenaeans, not long after the death of their most famous king, becomes an inevitable shift of history. As if a symbol of these troubled times, beside the other postern gate, at the far end of the citadel, is a **secret cistern**. A hundred steps lead down to a deep underground spring, a secure water supply and presumably bewildering to the enemy in time of siege. It's possible to descend the whole way but you will need a torch – matches make little impression on the immemorial darkness and there's a 70 metre drop into water at one turn in the passageways. It's an extraordinary sensation as you feel your way down the damp walls of this tunnel, constructed over 3,000 years ago. Nearby is the **House of Columns**, a large and stately building with the beginning of a stairway leading to an upper storey.

Outside the walls of the citadel lay the main part of the town; only the ruling elite of Mycenaean society could live within the citadel itself. Extensive remains of **merchants' houses** have been uncovered near to the road beside a second grave circle. In them Linear-B tablets, recording the spices used to scent oils, were found, along with large amounts of pottery; the extent suggesting that the early Mycenaeans may have engaged in a considerable trade in perfume. The discovery of the tablets has also caused a reassessment of the sophistication of Mycenaean civilisation for they show that, here at least, writing was not limited to government scribes working in the royal palaces, as had previously been thought, and that around the citadel may have been a commercial city of some size and wealth.

ARGOS

ARGOS, 10 km on from the Mikine turn-off (catch one of the regular buses there, coming from Korinthos), is said to be the oldest inhabited town in Europe. Passing through you wouldn't guess it – a drab, ramshackle industrial market centre. The **museum**, however, just off the main town square, is worth stopping off for if you've a serious Mycenaean interest – containing a good collection of tomb objects and armour along with extensive pottery from the region and Roman sculpture from the ruined local baths.

Apart from the medieval castle (massively cisterned and guttered, if you feel like climbing to the sprawling ruins) no ancient sites are particularly obvious. The principal **Roman ruins** are in fact a few minutes' walk down the Tripoli road, struggling to hold their own next to a tyre depot. Though very definitely a minor site they are surprisingly interesting. The theatre, built by classical Greeks and adapted by the Romans, looks oddly narrow from the road but climb up there and it feels immense. It's estimated to have held 20,000 spectators, 6,000 more than Epidavros and rivalled on the Greek mainland only by those at Megalopoli and Dodona. Alongside are the remains of an odeion and Roman baths, and presumably if the modern town could be cleared back an extensive site would be revealed. (Not entirely fenced off, the ruins have nominal opening hours from 9–2.30 Mon.–Sat., 10–3 Suns. and hols. Same for the Museum except it closes all day Tuesday.)

With NAFPLIO only a 15-minute bus-ride away – an elegant and stylish oasis amongst the generally functional modern centres of the Peloponnese – it's difficult to conjure any reason for staying in Argos. 4 kms before you get there the fortress of **TIRYNS**, companion site to Mycenae, rears up to the left of the road: buses will stop if you ask to be let off.

TIRYNS (Open Mon.–Sat. 9–1 and 4–6, Suns and hols 10–3)

Whilst all the tour coaches Greece can muster visit Mycenae, drawn by the magic of Homer's tale of Agamemnon, few bother with the equally impressive Tiryns; as a result you'll be able to see and feel this dramatic citadel in remarkable solitude.

The **fortress**, on a low dark hillock, once commanded the way from Nafplio to Argos, Mycenae and beyond but today the sea has receded a mile from its walls leaving it to stand bare and grim. Its mood of resilience and force is perpetuated by a modern prison which, by an eccentric quirk of planning, stands alongside; it was Easter Friday on my last visit and a sombre radio mass drifted eerily up from the exercise yard.

Homer wrote of the fortress as 'wall-girt Tiryns', an aspect so striking that Pausanias, coming upon it in the second century AD (when the walls stood at twice their present height), found it even more amazing than the Pyramids. The entrance is a superb example of Mycenaean military architecture. Climbing up the ramp, which allowed access to chariots, an invader's right (unshielded) side would be left exposed and at the top, forced to turn sharply, he would find himself again overlooked by defenders, with two considerable gateways to breach before eventually gaining access to the courtyard. The outer gateway at Tiryns is similar in size to the Lion Gate but, sadly, its lintel has gone so there is no heraldic motif to evidence any dynastic link between the two sites.

In the thickness of the courtyard's outer wall is one of the long stone vaulted corridors which are the citadel's most dramatic feature. A passage from the courtyard leads to a large forecourt and from there a staircase leads to the other network – a gallery 66 feet long, off which are numerous storage chambers. Sheep, throughout later ages, took refuge from storms in these galleries and the stone walls have been left brightly polished from their movements.

Of the **palace** itself only the limestone foundations survive but it is somehow more substantial than Mycenae and you can gain a clearer idea of its structure. The walls above would have been of sun-dried brick, covered in stucco and decorated with frescoes – fragments of which were found on the site, one depicting a boar hunt, the other a life-sized frieze of courtly women. Entering from the forecourt you are in the midst of a spacious colonnaded court, a round sacrificial altar in its midst. The familiar Mycenaean double porch leads directly ahead to the Megaron, or Great Hall, where the throne, its base surviving, is set before a massive round clay hearth. Royal apartments again lead off on either side: the women's quarters are thought to have been to the right whilst to the left is the bathroom, its floor – a huge single flat stone – intact. A tower, further off to the left, gives access to a secret staircase (not easy to find even today without the hindrance of walls) which winds down to an inconspicuous postern gate, no doubt useful in time of siege and again paralleling Mycenae. The site beyond the courtyard is separated by an enormous inner wall and has been rigged off the last few years for archaeological exploration after two underground cisterns were discovered at the far end.

Buses on to NAFPLIO stop by the roadside cafe if you wave them down; without luggage, though, it's under half an hour's walk.

NAFPLIO

Nafplio is a rarity amongst sizeable Greek towns. It is lively, beautifully sited and has a rather grand, fading elegance, inherited from the days when it was the fledgling capital of modern Greece. The seat of government was here from 1829 to 1834 and it was the initial residence of the Bavarian Prince Otho when he arrived in the country, put forward by the European powers to be the first King of Greece.

Beside the sea, spread beneath a great rocky headland, the town is an obvious place to stop over whilst exploring this whole region. It's within easy reach of Mycenae, Tiryns and Corinth, and there are two or three buses a day for the 27 km on to Epidavros. All of these leave from the **station** in Singrou street, near the base of the steps up to the Palamidi fortress; the train station has been purely ornamental for over a decade despite its continued appearance on route-maps. As a staging-post-resort the town gets fairly full in summer but there are over a dozen cheapish hotels (try the 'Leto' at Zigomala 28, or 'Tiryns' at Othonos 41) and loads of **rooms** places at the west end of town, just above Sintagma Square. The large **youth hostel** is a 10-minute walk to the outskirts on Odos Vizantiou (second turning to the left after the Argos turning).

The town is dominated by twin fortresses – **Palamidi** and **Its Kale**. Rich in historical exploits since medieval times, they were seen as the key to the Morea during the War of Independence, the Greek commander taking them in 1822 after nearly a year's siege. There's a statue of this majestically bewhiskered old hero in Nafplio's East Square and further notoriety is ensured him in Palamidi itself, where a cave-like room is pointed out as his prison. Ironically the actual imprisonment came after independence

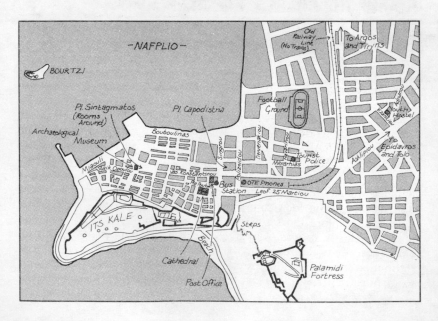

when Kolokotronis, objecting to the new Greek government's plans to curtail his powers, kidnapped four of its members as a warning stroke!

Open from sunrise to sunset (shorter hours on Sundays), Palamidi is an extraordinary place: perhaps the largest fort-complex in all of Greece, with its string of half a dozen self-contained Venetian castles. You can walk up to it – along some 899 steps hewn in the stone – from the south side of Plateia Nikitara, an excellent escape for an afternoon's reading or sunbathing. If you feel like cooling off there's a small pay **beach**, just between Palamidi and the ruined walls of Its Kale (now converted to house a government hotel). Or from here follow the road round a few hundred yards and you'll come upon a free and slightly longer rocky stretch.

There are few other monuments in Nafplio itself – and its appeal anyway lies much more in the provincial, easy-paced feel of the place. **Bourtzi**, third of the town's fortresses, is occasionally accessible by boat: an offshore islet, it was once the official residence of the Greek national executioner. Find time, though, for the **museum** – particularly if you didn't get to the one at Argos. Housed in a dignified old Venetian building on the main (Sintagma) square, it contains a unique suit of bronze Mycenaean armour, and the fragments of frescoes from Tiryns mentioned above. It's open 9–12.30 weekdays (which in Greece always includes Saturday), and 9–3.30 Suns. and hols. 10.30–2.30; closed Tuesdays.

ROUND THE COAST FROM NAFPLIO

There's not a grain of sand near Nafplio proper – you just swim off the rocks along the town's southern pine-backed promontory. Nearest real beach possibilities are at TOLO and KASTRAKI, 13 kms south.

TOLO, connected frequently by bus, is one of the Argolid's fastest growing resorts – its narrow sands thoroughly swamped in summer by some thirty or more hotels and campsites. Out of season it could be quite pleasant, and is reputedly a good place to find both painting and orange-picking work, but for pleasure you'll probably have much more time for **KASTRAKI BEACH**, 3 km out of Tolo on the far side of the road-fork to Nafplio (ask to be dropped on the way). Here too development is underway but it's a few years behind – limited to a manageable number of small hotels and two or three seasonal campsites. The beach itself is a beautiful long strand and if you get bored you can wander down and explore the scrub-covered rock towards the Nafplio road-junction. This is, or was, **ANCIENT ASSINE**, an important Mycenaean and classical city destroyed by the jealous and more powerful Argos in retribution for having sided with the Spartans against them. There's little to see other than the 300 yards of imposing ancient wall but it's somehow an oddly atmospheric spot.

The coast round the Argolid **towards Epidavros** has a series of beautiful (if rather small) beaches, looking out towards the Argo-Saronic islands a stone's throw away. However, since it is all so close to Athens and the villages also the obvious crossing points to these popular islands, it has for the most part become highly overdeveloped. Even the NTOG pamphlet admits 'the landscape itself is changing with the erection of new hotels and tourist resorts'; unless you have a car to explore the more secluded coves between resorts you'd probably do better elsewhere.

One possibility, if you're after a secluded beach not too far distant, is **PARALIA ASTROS**, 30 km south of Nafplio on the Tripoli side of the Argolic Gulf. There are very few direct buses (you need the one going to LEONIDIO) so you might have to end up taking one of the Tripoli buses and hitching from the turn-off. At last reports there were still just two small 'D' class hotels here, the 'Astros' and 'Chryssi Akti'.

EPIDAVROS (Site open weekdays 8–7, Suns and hols 10–4.30; Ancient Drama performances at weekends, late June-early September)

Epidavros is most famous, and most visited, for its remarkably preserved ancient theatre. Built by Polycleitus in the fourth century BC, it survived largely unaltered until recent years when, inspired by the perfect vision and acoustics from each of its 14,000 seats, the Athens Festival carefully restored it for performances of **ancient drama**. These take place every weekend from late June to early September and if you can possibly coincide it's worth doing so. As the light fades on the gentle rolling hills behind the stage a packed audience of Greeks spontaneously erupt into applause at poignant speech; it is the best place to see these timeless Greek tragedies and they really make sense dramatically – choruses and all – restored to their natural setting. Tickets can be bought before a performance but they do often sell out and it's wise to get them in Athens before you set out. You can camp on the rich green turf of the car park after a performance, although you're not allowed to put up a tent before it's finished.

Even without a performance **the theatre** is magnificent, a masterpiece of grace and beauty in its perfectly balanced shape and slope. Guides are constantly dropping coins and matches in the circular orchestra but this too has a curious fascination for the sound does indeed easily and clearly reach the highest of the 54 tiers of seats. Close by is a small **museum** which opens up an Epidavros unseen by most tourists; it displays finds from the Sanctuary of Asklepios, to whose cult Epidavros was dedicated as a spa and religious centre for over 800 years. Asklepios is reputed in some legends to have been the son of Apollo but it is more likely that he was a remarkable healer from the north of Greece. There were sanctuaries devoted to him throughout the Greek world but Epidavros was the most famous of them all; its renown so great that Rome, ravaged by an epidemic in 293 BC, sent for its sacred serpent. The finds in the museum show a progression of medical skills and cures used on the site – there are tablets recording miraculous and outrageous cures (like the man cured from paralysis after being ordered to heave the biggest boulder he could find into the sea) and also quite advanced surgical instruments. Additionally the museum have some excellent reconstructed models of the site – well worth visualising since most of the ruins are just foundations.

The **Sanctuary** is as large a site as Olympia or Delphi and in many ways it is equally fascinating, for the ruins here are of hospitals for the sick, dwellings for the priest physicians, and hotels and amusements for the fashionable visitors to the spa. Past the museum are the remains of Greek baths and a huge gymnasium with scores of rooms leading off a great colonnaded court – in its centre the Romans built an odeion. Beyond, to the left, is the Temple of Asklepios and, beside it, a fascinating rectangular building – the Abaton. Patients would sleep here to await visitation from the healing god – which probably appeared in a more physical manifestation than expected; harmless snakes are believed to have been kept in the building to be released at night to give a curative lick! The strong significance of the serpent at Epidavros (Asklepios was thought to take on its form) is extended in the next building you come to – the circular **Tholos**, one of the best preserved buildings on the site and designed, like the theatre, by Polycleitus. Its inner foundation walls form a labyrinth which it is thought was used as a snakepit and, according to one theory, a primitive form of shock therapy for mental patients. The patients would crawl in darkness through the outer circuit of the maze, guided by a crack of light towards the centre where they would find themselves surrounded by writhing snakes. Presumably, on occasion, it worked. The real healing elements at Epidavros, however, are still present – the sanctuary is set in a broad wooded valley, thick with the scent of thyme and pine and oddly devoid of the massed tourists thronging the theatre only a few hundred yards away.

The road for **ANCIENT EPIDAVROS** ('ARHEA' – *not* NEA or PALEA EPIDAVROS) branches off from the main Nafplio road at Ligourio (3 km away); the site is best reached by bus from Nafplio and can be visited from there as a daytrip. During the summer festival there are special boats and buses from Athens. Hotels and an official campsite are all at PALEA EPIDAVROS, some way distant. You can, however, **camp** on the car-park grass at any time of the week; bring some food if your money's light, the two nearby *tavernas* are both fairly expensive.

ONWARDS FROM NAFPLIO: THE TRIPOLI CROSSROADS

If you've only time for the Argolid, buses run back to Athens every hour from Nafplio and a couple of times a day from Epidavros. Both usually stop for a while at a cafe beside the **Corinth Canal**, begun under Nero but not completed until the 1890s. It's quite impressive.

Travelling deeper into the Peloponnese the main road climbs up through the Ktenias mountains, the Gulf of Argos brilliantly set out below you, to reach **TRIPOLI**. As so often it's a town which hasn't adapted with great dignity to modern industrial life: and the grand medieval buildings here were all razed to the ground in the Turkish retreat of 1828. For the traveller it makes a dull place, whose only importance lies in it being the central crossroads of the Peloponnese. Buses are plentiful and a choice must be made – south to Sparta and the Mani, west to Megalopolis or Kalamata and north-west to Olympia and Patras. For the purpose of this guide I'll begin with the route to the south – in my opinion much the most exciting alternative.

THE SOUTH: LAKONIA AND MESSINIA

Draw a line on a map from Kalamata over the Taygetus Mountains, through Sparti and across to Leonidio. This, broadly, is **Lakonia**, territory of the ancient Spartans. It's a dramatic country of harsh mountains and poor, rocky soil – terrain that has always maintained an isolation from most of the rest of the country. This, above all, is expressed by the Mani and by the two great ruined Byzantine cities of Mistra and Monemvassia: for virtually all travellers who get to them, the unexpected highlight of a stay on the mainland.

The third, western peninsula, the province of **Messinia**, is again dominated by dramatic medieval sites, the twin castles of Methoni and Koroni. It's also host to the third big Mycenaean site – Nestor's Palace near Pilos – and to some of the best beaches of the Peloponnese, strung upcoast almost the whole way to Pirgos.

SPARTA (SPARTI)

Thucydides predicted that if the city of Sparta were deserted, 'distant ages would be very unwilling to believe its power at all equal to its fame'.

The city had no great temples or public buildings and, throughout its period of greatness, remained unfortified – Lycurgus, architect of the Spartan constitution, declaring that 'it is men not walls that make a city'. The prediction has become partially endorsed for there are no great ruins to be seen at Sparta; yet, approaching the city through rocky hills clinging to the Parnon Mountains, one can sense much of the power and the strategic brilliance of its position. The modern town, **SPARTI**, occupies the main site of its ancient forbear and before it stretches the vast triangular plain of Lakonia – guarded on one side by the Parnon ranges, on the other by the Taygetus. The ancient city state occupied this whole area – there was no single great town but a string of villages clustered on the low hills to the right of the Eurotas river.

Traces of ancient glory are sparse but there are some ruins to be seen to the north of the city. A track behind the football stadium leads to the **acropolis**, on the tallest of the Spartan hills. An immense theatre was once built into the side of the hill but today most of its stone has gone – hurriedly adapted for fortification as the Spartans' power declined and, later still, used in the building of the Byzantine city of Mistra. Only the ridges can be seen but over to the left, about 500 m along the Tripolis road, a path descends to the remains of the Sanctuary of Artemis Orthia where Spartan boys underwent endurance tests by flogging. Pausanias records that young men often expired under the lash and adds that the altar had to be splashed with blood before the goddess was satisfied. Perhaps it was this aspect which attracted the Romans to revive the custom; the main ruins here are of the grandstand they built for spectators to watch the cruel spectacle. The site isn't enclosed, all movable artefacts and mosaics having been transferred to the town's small **archaeological museum** (weekdays 8.30–12.30 and 4–6, Suns and hols 9–3; closed Tuesdays). Among its more interesting exhibits are a number of votive offerings found on the sanctuary site – knives set in stone that were presented as prizes to the Spartan youths and solemnly re-dedicated to the goddess.

With its rough retsina, crude *taverna* food and rows of tractor dealers SPARTI itself isn't the most exciting place in Greece to stay and if you're camping you might as well press on to the official site at MISTRAS village (5 km) or find your own amid the ravines and orange groves on the way. For rooms, however, you pay well over the odds at Mistra and there's very little choice in season. Sparti has enough beds to go round at any time – cheapest in town are at the *Hotel Sparti*, Aghissilaou 46 (one block west of the central square).

MISTRA (Site open weekdays 8–7, Suns and hols 10–6.30)

A glorious, airy place, Mistra hugs a steep and rocky flank of the Taygetus – it is perhaps the most exciting and dramatic site that the Peloponnese can offer. Winding up this height is an astonishingly complete Byzantine city which once sheltered a population of some 42,000; you wander along winding alleys, through monumental gates, past the medieval houses and palaces and above all into its beautiful churches – each of which yields superb and radiant frescoes. It is, in effect, like wandering into a massive museum of architecture, painting and sculpture – only, unlike any ordinary museum, here you are physically placed within a different age.

That Mistra is here at all is an extraordinary quirk of history. The castle on its summit was built in 1249 by William II de Villehardouin, fourth Frankish Prince of the Morea, and together with the fortresses of Monemvassia and the Mani it guarded his territory. The Franks, however, were driven out in 1271 and this isolated triangle of land in the southeast Peloponnese became the Despotate of Mistra, a last province of the Greek Byzantine empire and for many years virtually its capital. Whilst the walls of Constantinople enclosed little more than a pillaged and half-ruined city here at Mistra emerged a defiant and splendid rebirth of Byzantine art and power. Much of the Peloponnese was recovered and was ruled from here by a son or brother of the eastern emperor, often

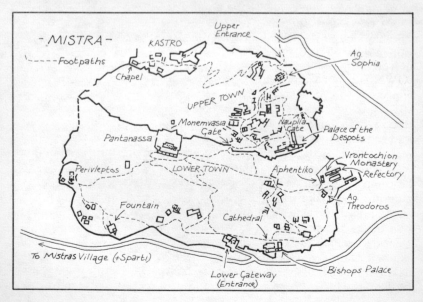

the heir presumptive. Mistra's most famous son, the last Byzantine emperor, Constantine XI Palaeologus, was crowned in the town's cathedral before he set out for Constantinople where, in 1453, he was to perish with his city and empire.

Mistra outlasted the capital by seven years, but for over a century before it had been the principal light of the Byzantine world. A glorious age of building was accompanied by a renaissance in painting and in scholarship; here, at the court of the Palaeologues, the humanist philosopher Gemisthus Plethon rediscovered Plato. But the confidence of this last great era of Byzantium is expressed in a more tangible form – the brilliant frescoes at Mistra, painted in the last decades before Christian Greece fell under nearly four centuries of Turkish rule.

From Sparti it's a 5 km walk – or occasional bus – to the modern village of **MISTRAS**, a beautiful place in itself, amidst dense groves of orange trees and with seemingly dozens of springs in any direction you decide to explore. (Incidentally if you're intending serious hikes around the Taygetus try and get a copy of Marc Dubin's *Backpacker's Greece* before you set out – or at least consult the Alpine Club in Sparti: it can be a treacherous range. The club operate a refuge near the summit of Profitis Ilias, a majestic peak whose trail begins beyond the village of Palaeopanagia.) The old **Byzantine town of MISTRA** (or Mystra) is a further 2 km up in the hills beyond Mistras village, so if you're on a bus and want to stay at the campsite get off before the bus rushes on (as they tend to do). Also don't reckon on staying anything less than a full day up here, wandering amidst the ruins: so if you want food take it, there are only a couple of seasonal drink stalls near the entrances.

The site is essentially in three parts: the Lower Town, with the city's earliest and most important churches, the Upper Town grouped around the vast shell of a royal palace, and the kastro, or castle. The **LOWER TOWN** is entered through an imposing gateway in the outer wall and immediately to the right stands the **Cathedral**, or Metropolis, built in 1309 and the oldest of Mistra's many churches. A marble slab set in its floor is carved with the double-headed eagle of Byzantium – commemorating the spot where the last Eastern Emperor was crowned. Of its frescoes the earliest, in the North Aisle, depict the torture and burial of St Demetrios (to whom the church is dedicated); it's interesting to note the comparative stiffness of their figures in contrast to the later works opposite. These, illustrating the Miracles of Christ and the Life of the Virgin, are less formalised, more intimate, lighter of touch and they date from the last great years before Mistra's fall.

Further uphill is the **Vrontochion Monastery** with its two churches: the centre of cultural and intellectual life in C15th Mistra it's still possible to make out the cells of the monks. Its beautifully restored **Aphentiko** church (furthest of the two) again has excellent frescoes executed late in Mistra's history, particularly striking in their bold juxtapositions of colour.

Retracing your steps slightly a path curves upwards to the Monemvassia Gate, entrance to the **UPPER TOWN**. **The Palace of the Despots** ('rulers') rears above you, an enormous complex of buildings with, principal among them, a great vaulted audience hall; built at right angles to the line, with ostentatious windows regally dominating the skyline, this was once heated by eight great chimney pieces and its façade painted. Behind it the ruins of official buildings edge down to the massive Nafplio Gate whilst, to the west, is the church of **Agia Sophia** which served as the Palace Chapel. Its frescoes have survived well, protected until recent years by coatings of Turkish whitewash from its period as a mosque.

The walls of the **Kastro** never seem to get any closer and it offers fewer revelations than the ordinary buildings of the town. When you do make it, though, the intricate panorama below rewards the climb.

Taking the other path down from the Monemvassia Gate the **Pantanassa**, now attached to a convent, stands on the right; the last families were moved from Mistra in 1952 and the nuns here remain alone in the town. Their church of 'The Queen of All' is perhaps the finest that survives; perfectly proportioned, it is best appreciated from the gallery reached by an external staircase. Some way further down on this side of the Lower Town is the old Monastery of the **Perivleptos** – its single domed church, partially carved out of the rock, contains the best frescoes in Mistra; at once humanised and spiritual they also offer an excellent idea of the iconography of a Byzantine church. The position of each figure had to depend upon its sanctity and so here upon the dome, the image of heaven, is portrayed the Pantocrator (the all powerful Christ, in glory after the Ascension). On the apse is the Virgin and on the higher expanses of wall are depicted scenes from the life of Christ in this world. Prophets and saints could only appear on the lower walls – decreasing in importance according to their distance from the sanctuary.

MONEMVASSIA (Site not enclosed)

After Mistra one expects to be disappointed but Monemvassia, one-time commercial capital of the Byzantine Morea, is no less thrilling than its spiritual counterpart. Again it has survived largely in its medieval form but here, instead of being evacuated of people to become a kind of museum of medieval art, it has remained inhabited; two of the surviving churches are still used and its streets are enlivened by shops and a *taverna*. The population fell to as low as 30 a decade ago but today it is rising as artists and writers are buying up and beautifully restoring its houses – setting up a community on the Hydra model, only one less pretentious and aglow with money. Ironically, given the conservatism of the region,

Monemvassia was also the birthplace of Yannis Ritsos, Greece's foremost Communist poet.

The name – 'moni emvasis' – means literally 'single entrance' and indeed this 'Gibraltar of Greece', as it's not inaccurately called, can only be approached by means of a long man-made causeway; not surprisingly it was invariably the last outpost of the Morea to fall to Greece's successive waves of invaders. It is visited by comparatively few Greeks and fewer foreigners, largely because it is, basically, miles from anywhere – stuck out on the first of the three great tongue-shaped peninsulas of the Peloponnese. Buses go only from Sparti (twice a day) so if you want to get there from Githio you'll have to pick up the bus at Krokees or Skala – there's a long wait at Molai and you may, as I did, find it quicker to hitch. It's also possible to come straight from Piraeus (or Nafplio) by one of the 'Flying Dolphin' hydrofoils, a dramatic approach to the Peloponnese, or on the ordinary weekly boat.

Boat and bus drop you at the modern village of **GETHIRA** where most of Monemvassia's population moved, a sleepy place with a narrow sandy beach and good clear water; there are two 'E' class **hotels** (the 'Akroyali' and 'Likinion') and along the waterfront to the right are **rooms** to rent. However a few of the private houses on the rock itself let out rooms and, if you can afford one, this is really the place to stay; as the light fades upon the town a ghostly and timeless air creeps upon it.

From Gethira nothing can be seen of the medieval town – it lies on the other side of the great rock, looming hazily across the water. Walking across the causeway and around, past a spectral-looking garage with a rattling Mobil sign, little more is revealed but an enormously powerful spirit of the place is asserted; when the road is suddenly barred by huge castellated walls you are prepared. Through the gate to the Lower Town, wide enough only for man or donkey, everything is revealed: piled upon one another amidst narrow stone streets and alleyways are houses with Turkish-style roofs and walled gardens, distinctly Byzantine churches and, high above, the long castle walls protecting the town on the summit. Standing there, taking it all in, you feel that same luxury and excitement as at Mistra – the prospect of being able to walk each street, explore every possible turn of this extraordinary town.

The **Lower Town** once sheltered 40 churches and 800 homes – an incredible mass of building which explains the intricate network of alleys. Down towards the sea is the restored church used today, the Chrysaphitissa, with its bell hanging from a bent-over old cypress tree in the courtyard. The other three remaining churches in the Lower Town are grouped around the tiny main square – with a well in its centre and a *taverna* taking up one side. The great vaulted Cathedral, the largest medieval church in this part of Greece, is dedicated to Christ in Chains; built in the thirteenth century it was heavily restored by the Venetians.

Across the square the domed church of Agios Paulos was transformed into a mosque – extraordinarily church and mosque must have functioned side by side for many years of Turkish rule; Agios Paulos is now a small museum, although it's rarely open.

The castle walls surrounding both levels of the town are well preserved and the gates into **Upper Town** retain their iron slats. These fortifications were well used since Monemvassia had a tradition of siege and fierce resistance over its years of shifting rule – originally Frankish, it became Byzantine for two centuries and was later to pass into the control of the Papacy, Venetians and Turks. The last conquest, by the Greeks in their struggle for independence, was, however, the most terrible. Mavromichalis and his Maniot army besieged the town for three months, reducing its Turkish inhabitants to eating rats and, allegedly, Greek children; on its surrender, as so often in this war, the population was brutally massacred.

The ruined Upper Town is astonishingly large, far greater than one can imagine from below, and it is suddenly possible to comprehend how the Byzantine city could have held a population of over 30,000. On the summit is the beautiful C13th church of Agia Sophia, its candles flickering anarchically in the wind, and beyond it the ruins extend for acres. There are Byzantine houses and public buildings and, perhaps most striking, a vast construction for the collection of water. Its cisterns are uncovered and elsewhere there are sheer drops down the cliffs so it's wise to descend before dusk. It's a glorious place, charged with a derelict grandeur, and most of the time you won't see another soul.

THE ISLAND OF KITHIRA

Kithira can be reached in an hour from either Monemvassia or Githio on the 'Flying Dolphin' hydrofoils. Monemvassia is more frequent with crossings every day from June to September (five a week April and May and September to October), the service from **Githio** is currently on Mondays, Thursdays and Fridays. Additionally hydrofoils go three times a week from **Neapolis** in low and mid season (the quickest crossing if you can get down there) and from here too there's an ordinary boat most days. Once or twice a week there's also a ferry from **Kasteli** on Crete, which after calling at Neapolis winds its way up to Monemvassia and Piraeus – and then back again. It's a complicated business, varying greatly from year to year and season to season: so ask as many people as far in advance as possible!

Isolated at the foot of the Peloponnese, **Kithira** is relatively large by, say, Cycladic standards. It is dry and rocky, though, and has lost much of its population over the last decades to Australia – from where the islanders keep many of the remaining Kithiran families going by the money they send home. This 'migrant economy' is evident in much of Greece – it's well known that the town with the largest Greek population is, after Athens and Thessaloniki, Melbourne; many Greeks, however, eventually return for their retirement and this explains why in almost any village in Greece there'll be someone who speaks English – often in a broad Australian or American accent.

On Kithira, this is almost ludicrously in evidence – and whilst you'll see very few 'tourists' you're quite likely to find most of the island's rooms and small hotels full with Australian family and friends. As a result attitudes are quite different to what you'd expect for a 'remote island': something most readers seemed to have found disappointing.

In many ways, though, it's a very attractive island. Historically part of the Ionian group, it was in Venetian hands for much of the C18th–19th, the occupiers leaving a strong influence on the houses of the main village **CHORA**, or KITHIRA, on the southern end of the island. Most people either stay here (or 2 km below at its port of KAPSALI) or at the other port of **AGIA PELAGIA** at the north end of the island. There are pensions, rooms and *tavernas* at both but Ag. Pelagia has the best swimming on the island and is probably the more attractive base. Note that if weather is rough boats dock *only* at KAPSALI/KITHIRA in the south; normally they call at both ports, sometimes going to Neapolis in between!

Around the island you'll find no long golden beaches nor ruins of any great note – it's likely to be one of the last outposts of Greece to fall before any mass tourist invasion. There is a large cave, 'Agia Sophia', but even this is far from becoming neatly sanitised as an 'excursion'. It's half an hour's walk beyond the village of Milopotamos, roughly in the middle of the island: ask there at the *taverna* for Andreas who will go with you and open it up.

GITHIO (GITHION)

Pronounced 'Yithio' (Greek g's are hard, like y's, if followed by an i or e), this is a small fishing town with a graceful waterfront, old tiled-roof houses and a certain almost Victorian charm. Githio was the ancient port of Sparta and, in a half-hearted way, has become the modern one, too; boats go from here to Kasteli on Crete (twice a week) and to Piraeus, via Kithira, Neapolis and Monemvassia (every Friday). It has a small beach, and outside of town on the Skala road there's a longer, sandy stretch. Along the front are some elegantly run-down hotels and a few **rooms** to rent. In the giant central Plateia a lively Friday **market** is held, drawing peasants from all over the Mani.

A hundred yards from the shore, tethered by a long narrow mole, is a low rocky islet known as **Marothinisi** – the site of Ancient Kranae. 'Kranae' may not perhaps be an immediately placeable Greek site but in fact it's one of Homer's most exotic locations. It was at Kranae that Paris, having stolen Helen from King Menelaus of Sparta, first dropped anchor – here the lovers spent their first night. Late into an evening, well drugged by wine, it isn't difficult to imagine.

The town later became prosperous under the Romans (it provided murex, the purple-producing mollusc for Roman togas) and there are some remains of the old town to be seen, now half a mile back from the coast. Follow the 'other road' near the road in from Sparti and you'll come to an army barracks – a great sign in the road says 'STOP' and there before you is a small but well preserved **theatre** cut into the hillside. It shows perfectly how ages blend into one another in Greece: built into the side of the theatre is a Byzantine church (now ruined) and that, in turn, has been adapted into the outer wall of the barracks. Back in town there's a small museum, thoroughly in keeping with this mood, displaying a mildly chaotic collection of local finds – it's closed on Tuesdays.

From Githio there are regular buses to Areopolis – a route through the Taygetus Mountains which until recently was the only road linking the Deep Mani with the rest of Greece. Today it's possible to continue up from Areopolis along the coast to Kalamata but first, to the south, lies the Deep Mani – the wildest and perhaps most fascinating area of Greece. A rocky land from which weird towerhouses ominously erupt, it is too remote for most tourists – only the caves at Pirgos Dirou (6 km south of Areopolis) are much visited.

THE MANI

Nowhere do you feel so compelled to find out the history of a place as in the Mani, the southernmost peninsula of the Peloponnese. An extraordinary region, quite unlike the rest of Greece, its boundaries are the last grey peaks of the Taygetus Mountains and it ends when they plummet into the sea at Cape Taenarus, the mythical entrance to the underworld.

It is these mountains, across which for centuries Greeks sought refuge from invaders, that offer the key to Maniot history. The region is, literally, several invasions behind the rest of the country – it was conquered by neither Romans, Slavs nor Turks, a tradition of independence which, with its feuding clans and wild landscape, evokes immediate comparison with Cornwall or the Scottish highlands. It remained pagan until the ninth century (some 500 years after the formation of a Christian Greek empire at Byzantium) and in 1830, when Greece became an independent state, the Mani had no schools and, beyond Areopolis, no roads.

In this isolated land of rocky soil and piracy a feudal society developed somewhere around the fourteenth century – its population divided into leading 'Nyklian' clans and peasants, or villeins. But the soil couldn't support the growing Maniot population and, as villages became occupied by several different clans, feuds broke out between the Nyklians for land, power and prestige.

These feuds were intimately bound up with the Mani's unique marble-roofed towerhouses (which could be built only by Nyklians) and developed a complex system of rules. The object was to completely annihilate the enemy clan and, when the church bells rang out war, each family would retreat to their towers – emerging only at night to bring in supplies of food and ammunition, or at such times as harvest when the rules decreed a temporary truce. Sometimes the feuds could last several years, during which the ordinary villagers would evacuate as the narrow village streets became the scene of constant battle and bombardment.

The favourite method of attack was to smash the prestigious marble roofs of the enemy's towerhouses, so the towers consequently rose to four or five storeys, often being extended or constructed at night. Feuds could end only in two ways – destruction of a family in battle, or by total surrender of a whole clan in *psychico* ('a thing of the soul'). In the latter instance the clan would file out to kiss the hands of enemy parents who had lost 'guns' (the Maniot term for male children) in the feud; the victors would then dictate strict terms by which they could remain in the village. Incredibly, the feuds continued in much the same way well after the formation of modern Greece – despite the efforts of King Otho to destroy the towerhouses, which he sensibly recognised as the root cause of the conflicts.

Today the region has become depopulated – it was never fertile enough to support large numbers and the traditional industry of piracy is long dead – but it is still fiercely resistant to change, retaining many of its old customs and traditions. It is also the notorious royalist stronghold of Greece – voting nearly 100 per cent to keep the monarchy in the 1974 plebiscite.

Deep Mani, which is still dotted with the pepperbox towerhouses, begins at **Areopolis**, a strangely austere town whose archaic C18th buildings set the mood for the region. Its beautiful Taxiarchis Cathedral, for example, has primitive reliefs above its doors which look twelfth-century until you notice their date – 1798. Similarly, many of the Maniot towerhouses could readily be described as medieval, though most of them were built in the early 1800s. You can stay in Areopolis (there are expensive rooms in a restored towerhouse, cheaper ones near the cathedral) but if you really want to explore the Mani, take one of the sporadic buses further south towards Gerolimena.

Eight kilometres along the road there's a turning to **Pirgos Dirou**, whose subterranean river caves are the Mani's single packaged tourist visit. They're open from 8.30am–7.30pm in summer, plenteously stocked with stalactites, and cost 120 drx for the half-hour punt trip. If you're staying at Areopolis, walk back along the donkey track by the coast: it's only 5 km, as against 11 km by road.

Beyond Pirgos you'll meet very few tourists and if you turn off to the right, a few kilometres on, you're likely to be alone in the tiny village and bay of **Mezapos** with, on its west side, Tigani ('Frying Pan') Rock – capped by the ruins of the Frankish **Castle of the Maina**, after which the region took its name. Still further, and just before you reach Gerolimana, major eruptions of towerhouses signify the depleted twin villages of **Nomia** and **Kitta**, set on either side of a great lunar rock. At Kitta was fought the last bitter feud – in 1870, between the families of Kaouriani and Kourikiani; it was eventually subdued by a force of 400 regular soldiers.

Gerolimena, after the journey from Areopolis, has the air of being the end of the world. With a couple of very simple and cheap hotels, it's an excellent place to stop over and explore the further extremities of the peninsula. In earlier times it was one of the harbours where Venetians would put in to buy slaves; the Maniots specialised in Turks but were not beyond attempts to capture each other, or certainly other's wives, if their families were at feud.

Beyond the town a good road continues to **Alika**, where it divides – leading either through the mountains to Laggia (and around the other side of the peninsula to Kotronas) or onwards to Vathia and Mianes. Between Alika and Vathia there are some good coves for swimming.

Vathia, a thick cluster of towerhouses set uncompromisingly on a great scorching mass of rocks, is one of the most dramatic villages in Deep Mani – though it's more or less deserted now, save for a minute *taverna*. Rather incongruously the NTOG are restoring some of the towers here, too, as guesthouses: they're likely to be expensive but it's hard to imagine anyone objecting to a tent.

The reason for staying at Vathia, or indeed Gerolimena, is to make the trek right down to **Cape Tenaro**, legendary entrance to Hades. From Vathia (a couple of hours' walk, or a just-possible hitch from Gerolimena) it is around three hours each way. Ask someone to point you in the direction of the footpath, since tracks seem to go off in most directions around Vathia, and take some water (and food); there's only one spring in between. It's a dramatic enough route, the land narrowing to a spit of stones on the final approach, waves lashing on each side. At the cape itself is a lighthouse, guarded rather oddly by a 'no camping' sign. The keepers may be glad of company but don't reckon on it – and it's not a track to return on at dusk so leave yourself plenty of time.

Taking the road to **Laggia**, high in the mountains, it's best to get yourself a lift: the route seems a completely open thoroughfare for bulls. It is, however, well worth the effort for this once grand village brilliantly exemplifies the feudal set-up of the old Mani. Four Nyklian families lived in the town and their four independently sited settlements, each with its own church, survive. Here, I was told, 400 men from one family built the highest of the towerhouses in a single night. There's a friendly *taverna* in the centre where you can stay but beyond, down to the east coast, transport is very sporadic.

If you want to complete a circle of this, before the road finally heads inland towards Areopolis, you might well end up doing a lot of walking in between lifts. At very worst this means some 50 kms, for Kotronas is the first community on this side of the Mani with a bus service to Areopolis. What villages there are on this stretch are mostly small and set beside the sea. **Kiprianos**, closest to Laggia, is tiny and inexplicably towerless and **Soloteri** is hardly more substantial. Nearing the lovely bay of **Kotronas**, however, the Mani seems to let loose its grip on the land – trees appear and the earth grows more fertile. The village itself, a small fishing port with good swimming, makes an excellent last stop in the region. Set high above it, as if placed to remind you that this is still Deep Mani, is the towered village of **Phlomochori**.

OUTER MANI: FROM AREOPOLIS TO KALAMATA

It's worth travelling this way simply for the road. Possibly the most beautiful in all Greece, it clings to the Taygetus and loops down to the sea. Additionally, this side of Kardamili (40 km from Areopolis) are some of the best villages in the Peloponnese to stay a few days, to swim and do nothing. The beaches are good and the great peaks of the Taygetus, still snow-covered in May, loom behind to create marvellously extravagant backdrops. Though little-developed it's an area just beginning to attract more offbeat-minded young travellers.

LIMENI, diminutive port of Areopolis, has a single taverna on a fine strip of beach whilst **ITILO** (where a ravine marks the official boundary of Mesa and Exa – Deep and Outer – Mani), has the added pull of its notorious strong wine. Beyond Itilo you can pick almost any village on the coast with the assurance of finding a fair beach and little development – some of the best are on the stretch before you reach Kardamili like **AGIOS NIKOLAOS** or **STOUFA** (where there's a small campsite and some rooms to rent in the village).

KARDAMILI itself is a beautiful place with a dense cluster of towerhouses and on the outskirts of the village a great long pebble beach fronted by acres of olive trees. But sadly it's beginning to change character – there are now tourist shops along the main road and hotels steadily creeping in. If you want a room ask at the grocery, 'B. K. Mantagan', who let out a wonderful old house; if you're after somewhere manifestly 'Greek' and unspoilt, however, you'll probably do better to stop before you get this far up-coast.

KALAMATA AND BEYOND

The most striking aspect about Kalamata are the approaches to the city. I've just outlined the tremendous road from Areopolis, but the route here through the mountains from Sparti is hardly less dramatic; a route, incidentally, that Telemachus takes in *The Odyssey* on his way from Nestor's palace at Pilos to that of Menelaus at Sparta. It took him a day by chariot – good going by any standards since the bus takes well over three hours.

KALAMATA itself you're likely to want to leave more or less as soon as possible; large, modern and industrialised, it lacks any particular charm or character. The beach here, as ever, is quite good but it's flanked by large hotels and there seems no other reason to stay. East of the city, at PETALIDI and beyond, there are some more excellent beaches but these seem mostly to have been turned into smart car-camping grounds where smart car-campers arrive and unload every imaginable piece of equipment. Unless you're perversely drawn to such places avoid them, for you'll end up paying as much as for a good hotel room.

If this sounds overtly gloomy, take comfort that Kalamata at least has a good bus service – and there's a wide choice of roads to take. Buses return regularly from here to Athens (via Megalopoli and Tripoli) and they veer off also to Sparti, Kiparissia and Pilos.

PILOS

PILOS, a stylish town with wide arcaded streets and a pair of medieval castles, slightly resembles Nafplio and like that town it's an attractive base for exploring the immediate region. *Rooms* here tend to be a little expensive but there are four modest 'D' class hotels to choose from – 'Astir', 'Galini', 'Trion Navarchon' and 'Navarinon'; they're not hard to find.

Arriving, your gaze is inevitably drawn to the really enormous natural harbour, virtually landlocked by the offshore island of Sphacteria. This is the famous **Navarino Bay**, site of the big budget movies and, more significantly, of the 'accidental battle' in 1827 which effectively secured Greek Independence. Nearly 200 battleships had been crowded into the bay as the allied forces of Britain, France and Russia blockaded the Ottoman fleet in order to negotiate a truce. But in the confusion of shipping an Egyptian, part of a fleet sent to support the Turks, fired cannon shots and a full-scale battle broke out. Without having intended to take up arms for the Greeks, the 'allies' found themselves responding to 'attack' and, extraordinarily, sank and destroyed fifty-three of the Turkish fleet without a single loss. There was considerable international embarrassment when news filtered through to the 'victors' but the action had nevertheless ended effective Turkish control of Greek waters and within a year their independence was secured and recognised.

Beyond what meets the eye there isn't a great deal else in Pilos of obvious interest. The Turkish **castle** overlooking the town is, however, curious. It was used until recent years as a prison and its inner courtyard is divided into a warren of narrow yards separated by high walls. Most Greek prisons — internally, at least — are fairly open and this peculiar feature is explained by the fact that it was the nearest garrison to the Mani. So frequently was it filled with Maniots imprisoned for vendettas, and so great was the crop of internal murders, that these pens had to be built to keep the feuding imprisoned clansmen apart!

NESTOR'S PALACE (Site open weekdays: 8.30–12.30 & 4–6; Suns and hols: 9–3; museum at Hora open same hours but closed on Tuesdays)

Nestor's Palace at 'sandy Pilos' is actually some 15 km from the modern town; you can get a sporadic bus from Pilos or follow the coastal road to Korifassi where, poorly signposted, it heads inland towards Hora. The Palace is on a long, low hill about 4 km from the turn-off; covered by a giant plastic roof, it looks a little like a bus station.

Set in one of the most beautiful and fertile parts of Greece, flanked by deep valleys, **the Palace** looks out towards the bay — a site which unerringly reflects the characteristics of wisdom and gentle courtesy that Homer ascribed to Nestor. One can without great difficulty imagine the arrival of Telemachus here (described in Book 3 of *The Odyssey*) to seek news from his father's old comrade at arms. Telemachus, accompanied by the disguised goddess Athene, comes upon Nestor with his sons and court making a sacrifice to Poseidon upon the beach. The visitors are welcomed and banqueted, 'sitting on downy fleeces on the sand', and although the King has no news of Odysseus he promises Telemachus a chariot so that he may enquire from Menelaus at Sparta. First, however, the guests are taken back to sleep in the palace and Telemachus is given a bath by Nestor's 'youngest grown daughter, beautiful Polycaste', emerging, anointed with oil, 'with the body of an immortal'. By some harmonious quirk of fate a bathtub actually survives intact at the palace, an oddly evocative reminder.

Despite its protective covering the palace ruins are potent ground for such imaginings and its walls standing to 3 feet are better preserved than either Tiryns or Mycenae. With forty-five rooms, halls, courts and lobbies in the main building alone, it is also far grander and more extensive. The palace was half-timbered (like Tudor houses), with its upper walls of sun-baked brick held together by vertical and horizontal beams. Covered in brilliant frescoes, these were once 11 feet high and perhaps as much again on their second storey but even in their diminished state they suggest a building of considerable prestige – as indeed might be expected, for Nestor sent the second largest contingent, 'ninety black ships', to Troy.

Remains survive of a massive complex in three main blocks, the main palace in the centre, on the left an earlier and smaller palace, and on the right either guardhouses or workshops. The basic design, if you've been to Mycenae or Tiryns, will be familiar – an internal court, guarded by a sentry box, giving access to the main sections of the building. The great throneroom with its traditional open hearth lies directly ahead, entered by a double porch, and here was found the finest of the Pilos frescoes – depicting a griffin (perhaps the royal emblem) standing guard over the throne. Around the room are grouped domestic quarters and storerooms and in the rooms directly behind literally thousands of pots and cups were found – this may have been a distribution centre for the produce of the palace workshops. Further back the famous bathroom, its terracotta tub in situ, adjoins a smaller complex of rooms, centred on another throneroom, which were probably the Queen's quarters.

Archaeologically the most important finds were made on the first day of digging in 1939 in the two small rooms to the left of the entrance courtyard – several hundred tablets inscribed in Linear B writing. These were the first to be discovered on the Greek mainland and proved conclusively a link between the Mycenaean and Minoan civilisations for, like those found by Arthur Evans at Knossos on Crete, the language of both was Greek. The tablets were baked hard in the fire which destroyed the palace around 1200 BC, perhaps as little as one generation after the fall of Troy.

The **museum** for the site is at HORA, 4 km further inland, and is well worth visiting; it contains superb frescoes from the palace (one, bearing out Homer's descriptions, shows a warrior in a boar's tusk helmet), much pottery and beautiful gold cups and objects from Mycenaean tombs in the region.

DOWN-COAST FROM PILOS: METHONI AND KORONI

Medieval castles often don't seem right in Greece, but the enormous fortress of **METHONI** (11 km from Pilos) is a justifiable exception. Its site is incomparable. Washed on three sides by the sea, it is cut off altogether from the land by a great ditch on its fourth. It was used by the Venetians as a main port of call for pilgrims travelling to the Holy Land and was heavily fortified by them with great gateways, awesome underground passages and, everywhere, the familiar Lion of St Mark motif. It is open weekdays 9–1 and 4–6, Sundays and holidays 10.30–2.30.

The **village** of Methoni, a rather nondescript three-street cluster of houses, gets crowded in season when hundreds of travellers descend to swim and windsurf off the shallow bay by the fort. *Rooms* are usually possible to find and if not there's a campsite near the east end of the beach; about 500 m west, too, there's usually another less official campsite, surprisingly well equipped with running water. Buses from Pilos leave three times a day but they're not well timed if you're thinking of a day-trip.

Methoni's twin fortress, **KORONI** is 29 km across the headland – connected by a rough road but no bus. It's a third the size and, after the seascape of Methoni, inevitably disappointing. If you set out to hitch or walk there are two fishing villages, each with long pebble beaches, in between – **LOUTSA** and **FINIKOUNDAS**. Both have *rooms* to let, as does Koroni from where you can take a bus back up to Kalamata.

UP-COAST TO PIRGOS

Cutting back from the coast at **Nestor's Palace** you can take a very rough and beautiful track, flanked by fields of oranges and olives, up towards **Kiparissia** and **Pirgos**. The road keeps within a couple of kilometres of the sea for most of its course and there are isolated villages along the way: unbothered by tourism, it's a tremendous route if you want to stop, swim, and stay maybe a day or a week. At **Filiatra** the track joins the asphalt road from Pilos (served on this stretch not by KTEL but by OSE, the railway's buses) but though it's a little more used the same thing goes really. Take a track down to the sea and you're likely to find a good beach, small village and a taverna that, if coaxed, will cook you something.

Kiparissia itself is a somewhat forlorn-looking modern town, stranded beneath a tiny castle. It actually has an organised campsite just back from the smallish beach. Travellers tend to favour **Kaiafas**, probably the best beach along the whole of this coast. Incredibly it is still definitely under-developed with its dozen or so hotels, all of them small-scale, failing to make much impression on the endless dunes and pine groves. Camping is no problem; the cheapest hotels are the 'Xenons' at Palea Laika.

ARCADIA AND THE NORTH

From Kaiafas, Olympia is within easy striking distance – but for the best part of Arcadia, the wooded, mountainous 'palm' of the Peloponnese, you should head inland well before this. Just beyond Kiparissia a good road takes you to the crossroads and theatre of **Megalopoli** and from there you can veer off to Andritsena and the **Temple of Bassae**, two of the few important ancient sites in Greece that you can take in, quite probably, on your own. It's this route, which continues towards Olympia, that is outlined below.

MEGALOPOLI (Site not currently restricted)

It's strange how so many of the most beautiful sites promise to be disappointing until the final approach. Getting off the bus at the modern town of **MEGALOPOLI** I couldn't figure out why I'd come here – it's a dull, dusty place, an empty joke on its adoption of the old name, meaning 'great city'. Perhaps this is in character with the ancient city, planned by Epaminondas to be the finest of a chain of towns built to contain the Spartans. No expense was spared on its buildings, enclosed by 5½ miles of wall, but the city never took root; its citizens, implanted from 40 local villages, preferred their old homes and within two centuries of its construction (371–368 BC) Megalopoli had been broken up and ruined.

The ancient site is a mile out of the town on the Andritsena road in a belt of glorious fertile countryside. It's a beautiful, peaceful place but, walking along the track signposted **Ancient Theatre** you see nothing; just a green valley stretching out beyond a dried-up river and, steadily closer, a graceful hill. Suddenly you round the corner and it clicks – the hill is carved out and there, set within it, the largest theatre in Ancient Greece. Only the first few rows are excavated but the rest is clearly visible, mounds and ridges of earth shelving right to the summit where, from the back rows, trees look on like immense spectators.

The theatre was built to seat 20,000 citizens and the Thersillion (Assembly Hall) at its base could hold 16,000, but today you're likely to be alone exploring the site. Only a few foundations remain of the strong walls and towers, the great temples, gymnasiums and markets, but the place itself is magnificent. 'The Great City', wrote Kazantzakis, 'has become a great wasteland', which in a sense is true; but it's the richest of wastelands – gently and resolutely reclaimed by nature.

Megalopoli, a central crossroads of the Peloponnese, has good bus connections to Pilos, to Kalamata and to the Argolid. There are only three a day onwards to Andritsena and Pirgos, however, so if you want to try the route below you'll probably end up hitching (not too difficult).

KARITENA, ANDRITSENA AND THE TEMPLE AT BASSAE

Beyond the ruins of Megalopoli the road stretches out into the heartland of Arcadia – a glorious route, curling around gentle hills and through lush green valleys. It's one of the most refreshing landscapes in Greece, varied enough to keep you surprised at its beauty but instilled with an obvious harmony and rhythm. After 15 km **KARITENA** appears, a wonderful medieval town spread about the tallest hill in the region and with the River Alpheus at its feet. It is visible for miles on each side but you must stop there to really take it all in. Narrow twists of lanes open out on to a Byzantine church or ancient plateia whilst, at its summit, a tremendous Frankish castle stands guard. Beyond Karitena the hills become mountains and **ANDRITSENA**, 28 km further on, clambers up a steep slope; a road stretches above it to Bassae so it's a useful place to stop over. The cheapest place is in the centre, the splendidly ramshackle Hotel Bassae (E), and there's an excellent restaurant up the stairs opposite it. Andritsena lacks the drama of Karitena but it has no less charm, wonderfully clear mountain water and brilliant air.

The **TEMPLE OF APOLLO AT BASSAE** (not fenced in) is the most spectacularly sited in Greece and, after the Hephaesteion in Athens, the best preserved. It stands roofless but otherwise virtually complete, nearly 4,000 feet above sea level amidst the peaks of the Arcadian mountains. The road begins to wind up from behind the church in Andritsena but be warned that it's a full 14 km to the temple and a fairly killing walk; taxis cost upwards of 600 drachmas for the return trip but if you wait around near the base you should get a lift. The best time to see it is early morning or late afternoon when the grey limestone takes on a shuddering glow, but if you're hitching don't get caught by dusk falling since there is nowhere for miles on either side.

The Temple was designed by the same architect as the Parthenon, Ictinus, and erected to Apollo Epikourios ('the succourer') by the Phigalians. We know that they built it in gratitude for being spared from plague but beyond this it is something of a puzzle. It is oddly aligned (facing north) and, although it's way up in the mountains, is only visible when you are comparatively near. Additionally there are oddities in the architecture – the columns on its north side are peculiarly thicker than elsewhere and incorporated into its long Doric colonnade was a single Corinthian column, the first known in Greece though now vanished save for its base. Unusually, again, the cult statue (probably a 12-foot bronze) would have stood in front of this pillar.

Whatever its eccentricities Bassae (the name, incidentally, means 'ravine' with which the mountains are studded) is a powerful and impressive place. It's impossible not to be struck by the contrasts between the temple and the wildness around it. Yet even this is half a paradox, for the temple is built from the same rock that it stands upon and seems to rise quite naturally from it. It's a lonely site, sometimes bleak and melancholic, sometimes triumphant; speculation that the temple sheltered an oracle feels right for, alone up here, you expect answers.

The road from Andritsena continues beyond Bassae over the other side of the mountain – though little used it's not impossible to hitch down and rejoin the Kiparissia-Pirgos coast road at THOLO (43 km). If you're making for **Olympia**, however, it's easier to return to Andritsena whence buses go towards **Pirgos** three times a day. If you get off at **Krestena** you'll probably save time – from here Olympia is only 12 hitchable (or even shared taxi) kilometres on.

OLYMPIA (Site open 7.30–6.30 in season, 8.30–6 out; museums open same hours but close 30 minutes earlier)

It's about half an hour by bus or train from Pirgos to Olympia but if you're heading there from some distance bear in mind that the last bus leaves Pirgos at 4 pm and the final train only two hours later. **PIRGOS** is a drab market town and **OLYMPIA**, although it's a blatantly tourist-geared village, is a far more pleasant place to stay. You only have to walk a little way beyond the hotels and souvenir shops to sense the harmony of this place chosen for the most important Sanctuary of Zeus in Ancient Greece and the site of its most famous quadrennial games.

The games have semi-legendary origins, with Apollo and Heracles reputed early victors, but they seem to appear historically in 776 BC. Astonishingly they were to continue uninterrupted by either war or disaster for over 1,000 years. For their duration an *Ekecheiria*, or sacred truce, was declared and it is a measure of their renown that this was almost universally honoured. There are only two recorded incidents of truce-breaking, the latter occasion, in 364 BC, chaotically erupting into a battle within the sanctuary itself before crowds gathered to watch the games.

Originally only free-born Greeks were allowed to compete, but as spheres of contact and conflict widened the rules were loosened to allow athletes from all over the Mediterranean – from as far afield as Sicily and Asia Minor. The great gathering of people and nations at the festival extended its importance well beyond the winning of olive wreaths; as-

For an excellent plan of the Olympia site pick up the NTOG's free pamphlet: preferably in advance since they run out locally

sembled under the temporary truce nobles and ambassadors negotiated treaties, and merchants contacts and foreign markets. Sculptors and poets, too, would seek commissions for their work and it is known that Herodotus read aloud the first books of his history at an Olympian festival. The Olympiads also came to form the basis of Greek chronology and Thucydides dates events after the winners of the Pancratiast event.

Today, thinking of the Greek contests, we probably most readily recall their Pentathlon, but this muffles the intense physical struggle which must have been evident. The Pancratiast was extraordinarily brutal, with its contestants fighting, naked and unarmed, by any means except biting or gouging out each others' eyes; on one occasion the olive wreath had to be awarded posthumously, the victor having died at the moment of his opponent's submission. The chariot races, similarly, were extreme tests of strength and command, for it was estimated that only one team in twenty could expect to complete the four-and-a-half-mile course without severe damage.

Under Roman influence the games became increasingly secular and corrupt, with professional athletes competing for rich prizes in place of the strictly honorary wreaths; a process strangely akin to that achieved in a mere century of our nationalistic revivals. Catching Nero's attentions, they became a complete travesty with the Emperor delaying the festival for two years so that he could contest and win special singing and lyre-playing events, in addition to the regular games like the chariot race which he was tactfully awarded despite falling twice and failing to finish. Still, for all this abuse, the tradition continued for a further three centuries until finally, in AD 393, they were suspended as pagan rites by the newly converted Emperor Theodosius I.

This suspension proved final, for Theodosius' successor ordered the destruction of the temples, a process completed by barbarian invasion, earthquakes and, lastly, by the River Alpheus fortuitously changing its course to cover the site completely. There it remained, covered by 20 feet of silt and sand, until the major German excavations of the 1870s.

The ruins of the **SANCTUARY** are at the far end of the village and it's worth taking along the free NTOG plan of the site. Olympia is probably the most visited site in Greece, but if you want solitude to recreate the glories you'll find it surprisingly quiet in the first couple of hours of opening and again before dusk. Personally I don't find the crowds too oppressive since the site is huge and absorbs people with a fair ease and, besides, there is a certain historical aptness in that this place where people from all over the Greek world would gather continues to draw people. There's also a perverse kick in walking out of the tunnelled stadium entrance to face a clicking mass of American photographers!

When they'd completed excavations the German archaeologists planted hundreds of trees in the sanctuary so the great temple columns lie today amidst pines and judas trees. The site is really divided into three although the distinctions are fast becoming more difficult to make out: the walled rectangular Altis or grove, the buildings outside and around its walls and, to the east, the stadium beneath Mount Kronos.

The most important buildings were contained within the *Altis*. Principal among them was the great Doric **Temple of Zeus**. Its enormous column drums now lie about the foundations but the building remains impressive. Completed in 457 BC, it was as large as the Parthenon and contained the great gold and ivory cult statue by Pheidias, one of the seven wonders of the ancient world. The smaller **Temple of Hera**, behind, is the oldest remaining Doric temple in Greece, dating from the seventh century BC – before the cult of the sun god Zeus – when the games were held in her honour. According to tradition the worship of Hera on this site was itself in turn predated by that of an Earth-Goddess; certainly Bronze Age occupation of the site has been confirmed by excavation.

Outside the Altis are the **Gymnasium**, with its covered practice track, and the **Palaestra** (wrestling school) where the athletes would practice for eight months before a festival. Beyond them are the priests' quarters, and the **workshop of Pheidias** – later converted into a Byzantine church but retaining its original proportions, exactly those of the west end of the Temple of Zeus where his great statue was erected. The **Leonidion**, an elaborate building which served as a hostel for distinguished visitors, stands in the south-east corner of the site, but the most interesting building in this section, the **Boulouterion** or Council House, lies towards the stadium. Here, before a great statue of Zeus, the competitors took their oaths to observe the Olympian rules and as they approached the stadium the gravity of this would be impressed upon them; lining the way were bronze statues, paid for with the fines exacted for foul play, bearing the name of the disgraced athlete, his father and his city.

Finally, though, it's neither foundations nor columns that makes sense of Olympia but the 600-foot track of the **stadium** itself. The starting and finishing lines are still there with the judges' seats in the middle and ridges rising up towards Mount Kronos (originally treeless and a natural grandstand) where 40,000 people could have watched. Here you can sweat to bring the ancient spectacle back to life – run up and down the track or climb up to gaze down. And it does seem to work.

There are two archaeological **museums** in Olympia, both of which it's essential to visit. Most of the artifacts and statues from the site, including the magnificent *Hermes* of Praxiteles, are in the new museum (200 yards from the entrance to the sanctuary) and everything is in the process of being moved there, but at the time of writing the finest sculpture – the beautiful *Winged Victory* of Paeonius and the evocative pediments and metopes from the Temple of Zeus – is still in the old museum further up the hill towards the village.

ARCADIAN BEACHES: PIRGOS TO PATRAS

There are some good beaches round the Gulf of Arcadia, the stretch of coast above Pirgos, and though the villages are fast turning into resorts their beaches tend to be long enough to handle things. Also it's not, on the whole, a very touristy area – most summer visitors being Greeks.

KATAKOLO, 12 km west of Pirgos, has a long beach not unlike that at Kaiafas. It spreads into the distance just before you reach the village, with a couple of 'D' class hotels and a small castle. For a quick escape to the sea after Olympia this would be about your easiest choice. AGIOS ANDREAS, a few kilometres north-west, has another long beach but it borders on the burgeoning bungalow resort complex of SKAFIDIA.

There's a lot of development going on at **LOUTRA KILLINI**, too, 50 km up-coast. At the north end of its beach you'll find a new rash of big hotels and a few stores: walk down to the southern part, though, and the dunes are fairly deserted. Usually this attracts quite a crowd of 'unofficial' summer campers, for whom the legitimate campsite nearby seems an unnecessary luxury. Standing guard over the beaches, at the village of KASTRI, is a vast hexagonal fortress, the Frankish CASTLE OF CHLE-MOUTSI. It's impressively sited, holding the straight to the island of Zakinthos and with views stretching even to Kefalonia and distant Ithaca.

LOUTRA KILLINI shouldn't be confused with **KILLINI**, the drab little port for ferries to Zakinthos (three times daily, 1½ hrs) and Kefalonia (once a day, 2 hrs). By road they're some 14 km apart, though you could cut most of this off by following a donkey track around the coast from Kastri – little more than an hour's walk. Connections of trains to Killini and ferries to Zakinthos seem to be perversely designed; you may find it useful, at least one way, to buy a combined bus/ferry ticket from Patras through to Zakinthos.

KALOGRIA, further round the coast towards Patras, has another vast beach (even bigger than Katakolo): a good bet for a last couple of days' camping before leaving for Italy.

PATRAS (PATRAI)

Patras is the largest town in the Peloponnese and, after Piraeus, the major port of Greece – you can go from here to Ancona or Brindisi in Italy as well as to the Ionian Islands. If your money is tight, however, bear in mind there are slightly cheaper ways to get to all these places – IGOU-MENITSA for Corfu or Italy and in season VASSILIKI (on Lefkada) for Ithaca and Kefalonia.

Virtually all the international **ferries** leave in the evening so you probably won't have to bother about lodging. It isn't, in any event, a problem with numerous cheap hotels and an excellent **youth hostel**, at Heroon

Polyteknik 68, who will keep luggage for you if you want to go island-hopping completely unrestricted.

As stressed in 'Basics', you'd be wise to check out a number of ticket agencies before settling on a ferry – and don't blow your last drachma, there's a 250 drx (maybe more by now) embarkation tax. If you read this too late you'll find the National Bank just back from the waterfront: it keeps special evening hours (6.30–8.30 pm) for **money exchange**.

For information on the more obscure possibilities of ferry and bus connections question the **NTOG**'s office by the customs house: they're more knowledgeable and helpful than the tourist police. **Buses** go almost everywhere from Patras: back to Athens, to most points of the Peloponnese, to the ferry at Rio-AntiRio and into central Greece to Lefkada, Ioannina and Delphi. For these buses across the gulf of Corinth you'll need the 'KTEL LEFKADOS', a separate terminal near the domed church above the international ferry dock.

Inevitably the hub of Patras is its seafront – around which you'll find some good, cheap restaurants, the 'Olympeion', for example, just behind the National Bank. If you've time to fill, though, there's a small heavily-restored Roman **odeion** and a pleasantly landscaped (if totally unremarkable) medieval **castle**. The nearest **beach**, connected by local bus, is 4 km out at ITIES.

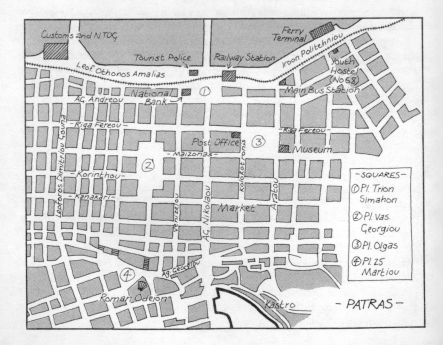

PATRAS TO CORINTH

There's a National Highway if you want to reach Corinth or Athens quickly but the old road, winding amidst the sheltered villages on the Corinthian Gulf, is more attractive. The whole stretch seems to be dotted with campsites (RIO is particularly popular) and, although it isn't for the most part especially dramatic or beautiful coastline, ease of access has led to quite a few resorts springing up. EGION and XILOKASTRO are now highly developed but the smaller towns and villages along the way are more manageable.

If you don't want to return to Corinth you can cross the gulf at **RIO** where a cheap car-ferry leaves every half hour – this, or the summer-only ferry at Egio-Eratini, is much the quickest approach if you're heading for Delphi.

Strangely the most exciting stop along this route is neither a historic site nor a beach but a railway line: it begins at **DIAKOFTO** (43 km from Patras), edges through a gorge to **KALAVRITA** and is quite unlike anything I'd experienced or expected in Greece.

THE KALAVRITA RAILWAY

Not remotely being a railway buff I was unprepared for the thrill of travelling on the rack and pinion line cut into the fantastic gorge between Diakofto and Kalavrita. Rising 2,300 feet in 14 miles (at gradients of up to one in seven) the tiny locomotives alternately push and pull their way through tunnels carved from the rock, along precarious ledges or loop down to cross narrow bridges over the Vouraikos River. The gorge narrows to a few feet at points then suddenly opens out into a brilliant, open shaft of light and the Vouraikos – the clearest and fastest-running stream I've seen in Greece – tumbles all along its course. It's a dreamlike journey which gets everybody rushing from one side of the carriage to the other like five-year-old kids. Perhaps more surprising is that, although it rivals Crete's famous Samarian Gorge, it's still far from packed with tourists – a state I can't see remaining for long.

Built by an Italian company in 1885–95, the railway is an extraordinary and eccentric feat of engineering; its steam trains were replaced some years ago but it still has all the charm of its period – the tunnels, for example, have delicately carved windows. It takes about an hour to get to Kalavrita, an unhurried pace which, when I travelled down, included a stop to let a chicken cross the line. **KALAVRITA** is beautifully positioned high up in the mountains but it was rebuilt after terrible destruction and the massacre of over 1,000 male civilians by the Germans in the last war and is now a sad, rather ugly town. The gorge also broadens out over this last part of the journey and to maintain the drama you should really stop half-way along the line at the minute village of **ZAKHLOROU**. The village echoes with the sound of the Vouraikos and, so long as you listen out for the trains, you can walk from here back down the gorge to Diakofto in about three hours. Alternatively it's a lovely, peaceful place to stay the night and the furthest of the two restaurants, the 'Messinia', will let you sleep on their roof if you can't afford a room.

Men can also sleep at the **Monastery of Mega Spilleon** ('great cave'), high above the village, but the monks like you to arrive before 8 pm. It's a three-quarter-hour walk up a rough donkey track and is reputedly the oldest monastery in Greece. Sadly it's been burnt down and rebuilt countless times and the present building is in remorseless 1930s style, erected after a keg of gunpowder left behind from the War of Independence exploded. Still, it's worth the climb, even if you're not staying, for the view of the gorge below and Mega Spilleon's small museum of icons. Their great treasure is a charred black Icon of Our Lady, one of only three paintings in Greece said to be by the hand of St Luke. It's a profoundly potent image and was found, after a vision, by St Theodore and St Symion in the great cave behind the church.

Trains run between Diakofto and Kalavrita six times a day.

TRAVEL DETAILS

1 Buses

Athens-Korinthos (hourly; 1½ hrs); Athens-Mycenae/Argos/Tiryns/Nafplio (hourly – last from Athens at 8.30 pm; 2 hrs/2½ hrs/2¾ hrs/3 hrs), Athens Sparti (7 daily, 6 hrs); Athens-Patras (hourly; 3½ hrs); Athens-Olympia (4 daily; 6 hrs); Korinthos-Mycenae/Argos/Tiryns/Nafplio (hourly; ½ hr/1 hr/1¼ hrs/1½ hrs); Nafplio-Tripoli (4 daily; 1¼ hrs); Tripoli-Megalopoli (5 daily; 40 mins); Tripoli-Sparti (6 daily; 1 hr); Sparti-Mistras (10 daily; 15 mins); Sparti-Monemvassia (2 daily; 3 hrs); Sparti-Githion (3 daily; 50 mins); Githion-Areopolis (5 daily; 35 mins); Areopoli-Kalamata (4 daily; 1½ hrs); Kalamata-Pilos (8 daily; 1 hr); Kalamata-Megalopoli/Tripoli (5 daily; 1 hr/1¾ hrs); Megalopoli-Andritsena/Pirgos (3 daily; ¾ hr/1¾ hrs); Pirgos-Olympia (7 daily; 35 mins); Pirgos-Patras (8 daily; 1½ hrs).

2 Trains

Athens-Korinthos (16 daily; 1½–2 hrs); Athens-Argos (6 daily; 2¾ hrs); Athens-Patras (26 daily; 3½–4½ hrs); Athens-Pirgos (6 daily; 5¼–7 hrs); Pirgos-Olympia (6 daily – last one at 6.12 pm currently; 35 mins); Korinthos-Mycenae (6 daily; 50 mins); Argos-Megalopoli (2 daily direct; 3 hrs); Argos-Kalamata (6 daily; 4½–5¼ hrs); Patras-Diakofto (20 daily; 1–1½ hrs); Diakofto-Zakhlarou/Kalavrita (6 daily; 1–1¼ hrs).

N.B. Duration of journey depends on whether you get an 'Express' – slightly more expensive but often far quicker.

Full timetable (in Greek) from any OSE station or from the OSE Booking Office, Karolou 1–3, Athens.

3 Boats and hydrofoils

Ordinary **ferry boat** from Piraeus every Thursday to Monemvassia (6 hrs), Neapolis (8¼ hrs), Agia Pelasgia (on Kithira; 9¾ hrs) and Githio (12 hrs). In season there are also ferries three times a week (currently Mons., Thurs., Fris.) from Githio, more or less everyday from Neapoli, and twice a week from Kasteli on Crete.

'Flying Dolphin' **hydrofoils** from the Zea Marina at Piraeus to Monemvassia (daily; 3½ hrs) and Kithira (daily except Mondays; 4½ hrs). Also every Friday from Githion to Kithira (1 hr). Details available from local travel agents at the relevant ports or in Athens from (among others) Thomas Cook at Kar. Servias 2, off Sintagma (2nd floor).

Patras has daily (usually evening) ferries to Brindisi, Bari and Ancona in Italy; in addition to ferries to the islands of Corfu (Kerkira), Kefalonia, Ithaca (Ithaki) and Paxi. **Killini** has daily ferries to Zakinthos and Kefalonia. There are ferries across the gulf of Corinth at **Rio-AntiRio** (every 20 mins; 30 mins at night) and at **Egia-Eratini** (hourly; summer only).

4 Planes

Daily flights in season from Athens to Kithira, Kalamata and Sparti; less frequently out of season. All operated by Olympic Airways (details from their office in Sintagma Square or in local towns).

Chapter three
CENTRAL AND WEST

Grouped together for simplicity, this is one of the more varied areas of Greece – and in **Delphi**, **Dodona** and the **Meteora** it has perhaps the most exciting and beautiful of all the country's historic sites. Delphi is well-known and rightfully well-frequented; the Meteora, an astonishing group of monasteries built 'in the air' on pillars of rock, much less so; and Dodona, a theatre larger than Epidavros and even more arresting, hardly at all.

Beyond these highlights it is not – as the Peloponnese – a land of constant scenic drama. Central Greece is dominated by the vast, drab plain of Thessaly, and for interesting journeys or hiking you must make for the corners – to the legendary peaks of **Parnassos** and **Olympus**, the dank woods of **Pelion**, or across the great mountainous backbone of the Pindus into northern **Epirus**. This last, a route which you can easily take after arriving at (or before leaving from) Igoumenitsa, is one of the most rewarding and least travelled parts. The Meteora lie at its end; Dodona, Metsovo and the remote Vikos gorge along its course; and for these alone it is hard to imagine a more impressive week's travel.

DELPHI AND THE CENTRE

THE OLD ROAD TO DELPHI

There are buses – and scores of tourist coaches – direct from Athens to Delphi, a fast new road for the most part and taking little over three hours. Unless you're heavily pushed for time, though, consider taking a rather slower approach: for, 12 km off the main route, is the **Monastery of Ossios Loukas**, one of the great monuments of Byzantine art. It will take you the best part of the day to get there and then on to Delphi but it really is worth every hour of the detour.

On the way, too, are a number of lesser sites completely off the tourist map of Greece. Some of the great ancient names – Thebes and Plateia, for example – are ignored with reason, but the lesser known fortresses of both Gla and Aigosthena have more than enough interest (and attractive isolation) to warrant a stop; certainly if you're travelling this ground for a second time on the way back from Pelion and the north.

The ancient road from Athens to Delphi began at the Parthenon as the Sacred Way to Elefsis – and from there climbed into the hills towards Thebes. Modern **ELEFSINA** is an incredibly hideous beginning if you're following the route but things improve fast as the road winds up and out into a quiet landscape of pines and grey stony hills. If you want to hitch to Delphi this is probably the best place to start: take the 282 bus from Athens's Plateia Eleftherias to the end of its route in Elefsina and follow the signs to THIVA, there's a fair amount of traffic.

The first place to tempt you off the route is **PORTO GERMENO**, a little resort at the extreme north-west corner of the Gulf of Corinth with just one ('C' class) hotel, and a few *tavernas* on the beach. Here, beneath Mount Kithairon, is the best preserved circuit of ancient walls anywhere in Greece – the obscure Classical fort of **Aigosthena**. Historically it is quite insignificant but the ruins themselves are tremendous – some of the towers rising 30–35 ft above the walls. As ever with isolated sites the problem is transport: it's 23 km from the main Thiva road, there's no regular bus and so you're dependent on hitching other committed tourists. . . .

Back on the highway you pass another Classical fortress 2 km on, C4th BC **ELEUTHERAI** eight of whose towers survive to varying degrees. The modern town of **THIVA** (**Thebes**) is 20 km beyond, built on the site of its ancient predecessor but – perhaps for this very reason – without important remains. The town **museum**, however, is excellent and well worth a look between buses; it is at the far end of Pindharou, the main street, open weekdays 9–3.30, Sundays 10–4, closed Tuesdays. Among many fine exhibits are a unique collection of painted Mycenaean sarco-phagi; these depict, in bold expressionistic strokes, women lamenting their dead.

There are no buses direct from Thebes to Delphi but they go frequently to Livadia, from whence there are regular connections. **LIVADIA** itself is a pleasant and prosperous town on the banks of the Herkyna – a river of ancient fame which emerges from a dark gorge at the foot of a Catalan fortress. Its waters rise from a series of springs (now channelled beside a Xenia Hotel) above which niches for votive offerings have been cut into the rock; in one of these, a large chamber with a bench, the Turkish governor would sit for a quiet smoke. In antiquity they marked the Springs of Memory and Forgetfulness in which all who sought to consult the **Oracle of Troiphonos** had first to bathe. The actual Oracle, a circular structure which gave entrance to caves deep in the gorge, has been tentatively identified at the top of the hill – near the remains of an unfinished Temple of Zeus. It was visited by Pausanias who wrote that it left him 'possessed with terror and hardly knowing himself or anything

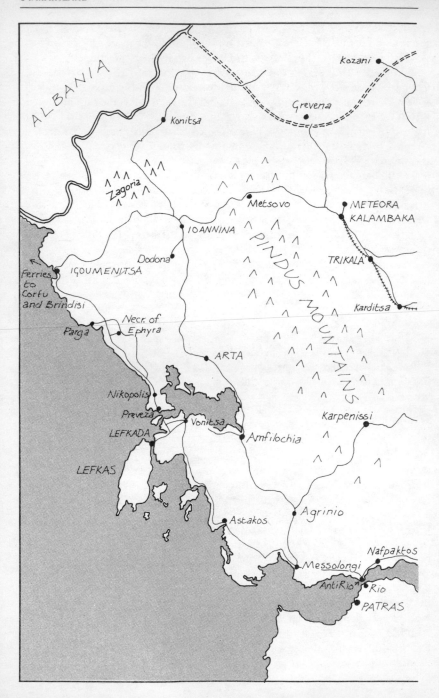

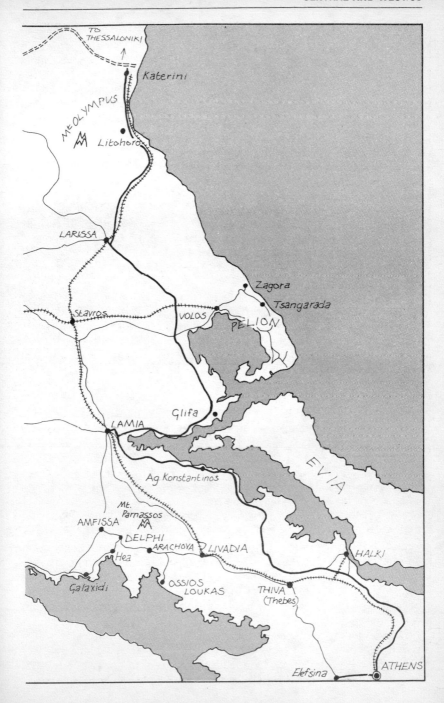

around him'. Today there's no particular reason to stay in the town but if you're stranded (it's the nearest train station to Delphi) there are a couple of cheap, very run-down hotels beside the river, near the main square, at nos 3 and 6 I. Lappa.

Just west of Livadia (10 minutes by local bus; every hour) is the site of **ANCIENT ORCHOMENOS** – inhabited from Neolithic to Classical times and, as the capital of the Minyans, one of the most important and wealthy Mycenaean cities. Near the centre of the drab modern village is the **Treasury of Minyas** (open weekdays 9–3, Sundays 10–2), a stone tholos tomb similar to that of Atreus at Mycenae; its roof has collapsed but it is otherwise complete and its inner chamber, hewn from the rock, has a beautiful and intricately carved marble ceiling. Beside it are the remains of a C4th BC theatre and behind, on the rocky hilltop, a tiny fortified acropolis from the same period. Across the road, built entirely of blocks from the theatre and column-drums from a Classical temple, is the ninth-century Byzantine **Church of the Dormition**. Note also the minute Byzantine church in the main square, again constructed from reused blocks.

Still continuing west, in a highly worthwhile diversion, it's a further 20 minutes by bus (five a day but they stop early) to the village of KASTRO – right next to the National Highway. Cross the highway and take the road (unsignposted) behind a large petrol station: a brief walk leads to the Mycenaean **CITADEL OF GLA** (unrestricted entrance) – an enormous and extraordinary site enclosed by 1¾ miles of 'Cyclopean' walls. Although it is far larger than either Tiryns or Mycenae almost nothing is known about it, save that it was once protected by Lake Copais and that it may have been an outpost of the Minyans. The walls and city gates still stand (some to a height of 15 feet) and on the highest point a huge Mycenaean palace has been revealed. Further down, and currently being excavated, is a vast walled area believed to be the market place, but almost anywhere you walk in this rarely visited site there are enigmatic traces of buildings. One word of warning, though – there are supposed to be snakes amongst the ruins so tread with care.

North from Livadia the scenery becomes ever more dramatic as Mount Parnassos and its attendant peaks loom high above the road. At 24 km, almost halfway to Delphi, you reach the **'Schiste' crossroads** where in ancient times the roads from Delphi, Daulis and Ambrossos met; here Oedipus, returning on foot from Delphi, met and killed his father Laius, King of Thebes. The old road lay in the gorge, the new thunders overhead, but it is still an important junction – leading straight on to Delphi or left to Distomo and Ossios Loukas.

Ossios Loukas can be reached easily (if not always promptly) by going first to Distomo (4 km from the crossroads) and then taking a further bus to the monastery itself (8 km from Distomo) or to the fork at Kiriaki, which is only ten minutes' walk before it.

THE MONASTERY OF OSSIOS LOUKAS (open daily 10–4)

Once you've seen Mistra or Monemvassia it's hard to believe that any single Byzantine monument would have an effect. Ossios Loukas docs. As a precursor of that last defiant flourish of Byzantine art it brings together a culmination of styles and in a setting as beautiful as it is remote. Hidden by trees along the approach from Kiriaki/Distomo its shady terrace suddenly opens out on to a spectacular sweep of Helikon peaks and countryside. Ten monks still live in the monastic buildings around the courtyard, but the monastery is today really maintained as a museum; a small seasonal hotel and restaurant have been built within the grounds.

The main structure comprises two domed churches – the larger Katholikon, or Ossios Loukas, and the attendant chapel of Theotikos. They are joined by a common foundation wall but otherwise share few architectural features.

The **Katholikon**, built in 961 and dedicated to a local beatified hermit, St Luke of Stiri (not the Evangelist), was the model of the octagonal style of church copied later at Dafni and at Mistra. Externally it is modest – rough brick and stone walls surmounted by a well-proportioned dome – and deceptively overshadowed by the older and smaller Church of Theotokos which culminates in an elaborate (and Eastern-influenced) marble panelled drum. The inside, however, is startling. A conventional cross-in-square plan, its atmosphere switches from austere to exultant as the eye moves along walls lined in red and green marble to the gold-backed mosaics on the high ceiling. Light filtering through marble-encrusted windows reflects across the curved surfaces of the mosaics in the narthex and the nave and bounces on to the marble walls, bringing out their soft and subtle shades. Sadly the mosaics of the dome were damaged by an earthquake in 1659 and replaced by unmemorable frescoes, but other quite superb examples testify to their effect.

The mosaic of *The Washing of the Apostles' Feet* in the narthex is one of the finest; its theme is an especially human one and the expressions of the Apostles, seen varying between diffidence and surprise, do it justice. This dynamic and richly humanised approach is shared by all the mosaics and is again brilliantly illustrated by the *Baptism* – high up on one of the curved squinches that support the dome. Here the naked Jesus reaches for the cross amidst a swirling almost animate mass of water, its illusion of depth created by the angle and curvature of the wall.

The frescoes are confined to the vaulted chambers at the corners of the cross plan and though less imposing than the mosaics are far more sympathetic in colour and shade to their subjects – particularly that of *Christ walking towards the Baptism*.

The **Church of Theotikos** is gloomy and crouched by comparison and apart from a couple of fine Corinthian capitals and a floor mosaic has little to seduce you away.

ARACHOVA AND MOUNT PARNASSOS

Whichever way you approach Delphi you'll pass through **ARACHOVA**, chief village of the Parnassos country and itself spectacularly poised on the edge of a deep gorge. Despite being carved in two by the Athens–Delphi highway – a contentious planning issue for many years – it remains a very beautiful place, most of its lanes and houses dating from the last century and the old clock tower in the schoolyard mimicking in miniature the nearby peaks. If you're not making for any other mountain areas it is well worth an afternoon's pause before continuing to Delphi (just 10 km on) and if you've transport you might consider staying here as a base for visiting the site. There are two 'D' class hotels (the 'Apollon' and 'Parnassos') and a very few *rooms* in private houses.

The village is famed for its strong wines, its 'flotaki' sheep hide rugs and (though these are getting dubiously traditional) its woollen embroidery. It is also the site of a tremendous festival on **Agios Georgios' Day** (23 April, or the Tuesday after Easter if this date falls within Lent), centred on the church at the top of the hill. If you can coincide it's one of the best events to catch genuine folk-dancing and almost 48 hours of unrelieved feasting! At other times you'll have to make do with one of the excellent local *tavernas* – try *Elatos* (the Fir Tree) 50 metres east of the fountain-cafe on the main street.

The **hike up Parnassos** is only feasible from around June through to mid-September and, Marc Dubin reports, is both tricky-going and one of the less interesting Greek mountain climbs. The one great reward – and if you get clear weather this could be incredible – is the view from the summit of Liakoura, stretching from the islands of the Sporades to Mount Olympos. The hike is described in detail in *Backpackers' Greece* – and if you haven't got this you'd be well advised to enlist a guide at the Arachova Alpine Club (phone Nikos Yorgakos, 31 391, if no one's around) or at least to get the 'Fthiotidhos' map from the Athens Statistical Service. The trail starts 11 km above the village at Arachova's Ski Centre, and you're unlikely to get a lift; from there it's roughly five hours to the summit.

Buses are fairly easy to pick up for the last stretch of road between Arachova and Delphi – though some from Athens are likely to go straight through full; have patience.

DELPHI (sites and museum open weekdays 8.30–7, Sundays 10–4.30; Museum closed Tuesdays)

Raised on the slopes of a high mountain terrace and dwarfed to either side by great and ominous peaks of the Parnassos, it's easy to see why the ancients believed Delphi to be the centre of the earth. But more than the natural setting or even the occasional earthquake and avalanche were needed to confirm a divine presence. This, according to Plutarch, was achieved through the discovery of a rock chasm which exuded strange vapours and reduced all who approached to frenzied, incoherent and undoubtedly prophetic mutterings.

The first **oracle** established on this spot was dedicated to Ge (or 'Mother Earth') and to Poseidon 'the Earth Shaker'. The serpent Python, son of Ge, was installed in a nearby cave and communication made through the Pythian Priestess. Python was subsequently slain by Apollo, whose cult had been imported from Crete (legend has it that he arrived in the form of a dolphin – hence the name 'Delphoi'), and the Pythian Games were instigated to commemorate the feat, perhaps also to placate the ancient deities.

The place was known to the Mycenaeans – their characteristic votive offerings (tiny striped statues of goddesses and worshipping women) have been discovered near the site of Apollo's temple – but it seems it was deserted in the 'Dark Ages' of Greece, between around 1100–800 BC. Historically it reappeared around the mid C8th BC and within a few decades became one of the major sanctuaries of Greece, its oracle tried and tested and generally thought to be the arbiter of truth. For over a thousand years a steady stream of pilgrims worked their way up the dangerous mountain paths to seek divine direction in matters of war, worship, love or business. On arriving they would sacrifice a sheep or a goat and, depending on the omens, wait to submit votive questions inscribed on leaden tablets. The Pythian Priestess (a simple and devout village woman of over 50) would chant her prophecies from a tripod positioned over the oracular chasm and an attendant priest would then 'interpret' her utterings and relay them to the enquirer in hexameter verse.

Though many of the answers were ambiguous and often equivocal (Croesus, for example, was told that if embarked on war against neighbouring Cyrus he would destroy a mighty empire – he did and destroyed his own) one can hardly conceive that the oracle retained its popularity and influence for so long without offering predominantly sound advice. We have, too, Strabo's word that 'of all oracles in the world it had the reputation of being the most truthful'. One explanation is that the Delphic Priests were simply better informed than any other corporate body around at the time. Delphi was the centre of the Amphyctionic League – a 'United Nations' of the Greek city states and, as Peter Levi describes it, 'a keystone of their disjointed unity'. Members of the League brought to Delphi not only their votive offerings but a wealth of political, economic and social information and additionally from around the seventh century BC Delphi had an actual network of informants throughout the Greek world.

The influence of the Oracle spread abroad with the age of classical colonisation and as its patronage grew so did its spectrum of informants. It reached a peak in the sixth century BC, attracting powerful benefactors such as Amasis, King of Egypt, and the unfortunate King Croesus of Lydia; many of the Greek state treasuries were also dedicated at this time. The Temple was elaborately rebuilt in 548 BC and the Pythian Games were reorganised (along the lines of Olympia) to become one of the major Panhellenic festivals.

Privileged position and enormous wealth had always made Delphi an obvious prey to Greek rivalries, and the first of a series of conflicts known as the 'Sacred Wars' broke out early in the sixth century BC. Then, it retained its autonomy but by the following century it had begun to be too closely identified with individual states. Worse, it maintained a defeatist, almost treacherous attitude towards the Persian invasions – only partially mitigated when a Persian force, sent by Xerxes to raid Delphi, was crushed at the entrance of the Sanctuary by a well-timed earthquake.

It never quite regained the same level of trust (and consequently of power) after these instances of bias and corruption. However, its prestige was still foremost in the Greek world and the stream of votive offerings continued undiminished.

Real decline set in with the resumption of the 'Sacred Wars' in the fourth century BC. Following prolonged squabbling amongst the Greek city states the Sanctuary was actually raided by the Phocians in 356 BC. Philip of Macedon intervened on this occasion to restore control to the Amphyctionic League but seven years later, when asked to do so a second time, he responded with the invasion of southern Greece. The independence of the city states was effectively brought to an end at the Battle of Chaeroneia and with it the intriguing role of Delphi.

Though the Oracle was maintained under Macedonian, and later Roman, control its influence was pathetically diminished. The Romans especially thought little of its utterances and much of its treasure; Sulla plundered it in 86 BC and Nero, outraged by its condemnation of his matricide, carted away some 500 bronze statues. Finally, with the demise of paganism under Constantine and Theodosius in the fourth century AD the Oracle became extinct, but for the last two centuries its authority had been over purely domestic issues such as marriage, loans and voyages.

When the French School leased the site in 1892 (in exchange for a French government agreement to buy the Greek currant crop) there was little more to be seen than the village of Kastri and the outline of a stadium and theatre. The villagers were persuaded with the help of an army detachment to move to modern Delphi and in the next decade most of the excavations and reconstructions visible today were completed.

The Site

Split by the road from Arachova, the ancient site divides essentially into three parts: the Castalian spring, the Marmaria, and the main sanctuary. There's a detailed map of the sanctuary in the free NTOG leaflet – available in advance or, here, from the tourist police at Friderikis 27.

Ignoring for the moment the main site and the museum, you reach a sharp bend in the road – here, marked by niches for votive offerings and by the remains of an archaic fountain house, the celebrated **Castalian Spring** still flows from a cleft in the Phaedriades cliffs. Visitors to Delphi (who originally had to be male) were obliged to purify themselves in its waters – usually by washing their hair, though murderers had to take the full plunge. Byron, impressed by the legend that it succoured poetic inspiration, jumped in.

Across and below the road is the '**Marmaria**' – the **Sanctuary of Athena**, whom the Delphians worshipped as Athena Pronoia ('Guardian of the Temple'); its nickname means 'marble quarry' and derives from medieval days when the ancient blocks were filched for private use. The most conspicuous building in the precinct (and the first to be seen from the Athens road) is the Tholos, a rotunda of the C4th BC. Three of its dome-columns and their entablature have been set up but though these amply declare the original beauty of the building (which has become *the* popular image of Delphi) its purpose remains a mystery. At the entrance to the sanctuary stood the **Old Temple of Athena**, destroyed by the Persians and rebuilt in the Doric order in the fourth century BC a hundred

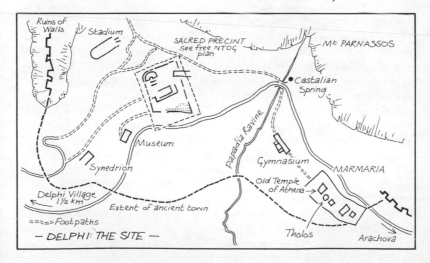

– DELPHI: THE SITE –

yards lower down; foundations of both can be traced. Outside the precinct on the north-west side (above the Marmaria) is the Gymnasium, again built in the C4th BC but later enlarged by the Romans who added a running track on the now collapsed terrace; prominent amongst the ruins is a circular (cold) plunge-bath used after training.

The **SANCTUARY OF APOLLO** is entered, as in ancient times, by way of a small **Agora**; it is enclosed by ruins of Roman porticoes and shops for the sale of votive offerings. The paved **Sacred Way** begins after a few stairs and zigzags uphill between the foundations of memorials and treasuries to the Temple of Apollo. Along each edge is a litter of statue bases where gold, bronze and painted marble figures once stood – Pliny counted more than 3000 on his visit and that was after Nero's infamous raid. The choice and position of these memorials, however, was dictated by more than religious zeal – many were used as a deliberate show of strength or often as a direct insult against a rival Greek state. For instance the 'Offerings of the Arcadians' on the right of the entrance (a line of bases which supported nine bronzes) was erected to commemorate their successes over the Spartans in 369 BC and pointedly placed in front of the Spartans' own 'Monument of the Admirals'. This large recessed structure, which once held 37 bronze statues of gods and generals, was built in celebration of their victory over Athens and by the same logic positioned directly opposite the 'Offering of Marathon', erected by the Athenians just 40 years previously.

Further up the path to the left is the **Siphnian Treasury** built around 525 BC; Siphnos had rich gold mines and intended the building to be an unrivalled show of opulence – the Caryatids which supported its west entrance and the fine Parian marble frieze which covered all four sides are now in the museum. Above it, at the corner of the path, is the **Treasury of the Athenians**, built after Marathon (490 BC) and reconstructed in 1905–6 by matching the inscriptions that completely cover its blocks. These include honorific decrees in favour of Athens, lists of Athenian ambassadors to the Pythian Festival, and a hymn to Apollo with its musical notation in Greek letters above the text.

Next to it are the foundations of the **Bouleuterion**, or council house, a reminder that Delphi needed administrators, and a little higher up is a circular area known as the **Threshing Floor** where a Morality Play enacting the killing of the serpents was presented every seventh year. Above is the remarkable **Polygonal Wall** whose irregular interlocking blocks have withstood, intact, all earthquakes. It, too, is covered with inscriptions but these almost universally refer to the emancipation of slaves; Delphi was one of the few places where such freedom could be made official and public by an inscribed register. An incongruous outcrop of rock between the wall and the Treasuries marks the spot where the Sibyl, an early itinerant priestess, was reputed to have uttered her prophecies.

Finally the Sacred Way leads to the Temple Terrace and you are confronted with a large altar, erected by the island of Chios. Of the main body of the **Temple of Apollo** only the foundations stood when it was uncovered by the French; they have, however, re-erected (from various rebuildings of the Temple) six Doric columns which give a vertical line to the ruins and provide some idea of its former dominance over the whole of the Sanctuary. In the innermost part of the Temple was the 'Adyton' – a dark cell at the mouth of the oracular chasm where the Pythian Priestess would officiate. No sign of cave or chasm has been found, nor vapours that might have induced a trance, but it is likely that such a chasm did exist and was simply opened and closed by the successive earthquakes. On the architrave of the Temple – probably on the interior – were inscribed the maxims 'Know Thyself' and 'Nothing in Excess'.

The theatre and stadium used for the main events of the Pythian Festival are on terraces above the Temple. The **Theatre**, built in the C4th BC with a capacity of 5000, was closely connected with Dionysus, god of the senses and wine, who reigned in Delphi over the winter months when the Oracle was silent. A path leads up through cool pine groves to the **Stadium** – a steep walk which discourages many of the tour bus trippers. Its site was artificially levelled in the C5th BC but it was only banked with stone seats (capacity 7000) in Roman times – the gift of Herodes Atticus. It easily swamps the crowds but if you want further (and very beautiful) solitude climb up to the pine trees which have engulfed the remains of C4th BC walls.

The **Museum** (admission included in Sanctuary ticket) contains a rare and exquisite collection of archaic sculpture matched only by finds on the Acropolis. Its most famous exhibit is *The Charioteer* – one of the few surviving C5th BC bronzes; its eyes, made of onyx and set slightly askew, give a startling realism to its demure confident expression.

Modern Delphi

The modern village of Delphi is unremittingly tourist-geared and a little on the expensive side. There's a **youth hostel** on the upper street (150 m down from the bus stop) and a fair number of 'C' and 'D' class **hotels**, but in mid-season you'll have to get there early to get a room. Best deal for a meal is usually at 'Vakkhas', below the hostel, or the un-named *psistaria* opposite Hotel Pan at the far end of town. If you're **camping** best find your own place because the two official sites are none too close; 'Camping Apollon' is 1½ km after the fork to Amfissa whilst 'Camping Delphi' is nearly 4 km down the Itea Road.

The **bus station** is in the lower street (though buses going north leave from the upper) and has a clear time-table; there are regular buses back to Athens, to Amfissa, and to Nafpaktos, probably the most attractive beach-resort in the area. Nearest **train station** is at Livadia and trains to Athens or north to Thessaloniki are reasonably well connected.

WEST OF DELPHI: THE COAST TO NAFPAKTOS

All buses heading north or west from Delphi stop first at **ITEA**, a gritty little town with two small beaches and vast oil tankers moored in its bay. Oddly it has a fairly popular campsite, 'Camping Kirrha', named after the ancient port of Delphi just to the east of Itea. From here, if you choose to stay, there's still a donkey track up to Delphi – probably the original approach.

GALAXIDI, 17 km southwest of Itea, is marginally more enticing – a quiet, rather lonely waterfront town of tall C19th houses. There's no real beach but some good walks: 3km out of town is the Byzantine monastery of Transfiguration with commanding views over Krissa bay and its islets. If you're stopping here there are 'B', 'C' and 'D' class hotels – the latter is 'Possidon' at Nea Mama 2.

Further round the coast is some of the sparsest scenery of the Greek coastline – villages are few and none of them seem to suggest any great reason to stay. At **ERATINI**, however, there's a summer (June–September) ferry across the gulf to **EGION**: an alternative to that at **RIO-ANTIRIO**, 60 km further on, which stays open throughout the year and operates virtually continuously.

The one place that really seems to break out of the languid feel of this stretch of coast is **NAFPAKTOS**, 2 hrs by bus from Delphi and an hour by bus and ferry to Patras. A small, lively resort, it sprawls along the seafront below an enormous and rambling Venetian *kastro*. The castle fortifications in fact run right down to the harbour and beach which they enclose – you enter them through one of the original gates. It's a good place to rest up – popular but not particularly overdeveloped; there are plenty of cheap hotels and on the outskirts of town a longer stretch of beach with a couple of *tavernas*.

THESSALY

AMFISSA, LAMIA AND THE COAST TO VOLOS

Heading north from Delphi through Itea, the road winds slowly up through wide expanses of olive groves to **AMFISSA**, set upon the first slopes of the Locrian Mountains. It's a nice enough place, with the ruins of a Frankish castle on its acropolis – a short and obvious walk if you've a few hours to wait for a bus, but of no especial interest. The castle is, however, the coolest place in town, its walls (containing a few stretches of Classical polygonal masonry) enclose shady pine trees.

Above Amfissa the road loops through the mountains which bisect central Greece – the only ancient pass was at Thermopylae to the east, off the National Highway, but there's no longer a pass there – before opening out on to the Plain of Thessaly. Here, beneath another medieval fortress (Catalan, this time, but closed for military use) is **LAMIA**, a thriving provincial town. It has little of note, though the central square, Plateia Laos, is attractive with an enormous plane tree filled with birds; some 'D' class hotels are grouped around. Lamia's bus stations are more tricky than most to find – for Larissa and Trikkala they leave from Odos Thermominon, for Volos from Odos Levaditou/Rozaki-Aggeli, and for Amfissa and Karpenissi from Odos Markou Botsari.

The coast road beneath Lamia (off the Highway to Athens) seems to be dotted with rather expensive resorts (particularly Arkitsa and Kanena Vourla); **AGIOS KONSTANTINOS** is no exception though it is the nearest port to Athens if you're going to the Sporades (daily ferries to Skiathos and Skopelos).

The National Highway extends above Lamia to Volos but the buses take the bonecracking old road along the coast – an attractive route through more olive groves with glimpses of Evia and, later, views across the Pagasitic Gulf. There are some small and agreeable resorts here amidst the little bays off the road – and for the moment tourist development seems distinctly half-hearted. **RAHES** and **GLIFA** (which has 6–8 ferries a day to Agiokambos on Evia) both have good beaches and rooms to let; **AHILIO**, further round, is more popular, less pretty, but has a campsite. At **NEA ANHIALOS** (17 km before Volos) five early Christian Basilicas have been uncovered; their mosaics and the small museum are worth stopping for if you've transport – less so if it means hanging about 3 hrs for the next bus.

VOLOS

VOLOS, the main port for the northern Sporades (but not to Skyros), is the newest industrial city in Greece and a major depot for truck drivers (who cross from here to Tartous in Syria). This makes hitching remarkably good but the place itself is dire; flattened by an earthquake in 1955, its ugly, modern rebuilding has already backed up to its natural limits against the Pelion Mountains. It is redeemed only as a ferry port, a gateway to the beautiful villages of the Pelion, and for its museum – which is quite superb and well worth a special visit (it's at the far end of town – 20 minutes' walk along the front towards the Agria road).

The **Museum** (open weekdays 9–1 and 3–6, Sundays 10–2.30), imaginatively laid out and clearly labelled in English, has a unique collection of painted grave stelai which depict, in now faded colours, the everyday scenarios of C5th BC life. It also has one of the best collections in Europe of Neolithic pottery, tools and figurines; these are from the local sites of Sesklo and Dimini and, exhibited with models and diagrams, really give an insight into the sophistication of fourth and fifth millennium civilisation. (The Sesklo and Dimini sites can be visited – they're respectively 15 and 3 km from Volos – but are of essentially specialist interest.)

The **bus station** in Volos is just off the main square (Plateia Riga Fereou) but if you have to stay the night there are cheap **hotels** in the streets parallel to it (i.e. Sarakinou, Solonos and Korai). There's a **town plan** printed on the 'Volos-Pelion' leaflet – available free from the NTOG who have an office on the waterfront side of the main square.

A town plan of Volos and detailed map of the Pelion area is printed on the NTOG's free "Volos-Pelion" leaflet: pick it up in advance

---

THE PELION VILLAGES

Rising up behind Volos the long Pelion mountain range sweeps round the Pagasitic Gulf to form the Pelion Peninsula. There is something decidedly un-Greek about the whole of this area. The slopes are exceptionally green with hardly a rock visible amongst the apple, walnut and chestnut trees and almost everywhere there is the sound of water, bubbling out from rock crevices. Its beauty is peculiarly like that of an English country lane – only the Pelion has more to offer, its air and water are exquisite and the beaches are good.

There are twenty-four villages on the peninsula, most of them founded in the C18th when the area, gaining certain concessions from the authorities, became a nucleus for those seeking refuge from Turkish oppression; a tradition of folk art was established at this time and the villages of Zagora and Milies were the main cultural centres in Thessaly. Their structure is unique in Greece for instead of being gathered around a central 'plateia' they consist of long meandering lines of whitewashed stone houses; occasionally these form a cluster around a church or *taverna*, and these small plateias (often half a mile or so apart) are connected by stone paved paths that wind through the woods and gardens. The churches, too, are different – low and wide, they are built in the old basilica style with wooden cloisters and detached bell towers. In many of the villages the grand old mansions of the C18th survive, too, providing an elegant focus for the Pelion backdrop, and in **Vizitsa** (near Milies) and **Makrinitsa** (above Portaria) these have been restored as guesthouses by the NTOG.

Both are definite 'showplaces' of the Pelion and can get a little over-exploited in midsummer – but **Makrinitsa**, just 17 km from Volos (and 2000 feet up the mountain), is probably the best single target if your time is limited. Founded in 1204, presumably by refugees from the first sack of Constantinople, it boasts six outstanding churches and a monastery in addition to the much-touted mansions. There's a 600 ft altitude difference between the top and bottom of the village so to get a full sense of the village takes a full day's rambling. Most impressive of the churches are Agios Georgios, 10 min walk downhill from the shady main plateia, and the monastery of Theotokou, right under the clock tower. Many of the sanctuaries and frescoes here are only a few centuries old but the marble relief work on some of the apses (the curvature behind the altar) is the best work of its type in Greece.

Makrinitsa's NTOG lodges are expensive – and for rooms only a little above normal prices you'll need to try *Yanni's Rooms*, a red-fronted house 150 metres above the main square. *Kafe-Bar Pakoulorizos*, again just above the square, is the place to eat, specialising in the local *spedzofai*, a kind of sausage and pepper stew. Close by Makrinitsa is the village of **Portaria**, again with some very fine churches and an incredible tone of running water: there are more rooms here, useful if you've just completed a circuit of the peninsula and want to pass straight through Volos next day: it's one of the best connected villages by bus.

The villages close to Volos on **the Pagasitic coast** – especially between AGRIA and KALA NERA – are extremely popular beach resorts for Greeks from Volos and even Athens, particularly at weekends. For this purpose they are all quite pleasant but for the 'real Pelion' you need to take one of the loops across the peninsula to the eastern half. Buses from Volos to either MILIES or ZAGORA are fairly frequent – though most of the other villages are served only two or three times a day, usually in a complete circuit from Volos. Hitching is easy enough but you'll often wait for some hours on the minor roads so plan on walking for much of the time and don't expect to cover too much ground too quickly; the roads are forever bending and backtracking around the mountain slopes and being in sight of a place is not as encouraging as you might think!

TSANGARADA and **ZAGORA** are two of the best bases to head for. They have plenty of rooms to let (which isn't universally true of the villages), are well served by buses and both have excellent beaches 8 km by road (shorter by track) beneath them. Tsangarada also has the largest plane tree in Greece in the second of its four plateias, said to be 1000 years old and to take eighteen men to encircle its monstrous trunk. Between these two villages is **Agios Ioannis** – the best beach in the Pelion and a growing resort (rooms and all classes of hotels). Completing the circuit back to Volos there's a tremendous twisting drive up to **Hania**, a plush ski-resort at the highest pass of the Pelion, and onwards to **Portaria** and the road up to **Makrinitsa**.

One thing to remember when travelling through the area is that nearly all the villages are substantially hidden amidst trees off the road; you simply have to aim for a place on the map and explore.

There are no Classical sites in the Pelion although it figures often in legend as the home of the Centaurs. Both Achilles and Jason were nurtured to manhood here under the tutelage of the wise centaur Chiron. The wooded slopes also provided the timber for Jason's ship *Argo* which sailed from Volos.

LARISSA AND THE ROUTE NORTH

Buses and trains are frequent between VOLOS and LARISSA, a dull journey across the cornfields of Thessaly. **LARISSA** itself is a large, thriving and unremarkable town, but for travellers it's an important junction, well connected with TRIKALA (for the Meteora and Epirus), and the principal gateway to the north. If you have to stay overnight there are 'D' class hotels in the streets just off Plateia Stratou (the main square) and in the square by the railway station, 1 km from the centre. If desperate there's also a park, the 'Alkazar', on the far bank of the river.

The **National Highway** from LARISSA to THESSALONIKI is much the quickest route north – even if you're coming from Kalambaka – and it's also much the most interesting scenically, flanked on one side by the peaks of Mount Olympos, on the other by the Thermaic Gulf. If you plan to **hike Olympos** the base to head for is LITOCHORO, but see the following section for specific details.

If you've got time or your own transport, one of the more interesting places along the highway is **AMBELAKIA**, a small town on the slopes of Mount Ossa – and itself a good hiking base if you want to explore the Vale of Tempe. Buses go here direct from Larissa, or the town is 5 km above the 'Tempe' railway station. A dignified place, it was the world's first-ever industrial co-operative, thriving in the C17th–18th under an enlightened association of capital and labour, exporting its own textiles to Europe and maintaining branch offices as far afield as London. At a time when most of Greece lay stagnant under Turkish rule Ambelakia was largely autonomous; it held democratic assemblies, operated free education and medical care and even subsidised weekly performances of ancient drama. Tragically the town was destroyed by Ali Pasha in 1811 and any chance of recovery crushed by the bankruptcy of the Viennese bank in which its collective wealth was deposited. Today you can get some idea of its former prosperity by visiting the restored **Mansion of George Schwarz** – home of the co-operative's last president.

Continuing along the National Highway you enter the **Vale of Tempe** about 2 km after the Ambelakia turn-off. This is a particularly beautiful valley, about 10 km long, formed between the steep cliffs of the Olympos and Ossa ranges; the River Peinios follows its course. In antiquity it was sacred to Apollo and one of the few possible approaches into Greece: this was the path taken by both Xerxes and Alexander the Great. It remained an important pass during the Middle Ages and halfway down (on the right) you can see the ruined 'Kastro tis Orias' (Castle of the Beautiful Maiden), one of four guardposts erected by the Franks. Another medieval fortress (this time built by the Crusaders) rises high above the village of Panteleimonas, as you emerge from Tempe, and at this point, too, there are the best beaches on the Thermaic Gulf – at PLATA-MONAS, PARALIA SKOTINAS, GRITSA and PLAKA. They're beauti-fully situated, with Olympos rising impressively behind, but, sadly, are now very developed resorts; in the space of a dozen or so kilometres there are as many organised campsites – an overblown and soulless concentration.

MOUNT OLYMPOS

At nearly 10,000 ft the peaks of Mt Olympos are the highest in Greece. The mythical home of the gods, they are also the most dramatic of the country's ranges – rearing suddenly above the sea, from a low narrow plain. Surprisingly one of the highest groups of peaks, centred on Profitis Ilias at 9145 ft, is not a particularly difficult hike. From LITOCHORO, the main base-camp, you'll need a couple of full days – and the summer, for from October through to March Olympos is snow-covered and hazardous.

LITOCHORO, or Litohoron, is connected by bus with both Katerini and Thessaloniki. It has a railway station, too, though this is actually 9 km distant so you'll need to wait for a connecting bus. A small, rather dreary town, it is simply a functional base for the ascents. There's a **youth hostel**, the only cheap place to stay, at the bottom of town (behind Hotel Park) and this, even if you plan to press onwards should be your first stop: there are maps of the trails available here, or if they've run out you can at least make a copy – it's a fairly simple route, though confusing if you're going purely by nose. You can stock up on provisions in Litochoro.

The Profitis Ilias peaks have two possible approaches – which many hikers choose to combine into a three-day circuit. Both trailheads are reached by the road leading out above Litochoro: **route one** (the most popular) starts right at the end at the Prionia Spring (18½ km from Litochoro) and is indicated with red dots; **route two** (blue dots) starts at the 11 km marker, signposted with a fairly accurate map of the area. Between the two trailheads, and probably the best place to spend the night before you start, is the monastery of **Agios Dionisios**, 20 mins walk below the road and equipped with water and rooms for visitors.

Taking **route one** it's about a 3½ hr hike from the Prionia spring to

Refuge A of the Hellenic Alpine Club (open 15 May–15 Oct; also known as 'Katafiyo Spilios Agapitos') and from here you can reach one of the summits (Skala 9400 ft; Mitikas 9570 ft; Stefani 9545 ft; Profitis Ilias 9145 ft) in three to four hours. Information is usually available from the warden or fellow hikers at this refuge; so too are the keys for Refuge C, 'King Paul', half way up to Profitis Ilias. Just beyond 'C' is another refuge, 'SEO', usually locked but offering some shelter if you want to camp.

Route two also brings you out at the 'SEO' refuge below Profitis Ilias (and its summit chapel). From the 11 km trailhead it's a fairly hard-going 3 hr hike to Petrostounga, a beautiful high mountain pasture and from there the refuge is about another 2½ hrs.

For additional information once again see Marc Dubin's hiking book, or consult the **Hellenic Alpine Club** (SEO) information office in Litochoro – on the main square beside the church.

WEST FROM LARISSA: TRIKALA AND KALAMBAKA

TRIKALA, spread along the banks of the River Lethaios, feels quite a lively metropolis after the drab agricultural plains towns of central Thessaly. Many of its old Turkish houses survive, too, stacked about the Byzantine fortress at the far end of town. There isn't, however, a lot to actually hold you here and if you're making for the fantastic landscape of the Meteora there seems no particular reason not to continue the remaining 21 kms to Kalambaka. Buses run this way every half hour, trains four times a day.

There are few more exciting places to arrive than **KALAMBAKA**. The town itself you hardly notice for the eye is drawn up in an unremitting vertical ascent to the weird grey cylinders of rock overhead; these are the outlying monoliths of the extraordinary valley of the Meteora. To the right you can make out the Monastery of St Stephen, firmly entrenched on a massive pedestal; beyond stretch a chaotic confusion of spikes, cones and cliffs – beaten into bizarre and unworldly shapes by the action of a prehistoric sea that covered the Plain of Thessaly around fifty million years ago.

Kalambaka is the standard place to stay when visiting the Meteora and it enjoys a quiet prosperity from the stream of tourists. Though quite a pleasant base it's not in itself a very beautiful nor interesting place, burnt by the Germans in the last war, its buildings are mainly functional and modern. The one notable exception is its old Byzantine Cathedral, the **Church of the Assumption of the Virgin**, at the top of the town a couple of streets above its large modern successor. It was founded in the C7th on the site of a Temple to Apollo and incorporates various classical drums and fragments in its erratically designed walls. Well worth a visit, it's a lovely church with some good C14th frescoes and, most unusually, a great marble pulpit placed in the central aisle.

Cheapest of Kalambaka's many small hotels is the 'Acropolis', the first place you meet after leaving the train station. Equally good value is the lone rooms establishment near the bus terminal downtown, or the nearby Hotel Epirotikon. But if you're happy to camp, or have arrived earlyish in the day (or out of season) head instead to the village of **KASTRAKI**, 20 mins walk out of town and right in the shadow of the main rocks. There are a number of café-restaurants here and a couple of campsites – the most convenient right at the far end of the village. Here too is the fabulously-sited, 'E' class 'Hotel Kastraki', much the best place to stay if you can get a room; telephone 2 2286 before setting off from Kalambaka if you definitely need a bed – there's nowhere else, except the camping opposite.

Some years one of the monasteries, the GREAT METEORON, actually operates a summer hostel/café. It's quite expensive, and if you want to stay check first with a major NTOG office that it will be open.

THE METEORA

The monasteries of the Meteora are a spectacular enigma. Perched high on detached and seemingly inaccessible pinnacles of rock, nobody is quite sure how they were established. Legend has it that St Athanasios, who founded the first – the Great Meteoron, flew up there on the back of an eagle. Cynics suggest that the villagers of Stagi (the medieval precursor of Kalambaka) became adept at climbing and helped the original monks up.

Their name, 'Meteora', means literally 'rocks in the air' – an apt description; by the C16th some twenty-four of these had been surmounted by monasteries and hermitages. Today six of them survive, of which four can be visited. They have lost their isolation (and many of their monks) to the ravages of an asphalt road and seasonal coachloads of tourists; however they remain at all times an awesome monument of medieval religious spirit and if you can possibly visit them in spring or winter they are something more.

The earliest religious community in this weird and powerful valley emerged in the late C10th when hermits, seeking refuge from the turbulence of the age, made their homes in the caves which score many of the rocks. In 1336 they were joined by one Athanasios and his Abbot Gregorius from the skete of Magoula on Athos; they had fled from repeated attacks on the Holy Mountain by pirates and had been directed to this rocky district by Jakolos, Bishop of the Serbs. Gregorius shortly returned to Athos but saw in his companion an affinity to the isolated rocks and ordered him to stay and found a new monastery. This Athanasios did, whether supernaturally aided or not, and despite imposing a particularly austere and ascetic rule he was quickly joined by many brothers and in 1371 by John Palaeologos, who refused the throne of Serbia to become the monk Ioasaph. More monasteries followed on all the accessible, and many of the inaccessible, rocks and for the next three centuries they flourished upon the revenues of estates granted to them in distant Wallachia and Moldavia, and in Thessaly itself. They probably reached their zenith in the reign of Suleiman the Magnificent (1520–66) and did not markedly decline – despite some shameful internal squabbling over superiority – until the C18th. It was largely the loss of land and revenues which brought about the ruin of the monasteries – although some were simply not built to withstand the centuries and just slowly disintegrated in the air! By the C20th they were scarcely populated and in the 1920s lost most of their estates in Greece under the reforms of Eleftherios Venizelos, who nationalised church lands for the use of refugees.

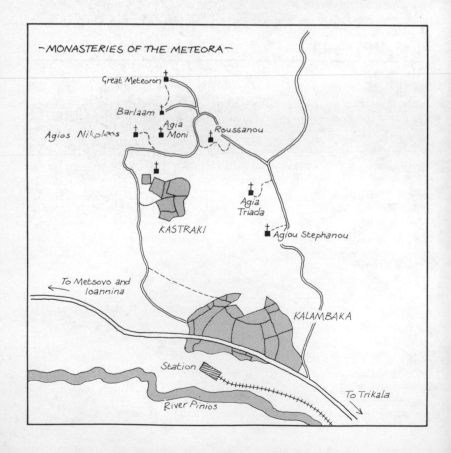

─ MONASTERIES OF THE METEORA ─

Great Meteoron

Barlaam

Agios Nikolaos

Agia Moni

Roussanou

Agia Triada

Agiou Stephanou

KASTRAKI

To Metsovo and Ioannina

KALAMBAKA

Station

River Pinios

To Trikala

In the 1950s five of the monasteries struggled on with little more than a dozen monks between them (for a superb account of them at this time see Patrick Leigh Fermor's *Roumeli*) but ironically, just before their expropriation in the late 1960s as a tourist attraction, they had begun to revive, attracting a number of young and intellectual brothers. Today only two seem to function principally as monasteries.

From **KASTRAKI** it's possible to complete the circuit of the valley in a good day's walking – much the best way to visit them, especially if you ignore the road and strike across some of the old tracks; there are also a few irregular buses and it's easy to hitch lifts. A couple of points, however – take some food and water as there are only a couple of occasional fruit stalls along the way and, most important, *WOMEN MUST WEAR SKIRTS NOT TROUSERS AND MEN MUST NOT WEAR SHORTS; BOTH MUST HAVE THEIR ARMS COVERED* (these rules are strictly enforced at Barlaam and the Great Meteoron – if you don't comply you won't be admitted). Lastly don't forget to take money with you – there's an admission charge (currently 30 drachmas) at each monastery.

About 20 mins walk from Kastraki you reach a track which leads left to a low rock on which stands **AGIOS NIKOLAOS TOU ANAPAVSA** – a small monastery with reputedly excellent frescoes by Theophanes the Cretan (1527); it was restored in 1960 and again in 1983–4; recently re-opened, it should definitely be worth the climb. Next to it, on a needle-thin shaft, is **AGIA MONI**, inaccessible now and ruined and empty since an earthquake in 1858. Bearing off to the right, 15 mins or so further on, a barely visible path ascends to the tiny and compact **ROUSSANOU** (or Convent of St Barbara), approached across dizzying bridges from an adjacent rock. Again it is closed (although work was being carried out when I was there) but you can at least go as far as its main doorway. It is perhaps the most extraordinary of all the monasteries, with walls built right on the edge of a sharp and imposing blade; its frescoes, particularly bloody scenes of martyrdom and judgment, were painted in 1560. (Roussanou can also be reached from the upper fork of the road – there's a track.)

A short way beyond Roussanou the road divides – swinging left to Barlaam and the Great Meteoron. **BARLAAM** (open 9–1.30 and 3.30–6; closed Fridays) stands on the site of a hermitage established by St Barlaam shortly after Athanasios arrived. These two, along with the royal Ioasaph, are the principal figures of Meteorite history. The monastery, the most beautiful in the valley, was built in 1517 by two brothers from Ioannina and was dedicated to All Saints. Its Katholikon (chapel) is small but glorious – supported by painted beams and with walls and pillars totally covered in frescoes. A dominant theme (well suited to the Meteora) are the desert ascetics, but there is also a vivid Last Judgment with a gaping Hell's Mouth and a great Pantocrator in the dome; they were painted in 1548 and 1566. There's a small museum of icons in Barlaam's Refectory but of more interest is the old Ascent Tower with its precipitous reception platform and dubious windlass mechanism. Until the 1920s the only way of reaching the monasteries was by being hauled up in a net drawn in by rope and windlass or by the equally perilous retractable ladders; a former abbot asked how often the rope was changed is reputed to have replied, logically enough, 'Only when it breaks.' Steps were eventually cut to all of them on the orders of the Bishop of Trikala and the mechanisms are used today only for supplies and building materials.

The **GREAT METEORON** (open 9–1.30 and 3.30–5.30; closed Tuesdays) is the grandest and highest of the monasteries f built on the 'Broad Rock' 1,752 feet above the ground. It had extensive privileges and held jurisdiction over the area for several centuries; in a fine C18th engraving (displayed in the museum) it is depicted literally towering above the others. Its Katholikon is certainly the most magnificent, a beautiful cross-in-square church surmounted by a lofty dome; it was rebuilt on this scale in the C16th – the original, constructed by Athanasios and Ioasaph, forming just the *hieron*, the part behind the iconostasis. The monastery itself is a vast arched cluster of buildings – you can see the refectory (now a museum, with some exquisite wood carved crosses) and the ancient domed and smoke-blackened kitchen, but its power really lies in the position and the mystery of how Athanasios ever got on to the rock.

Returning to the main branch it's about 2 hours' walk to **AGIA TRIADA,** the Holy Trinity (open 8–12 and 3–6), entered by 130 steps carved into a tunnel in the rock. You emerge to a light and airy cloister where the monks are hard at work building and renovating. Although the Katholikon is poor and its frescoes dark with age it's a refreshing change for the coaches do not stop here and life is still essentially monastic. It stands above a deep ravine and at the back a little garden ends in a precipitous drop; again it is impossible to work out the original means of access. **AGIOU STEPHANOU** (open 8–12 and 3–5; closed Mondays), the last and eastern-most of the monasteries, is three-quarters of an hour on – appearing suddenly at a bend in the road. Again it is active (occupied this time by nuns) but it is a little disappointing; the Katholikon is whitewashed and simple whilst the rock on which it stands is spanned by a bridge from the road. Its view, of course, is amazing – like every turn and twist of this valley – but if you're pushed for time it's the best one to miss out.

NORTH FROM KALAMBAKA: TOWARDS VERIA

Despite its uncertain appearance on most maps the road from KALAMBAKA to GREVENA is quite reasonable; its only drawback is that there's just one bus a day (currently at 11am) and not a lot of other transport. There's no particular reason to take this route other than to get to VERIA (and thence to the important Macedonian sites of VERGINA and LEFKADIA) – **GREVENA**, once a Klephtic stronghold against the Turks, is now just another dull concrete town and **KOZANI** no less forgettable. There are, however, regular buses from both these towns to VERIA and there's a certain grandeur in the last section of this journey; the road, previously through scrubby hills and dismal plain, ascends and twists through outlying flanks of Mount Olympos (or 'Ollybus' as the Greeks pronounce it). Veria is covered under 'The North' (see p. 145).

EPIRUS: THE WEST

ACROSS THE PINDUS TO METSOVO AND IOANNINA

West of KALAMBAKA lies one of the few roads that cross the Pindus Mountains into Epirus. It's actually the quickest and shortest east–west route across Greece but distances here are distracting – the road switchbacks and zigzags through folds in the enormous peaks and from November to March the snowline must be crossed. If you're driving allow half a day for the journey to IOANNINA (114 km) and if you're hitching don't take a lift that's not going either there or to METSOVO (59 km) for there's little but mountain forest in between. Three buses a day make the route in each direction.

METSOVO, almost astride the 5600 ft Katara Pass, encapsulates the most striking and picturesque facets of Epirot tradition. Built in steep terraces on two sides of a ravine, it's encircled by a crown of mighty peaks. Its stone houses with wooden balconies and quartered tile roofs begin just below the main road, winding down an intricate network of rock-paved paths to the main **plateia**. Here the old men loiter – magnificently garbed in full traditional dress, from flat black caps to pompommed feet; the women, ensconced in rich blue weave, have a rougher attire. 'The best dressed people in the world', Byron described the Epirots and in Metsovo – where it all seems entirely natural, you get an idea of what he meant. Many of the villagers here, and elsewhere in the Pindus, are descendants of the Koutsovlachs – Romanian nomads who settled the mountain valleys in the Middle Ages. In some of the more remote parts the old people are still bilingual in their native tongue.

The finely woven cloth, rugs and blankets are still produced on household looms – handicrafts of rare taste and quality in modern Greece – whilst a fine collection of Epirot crafts and costumes are housed in the restored C18th **Tossitsa Mansion** (open 8–1 and 3–5.30; on request). Its rooms, lined with carved wood panelling and terrific weaves, recreate the wealth and grandeur of the town in the C17th and C18th. Then, in a bizarre and dignified episode of history, it enjoyed independence from Turkish rule, becoming the refuge of several prominent Christian families. This was the reward of a Turkish vizier who, causing offence to his Sultan, sought anonymous asylum in Metsovo and was given hospitality. Later returning to favour at court he offered his former host anything he desired; the man chose freedom for the town – which was honoured by four successive sultans before being violated by Ali Pasha.

Although it stands in some danger of being developed as a chic ski-resort (the slope above is open January to March) Metsovo remains one of the most beautiful and disarmingly friendly villages in Greece. It's a superb place to stay and there are a handful of good small hotels, cheapest of them the 'Acropolis', right at the top, and the 'Athinae' in the central square. To catch the bus on to IOANNINA it's wise to walk up to the main road: they don't always go down to the village itself.

IOANNINA

After an hour and a quarter's swirling descent through even more spectacular folds of the Pindus you emerge high above the great lake of Pambotis – **IOANNINA**, once the capital of Ali Pasha, stands upon its edge. A rocky promontory juts confidently out from the town, its fortifications punctuated by towers and minarets as if to declare its history. For from this base Ali, 'the Lion of Ioannina', carved from the Turks a kingdom encompassing much of western Greece, an act of contemptuous rebellion that portended wider defiance in the Greeks' own War of Independence.

As an 'heroic rebel' **Ali Pasha** assumes an ambivalent role – for his only consistent policy was that of ambition and self-interest, and as frequent as his attacks on the Turkish Porte were acts of appalling and vindictive savagery against his Greek subjects. He was born in 1741, in Albania, and rose to power under Turkish patronage, being made Pasha of Trikala in reward for his efforts in the Sultan's war against Austria. His ambitions, however, were of a grander order and that same year, 1788, he seized Ioannina – an important town since the C13th and with a population of 30,000, probably then the largest in Greece. Paying sporadic and usually token tribute to the Sultan, he operated from this centre of power for the next 33 years, allying in turn and as the moment suited him with the British, French or Turks.

In 1809, when his dependence upon the Porte was nominal, Ali was visited by the young Lord Byron – whom he overwhelmed with hospitality and attention. Byron, impressed for his part with the rebel's daring and stature, and by the lively revival of Greek culture in Ioannina (which, he wrote, was 'superior in wealth, refinement and learning' to any town in Greece), commemorated the meeting in *Childe Harold*. The portrait that he draws, however, is an ambiguous one, well aware that there are 'deeds that lurk beneath' the Pasha's splendid court and deceptively mild countenance which 'stain him with disgrace'. In a letter to his mother Byron was still more explicit, concluding that 'His highness is . . . a remorseless tyrant, guilty of the most horrible cruelties, very brave, so good a general that they call him the Mahometan Buonaparte . . . but as barbarous as he is successful, roasting rebels, etc., etc.'

It is in fact the stories of Ali Pasha's cruelties rather than the glories of his success which seem to hang about the surviving vestiges of his capital. Disappointingly, most of the city is modern and undistinguished – in itself testimony to Ali for, under siege in 1820, he burnt most of it to the ground. Outside the fortifications only a few crumbling mosques – the Turkish presence persisted into the late 1920s – give atmosphere to the place, their minarets long taken over by storks. But the walls of the **Frourion**, the great citadel, remain impressively complete – although they no longer drop abruptly to the lake and the moat on their landward side has been filled in. Once inside, signs direct you to the 'Popular Museum' (open weekdays 8.30–1 and 4.30–6.30, Sundays 11–1), a splendidly ramshackle collection of Epirot costumes and jewellery along with photographs and relics from the liberation of Ioannina from the Turks – just 70-odd years ago in 1913, a sobering reminder of the closeness of foreign rule in Greece. The museum itself is housed in the well-preserved **Cami of Aslan Pasha**, allowing a rare glimpse of the interior of a mosque; it retains the decoration on its dome and the recesses in the vestibule for the shoes of worshippers. Here, in 1801, tradition places Ali's rape and murder of Kyra Phrosyne, the mistress of his eldest son. Her 'provocation' had been to refuse the 62-year-old tyrant's sexual advances and, together with seventeen of her companions, she was bound, weighted and thrown alive into the lake. Later, Ali was to rape the wife of his second son.

From the courtyard of the Cami you look down upon the **inner citadel** of the fortress. This was used for some years by the Greek military and most of its buildings are gone or, like Ali's palace (where Byron was entertained), restored past recognition. A circular tower remains, however, along with the fine old Fetihie Cami ('Victory Mosque') – now sealed up and consigned to silent decay; close by is supposed to be Ali Pasha's tomb, though hunting around I failed to find it.

A more obvious and dramatic site survives on the **Island of Nissi** in the centre of Lake Pambiotis. This is the Monastery of Pantaleimon where in January 1822 Ali Pasha was finally assassinated, shot from the floor below his rooms by a Turkish soldier. The fateful bullet holes in the floorboards form the centrepiece of a small museum to the tyrant, along with a few prints and knick-knacks like Ali's splendid hubble-bubble. It stands a little to the east of the beautiful old island village – the best place to stay if you can find a room – whilst to the north are three other monasteries, signposted and spread within a few hundred yards of each other along a lovely treeswept lane. All are maintained by a few nuns and their frescoed **Katholikons** (chapels) can be visited; the finest is Agios Nilolaos, with extraordinarily bloody and graphic C17th scenes of early Christian martyrdoms. Boats ply every hour between the island and the Ioannina quay (beneath the Popular Museum); they're inexpensive and the last one returns at 9pm.

Ioannina details

The modern capital of Epirus, Ioannina is a strategic base for travel in the region. **Dodona**, site of the oldest oracle in Greece and of (arguably) the country's most beautiful surviving ancient theatre, lies 22 km to its west. **Igoumenitsa**, port for Corfu and Italy, is under two hours away, and there are buses returning to **Athens** (via Arta) in a little over seven hours. Perhaps most tempting, though, if you have three or four days, is the remote area of the **Zagoria** immediately north of the town. Here, along with a fantastic hike through the dark Vikos Gorge, you'll find some of the most unspoilt (indeed unvisited) villages in Greece: made entirely of local schist and wood and perfectly adapted to their wild mountainous environment.

More of all these options in the sections that follow: but heading out from Ioannina (especially to the Zagoria) be sure to plan **buses** well in advance. Terminals are spread about town. For buses to Dodona you'll need the Bizaniou 28 terminal, beyond the larger one for Arta and the south. Other local destinations are served by the Epirus Provincial Station at Zozimadou 4. If you're confused check out times and departure points at the very helpful tourist police or NTOG office.

Cheap **hotels** in Ioannina are mostly called *pandoheia*, or inns, and they're gathered into a small area around Kentriki Plateia, the main square. Try the *Agapi* at Tsirigoti 6 – easiest found by following the signs to 'D' class *Hotel Paris*, run by the same people. Alternatively, there are a couple of 'D' class places in the Kentriki Plateia itself. The Ioannina **campsite** is a couple of kilometres out of town – but very nicely positioned on the edge of the lake; to get there take bus no. 8 from the centre. The same bus, incidentally, continues around the lake to **Perama** where you can visit a vast complex of **caves**. Said to be the largest in Greece, they really are very impressive – grand echoing chambers spread for over a mile beneath a low dank hill. They are open fairly continuously through the day in summer, closing earlier at around 4 pm out of season.

Lake Pambotis also produces the town's culinary specialities – trout, eels and frogs' legs, all of which are served at the two *tavernas* on the island. For solid, cheaper fare try the *Pantheon* restaurant, just beside the main gate to the Frourion at the end of Averof Street.

Last, if you're visiting Dodona be sure to take a look at the **Archaeological Museum** (weekdays 9–3.30; Suns 10–4), one of the best you'll find in the provinces. Displayed here – along with some exceptional crafted bronze seals (note that of Clytemnestra being slain by Orestes) – are a fascinating collection of lead tablets inscribed with questions to the Oracle. Memorable also, but unlabelled in the corner by the door, is an object that looks like an anchor chain: this is in fact the windlass mechanism from the extraordinary Necromanteion of Ephyra (see p. 124).

DODONA (Open daily 9–5; closed Tuesdays)

There is a certain romantic egocentrism in being a tourist which demands that a site should not only be beautiful beyond one's expectations but should also be a personal and private discovery. If you ever feel like this go to Dodona. Here in the wildly mountainous and once isolated region of herdsmen lie the ruins of the Oracle of Zeus – reputedly the oldest in Greece – dominated by a vast and elegant theatre.

Few people bother to make the 22 km detour from Ioannina so the site and the little village to the west of it are completely unspoilt. **Transport**, however, is accordingly sparse – there are only two buses a day from Ioannina and if you want to see the ruins and return the same day the only practicable one goes at 6am. It's probably best to take the afternoon (2pm) bus and stay the night, there are some lovely spots to camp and a friendly if basic *taverna* in the middle of the nearby village. For the affluent there's also a tiny 'B' class 'Xenia' hostel at the site.

'Wintry Dodona' was already known to Homer but **the Oracle** is probably far older; the worship of Zeus and of the sacred oak tree at Dodona seems to have been connected with the first Hellenic tribes who arrived in Epirus (around 1900 BC). Its origins are fairly undecided – Robert Graves says that patrilineal invaders replaced the resident Earth Goddess with Zeus, and Herodotus gives an enigmatic story about the arrival of a dove from Egyptian Thebes which settled in an oak tree and ordered a place of divination to be made. Significantly the word *peleiae* meant both dove and old woman so it's possible that the legend Herodotus heard refers to an original priestess – possibly captured from the East and having some knowledge or practice of divination. The oak tree, stamped on the coins of the area, is central to the cult. Herodotus recorded that the Oracle spoke through the rustling of its leaves in sounds amplified by copper vessels suspended from its branches; these would then be interpreted by frenzied priestesses and by strange priests who 'slept on the ground and never washed their feet'.

You enter the *SITE* through the outline of a third-century BC **Stadium** and are immediately confronted by the massive western retaining wall of the **Theatre**. One of the largest on the Greek mainland and rivalled only by Argos and Megalopolis, it was built during the time of Pyrrhus (297–272 BC). Later, the Romans made adaptations necessary for their bloodsports, building a protective wall over the lower seating and a drainage channel, cut in a horseshoe shape around the Orchestra. At the top of the Cavea, or auditorium, a grand entrance gate leads into the **Acropolis**, an overgrown and largely unexcavated area. Its walls, mostly Hellenistic, are a remarkable 10–15 feet wide but rarely stand higher than 10 feet.

The theatre is used annually in August for a couple of performances of **Ancient Drama**; details from the NTOG office in Ioannina at Napoleontos Zerva 2. These must be terrific for it is one of the most glorious settings in Greece – the seats face out across a green, silent valley to the slopes of Mount Tomaros, like one peak challenging another.

Beside the theatre, and tiered uncharacteristically against the same slope, are the foundations of a **Boulouterion** (council house), beyond which lie the complex ruins of the **Sanctuary of Zeus** – site of the ancient oracle. There was no temple here at all until the end of the C5th BC. Worship centred upon the Sacred Oak, within which the god was thought to dwell, standing alone within a circle of votive tripods and cauldrons. Building began modestly with a small stone temple surrounded by a peribolos wall, though by the time of Pyrrhus this enclosure was made of Ionic colonnades. In 219 BC the Sacred House was sacked by the Aetolians and a larger temple was built with a monumental propylon. This survived until the C4th AD, when the oak tree was hacked down by Christian reformists and it is the remains of this precinct that can be seen today. It is easily distinguishable by an oak planted at its centre by a reverent archaeologist. Remains of an early Christian **Basilica**, constructed over a Sanctuary of Herakles, are also prominent nearby.

Many oracular inscriptions were found scattered around the area when it was excavated in 1952 – now displayed in Ioannina Museum, they give you a good idea of the personal realm of the Oracle's influence in the years after it had been eclipsed by Delphi. Perhaps more interestingly, they also offer a glimpse of the fears and inadequacies that motivated the pilgrims of the age to journey there – asking questions like 'Am I her children's father?' and 'Has Pleistos stolen the wool from my mattress?'!

ZITSA AND THE ZAGOROCHORIA

Leaving IOANNINA on the IGOUMENITSA road there's a turning after 21 km to ZITSA, a rather time-consuming excursion. With its unique champagne-like wine, its stone mansions and cobbled streets, this is one of the most attractive villages in Epirus. Byron stayed here, at the **Monastery of Profitis Ilias**, whose situation he thought 'the finest in Greece'. In the valley below flows the River Kalamas – anciently the Acheron, legendary river of Hades. 'If this is hell,' wrote Byron in *Childe Harold*, 'close shamed Elysium's gates.'

Beyond, a small road takes you north-east, through exceptional scenery to ASFAKA, and a couple of kilometres beyond a turning to the right opens into a network of beautiful stream-crossed lanes and unbelievably rustic and distant-aged villages. These are the **Zagorachorio**, the forty-five remote hamlets of the Zagoria mountains. If you've upwards of two to three days and enjoy hiking or just rambling amid the wooded hills make all efforts to come here and explore: hardly anyone does at present, except one small British trekking company, and there are still no modern hotels. You can, however, get basic rooms at most of the village *pandoheio* – and there are two buses daily from Ioannina to both Vitsa and Monodendri, at the heart of the region. Vitsa has rooms to let.

MONODENDRI, one of the largest and most spectacular of the villages, is the place to head for if you want to hike the Vikos Gorge, 'a dark chaos of boulders and spikes' (to quote Leigh Fermor) and every inch a rival to the famous Gorge of Samaria on Crete. There are no rooms here but a good *psistaria*, and, 10 mins walk on, the **Monastery of Agia Paraskevi**, fabulously poised on the lip of the gorge. Even if you go no further, at least walk out here – and cautiously along the track beyond, which suddenly stops sheer in a 1,000 ft drop! The monastery itself is disestablished but is currently being converted to house a small hostel – a fabulous place to wake if the NTOG don't impose some ridiculous tariff.

The trail down to the **Vikos Gorge** begins back by the village church, and is signalled by some red dots. It isn't an easy hike, particularly on the initial descent, and should only really be attempted in summer – spring can see parts of the route under several feet of water. It takes about an hour to get down to the bottom of the gorge, around five and a half to reach the mouth of the river bed at its end (where there's a farmhouse and pasture). Here the trail turns into a rock stairway leading off to the left to the tiny village of **Vikos**. You could stop here, stay the night at the Vikos inn, and get back to Ioannina by walking (possibly hitching) along the 5 km dirt road to ARISTI, the first village connected by bus. Alternatively – and as Marc Dubin urges in detail, again in *Backpacker's Greece* – it's possible to take the (blue-dotted) trail, from the opposite bank to the Vikos stairway, 2½ hrs on to the villages of Micro and Megalo (big and little) **Papingo**. This isn't an easy trailhead to find but once you're on to it and over the ridge it's not too strenuous. Beyond the Papingo villages, where there are rooms and food, still more tempting trails lead on to the Gamila range and the mountain lake of Drakolimni.

Getting back on to the bus routes at either Aristi or Papingo, you can continue north instead of doubling back to Ioannina. Skirting the Albanian border the road winds up and around to **KONITSA**, another magnificent Epirot village built above a dark river gorge emerging from the Pindus – this time the Aoos, and eventually to KASTORIA. A rather forlorn sort of place, **KASTORIA** is a centuries-old fur centre (its very name means 'beavers') and must once have been among the finest towns in the country, marvellously set on a peninsula that extends deep into a chill-blue lake. Amidst its narrow cobbled streets elegant C17th and C18th mansions survive, along with some fifty churches – many of them medieval and Byzantine. In recent years, though, these have been immersed on all sides into a drab mire of modern building and the lake itself has become pretty unwholesome. It's still an interesting place to stop over if it fits in with your route but isn't really worth any special planning. The best concentration of mansions are on Bizantiou Street, running down to the lakeside from Plateia Emmanou I; finest of the churches are along Kommenou and Mitropoleou Streets, which lead from the bus station into the centre of town. If you're here outside the summer it could be bitterly cold – 'D' class *Hotel Palladion* (Mitropoleou 40) has central heating; cheaper places can be found further into the centre.

Kastoria has reasonable bus links with Thessaloniki – and also with **FLORINA**, border town for the quieter, more interesting crossing into Yugoslavia at Bitola, a good approach to the Yugoslav coast and the (ethnically) Albanian province of Kosovo. The town itself has absolutely nothing to delay your progress – except its trains to Bitola, which are quite amazingly slow – but it's useful for changing money. Here, with free-market rates, you get a much better exchange from drachmas to dinar: change as much as you possibly can, bearing to some extent in mind the official Yugoslav maximum import of 1500 New Dinar.

DOWN TO THE COAST: IGOUMENITSA AND PARGA

IGOUMENITSA, 100 km on from Ioannina, is the cheapest and quickest port for the islands of **Paxi and Corfu** and for southern Italy – a function that dominates the town and provides virtually all its character. It's also possible to sail from here to **Ithaca and Kefalonia**, though both are easier (and cheaper) reached from Patras. If you want to go to Italy and stop off at Corfu en route it is sometimes possible to have this specified on your ticket (as is routine at Patras); often, however, boat companies don't seem able or willing to do this since it competes with the local (6 times daily) ferry to Corfu.

Buying a **ticket to Italy** as ever demands a little hunting about since there are widely varying deals and operators. From 1 June to 1 October (or thereabouts) the cheapest crossing tends to be on the *Roana* to Otranto, via Corfu: this is operated by 'R-Lines' and tickets sold by the G. Pitoulis agency on the seafront. The route has the added advantage of being a night ferry, cutting down on boredom and hotels. Second choice is usually Hellenic Mediterranean/Adriatica who run a more or less daily service to Brindisi; they give reductions if you have Eurail or student/youth cards. For all these departures, however, remember that you'll be paying 250 drx or so **embarkation tax**.

On the subject of ferries it's also worth recording that once or twice weekly, depending on season, 'Jadrolinija Lines' operate a ferry connecting Igoumenitsa and Corfu with **Yugoslavia's Dalmatian coast**. This is relatively costly (nearly double the fares to Italy) but it does take in some of the most beautiful maritime scenery in southern Europe, and it is

sometimes possible to buy a ticket with stopover possibilities, turning it
into more of a budget cruise. The route is Igoumenitsa–Corfu–Dubrov-
nik–Split–Zadar–Rijeka.

The Igoumenitsa youth hostel has closed but there are dozens of cheapish **hotels** and a **campsite**, 'Sole Mar', at the south end of town. Unless
you've arrived from Brindisi late at night, however, there's little reason
to linger. Far better to head down-coast a little to the clearer waters of
PLATARIA, a good beach (8 km by bus) with a few tavernas and
unofficial camping, or to PARGA.

PARGA is the fastest-growing resort on this west coast and if you're
around in peak season the crowds will probably be a little over the top.
At other times though it's a wonderful place – a little circular bay beneath
a Norman castle, looking out towards a spattering of rocky islets and,
12 km offshore, the island of **Paxi**, accessible from here by daily caique.
Greek cement is beginning to make inroads but old Epirot houses still
predominate among the arched lanes. The beaches, too, are excellent –
three consecutive bays, split by the headland of the fortress hill. Immediately beyond the castle (and on foot easiest reached by the long
stairway from the castle gate) is **Valtos beach**, over a kilometre in length
as it sprawls round to the hamlet of the same name; there's a small
campsite here, as also at **Lihnos**, 3 km in the opposite (south-east)
direction.

Rooms in Parga are fairly plentiful and a little above usual prices; as
so often a costly business if you're travelling/sleeping singly. The main
town **campsite** is a good fallback – non-plastic and pleasantly sited amid
olive groves 500 m inland (just off the access road). Four buses a day run
between Parga and both Igoumenitsa and Preveza: but if you're heading
here after the last one has gone you can take any of the Igoumenitsa–
Preveza buses to the road junction at MORFI, a fairly routine 12 km
hitch.

Beyond Parga there are other fine beaches along with a handful of
small, isolated stony villages. The main road, however, runs some way
inland and you really need a car – or time and determination – to reach
them. One of the best beaches, and a relatively easy one to get to (by bus
from Parga/Morfi), is at the village of **AMMOUDIA**. Here it is possible
to camp and also to visit the extraordinary **Necromanteion** in the village
of **Mesopotamo**, a few kilometres inland.

THE NECROMANTEION OF EPHYRA (Open weekdays 9–3.30, Suns 10–4.30)

The **Necromanteion of Ephyra**, Oracle of the Dead and Sanctuary of
Persephone and Hades, stands on a rocky hill just above Mesopotamo.
It is signposted also from the village of Kastri on the main road from

Igoumenitsa to Preveza, 4 km before you come to Kanelaki; buses stop at Kastri and you can hitch the last 5 km without difficulty. Though small, the Necromanteion is a fascinating site, enough of its peculiar structure remaining to give a clear insight into the cynical machinations of the Oracle, scene of the 'Journey to the Dead' in Homer's Odyssey.

Pilgrims came here to consult the souls of the departed and were rooted no doubt in the fears and sanctity of their task. On arriving at this forbidding and ominous place they would be accommodated in window-less rooms and relieved of their votive offerings. Then, as their turn came, they would be sent groping along a labyrinth-corridor into the heart of the Sanctuary where, further disorientated by hallucinogenic vapours, they were lowered into the antechamber of Hades itself to witness what-ever spiritual visitation the priests might have devised.

The remains of the Sanctuary are impressively complete and each room can be easily identified by a plan inscribed at the entrance. At the centre is a long room with still high walls, flanked by stores for votive offerings; metal steps lead from here to the underground chamber where the nec-romantic audiences took place. Originally this descent was by means of the precarious windlass mechanism – now kept at Ioannina Museum.

Although the ruins, crowned uneasily by a tiny C2nd basilica, are mainly Hellenistic, the site and oracle are, like Dodona, much older. It was chosen for its position on the waters of the Acheron, mythological river of the underworld, which in ancient times formed a great lake around its base. Its fame must have been widespread by the C9th BC for Homer to have placed Odysseus' visit to Hades here – and this he does, unequivocally, Circe giving explicit directions to the place in Book 10:

> You will come to a wild coast and to Persephone's grove, where the hill poplars grow and the willows that so quickly shed their seeds. Beach your boat there by Ocean's swirling stream and march on into Hades' Kingdom of Decay. There the River of Flaming Fire and the River of Lamentation, which is a branch of the Waters of the Styx, unite around a pinnacle of rock to pour their thundering streams into Acheron. This is the spot, my lord, that I bid you seek out . . . then the souls of the dead and departed will come up in their multitudes.

The trees are still there but the lake has now receded to a vague line of the Acheron skirting through the plain – one can pick out its course from the walls of the Sanctuary by linking the bridges. Here it seems impossible to think of the river as a pathway to hell but high up in the Barrier Mountains it is said still to cut through plunging ravines and disappear through mysterious rock chasms.

PREVEZA AND NIKOPOLIS

Thirty km on from KASTRI the main road west reaches **Preveza** at the gate of the land-locked Ambracian Gulf. Here at the Battle of Actium in 31 BC Octavian defeated the combined forces of Antony and Cleopatra to become the Emperor Augustus. To commemorate this triumph he founded **NIKOPOLIS** ('Victory City') on the site where his army had camped. An arrogant gesture, it made little geographical sense; water had to be transported by aqueduct from Louros and it was forcibly populated from towns as far afield as Nafpaktos, built on far more secure ground. Sacked by Vandals and Goths, it was restored in the C6th by Justinian and flourished for a while as a Byzantine city; but within two centuries it had sank again into the earth, devastated by the combined effect of earthquakes and Bulgarian raids. Its far-flung and overgrown ruins lie 5 km before Preveza.

From the road the ruins look impressive – a great theatre stands to the left and as you approach the museum, past remnants of the baths, there is a formidable stretch of fortified walls. But, walking round, the promise of this enormous site is unfulfilled; there are few remains that reward closer inspection and the most interesting of these are the mosaics of an early Christian basilica beside the museum. The **Museum** itself (open – like the site – weekdays 9–3.30, Sundays 10–4.30) displays sundry Roman sculpture and the caretaker's main function is to unlock the Roman and Byzantine mosaics unearthed amidst the foundations of the C6th **Basilica of Doumetios**. The finest and best preserved depicts the Creation – crowded with trees, flowers, fruits and birds and framed by a well-stocked sea. The caretaker will then point you in the direction of the one other significant remain, a Roman **Odeion** dating from the original construction of the city; it has been well restored for use in a small annual drama festival.

Backtracking past the scant foundations of another C6th church (the double-aisled **Basilica of Bishop Alkyson**) it's a 3-km walk to the threatre, its arches still standing amidst dangerously crumbling masonry. To the left the sunken outline of the **stadium** can just be made out, below the village of Smyrtouna. Octavian's own tent was pitched upon the hill above and a massive podium remains from the commemorative monument that he erected.

The modern town of **PREVEZA** is drab and insignificant, although its ferries that cross the gulf to **ACTION** (every half hour; small charge) offer the quickest access to the quasi-island of **Lefkada** (connected frequently by bus). If that's not your plan you can by-pass the town altogether, the road past the Nikopolis theatre leads to Arta.

ARTA

A small, pleasant and quite interesting town, **ARTA** lies in a loop of the broad river Arakthos. Its approaches are all rather majestic and best of all the road from Ioannina following the plane-shaded Louros river gorge – a 2 hr journey, moodily impressive in the early evening. Still straddling the river as you enter the town, though no longer used by traffic, is a humpbacked old **Turkish bridge**, subject of folk-songs throughout Greece. Legend maintains that the builder, continually thwarted by the current, took the advice of a bird and sealed up his wife in the arch: the bridge held but the woman's voice haunted the place everafter. Inside the town, there are a number of important Byzantine churches, well worth wandering around. And it's an easy, friendly place if you want to stay – there's a reasonable 'D' class **hotel** opposite the bus station (*Hellas* at Skoufa 185) and a couple of others further down the same street, *Pantheon* (126) and *Rex* (9).

Anciently, known as Ambracia, the town was capital of Pyrrhus, King of Epirus, and the base for his hard-won ('Another such victory and I am lost') campaigns in Italy. Foundations to a sizeable Temple and part of a theatre have been unearthed (both off Odos Pyrrhou, the street leading from bus station/central square to the *frourion* or castle) but neither are very notable. Much more impressive are the churches from the town's second period of greatness, after the Fall of Constantinople, when it became the cultural centre of an autonomous '**Despotate of Epirus**'.

Most striking and certainly most bizarre of the churches from this epoch is the **Panagia Paragoritissa** (weekdays 9–3, Sundays 10–1; small charge), a grandiose multi-domed cube that dominates Plateia Skoufa, the central town square. Its interior is perhaps best described as 'Byzantine Gothic' – the main dome being held up on an extraordinary cantilever system that looks unwieldy and unsafe, its insecurity exaggerated by a looming Pantocrator mosaic. It was erected in 1282–9 as a monastic church; today a small archaeological museum occupies part of the old refectory. Two smaller Byzantine churches also survive – both of more standard structure but with brilliant designs of elaborate brick and tile decorations on their outside walls. **Agia Theodora**, containing the fine marble tomb of Michael II's consort, stands in a courtyard half-way down Odos Pyrrhou; a little further, opposite the market, is the small but very beautiful C14th **Agios Vassilios**.

Amidst the orange groves surrounding Arta are also several monasteries, many of them founded by members of the imperial Angelos dynasty. Within easy walking distance (2 km out on the Kominon Road) is **Kato Panagia** – perhaps the only monastery in Greece with an automated electric door-opener! Its C13th Katholikon, in a shaded courtyard guarded by peacocks, again has good exterior decoration.

DOWN-COAST TO MESSOLONGI AND THE GULF OF CORINTH

There are regular buses onwards from ARTA to AMFILOHIA – and thence to the island of Lefkada (Lefkas) – and to AGRINIO (for Messolongi) but there really isn't much to delay you on the way. AMFILO-HIA, promisingly situated at the mouth of the Ambracian gulf, is a very drab, dead place with murky swimming; STRATOS stands amidst ruins of its ancient city – once a provincial capital but with little more than a few stretches of wall to show for it; and AGRINIO is simply a modern commercial town, important mainly for its local tobacco trade.

Were it not for Byron's death, MESSOLONGI, too, would be no less forgettable: it's really neither an interesting nor a pretty place. Unless you've a strong fascination for the poet and the events of the Greek War of Independence give it a miss – or take another bus out to the less limpid waters of ASTAKOS or MITIKAS, two small but growing resorts midway to Vonitsa (and each, incidentally, with surprisingly un-Greek long, rambling beaches).

Staying on the Ioannina–Arta–Athens highway the liveliest resort to head for is NAFPAKTOS, covered earlier in this chapter (p. 104). If you're heading for Patras (and hence to Ithaca or Kefalonia), Olympia or the Peloponnese the best plan is to cross over at ANTIRIO–RIO, an almost continuous ferry link a few kilometres before Nafpaktos, each side guarded by the twin medieval 'castles of the Roumeli'. The ferries are extremely cheap and, if you're not on one going straight through, there are frequent local buses from RIO to PATRAS. Storming back by train this way to Athens, don't forget the possibility of the Diakofto–Kalavrita railway (see p. 89), far the most beautiful line in Greece.

MESSOLONGI: O LORDOS VIRONOS

In January 1824 Lord Byron joined the Greek mainland forces at Messolongi, a squalid and inhospitable town surrounded by marshland that comprised the western centre of resistance against the Turks. He was enthusiastically greeted with a 21-gun salute and on landing was made commander-in-chief of the 5,000 soldiers gathered at the garrison.

Byron had come to Greece determined to do his utmost for Hellenic freedom and, whilst never under the illusion that his service would be easy, was hardly prepared for the incessant and exasperating setbacks to follow. The Greek forces, led by Klephtic brigand-generals, were split amongst themselves and each faction separately and persistently besought him for money. Already he had wasted months in Kefalonia trying to assess their claims and calm their quarrels before finalising his own military plan – to march full force on Nafpaktos and from there take control of the Gulf of Corinth – but in Messolongi he was again forced to delay. Occasionally he despaired ('Here we sit in this realm of mud and discord') but whilst other Philhellenes were returning disgusted by the squabbles and larceny of the Greeks, he stayed, campaigning eloquently and profitably for the cause.

Though repeatedly urged by his friends to leave the damp, stagnant town he would not; he worked ceaselessly for the next few months, planning his offensive and drilling soldiers outside his house until eventually he fell ill of a fever. On 19 April 1824 Byron died – pronouncing a few days earlier, in a moment of lucid resignation, 'My wealth, my abilities, I devoted to the cause of Greece – well, here is my life to her!' In the outcome it was this last contribution, swelled to heroic proportions by his admirers at home and abroad, that changed the course of the war. When Messolongi itself fell, two years later, a public outcry reverberated across Europe and the French and English forces were finally galvanised into action.

While he lived, Byron could never be more than a Philhellene, though a generous and enduring one, but his death turned him into a national hero and the unassailable property of every Free Greek. Almost every town in Greece has a street named after him – *O Lordos Vironos* – and there's even a brand of cigarettes; furthermore, the respect he inspired was for many years generalised to his fellow countrymen, although the Cyprus issue effectively reversed such feelings.

You enter **MESSOLONGI** by the '**Gate of Sortie**' where, in 1826, 9,000 men, women and children attempted to break out from the year-long Turkish siege. In one wild dash ('The Exodus') they managed to get free of the town, leaving a group of defenders to destroy it in their wake; but they were betrayed and in the supposed safety of nearby Mount Zygos were ambushed and massacred by a large Albanian force. Just inside the gate on the right is the **Garden of Heroes** where a tumulus covers the bodies of the town's unnamed defenders; beside it is the Statue of Byron erected in 1881 under which is buried the poet's heart.

In the town traces of Byron are sparse. **The house** in which he lived and died was destroyed in the Second World War and its site is marked by a clumsy memorial garden enlivened only by socialist graffiti (suitably the word 'allagi', change); it's on Odos Levidou which is reached from the central square by walking down to the end of Odos Trikoupis and turning left. Back in the central square (Plateia Botsaris) the **Dhimarkion** houses a small 'Museum of the Revolution' with some emotive paintings of the Exodus and a rather desperate collection of Byronia – padded out with postcards from Newstead Abbey and the branch of an elm from his old school, Harrow.

It is tempting to draw analogies between the modern town and that which Byron knew: both are desperately unromantic places, wet through autumn and spring, and conspicuously drab. If you come here as a pilgrimage reckon on moving out before long: cheap hotels are few and poor.

TRAVEL DETAILS

1 Buses

Athens–Delphi (5 daily; 3½ hrs); Athens–Ossios Loukas (2 daily; 4 hrs); Athens–Thebes (hourly; 1½ hrs); Athens–Volos (9 daily; 5 hrs); Athens–Trikala (7 daily; 5¼ hrs); Delphi–Itea/Amfissa (4 daily; 20 mins/1 hr); Delphi–Nafpaktos (3 daily; 2½ hrs); Lamia–Volos (2 daily – 9am & 2pm; 3 hrs); Lamia–Trikala (4 daily; 3 hrs); Lamia–Larissa (4 daily; 3½ hrs); Volos–Larissa (hourly; 1¼ hrs); Volos–Kalambaka (3 daily; 2½ hrs); Trikala–Kalambaka (hourly; 25 mins); Kalambaka–Larissa (8 daily; 1¾ hrs); Kalambaka–Metsovo/Ioannina (4 daily; 1½ hrs/2¾ hrs); Ioannina–Dodona (daily – 6.30am & 4.30 pm; 35 mins); Ioannina–Arta (10 daily; 2½ hrs); Ioannina–Igoumenitsa (7 daily; 2 hrs); Igoumenitsa–Parga (4 daily; 50 mins); Igoumenitsa–Preveza (2 daily; 2½ hrs); Igoumenitsa–Athens (3 daily; 8½ hrs); Arta–Preveza (5 daily; 1 hr); Arta–Amfilochia/Agrinio (10 daily; 1 hr/2 hrs); Amfilochia–Lefkada (6 daily; 1½ hrs); Agrinio–Messolongi (6 daily; 1 hr); Agrinio–Patras (9 daily; 1¼ hrs); Messolongi–Nafpaktos (4 daily; 1 hr); Nafpaktos–Athens (4 daily; 1 hr).

N.B. Buses for Delphi and Ossios Loukas leave Athens from the **Liossion 260** terminal; most of the others from **Kifissou 100**. See Athens travel details.

2 Trains

Athens–Thebes/Livadia/Larissa (8 daily; 1½ hrs/2 hrs/5½–6 hrs); Athens–Volos (2 daily; 7–8 hrs); Larissa–Volos (12 daily; 1 hr); Volos–Kalambaka (only 1 daily, direct by 3 other connections via Palaiofarsalos; 4–5 hrs); Trikala–Kalambaka (4 daily; 25 mins); Larissa–Thessaloniki (9 daily; 3 hrs).

N.B. Though there are no trains to western Greece you can go by train to Patras (hourly; 3½–4 hrs) and thence by bus to the Rio-Antirio ferry.

3 Ferries

Ferry link every 20 mins (30 at night) between **AntiRio** and Rio on the Peloponnesian bank of the Gulf of Corinth; takes just 10 mins and nominal charge for passengers, cars around 200 drx.

From June to September there is also an hourly ferry between **Eratini** and Egio; 25 mins and a little more expensive.

Chain-ferry to the island of **Lefkada**, included in the buses from Vonitsa.

Ferries from **Igoumenitsa** to Brindisi, Bari and Ancona in Italy (most daily, or more often nightly); to Corfu six times daily (2 hrs); to Yugoslavia's Dalmatian coast (twice weekly in season); and at least weekly to the islands of Paxi, Ithaca and Kefalonia.

Daily caiques in season from **Parga** to the island of Paxi.

Chapter four
THE NORTH

The north of Greece was liberated from Turkey comparatively recently – **Macedonia** (Makhedonia) in 1912 and easterly **Thrace** (Thraki) only in 1920. As such it's the one area of Greece that retains a significant Turkish character and indeed in parts of Thrace Turkish communities also remain, the only ones allowed to do so in the 1922 exchange of populations. Constituting nearly a quarter of the Thracians, they are strongly in evidence from Kavala onwards: mixed with Greeks in the towns but maintaining strict independence in their villages.

Historically it is the Macedonian, Roman and Byzantine sites which provide the region's main interest. Only a part of the ancient Macedonian kingdom is now within the modern Greek state but there are striking excavations at its two capitals, Aigai (**Vergina**) and **Pella**. Roman remains are worth a detour at **Philippi** and are also scattered about **Thessaloniki** (Salonica), later the second city of the Byzantine Empire from which age it boasts a number of beautiful and important churches.

Thessaloniki is also very much the modern capital of northern Greece – a less lively and interesting place than Athens, though a far cleaner,

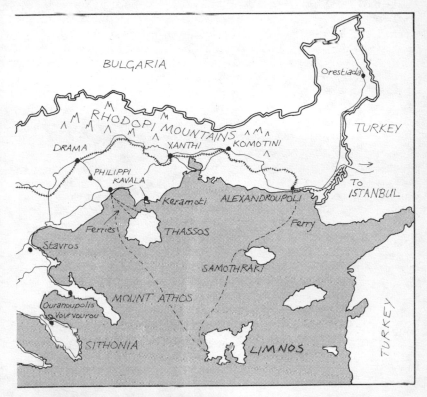

more relaxed city to live and get around. From here it's a relatively short journey to Istanbul, or Constantinoupoli as the Greeks still call it; or, if you want to loop down to the islands, **Kavala** provides access to Thassos and Limnos, **Alexandroupoli** to Samothraki. The north itself, with its rather muggy hot summers and bitterly cold winters, is more a region to travel than to 'holiday': beaches are generally disappointing and the best (on Halkidiki) have been rigorously developed.

Lastly, the monastic peninsula of **Mount Athos** must be mentioned – an autonomous community where no women have been allowed since a Byzantine edict of 1060. Men over 21 *are* allowed to visit and to stay in the monasteries after completing a marathon of bureaucracy (details later: plan well in advance), and for many it proves the most rewarding experience of all Greek travel. The most that women can do is take a caique ride from the secular athonite ports of Ierissos or Ouranoupoli – most of the monasteries are visible from the sea.

THESSALONIKI

Second city of Greece and administrative centre for the north, **Thessaloniki** has a very different feel to Athens: more modern, cosmopolitan and, for the most part, wealthier. Situated right at the head of the Thermaic Gulf, it also seems much more open – you're never far from the sea and the air actually circulates. This 'modern' quality of the city is partly due to the fire of 1917 which levelled most of the old twisting Turkish streets; it was rebuilt eight years later on the ancient chess board plan so there's an underlying logic with three main roads (Egnatia, Tsimiski and Konstandinou) running parallel to the sea. Although lacking any single great monument it does have an unrivalled collection of Byzantine churches, brilliantly exemplifying each of the subtle transitions of their form over more than ten centuries.

Macedonia became a **Roman** province in 146 BC and Thessaloniki, with its strategic position both for land and sea access, was the natural and immediate choice of capital. Its fortunes and significance were further accelerated by the building of the 'Via Egnatia', the great road linking Rome (via Brindisi) with Byzantium and the East, along whose course Philippi and Kavala were also to develop. St Paul deemed the city important enough to visit but was badly received and his house attacked by the large Jewish community whom he had provoked; nevertheless he founded a church, revisited the city (in 56) and later wrote from Athens the two Epistles to the Thessalonians.

By the late C3rd the first subdivisions of the Roman Empire had begun under the direction of Diocletian, and Galerius, who succeeded to the eastern part, made Thessaloniki his residence. From his reign date virtually all the surviving Roman monuments and, perhaps more significantly, he also provided the city with their patron saint Dimitrios, whom he martyred in 306. In 330 Constantinople was founded and the eastern, **Byzantine** half of the Empire rose to a pre-eminent position – and with it, Thessaloniki. Theodosius the Great spent much of the time here during his reign (379–95) and was converted to Christianity, issuing in 380 his 'Edict of Thessaloniki' which officially ended paganism.

Under Justinian's rule (527–65) Thessaloniki became the second city of Byzantium and it remained so, under constant pressure from Goths and Slavs, until 904 when it was sacked by Saracens. The storming and sacking continued under the Normans of Sicily (1185) and the Fourth Crusade (1204) when it became for a time the Latin Kingdom of Thessalonica. It was, however, restored to the Byzantine Empire of Nicea in 1246 – reaching a cultural 'Golden Age', amidst theological conflict and political rebellion, during the next two centuries. The long period of **Turkish occupation** began in 1430, when the Ottomans at their third attempt took the city; it lasted until 1912, proving a key city in the First

Balkan War which preceded its liberation. Under the Turks virtually all the churches were converted for use as mosques, a fate which has obscured many of their original features and destroyed (despite judicious restoration over recent years) the majority of their frescoes and mosaics. This disappointment acknowledged, they remain an impressive and illuminating group.

The churches

Almost all of the main Byzantine churches can be found amongst the centre streets so a Grand Tour of them is neither grand nor difficult. With this in mind it's more interesting to consider them in turn according to the changing tastes of architecture rather than the vagaries of city planning.

The church of **Agios Georgios** (popularly known as the *Rotunda*) is the oldest and strangest of the collection. It was designed, but never used, as an imperial mausoleum (possibly for Galerius) and converted to Christian use in the late C4th by adding a sanctuary, narthex and rich mosaics. It is the largest surviving circular Roman building after the Pantheon and its mosaics of martyred saints, peacocks and elaborate temples are superb. Sadly the structure – like so many of Thessaloniki's churches – was very badly damaged in the 1978 earthquake and at present it's closed for an indefinite period whilst the drum is strengthened. It served as a mosque and its minaret, one of the few that survive in the city, is preserved with the rest as a museum.

More prevalent in the early Christian world and far better suited for adaptation was the Roman Basilica. The large wooden-roofed hall with its three aisles and two rows of columns was ideal for congregational worship. Conversion was simply achieved by placing a canopied altar in the apse and dividing it from the main body of the church (the nave) by a screen (a forerunner to the iconostasis); the baptistry, a small distinct building, was then added to one side. The upper reaches of wall were adorned with mosaics illustrating Christ's Glory and Man's Redemption, whilst at eye level stood a blank lining of marble. (Frescoes, by far the more economical medium, did not become fashionable until much later – around the C13th and C14th – when their scope for showing expression and movement was realised.) Two fine examples of these massive yet simple churches are **Agios Dimitrios** and the **Ahiropiitos**; both originate in the C5th though they have been heavily restored and indeed rebuilt since.

Agios Dimitrios is dedicated to the city's patron saint and stands on the site of his martyrdom. Even knowing that it is the largest church in Greece its immense interior comes as a surprise. Tall façades supported on red, green and white columns (with the occasional Theodosian capital) run alongside the nave. However amidst so much space and white plaster

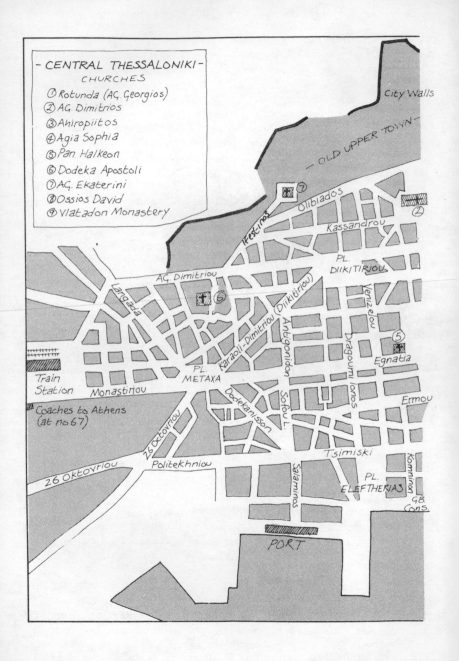

- CENTRAL THESSALONIKI -
CHURCHES
① Rotunda (Ag. Georgios)
② Ag. Dimitrios
③ Ahiropiitos
④ Agia Sophia
⑤ Pan. Halkeon
⑥ Dodeka Apostoli
⑦ Ag. Ekaterini
⑧ Ossios David
⑨ Vlatadon Monastery

City Walls

OLD UPPER TOWN

Olibiados

Kassandrou

PL. DIIKITIRIOU

Ag. Dimitriou

Yenizelou

Karaoli-Dimitriou (Diikitiriou)

Antgonidon

Dragoumi

ionos

Egnatia

Langada

Monastiriou

PL. METAXA

Dodekanisson

Sofou L.

Ermou

Train Station

Coaches to Athens (at no 67)

26 Oktovriou

Politekhniou

26 Oktovriou

Salaminos

Tsimiski

PL. ELEFTHERIAS

Komninon

98. Cons.

PORT

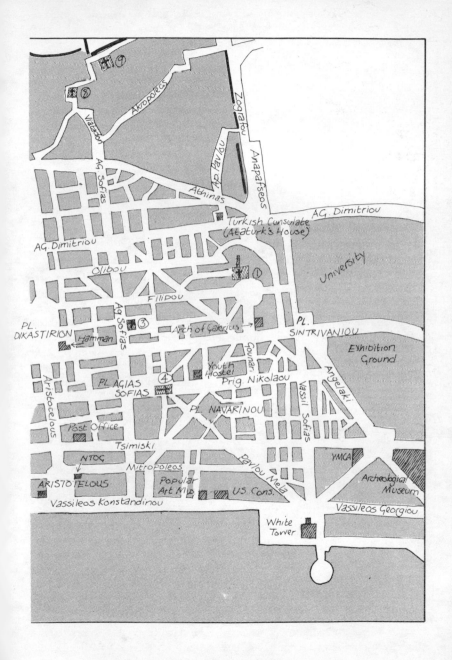

the few and small surviving mosaics make an easy focal point; five are grouped to either side of the iconostasis and, of these, three date back to the church's second building in the late C7th. The mosaic of St Dimitrios with the church's founders was described by Osbert Lancaster as 'the greatest remaining masterpiece of pictorial art of the pre-iconoclastic era in Greece'; it contrasts well with its contemporary, a warm and humane mosaic of the saint with two young children. The *crypt*, unearthed after the great fire, contains the martyrion of the saint – probably an adaptation of the Roman baths in which he was imprisoned – with its famous Peacock mosaic.

Panagia Ahiropiitos, a basilica of the Syrian type, is less well endowed. Its arcades can also boast monolithic columns with (here, often elaborate) Theodosian capitals but only the mosaics in their arches survive; these depict birds, fruits and flowers in a rich Alexandrian style.

By the sixth century the architects had succumbed to eastern influence and set about improving their basilicas with the addition of a dome. For inspiration they turned to the highly effective Agia Sophia in Constantinople – the most striking of all Justinian's churches. Aesthetic effect, however, was not the only accomplishment, for the structure lent itself perfectly to the prevailing representational art. The mosaics and frescoes adorning its surfaces became interrelated as a whole and powerful spiritual aid. The eye would be at once uplifted to meet the gaze of the Pantokrator (God Almighty) illuminated by the windows of the drum. Between these windows the prophets and apostles would be depicted and as the lower levels were scanned the liturgy would unfold amidst a hierarchy of saints. Thessaloniki's **Agia Sophia**, built early in the C18th, follows closely its more illustrious namesake – providing a good example of the transitional domed basilica. Its dome, 33 feet in diameter, carries a splendid mosaic of the Ascension – Christ, borne up to the heavens by two angels, sits resplendent on a rainbow throne; below them a wry inscription reads 'Ye Men of Galilee, Why stand ye Gazing up into Heaven?' Sadly, once more, the dome is in the process of restoration; the rest of the interior decoration was repatched after the fires.

The most successful shape to emerge during all these later experiments with the dome was the 'Greek Cross in Square' – four equal arms that efficiently absorb the thrust of the dome, passing it from high barrel vaults to lower vaulted chambers fitted inside its angles. Architecturally it was a perfect solution, a square ground plan was produced inside the church with an aesthetically pleasing cruciform shape evident in the superstructure and, best of all, it was entirely self-supporting. By the C10th–C11th it had become the conventional form. Architects, no longer interested in new designs, began to exploit the old and it proved remarkably flexible – subsidiary drums were introduced above corners of the square, proportions were stretched ever taller and the outer walls became refashioned with elaborate brick and stone patterning. The C11th **Panagia Halkeon** is a classic though rather unimaginative example of the form. Far more beautiful is the church of **Dodeka Apostoli**, built with three more centuries of experience and the bold influence of the Palaeologan Renaissance (which centred on Mistra); its five domes rise in perfect symmetry above walls of fine brickwork, though its interior no longer does it justice. **Agia Ekaterini**, its contemporary, has still finer brickwork – exploiting all the natural colours of the stones.

The tiny C5th church of **Ossios David** does not really fit into this architectural progression as the Turks, over-zealous in their conversion, hacked most of it apart. It's well worth visiting, however, for it has arguably the finest mosaic of all – depicting a beardless (C5th-style) Christ appearing in a vision to the amazement of the prophets Ezekiel and Habakkuk. The frescoes on the arch – of the Baptism – are probably C12th.

Other sites

Sections of the C14th **Byzantine Ramparts**, constructed with brick and rubble on top of old Roman foundations, crop up all around the north of the town. The best portion (marked, logically, 'the walls' on the NTOG map) begins at a large circular keep in the north-east angle and rambles on to become the south wall of the Acropolis. The C15th Keep, known as the 'Chain Tower' due to its encircling stringcourse, is perhaps the best place to sit and scan the town. The Acropolis, entered through a large gate, is now the City Prison – a rather nervous armed guard discourages you from showing too much interest. The **White Tower**, a contemporary of the Chain Tower, stands out on a limb at the sea front; you can climb it. Though hardly an inspiring Byzantine monument, it's come to symbolise the town, Big Ben fashion, on the TV news.

Clumped below the northern corner of the ramparts (and quickly being swamped by new apartment blocks) stands the old **Turkish quarter** – a labyrinth of timber-framed houses and winding steps. It's probably the only area which retains the ramshackle if squalid atmosphere of the old, pre-fire C19th city. Further down, beside the Turkish Consulate at the bottom of Apostolou Pavlou, is an indecorous pink building in which **Kemal Ataturk**, first President and creator of the modern state of Turkey, was born. Here, on 19 May 1981, a bizarre and farcical attempt was made by the Turks to celebrate his centennial. Halfway through the proceedings the whole area had to be evacuated due to the repeated 'kamikaze' dives of a patriotic Greek stunt pilot who threatened to fly straight at the house unless the ceremony was called off; it was! If you want to see the house, which is preserved with its original fittings and furnishings, you must ask at the consulate – and you'll need to take your passport along; it's open 9–1 and 4–6.

Remains of the town's formative years in the early eastern empire are scant. The Rotunda is much the most striking but it once formed part of a larger complex linking the **Arch of Galerius** with a palace and hippodrome. The Arch, the surviving half of a great double gate, was built to commemorate the Emperor's victories over the Persians in AD 297; its piers contain reliefs of the battle scenes interspersed with symbolic poses of Galerius himself. The ruins of the **Roman Agora** were recently unearthed in the vast Plateia Dikastrion; although they're still being excavated they don't seem particularly exciting – most prominent is an **Odeion** in the north corner.

The Archaeological Museum
Whatever else you do in Thessaloniki find time for the superb **Vergina exhibition** at the Archaeological Museum: it's open weekdays 9–5 and Sundays 10–5, closed Tuesdays.

Displayed – and clearly labelled in both English and Greek – are the vast majority of the finds from the Royal Tombs of Philip II of Macedon (father of Alexander the Great) and others at Vergina, around 60 km to the west of Thessaloniki. They are pieces of extraordinary craftsmanship and often astounding richness.

Through these, and other local finds, the history of the Macedonian dynasty and empire is imaginatively traced – a surprisingly political act for the discoveries at Vergina have been used by Greece to emphasise the fundamental 'Greekness' of Makhedonia and Thraki. Although these territories would seem obviously and inviolably part of Greece to an outsider, their occupation by Turks and Bulgarians is still very much part of Greek political history and memory. During the Bulgarian occupation of Macedonia in the Second World War, for example, there was a deliberate policy of vandalism towards many of the region's ancient sites – and above all the one-time capital of Pella.

There is also a **Popular Art Museum** (open 9–1.30, closed Tuesdays) on the seafront. I've never been there but one might well expect a similar emphasis.

Living: a few points
Cheap **hotels** are easy to find – if none too glamorously sited. Most are grouped along the busy Egnatia Avenue, between the railway station and Aristotelous Street. These include, in roughly ascending price order, the Thessalonikon (at Egnatia 9: and pretty dire), Atlantis (14), Argo (11), Nea Niki (15), Ilissia (28), Ilios (27), Atlas (40), Alexandria (18) and Thessalikon (60). If they've rooms Hotel Tourist at Mitropoleos 21 (near the NTOG office) is a generally more wholesome location.

Youth hostels in cities are usually last resorts and miles out but the one here, at Prinkipou Nikolau 44, is excellent and within walking distance of most points of interest. To get to it from the railway station take bus 10 or 11 to the 'Kamares' stop on Egnatia; the 10pm curfew is unlikely to worry you, Thessaloniki closes early. Also well placed are the **XEN (YWCA)** at Ag. Sofias 11, and **XAN (YMCA)** across the square/road-junction from the Archaeological Museum.

Restaurants, at least in the central area, are harder to come by. Try the old market area on and around Komninon, which leads up from the seafront between plateias Eleftherias and Aristotelous. There are a few *tavernas* here and some excellent *souvlaki/kefta* stalls – as also around Politehniou 50 (to the west: the continuation of Tsimiski). *Hrisi Pagoni*, half a block from the youth hostel on Prinkipou Nikolau, is slightly pricier but really good. Just beyond it (at no. 42) *Vivoli's* serves the best ice cream I've tasted in Greece.

'*Shic*', at Layamarguerita 5, is a piano bar/women's entertainment/*feminist* meeting place, open most evenings.

The **Central Post Office** (for poste restante) is at Tsimiski 45: it's closed on weekends – beware. **American Express** have an office at Venizelou 10, three blocks from the **Tourist Office**, just back from the seafront at Plateia Aristotelous 8. The NTOG here are very helpful – particularly with the complex system of bus departures – and can give you a rather larger **map** of the city than the one we've printed. If you're heading east, through Kavala, pick up their 'Kavala-Thassos' leaflet with its invaluable townplan; same goes for Volos if you're moving down south. If you want to read British newspapers there's a library/reading room at the **British Council** (Leof. Vas. Konstantinou 3); various cultural events take place here too but not through the summer months. There's also a terrific English-language **bookshop** – *A. Samixos* at Ag. Sofias 28 – good for novels and magazines; you can browse uninterrupted for hours over everything from the *New Statesman* to *New Musical Express*. If you're after traditional/regional/contemporary Greek music, *Studio 52* at Gounari 46 is one of the best **record stores** in the country.

Consulates, which you'll need for letters of introduction if applying for an Athos permit, include: BRITAIN (Vass. Konstantinou 39), USA (Vass. Konstantinou 59), NETHERLANDS (Komninon 26). The **Ministry of Northern Greece**, next stop in the Athos quest, is on Plateia Diikitiriou; find your way to Room 218. And finally, for getting the date of a visit registered, you'll have to get a stamp at the **Aliens Bureau** (Politehniou 41: the continuation of Tsimiski). See the Athos section for details on all these procedures and pitfalls.

Bus terminals for different destinations are spread all over the city. They include:

ATHENS   Ktel buses from Monastirion 67, or OSE coaches from the train station (bookable in advance at Aristotelou 18).

ATHOS/HALIKIDIKI   Karakassi 68 (some way out – take bus 10 from Egnatia to the 'Botsari' stop).

PELLA/VOLOS   Anagenisseos 22 (continuation of Tsimiski, beyond Politehniou).

Details of times and other terminals are available from the NTOG office. There is usually a direct coach to Istanbul four or five times a week – again check departures (all privately operated) with the NTOG. Thessaloniki is next to useless as a **ferry port** with just one weekly boat to Limnos, Lesvos and the larger Dodecanese: the main northern port is Kavala, and (for Samothraki) Alexandroupoli.

Lastly avoid Thessaloniki during **September** when it's host to an International Trade Fair. Hotels will be universally full and their prices automatically rise by 20 per cent. The city's main **festival**, with large religious processions, marks St Demetrios' Day (26 October); since Ohi day follows on the 28th there's a three-day holiday, all banks, etc. closing for the period. If you happen to be in the city around **21 May** see below.

ANASTENARIA: THE FIRE WALKERS OF LANGADA

On 21 May, the feast day of Saints Constantine and Helen, villagers at **LANGADAS** (12 km from Thessaloniki) perform a ritual dance, barefoot across a bed of burning coals. The festival rites are of unknown and strongly disputed origin – it has been suggested they are remnants of a Dionysiac orgiastic cult, though devotees assert a purely Christian tradition. This seems to relate to a fire, around 1250, in the Thracian village of Kosti: holy ikons were heard groaning from the flames and were rescued by villagers, who emerged miraculously unburnt from the blazing church. The ikons, passed down by their families, are believed by them to ensure protection. The official Greek church thinks otherwise, refuses to sanction any service on the day of the ritual, and has even been accused of planting glass among the coals to try and discredit this 'devil's gift'.

Whatever the origin, the rite is still performed each year – now something of a tourist attraction with an admission charge and repeat performances over the next two days. It is nevertheless strange and impressive, beginning around 7pm with the lighting of a pile of hardwood logs. A couple of hours later their embers are raked into a circle and, just before complete darkness, a traditional Macedonian *daouli* drummer and two *lyra* players precede about sixteen women and men into the arena. These *anestenarides*, in partial trance, then shuffle across the coals for around a quarter of an hour. In recent years they have been the subject of various scientific tests – but the only established clues are that their brain waves indicate some control taking place (when brain activity changed they immediately left the embers) and that their rhythmical steps maintain minimum skin contact with the fires. There's no suggestion of fraud, however: in 1981 an Englishman jumped into the arena, was very badly burned and had to be rescued by the police from irate devotees and dancers.

If you go to the **Langada** *anastenaria* arrive early (at least by 5.30pm) in order to get a good seat, and expect the circus-like commercialism, which itself can be quite fun. Other communities of *anastenarides* (literally 'groaners') perform at **MELIKI**, near Veria, and at the **AYIA ELINI** and **AYIA PETROS** villages near Seres: crowds, though, are reputed to be just as large and fire-walkers fewer – there doesn't seem much advantage in their remoteness. If you're in Greece, anywhere, and moderately interested just catch the show on the ERT TV news at 9pm, their cameramen are at Langadas too!

PELLA (Open weekdays 9–3, Sundays 10–4)

PELLA, capital of Macedonia throughout its greatest period, was in fact the first real capital of Greece – after Philip II had forcibly unified the country around 338 BC. It had been established some sixty years earlier under one King Archelaus, who transferred his court here from Aigai (Vergina) to create an unrivalled new centre of culture. His palace, decorated by Zeuxis, was said to be the greatest artistic showplace since the time of Classical Athens; Euripides wrote and produced his last plays at the court; and here too Aristotle was to tutor the young Alexander the Great – born, like his father Philip II, at this city.

When Archelaus founded **Pella** it lay at the head of a broad lake, connected to the Thermaic Gulf by a navigable river; by the second century BC the river had begun to silt up and Pella fell into decline. It was destroyed by the Romans in 146 BC and never rebuilt. Today its **ruins** stand in the middle of a dull expanse of plain, 40 km from Thessaloniki and the sea; buses stop in the centre of the site, which is cut in two by the main road to Edessa.

The city was located by chance finds in 1957 and preliminary excavations have revealed a vast site covering over one and a half square miles. As yet, only a few blocks of the city have been fully excavated but they have proved exciting. To the right of the road is a grand official building, probably a government office; it is divided into three large open courts, each enclosed by a *peristyle*, or portico (the columns of the central one have been re-erected) and bordered by wide streets with a sophisticated drainage system. The three main rooms of the first court have patterned geometric floors in the centre of which were found superb and intricate **pebble-mosaics** depicting scenes of a lion hunt, a griffin attacking a deer, and Dionysus riding a panther. These are now in the museum (across the road) but in the third court three have been left in situ; one, a stag hunt, is complete – and astounding in its dynamism and use of perspective. Others represent the rape of Helen and a fight between a Greek and an Amazon.

It is the inherently graceful and fluid quality of these compositions which sets them apart from later Roman and Byzantine mosaics and more than justifies a visit. The uncut pebbles, carefully chosen for their soft shades, blend so naturally that the shapes and movements of the subjects seem gradated rather than fixed – note the action of the hunting scenes and the sloping movement of the leopard with Dionysus. Strips of lead or clay are used to outline special features; the eyes, all now missing, were probably made of semi-precious stones.

The **acropolis** at Pella is a low hill to the left of the modern village. Excavation is in progress on a sizeable building but at present it's illuminating mainly for the idea it gives you of the size and scope of the site.

VERGINA (Site partially open: weekdays 9–5, Sundays 10–5, closed Tuesdays)

Excavations at **VERGINA**, 20 mins by bus from the town of VERIA, have over the past six years revolutionised Macedonian archaeology. A series of chamber tombs, unearthed here by Professor Manolis Andronikos, are now widely accepted to be those of Philip II and members of the Macedonian royal family. This means that the site itself must be that of Aigai, the original royal capital and later necropolis. Finds from the site and tomb – the richest in Greece since, perhaps, the discovery of Mycenae – are exhibited at Thessaloniki's archaeological museum. The tombs, however, are still in the process of excavation and documentation and the sites which you can see are inevitably somewhat minor and disappointing. If you're travelling this way, though, it's a worthwhile detour, and Veria itself is quite an interesting town.

Ancient Aigai is documented as the sanctuary and royal burial place of the Macedonian kings. It was here that Philip II was assassinated and buried – and tradition maintained that the dynasty would be destroyed if any king were buried elsewhere, as indeed happened after the death of Alexander the Great in Asia. The site, until Andronikos' finds in 1977, had long been assumed to be lost beneath modern Edessa: a theory which is now completely discarded.

What Andronikos unearthed, under a tumulus just outside the village of Vergina, were two large and undoubtedly Macedonian **chamber tombs**. The first had been looted in antiquity but retained a wall painting of the Rape of Persephone by Hades, the only complete example of an ancient Greek painting that has yet been found. The second, a grander vaulted tomb with a Doric façade supported by a superb painted frieze of a lion hunt was – incredibly – intact. Among its treasures was a marble sarcophagus containing a gold casket of bones with the exploding star symbol of the royal line engraved on its lid and, still more significantly, five small ivory heads – among them representations of both Philip II and Alexander. It was this definitive clue that has led to the identification of the tomb as that of Philip II.

Buses to the **village of Vergina** stop at the crossroads – from where the 'Royal Tombs' and other sites are grandiosely and frustratingly signposted. As yet the village hasn't been exploited for the growing number of hopeful tourists but there are a few tentative *tavernas* and rooms to let; camping is easy too, the surroundings are good.

The '**Tomb of Vergina**', which you can visit, lies some way from the recent discoveries – about half a kilometre up the hill from the village. Excavated by the French in 1861 it is said, though, to be not dissimilar to its royal neighbours. Characteristically its form is that of a temple, with an Ionic façade of half-columns closed by two pairs of marble doors. Inside stands an imposing marble throne with sphinxes carved on the sides, armrests and footstool.

A few hundred metres further on, occupying a low hill, are the ruins of the '**Palace of Palatitsa**', probably built in the C3rd BC as a summer residence for the last great Macedonian king, Antigonus Gonatus. It is now little more than foundations, but amidst the confusing litter of poros drums and capitals you can make out a triple propylaia opening on to a central courtyard. This is framed by broad porticoes and colonnades which, on the south side, preserve a well-executed if rather unexciting mosaic. For all its lack of substance it is an attractive site, dominated by a grand old oak tree looking out across the plains of Vergina – scattered with Iron Age tumuli (C10th–C7th BC) and who knows what more.

VERIA, LEFKADIA AND NAOUSSA

Vergina apart, **VERIA** has no particular site or monument. It is, though, one of the more interesting towns of northern Greece – preserving much of the old Turkish atmosphere of its streets and market quarter. Amid these, too, are a number of old mosques and over fifty churches, built during a particularly oppressive period of moslem rule and disguised as (or behind) townhouses. These, inevitably, are tricky to find and many are now decaying and kept locked. One that's not – and which gives a good idea of their long, low structures – is near the new cathedral on Odos Mitropoleos, the main road out of town to Kozani.

For the most part, however, Veria seems more a place to wander about: particularly in the streets off Odos Vassileus Konstantinou (the main thoroughfare down into town from the bus station). Midway down this street is the old Metropolis (cathedral) and opposite it a gnarled plane tree from which, in 1436, the Turks hung the town's archbishop. Further down – past some great *kafeneions* in the old bazaar section – narrow dark streets of balconied wattle and timber houses sprawl down towards the river.

The town's **archaeological museum** (weekdays 9–1 and 3–5, Suns. 10–4; closed Tuesdays) has a few of the lesser finds from Vergina but contains mostly Roman oddments from the area; it's about ½ km out of town on Leoforos Anoixos, the beginning of the road to Vergina. Cheap **hotels** here are a problem – the two 'D' class ones (Aristidis and Veroi, both in the Kentriki Plateai) are at the pricey end of their scale. Ask around and you might find a room – as we did; otherwise your options are camping near Vergina or moving on to Naoussa or Thessaloniki.

At the village of **LEFKADIA**, 16 km from Veria along the Edessa road, can be seen the '**Great Tomb**' – the largest Macedonian temple tomb that has yet been discovered. It too is C3rd BC and was probably built for a general – depicted in one of the surviving frescoes with Hermes (the Conductor of Souls); the other fresco represents the Judges of Hades. The tomb has an elaborate and grand façade – double storeyed, one half Doric, the other Ionic; the frieze on its entablature shows a battle between Persians and Macedonians. Nearby there are three other tombs, one with a huge Ionic front, but they are not open to the public. Lefkadia itself has not been positively identified with any Macedonian city but it is thought possibly to have been Mieza, where Aristotle taught.

The 'Great Tomb' is signposted to the left of the main road a couple of kilometres after the **NAOUSSA** turning. This town, although of no historic interest, must be mentioned – it has the finest wine in Greece (try the Boutari red), and the best apples and peaches too. With three cheap hotels it makes a fine watering hole; more than that if you can coincide with its pre-Lenten carnival, famed for elaborate *boules*, or masques. As at Veria there are regular bus connections to Thessaloniki.

HALKIDIKI: KASSANDRA, SITHONIA AND SECULAR ATHOS

The Halkidiki, a strikingly squid-shaped peninsula, begins at a perforated edge of lakes east of Thessaloniki and extends into three prongs of land – Kassandra, Sithonia and Athos – trailing like tentacles into the Aegean sea. **Athos**, the Holy Mountain, is in all ways separate – forbidden to women and not easy of access to men. Practicalities for staying on the twenty monasteries there are dealt with in the following section. If you want just to get some glimpse of the buildings, however, it is possible to take a caique ride from either of two small resorts on the periphery of Athos: Ierissos and Ouranoupoli. **IERISSOS**, with a good long beach facing the rising sun and a coastline which extends towards the Great Lavra, grandest of the monasteries, is probably the more satisfying. Boats have to stay 500 metres from the coast, though, unless they're all-male when they can actually dock at the monastery of Iviron. There are two 'E' class hotels (*Akanthos* and *Akroyali*) at Ierissos, and sometimes a few rooms to let. **OURANOUPOLI**, across the isthmus, is surprisingly a little more developed but again a very attractive place: boats from here loop the forested west coast of Athos but don't normally stop at any of the monasteries. On a more easy-going level you can also get taken out to the lovely islet of Amoliâni, just offshore. Cheapest of half a dozen hotels is the *Ouranoupoli*. Buses to both villages leave Thessaloniki fairly regularly through the day: as with all the Halkidiki buses from the terminal at Karakassi 68.

Athos aside, **the rest of Halkidiki** is one of the fastest growing holiday resorts in Greece – as much for Greeks as anyone else, although it's also heavily frequented by Germans, Yugoslavs and numerous international package companies. Almost any reasonable beach is now accompanied by a crop of villas or a hotel complex, and a rash of vast plastic campsites are advertised miles in advance by huge billboards. A still larger billboard at the entrance to the Kassandra peninsula reminds you that camping outside authorised sites is strictly prohibited.

Both Kassandra and Sithonia are connected to Thessaloniki by a network of fast new roads which extend around their coastlines; buses run often to all the larger resorts but in spite of this it doesn't seem an easy area to travel around. You really just have to pick a place and stay there.

Preferably don't pick somewhere on **Kassandra** – the nearest prong to Thessaloniki and much the most developed. On its west coast there are massive and depressing-looking campsites at both **SANI** and **POSSIDI** and between the two an interminable stretch of villas cramping some rather ordinary beaches. There were never many villages on this coast before development and the few real fishing hamlets are all fast being crowded out; a little more life surfaces on the east coast – **HANIOTIS** has a good long beach and a few ordinary-sized hotels and tavernas – but at **PALIOURI** and **KRIOPIGI** it's back to the huge 'holiday-campings'.

Things improve considerably as you move east across the peninsula and, away from the frontline of tourism, the landscape too becomes increasingly green and hilly, culminating in the isolated and spectacular scenery of the Holy Mountain itself. **Sithonia** stands midway in this progression: more rugged but better cultivated than Kassandra, and with more pre-tourist village communities. Pine forests cover much of its slopes, giving way to olive groves at its coast, which instead of sprawling beach resorts tends to be small pebbly inlets with relatively discreet pockets of hotels. On the east coast **VOURVOUROU** is probably the best beach, set in a tremendous bay with (as yet) only three small hotels. Neighbouring **ORMOS PANAGIA** is also on a human scale, slowly developing around its tiny harbour village; rooms are easier to come by than at Vourvourou and there are beaches in walking distance. Excursion boats also leave from Panagia to sail round Athos though they're usually crammed with tourists coached in from the big Halkidiki resorts. And further down the coast of Sithonia, **SIKEA** and **SARTI** have both had good reports – a pair of fairly unaffected villages with possible camping and short beaches. Round on to the east coast, however, it's a different story. **PORTO CARRAS**, 'the Greek Marbella', has its own conference hall, shopping centre and vineyards; whilst at **NEA MARMARAS** there are no less than six campsites (capacity over 3000) in the space of a few kilometres.

Heading **towards Kavala** from Athos or Sithonia is surprisingly tricky, since buses from Poligiros or Ierissos/Ouranoupoli run back only to Thessaloniki. You can, however, take the bus to **STRATONI** on the eastern coast (paying passing homage to Aristotle's birthplace at **STAGIRA**) from where a rough road twists 19 km through the hills above the coast to **OLIMBIADA**. This is hitchable, or you can negotiate in Stratoni (an ugly seashore mining town) for a shared taxi; don't try the mountainous road that heads inland just before Stagira; though well drawn on the NTOG map it's really no more than a forest track and lifts were none too forthcoming! **STAVROS**, a further 20 km beyond Olimbiada, is the first village on the busroutes and a tremendous place to emerge – a gentle resort with a beautiful seafront terrace of plane trees. It's becoming popular but isn't at all spoilt; finding rooms or camping here shouldn't prove a problem. From Stavros the best approach on to Kavala is to take a local bus to **ASPROVALTA** on the main highway and hitch or take another bus from there.

MOUNT ATHOS: THE MONKS' REPUBLIC

The population of Athos has been exclusively male – animals included – since an edict, the *avaton*, issued by the Byzantine Emperor Constantine Monomachos in 1060. It is an administratively autonomous part of Greece, a 'monks' republic', and also one of the most beautiful parts of the country, densely wooded and mountainous, climaxing in the 6670 ft *Agion Oros* (Holy Mount) itself. Twenty monasteries survive on its slopes, most of them founded in the C10th and C11th; all are in a state of comparative decline but remain unsurpassed in their general and architectural interest and for the art treasures that they contain.

Permits and practicalities

Until a few years ago it was possible for foreigners to visit Athos quite easily but in the early 1970s the number of tourists grew to such an extent that the monasteries could no longer cope. Nowadays a considerable amount of bureaucracy surrounds a visit for all non-Greeks: you must also be over twenty-one, though the old stipulation that all visitors must be bearded has been withdrawn.

First step in acquiring a permit to visit and stay on Athos is to get a letter of recommendation from your consulate in Athens or (if there is one) in Thessaloniki: see listings for addresses. This is purely a formality, though most embassies make a charge – £6 in the case of Britain. Your consulate will also give you a list of regulations and information, not all of which are correct or relevant; don't be alarmed by the standard phrase 'the entry of "student" against "profession" in a passport is not regarded as a sufficient qualification' – it generally is. If you're wary, and planning in advance, a letter from an art/history/theology tutor, or from a local bishop, will guarantee co-operation.

In Athens take the consular letter to the Ministry of Foreign Affairs at Zalakosta 2 (Mon.–Fri. 11am–1pm: be persistent, this is the right place); or, if you've obtained your letter in Thessaloniki, to the Ministry for Northern Greece (room 218) in Plateia Diikitiriou. You will there be issued with a permit valid for four days' residence on Athos, which must be used within a month. Lastly – and this tends not to be mentioned – you must take the permit to the Aliens Police in Thessaloniki at Polytehniou 41 (a continuation of Tsimiski). They then give you a second permit specifying the first day of your visit; if you're going in a group or in summer this might not be on the date of your choice since only ten non-Greeks are allowed to enter each day.

To get to Athos take one of the buses from Thessaloniki (Halkıdiki terminal, Karakassi 68) to **Oranoupoli**. There are several departures through the day from 6am–5pm but only one boat a day from here on to **Daphne**, the port of entry for Athos. This leaves at 10am so you'll have to either get the 6am bus from Thessaloniki, or spend the previous night here – no great hardship (see the previous section on Halkidiki).

As you board the boat to **Daphne** you'll be asked for the permit issued by the Aliens Police and for your passport, which you later collect in Karyes, the capital of Athos. The 2-hour boat-ride costs around 200 drx, followed by a 150 drx bus journey straight to **Karyes** where you must first visit the Aliens Police (for your passport), and then the government buildings across the central square. Here you will receive your final permit – the *diamonitirion* – which admits you to any of the Athonite monasteries. It costs a further 750 drx (500 drx for students) but you will be staying in the monasteries free of charge – if you offer money it will be refused, though some idiorythmic monks are very eager to sell you candles and religious ikon-pictures. The permit lasts for four days but if you want to stay longer ask at this stage and you will probably be granted a few days more at no extra cost. You will also be given a card to return to the police at Ouranoupoli after you leave Athos: failure to do so may disqualify you from a return visit.

Ideally, you should have bought the ESY (Statistics Office) **map** of 'Halkidikon' in Athens. If you haven't there are vaguely helpful tourist-pamphlet maps on sale in Karyes. Either way you'll still need to ask specific instructions from the monks for each stage of your hiking; the old paths are often difficult to find.

Monasticism and the way of life

The development of monasticism on Athos is a matter of some controversy and foundation legends abound. The most popular is that the Virgin Mary was blown ashore on her way to Cyprus and whilst overcome by the great beauty of Athos a mysterious voice consecrated the place in her name. Another tradition asserts that Constantine the Great founded the first monastery in the C4th but this is certainly far too early. The earliest historical reference to Athonite monks is to their attendance at the Council of the Empress Theodora in 843 but there were probably some monks by the end of the C7th. Athos was particularly appropriate for early Christian monasticism, its deserted and isolated slopes providing a natural refuge from the outside world and especially from the Arab conquests in the East and the iconoclastic phase of the Byzantine Empire (C8th to C9th). Moreover, its awesome beauty, which had so impressed the Virgin, facilitated communion with God.

The most famous of the earliest monks were Peter the Athonite and St Euthymios of Salonica, both of whom lived in caves for many years in the mid-C9th. In 885 an edict of Emperor Basil I recognised Athos as the preserve solely of monks and gradually hermits came together to form communities known as *coenobia* (literally, 'common living'). The year 963 is the traditional date for the foundation of the first monastery, the Great Lavra, by Athanasios the Athonite; the Emperor Nicephoros Phocas provided considerable financial assistance. Over the next two centuries, with the protection of further Byzantine emperors, foundations were frequent, reaching forty in number (reputedly with 1,000 monks in each) along with many smaller settlements, or *kellia*. At the end of the C11th they suffered from pirate raids and from a settlement of 300 Vlach families but after a time these shepherds were ejected and a new Imperial *Chryssobul* was issued, confirming that no female – human or animal – was allowed to set foot on Athos. The C12th saw an international expansion as Iberian, Latin, Russian and Serbian monks flocked to the mountain.

Athos was subjected to Frankish raids during the Latin Occupation of Constantinople (1204–61) and even after this faced great pressure from the Unionists of Latin Salonica to unite with Western Christians; in the courtyard of Zographou there is a monument to the monks who died to preserve the independence of Orthodox Christianity. In the early C14th it suffered two disastrous years of pillage by Catalan mercenaries but recovered, primarily with Serbian benefactors, to enjoy a period of great prosperity in the C15th and C16th; the Fathers wisely declined to resist the Turks after the fall of the Byzantine Empire and maintained good relations with the early Sultans, one of whom paid a state visit. The later middle ages brought economic problems, with taxes and confiscations, and many of the monasteries reverted to an *idiorythmic* system – a self-regulating form of monasticism whereby monks live and worship in a community but work and eat individually. However, Athos remained the spiritual centre of orthodoxy and in the C17th and C18th built and maintained its own schools. Its real decline came in the C19th after the monks fought alongside the rest of Greece in the War of Independence (1821); easily subdued by the Turks, they paid the penalty under a permanent garrison during which numbers fell sharply. Foreign monks, especially Russian, tried to step in to fill the vacuum but the Athonite Fathers managed to preserve the Greekness of the Holy Mount. In the C20th numbers have continued to drop (current population is estimated at 1,700 – compared to 20,000 in its heyday) although today some monasteries – notably Philotheou – are experiencing a modest revival with young monks.

By a legislative decree of 1926 Athos has the status of 'Theocratic Republic'; it is governed from Karyes by the 'Holy Community', a council of 20 elected representatives from each of the monasteries. At the same time Athos remains a part of Greece. All foreign monks must adopt Greek citizenship and the Greek government is represented by a governor and a small police force. Each monastery has a distinct place in the Athonite hierarchy – the Great Lavra holds the prestigious first place, Konstamonitou ranks twentieth. All other monastic settlements are attached to one or other of the twenty monasteries; these range from *skiti* (a group of houses, often scarcely distinguishable from a monastery), through *kellio* (a kind of farmhouse) to *hesychasterio* (a solitary hermitage, often a cave). As many laymen as monks live on Athos, mostly employed in agriculture by the monasteries.

The monasteries welcome visitors who are genuinely interested in their **way of life** and show respect for their customs. I spoke with one monk who classified about half the visitors as 'tourists, running the one behind the other, as muttons go to butchers'. You should observe a few points – be fully clad at all times (even going from dormitory to bathroom), don't take photos of the monks without asking them and, less obviously, try not to stand with your hands behind your back (taken as an overbearing stance) or to cross your legs in church. Each monastery has an *arhontaris* (guestmaster) who is responsible for you – when you arrive at a monastery he will usually welcome you with an ouzo and *loukoumi*.

Accommodation is in dormitories and fairly spartan but you're always given sheets and blankets – you don't need to haul a sleeping bag around. The monasteries are largely self-sufficient in food and the diet is based on tomatoes, beans and other vegetables; wine is served with every meal, including breakfast. You might want to take some of your own provisions (like ION chocolate) for the long walks between monasteries; there are a few shops in Karyes. Some knowledge of Greek is obviously useful but you can get by at most monasteries on a combination of English and French. The standard greeting, on your part, is *'evlóyite'*, to which monks reply *'O Kyrios'* (the Lord's blessing on you).

You will find that your whole day is shifted around to fit in with sunset and sunrise. Quite apart from being 13 days behind the outside world (the Julian Calendar is still observed), the Athonite day *begins* at sunset. Very few monasteries have electricity and you will be expected to go to bed early. Obviously you can't see all 20 monasteries on a short visit (and space here permits notes only on a handful); travel is usually by foot – though there are some boats – and takes a long time.

The Monasteries

Having obtained your *diamonitirion* in **Karyes** take a look inside the church in the main square – the *Protaton*. The oldest on Athos, it dates from 995 and has exceptional C14th frescoes. On the outskirts of the village – and dominating the capital – is the magnificent *skiti* of **Agiou Andreou**, a Russian dependency of the great Vatopedi monastery but today virtually deserted. If you've a lengthy permit, or plan to cross the peninsula in a first day's walk over to Gregoriou or Simonopetra, you might want to make use of one of the inns in Karyes. But for most visitors there seems no reason not to walk straight on out to a monastery: the nearest three are Koutloumousio, Iviron and Stravonikita, all of which you can easily reach before sunset – the hour when Athonite monasteries close their doors. Check the noticeboard at government house before setting out, however, as from time to time some monasteries are closed to visitors. This was the case with **Koutloumousio**, for example, on my last visit – due to recent damage from one of the all too frequent fires on the peninsula.

Around half an hour's walk from Karyes, **Iviron** was founded late in the C10th by Iberian (Russian Georgian, not Spanish) monks. It ranks third on the Athonite hierarchy, possessing an immensely rich library and treasury – though the monks, perhaps jaded by being an easy 'first stop', seem reluctant to show visitors around. As an idiorythmic monastery – where each monk is responsible for his own food, property and to some extent discipline – its hospitality relies very heavily on the individual *arhontaris*, or guestmaster. **Stavronikita**, in contrast, is a small and very friendly *cenobium* (shared meals, property and communal living) an hour and a half's walk out of Karyes. If you fix your sights here make sure you come early: it's been known for the guesthouse to be full in midsummer. Typical of the Athonite structures, the monastery is built like a fortress perched on rocks above the sea – a pleasant introduction although it holds little interest in art or architecture.

From Stavronikita it is a short walk north along the coast to **Pantokrator**, very similar in design and again with many buildings restored and replaced after a series of fires. Only eighteen monks live here but they are exceptionally kind, particularly Father Petra, the guestmaster. Since this is another idiorythmic monastery he'll be cooking solely for himself and any guests.

Whilst not conspicuously hospitable, **Vatopedi**, a couple of hours' walk further north, is one of the most worthwhile visits to be made. Second in the hierarchy and fabulously sited above the sea, this grand complex seems more like a fortified town. It is also the most modernised establishment – electricity has been installed and there were rumours of colour television. It was founded in the C10th, has superb Byzantine mosaics in its Katholikon (principal chapel), an impressive display of relics and ikons in its treasury, and a library of over 10,000 volumes and illuminated manuscripts. Incidentally, here (as everywhere on Athos) you'll find difficulty in seeing the treasury and library. The usual system is that one monk only has the keys and he is invariably busy: the best times to request a look are immediately after a main service or (if you're in a *cenobium*) during meals.

About 2½ hours' walk west of Vatopedi lies **Zographou**; the road is difficult to find so get clear instructions. It's a very hospitable Bulgarian monastery of only twelve monks; the buildings are mainly C17th and once accommodated hundreds of monks – a walk down the empty corridors past old, uncared-for cells is a stirring experience and helps you appreciate the enormous workload (not least the upkeep of buildings) which now falls on so few monks. The monastery is dedicated to St George, and 'Zographou' means 'of the painter'; the legend goes that when it was founded by Slavs in the C10th they couldn't decide on a patron saint, so they put a wooden panel by the altar and after lengthy prayer a painting of St George appeared. Another foreign monastery is **Agios Panteleimon**, or simply 'the Russian monastery', across the peninsula towards Dafni. It's inhabited by twenty Russians, four Romanians and one Greek – an ethnic predominance strongly reflected in the onion-shaped domes of the architecture and in the softer and more angelic faces of the frescoes. Do not miss the early morning service held here in the church on the top storey of the building next to the bell-tower; the church is exceptionally rich in gold which looks even more impressive when illuminated by candles. The service is in Russian. In many monasteries non-Orthodox people are not permitted to enter the main body of the church during services but here you are allowed this privilege. Panteleimon's library contains several illuminated manuscripts and some interesting photograph albums documenting its more recent history.

The **Great** (**Megisti**) **Lavra**, oldest and foremost of the monasteries, lies towards the end of the east coast. It can be reached by land via the extremely hospitable PHILOTHEOU, high up on a plateau in the centre of Athos; from there Lavra is about 4 hours on foot. A less tiring, though less rewarding, way of reaching Lavra is by boat. The *boat times* vary occasionally but usually there is one a day along the west coast and three a week along the east; prices are reasonable. LAVRA is the most impressive monastery on Athos with no less than fifteen chapels inside its walls; unique among the 20, it has never suffered from fire. The Katholikon was completed in 1004 and its plan copied in all the other Athonite Katholika; its frescoes, painted by Theophanes the Cretan in 1535, are particularly fine. Theophanes also executed the frescoes in the refectory – the most notable is of the Last Supper, not surprisingly a very popular theme in refectories. The Great Lavra's treasury and library are both extraordinarily rich, the latter containing over 2,000 manuscripts.

To return to **OURANOUPOLI** you can take the morning boat from Lavra and connect with the main ferry at Dafni – which leaves around 12.30am. The coastline between Lavra and Dafni is magnificent. Mount Athos towers above everything and for most of the year is capped with snow; on its summit is a chapel with stone icons where monks hold an annual service on 6 August. Nowadays some of the most ascetic settlements on the peninsula are to be seen on the slopes of the mountain, notably at Eremis and Karilia. The actual monasteries along this western coast to Dafni – Agiou Pavlou, Dionisiou, Gregoriou and Simonopetra – are all in stunning green and mountainous settings.

Simonopetra is the most impressive – and an excellent last stop, a short boat ride away from Dafni. Its several-storeyed buildings, perched over 1000 ft above the sea, drop sheer all around held by vast supporting walls. A cenobitic community of some forty monks, it is another monastery where you may be granted the privilege of attending a service. If you start out from here on an exploration of Athos it is roughly an hour to **Gregoriou**, an hour and a half more to **Ayiou Dionisiou** (cenobitic, with reputedly the best wine and frescoes on the mount), and finally a hard 45 mins trek to **Ayiou Pavlou**, least spectacular of the three but, with a growing number of monks (currently 125), probably the most active of all.

KAVALA

KAVALA, backing on to the lower slopes of Mount Symbolon, is the second largest town of Macedonia and principal port for northern Greece.

Its old harbour area is remarkably pretty – an old citadel towering over it from a rocky promontory to the east and an elegant Turkish aqueduct curving through the centre. Known anciently as Neapolis, it served as the terminus of the Via Egnatia and first port of call to Europe until the conquest of Thrace in AD 46; St Paul landed here on his way to Philippi. Keeping in step with the vicissitudes of Byzantium it was sacked by the Normans, occupied by the Franks and Venetians, and remained under Turkish rule till as late as 1912. Mehmet Ali, Pasha of Egypt and head of the dynasty which ended with King Farouk, was born here in 1769; his birthplace, maintained as a monument, provides a rare opportunity to look over a Turkish house, but his main legacy to the town is an astonishing multi-domed 'Imaret', built as an almshouse for 300 softas.

> There's a good free map of Kavala printed on the NTOG's
> "Kavala-Thassos" pamphlet: pick it up before you arrive

The **Imaret** can be seen in the old 'Panagia' section of town – beneath the citadel. It's on Odos Poulidou (which winds up from the quay), an amazingly elongated building covered in Islamic inscriptions and topped by a mushrooming roof of domes; sadly it's been allowed to decay and is now used as a warehouse. At the far end of the street, and in excellent repair, is the **Birthplace of Mehmet Ali**, built on two levels with stables and kitchen below and the living quarters above (offering an insight into the restrictions of harem life); a caretaker opens it up for you and expects a small tip. Another caretaker will unlock the **Citadel** so you can explore the Byzantine ramparts and dungeon; in season there are dance performances in its main court.

Down in the centre of town the **aqueduct**, built in the reign of Suleiman the Magnificent (1520–66) on a Roman model, stands at the far side of Panagia's narrow maze of streets. The **Archaeological Museum** (open weekdays 9–3.30, Sundays 10–4.30; closed Tuesdays) is at the opposite end of the bay, just off the front; it's worth a visit, containing a fine dolphin mosaic, a reconstructed Macedonian funeral chamber and many terracotta figurines still decorated in their original paint.

There's a **NTOG Office** in the main square where you can get tickets for the Thassos and Philippi Drama Festivals (mid-July to mid-August) and a good town plan. The only **rooms** are at Anthemion 37, in the heart of the old Panagia quarter. Otherwise try a handful of 'D' class hotels grouped in the streets around the main square: *Pageou* at K. Palama 12, *Attikon* at Meg. Alex. 8, *Parthenon* at Spetson 14 and *Rex* at Kriezi 4. Most tourists stay at the suburb of Kalamitsa, which has become a major beach resort, or at the string of **campsites** along the beaches to the west of the port – nearest and largest of these is at 'Bati Beach', 5 km from the centre. A good cheap **restaurant** in central Kavala is *Zythestiatorion*, opposite the bus station on Venizelon street.

There are several **ferries** a day from Kavala to Ormos Prinou on Thassos (though it's quicker and cheaper to go direct to Limin from KERAMOTI – connected frequently to Kavala by bus) and there are weekly boats (currently Wednesdays am) to Samothraki, and to Limnos and Lesvos. The main **bus station** is at the corner of Odos Eterias, near the main anchorage, but buses for Alexandroupoli leave by a cafe called 'Poda' on the adjoining Odos Filkis.

PHILIPPI (14 km from Kavala)

As you might expect, Philippi was named after Philip II of Macedon, who wrested the town from the Thracians in 356 BC. However, its importance and prosperity, like so many of the northern towns, was linked to the building of the Via Egnatia. With Kavala-Neapolis as its port it was essentially the first town of Roman-occupied Europe. Here also, as at Actium and Farsala, the fate of the Roman Empire was decided on Greek soil. Brutus and Cassius had fled east of the Adriatic after assassinating Julius Caesar, and late in the year 42 BC were forced against their better judgment to confront the pursuing armies of Antony and Octavian on the Plains of Philippi. The 'honourable conspirators', who could have successfully exhausted the enemy by avoiding action, were decimated in the two battles and as defeat became imminent first Cassius then Brutus killed himself – the latter running on his comrade's sword with the Shakespearian sentiment 'Caesar now be still, I killed thee not with half so good a will'.

St Paul visited Philippi in AD 49 and so began his mission in Europe. Despite being cast into prison he retained a special affection for the Philippians, his first converts, and the church that he established was one of the earliest to flourish in Greece. It provides the principal remains of the site – several impressive, although ruined, basilican churches. Most conspicuous is the **Direkler**, on the left of the modern road. This was an unsuccessful attempt by its C6th architect to improve the basilica design by adding a dome; in this instance the entire east wall collapsed under the weight, leaving only the narthex convertible for worship. The central arch of its west wall and a few pillars of reused antique drums stand in their old redundant state amidst the Roman forum. A line of C2nd AD porticoes spread outwards in front of the Direkler and on their east side are the foundations of a colonnaded octagonal church which was approached from the Via Egnatia by a great gate. Behind the Direkler, and perversely the most interesting and best preserved building of the site, is a huge monumental **public latrine** with fifty of its original marble seats still in situ.

Across the road, near the further of the two entrances, stone steps climb up to a terrace passing midway on the right a Roman crypt reputed to have been the **prison of St Paul** and appropriately frescoed. The terrace flattens out on to a huge paved atrium that extends to the foundations of an awesomely large basilica church. Continuing in the same direction round the base of a hill you emerge above a **Theatre** cut into its side. Though dating from the original town, it was heavily remodelled as an amphitheatre by the Romans – the bas reliefs of Nemesis, Mars and Victory (on the left of the stage) all belong to this period. It is used for the annual Ancient Drama festival – every weekend from mid-July to early August. The **Museum**, above the road at the far end of the site, is rather uninspiring.

Naturally the best impression of the site (which is very extensive, despite a lack of obviously notable buildings) and of the battlefield behind it can be gained from the **Acropolis**, a steep climb along a path from the museum; its remains, though predominantly medieval, are unrelated.

HEADING EAST INTO THRACE: XANTHI, KOMOTINI AND ALEXANDROUPOLI

Shortly after the turning to KERAMOTI (the port for Thassos – small, rather drab but with a fair beach, campsite and two 'E' class hotels) you cross the Nestos River and enter Thrace. Most of the province's interior is covered by the forbidding Rhodope Mountains but even on the main highway you immediately sense the shift towards Turkish influence.

Approaching Xanthi the first moslem villages appear – an interesting change from the poor, drab Greek settlements built for refugees in the 1920s. XANTHI itself has the strongest Turkish feel in Thrace – and indeed in Greece – along with a considerable population of Bulgarian *pomaks*, their men decked in baggy Arabic trousers, the women veiled like the Turks. Sprawling below a massive rocky outcrop of the Rhodopes (topped by a Byzantine castle and a couple of monasteries) it's an interesting if none too pretty market town.

KOMOTINI, 48 km on, has a similar but richer feel to it – the capital of modern Greek Thrace its population, too, is over half Turkish. On the left of the road leading into town (and prominently signposted) is a surprisingly interesting **Archaeological Museum** (open daily 9–5) giving a lucid explanation of Thracian history through plans and finds from local sites. It's especially helpful for understanding the extent and influence of Ancient Samothraki – presumably your target from here unless you're going on to Istanbul.

Ferries for Samothraki leave from **ALEXANDROPOULI**, the last sizeable Greek town before the Turkish border. Inevitably there's a heavy military presence – but rather inexplicably the town has also become a considerable seaside resort, with an enormous NTOG **camping site** by the beach on the outskirts of town. This is probably the best place to stay, impersonal in the extreme but redeemed by the sands and a nightly **wine festival** from July through to mid-August. The Samothraki **boats** leave twice a day in season, every other day out; on Tuesdays there is also a ferry to Limnos and Lesvos, currently leaving around 3pm.

Beyond Alexandroupoli it is 43 km to the Turkish frontier at KIPI: there's a daily bus, which takes an hour. Walk across and you can get a Turkish coach to Istanbul (260 km). Alternatively there's a rather slow train, twice a day, coming from Thessaloniki.

TRAVEL DETAILS

1 Buses

Volos–Thessaloniki (4 daily; 3½ hrs); Larissa–Thessaloniki (hourly; 2½ hrs); Kalambaka–Grevena (one a day at 10am; 1½ hrs); Grevena–Thessaloniki (3 daily; 3½ hrs); Grevena– Kozani (8 daily; 1 hr); Kozani–Veria (8 daily; 1½ hrs); Veria–Vergina (every 1½ hrs; ½ hr); Veria–Thessaloniki (hourly – last at 10pm; 1¾ hrs); Thessaloniki–Pella (every 45 mins; 45 mins); Thessaloniki–Kavala (hourly; 3 hrs); Thessaloniki–Kalambaka/Ioannina (5 daily; 3½ hrs/7 hrs); Thessaloniki–Istanbul (at least one privately operated coach a day; 8 hrs); Kavala–Philippi (every 20 mins; 20 mins); Kavala–Xanthi/Komotini (every ½ hr; 1 hr/1¾ hrs); Kavala–Alexandroupoli (5 daily; 2½ hrs); Alexandroupoli–Turkish frontier (2 daily in 30 mins; thence to Istanbul by Turkish coach in 3½ hrs).

2 Trains

Larissa–Thessaloniki (9 daily; 2½–3 hrs); Larissa–Plati (for Vergina, Kozani, Florina; 6 daily; 2 hrs); Kozani–Edessa/ Veria/Plati/Thessaloniki (3 daily; 2 hrs/3 hrs/3½ hrs/4 hrs); Thessaloniki–Drama/ Xanthi/Komotini/Alexandroupoli (4 daily; times very variable – 4–6 hrs/6–8½ hrs/ 8–9½ hrs/8–11 hrs); Thessaloniki–Athens (6 daily; 7½ hrs); Thessaloniki–Istanbul (2 daily; 21 hrs); Alexandroupoli–Istanbul (2 daily; 14 hrs); Thessaloniki–Sofia (2 daily; 13 hrs); Thessaloniki–Belgrade/Venice (4 daily; 12 hrs/32 hrs).

N.B. Greek Railways (OSE) also operate long-distance coaches from Athens and Thessaloniki to Sofia, Belgrade, Milan, Paris, London, Vienna and Germany.

3 Ferries

From **Kavala**: 8 times daily to Thassos (and 7 daily from Keramoti); twice weekly to Limnos, Lesvos (and major Dodecanese islands); weekly to Samothraki.

From **Alexandroupoli**: Twice daily in season (every other day, out) to Samothraki; weekly to Limnos and Lesvos.

From **Thessaloniki**: Weekly to Limnos, Lesvos and major Dodecanese – but generally unpredictable service.

4 Planes

There are 8–10 flights a day from Athens to Thessaloniki (and vice versa); also on most days from Athens to Alexandroupoli and Kavala. Additionally there are regular flights from Thessaloniki to Alexandroupoli, Ioannina, Kastoria, Limnos and Mitilini (Lesvos). Details of all of these from Olympic Airways.

Thessaloniki has direct international flights to Amsterdam, Budapest, Dusseldorf, Istanbul, Larnaca (Cyprus), London, Munich, Paris, Stuttgart, Vienna and Zurich.

Part three
THE
ISLANDS

IONIAN

SPORADES
+ EVIA

EVIA

NORTH
AND EASTERN
AEGEAN

ARGO
SARONIC

CYCLADES

DODECANESE

CRETE

INTRODUCTION TO THE ISLANDS

Whilst it's fair to talk about 'mainland regions', the isles of Greece often seem to defy even this degree of generalisation. Each one has a different feel, character and life – and, whatever you've heard, there is no such thing as a 'typical Greek island'. All have far more to be considered than a mere proximity of beaches.

Histories, for a start, are diverse – Corfu was British-ruled for much of the last century, Rhodes by the Italians until 1947, even Crete (one of the last islands liberated from the Turks) was only reunited with Greece in 1912. And beyond these wild fluctuations of history, politics and culture there are the ever-changing island landscapes and colours, architecture, music and people. Tourists too, these days, vary enormously from island to island – Ios sees only young and mainly Irish backpackers, Hydra is exclusive and expensive, Mykonos has a strong gay presence.

In all there are 1,425 islands and islets in Greek waters – of which 166 are to some degree inhabited. A few are privately owned and many shelter only a handful of shepherds or monks but a good 80 can be visited if you've time and inclination to fit in with the sometimes sparse boat schedules. As always the real rewards of travel come in direct ratio to the effort that you put in and the level of isolation that you're happy to take. Islands on the main ferryboat routes become incredibly crowded in midsummer but there are dozens much less known and still many where the caiques don't call that often and which are penetrated only by the determined. If you do decide to visit some of the really obscure islands it'll help if you can speak a few bare phrases of Greek and it's essential to change money in advance. But outside the peak season you'll find even the most popular – like Corfu or Paros – retain many of their traditional elements and much of their charm.

Wherever and whenever you go, however, there is an art to be learnt: to fall into the natural pace of Greek life, to learn how to do nothing – Greece by absorption, it shouldn't take long.

Points

BOATS We've indicated most of the boat connections possible in the Travel Details at the end of each chapter. Don't take this as an exhaustive list, however, since there are often additional services operated locally. The most reliable, up-to-date information is available from the local port police (*limenarheio*), who maintain offices at Piraeus and on most fair-sized islands. Ferry services from Piraeus are listed in weekly schedules available from the NTOG bureau inside the National Bank on Sintagma, Athens; these are a fairly reliable guide though there are frequent last-minute changes.

Usually your only consideration will be getting a boat that leaves on the day, and for the island, that you want, but when sailing from Piraeus to islands of the Cyclades or Dodecanese you should have quite a degree of choice. Bear in mind that routes taken and the speed of the boats vary enormously – and a journey from Piraeus to Thira, for instance, can take anything from 9 to 14 hours. Before buying a ticket make sure you've established how many stops there'll be before your island and the reckoned time of arrival. Many agents act only for one specific boat so you may have to ask around before getting alternative choices – they'll happily tell you that their ferry is the only one going! Most sailings from Piraeus are in the early morning, around 7–10am, though there are a number of evening departures for Crete.

In season there are also several smaller caiques (*kaikia*) sailing between adjacent islands and to a few of the more obscure. These are no cheaper than main services but can be extremely useful and often very pleasant. They have a good safety record, indeed it's often the larger overloaded car ferries that run into most trouble.

BOATS TO AVOID It's always good policy to ask ferry agents which boat they're trying to sell you a ticket for: if it's new, fast and efficient they're likely to show you a photo immediately. Two to avoid, if at all possible, are the *Mioulis* and the *Elli*; the former was said to be already 15 years old when the Greeks got it as part of Italian war reparations in 1948!

BOAT TICKETS Don't buy them far in advance because they'll tie you down to a particular ferry at a particular time – and innumerable factors can make you regret that. Most obviously there's bad weather, which, particularly off-season, can play havoc with the schedules causing some small boats to stay in harbour and others to alter their routes drastically. The cheapest class of ticket, which you'll probably automatically be sold, is *deck class* – sometimes also called *triti, gamma* or *touristiki*. This gives you the run of most boats except for the first class restaurant and bar. Talking of which, **food** sold on board is usually pricey and poor – take some along on any lengthy journey.

CHEAP ACCESS Mainland port-to-island connections aren't expensive (the NTOG prints a schedule with prices) but inter-island hopping can work out comparatively pricey; you won't pay very much more, for example, for a ticket from Thira–Piraeus than for Thira–Siros. If your money is very tight consider some of the islands scattered close to points of the mainland other than Athens. For under £3 you can currently get from Killini to Zakinthos, Kavala to Thassos, or Igoumenitsa to Corfu. All these ports are hitchable, or you can try hitching all the way to the island of Lefkada, separated from the mainland only by a 100 m chain ferry!

FLYING DOLPHINS These are hydrofoils, roughly twice as fast and twice as expensive as ordinary ferries. They operate mainly among the Argo-Saronic islands close to Athens, though there are also services in the Cyclades between Siros, Tinos, Mykonos, Naxos and Paros.

BIKES, BUSES AND MOPEDS Most islands have some form of bus service, usually timed at least to connect ferries with the main village. For more freedom you can rent bikes (around £2 a day), mopeds (from £6) and occasionally motorbikes (£8 up and you'll need to show a licence). Bikes can be ideal, especially if you get a deal for a week's rent. Mopeds should always be very thoroughly looked over before riding off – some I've used have literally fallen apart – and dirt tracks treated with caution. There are scores of accidents each year and, on top of your own wounds, you can get landed with a criminally high bill for 'repairs'.

ROOMS Along with beach-camping, privately let rooms (*dhomatia*) are the standard island accommodation. Owners will usually descend upon you as your ferry pulls in – bargain a little and yield, you'll rarely do better for a first night.

BANKS All but the smallest and remotest islands have a bank, though often only in the island capital. You will always, however, find a post office (*tahidhromio*) and armed with a giro account can gain freedom and save a lot of queueing.

CHORA Pronounced (and sometimes written) 'Hora', this is the local name given to many island capitals; literally it just means 'the place'. The Chora is also often known by the same name as the island – as with Tinos, Skopelos, Thira, Kerkira, etc.

OUT OF SEASON TRAVEL Reckon on severely reduced ferry services, with many daily services falling to once or twice weekly, and on unpredictable cancellations due to stormy weather. Most island hotels close down through the winter, and *rooms* are actually required to do so, but you'll usually find one hotel and a place to eat open at the port and island capital.

Chapter five
CYCLADES

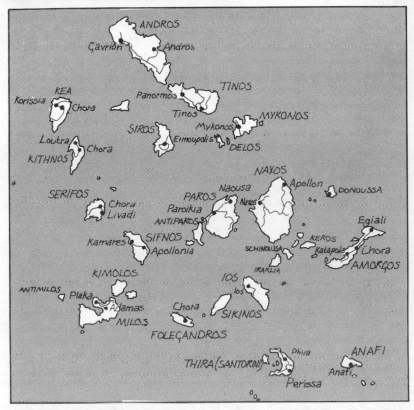

Named from the circle they form around the sacred island of Delos, the **Cyclades** are probably the most satisfying archipelago for island-hopping. On no other group do you get quite such a strong feeling of each island as a microcosm, each with its own distinct traditions, customs, and (very definitely) path of modern development. And most of these small worlds are small enough actually to walk round in a few days, giving you a sense of completeness and identity impossible on, say, Crete or the Ionian islands.

There is some unity. Most of the islands – Andros and Naxos notably excepted – are arid and rocky, and most share the 'Cycladic' style of brilliant white cubist architecture. The extent and impact of tourism, however, is dramatically haphazard – and there are only two islands where it has come to completely dominate the character. These are **Ios**, the original hippy-island and still a paradise for hard-living packers, and **Mykonos**, way the most popular of the group with its cute-derelict windmills, nude beaches (one exclusively gay) and highly sophisticated clubs and bars. After these two, **Paros, Sifnos** and **Thira** (Santorini) are currently the most popular – all with good reason. They get drastically overcrowded in August but, for the most part, seem to absorb visitors with remarkable ease. For isolates the most promising are probably **Sikinos** or **Folegandros**, or even (going to extremes) the minor islets around Naxos. **Delos**, commercial and religious centre of the Classical Greek world, is the one major ancient site; it is on a few of the ferry routes but is easiest visited by caique from Mykonos.

Two general points: the Cyclades can often get frustratingly windy, particularly in early spring, and they're the worst affected by the Meltemi or sirocco which blows sand and tables about with equal venom through much of August. If you're heading back to Athens to catch a flight leave yourself a day or two in hand. Many of the islands have connections onwards to Crete and from Thira or Amorgos you can loop on to the Dodecanese ferry-circuits.

KEA AND KITHNOS

Kea, the closest of the Cyclades to the mainland, is popular with Athenians, but its rugged interior has condensed the resorts into small crowded pockets so that even in the summer much of the land is quiet, while out-of-season shuttered holiday villas give the coast a ghostly air.

The small port of **Korissia** has hotels and rooms: it is expanding to accommodate tourists and has little beauty to lose. Around the bay to the north is **Vourkari**, where the church of Agia Irene stands on a promontory near the beach. In 1960 the site of a Minoan colony was excavated here, revealing the remains of a palace, temple and road in good condition. Beyond Vourkari **Otzias** also has beaches, tavernas, rooms and summer crowds.

The island bus goes from Korissia to **CHORA** (ancient Ioulis), birthplace of Simonides and Bacchylides, renowned poets of the fifth century BC. It is not a typical Cycladic village, but it is beautifully situated in an arc-shaped fold of the hills. Its lower reaches stretch across a spur to the

Kastro, site of the ancient acropolis. The Venetians built a castle here reusing stones from the Temple of Apollo, which you can still see, but the remains now have to share the Kastro with a modern hotel. Fifteen minutes east of town the road passes the **Lion of Kea**, carved out of the solid rock with crudely powerful haunches and a bizarre expression. There are steps down to it, but the effect is most striking from a distance.

Down the west coast there are beaches at **Pisses** and **Koundoros**, but they tend to be spoilt by overdevelopment. The scant ruins of ancient Poiessa are at Pisses, and inland at **Agia Marina** a restored Hellenistic tower soars dramatically out of the ruined monastery.

Kea is connected regularly with *Lavrio* on the mainland – an hour's bus ride from Athens – but only once a week with neighbouring *Kithnos*. This, if you want a first or last island-stop, is a much more practical possibility – with ferries onwards to Serifos, Sifnos and Milos several times a week.

Close as it is to the mainland *KITHNOS* remains an oddly quiet island even in midsummer. The people are outwardly friendly and it makes an attractive, even if brief, refuge from the manic crowds elsewhere. The west coast port of **MERICHAS** is a fishing harbour with a small beach – you can sleep on it but there's no fresh water. The town offers plenty of cheap rooms, though, and a large modern hotel: food is excellent, if sometimes pricey. The bus goes to most places, but you can also walk almost anywhere on this island. By the quay, notices about the boat to Lavrio are only in Greek, so ask.

Roads lead across the island to the capital at **CHORA** (which is where the Post Office is) and to **Loutra**, named after its thermal baths, which has a couple of *tavernas* by the beach and a few rooms to let. **Driopis** has another beach and more *tavernas* by one of the island's many caves.

SERIFOS

Serifos has remained outside the mainstream of both history and tourism – its only fame is in myth as the island kingdom to which Perseus returned with the Gorgon's head. Most visitors are deterred by the barren hilly interior and stay in the port, **LIVADI**. Set in a wide green bay overlooked from the distance by Chora, it is the easiest place to find rooms (which are very sparse on the island) if not the most attractive. To the south the further of two beaches is cleaner and better for camping, while the best of the restaurants is a long walk to the last house round the bay. A bus connects the port with the capital at Chora, and less frequently with Megalo Livadi and Galini.

CHORA, pouring like milk from a rocky hogback above the harbour, is one of the most spectacular villages of the Cyclades. At odd intervals along its alleyways you'll find part of the old castle making up the wall of a house, or a marble statue leaning incongruously in a corner. It's a quiet place, with a couple of *tavernas* (near the bus stop), the island's post office, but no rooms at all to let. For these, the best bet is down by the beach of **Megalo Livadi** – to the west of Chora. Once, iron and copper were exported from here but cheaper African deposits sent the mines into decline and the machinery stands there rusting.

North from Chora you can walk across the hills to **Panagia**, named after its Byzantine church, **Galini**, and the medieval Monastery of Tax-iarchos. The road circles round through **Kallitsos** and its verdant valley before getting back to Chora. On foot the whole circuit takes as much as three hours, but there are *tavernas* at Galini and Kallitsos, as well as isolated beaches where you can sleep undisturbed. Serifos's best beach, however, is at **Psili Ammos** – below Chora to the east or an hour's hike over the hills from Livadi. There's a *taverna* behind the quiet stretch of sand.

SIFNOS

Sifnos is a more immediately appealing island than its northern neighbours – greener and with some fine local architecture – and it's much more popular. No bigger than them, it does often get crowded: buses can be packed, and if you want a room be quick to take any offered as you land. On the other hand the size means that wherever you stay, you can reach the rest of Sifnos on foot – over an excellent network of old stone pathways. And in spite of the crowds, it remains the friendliest of islands.

KAMARES, the port, is set between high bare cliffs in the west: it can be an expensive town, and it is well worth haggling over the price of rooms, or there is a beach with showers and a certain amount of shelter to camp on. Like so many islands, Sifnos is short of both water and fresh produce; most of the shops only stock tins, so if you want fruit, cheese or fresh bread you should bring your own.

A steep 20-minute bus ride takes you up to **APOLLONIA**, the capital, a rambling collage of flagstones, belfries and flowered courtyards. The island bank, post office and tourist police are all found here but rooms, though plentiful, are even more likely to be full than at Kamares – try the outlying districts of Katavati or Artemonas, once distinct villages around half a kilometre north and south of the central plateia. The town is beginning to get commercialised but there are some good genuine *tavernas*, best of all O Manganas at Artemonas. The Folk Museum, in the square by the bus stop, is also well worth a look since Sifnos produces some of the finest pottery and fabrics in Greece; it's open in the mornings and again in the evenings from around 7.30pm.

As an alternative base for rooms you could try **Kastro**, half an hour's walk below Apollonia on the south-east coast. Built on a rocky outcrop with an almost sheer drop to the sea on three sides, this, the ancient capital, retains much of its medieval character; parts of its walls survive, surrounding tortuous narrow streets and some fine old churches. Venetian coats of arms can still be seen on some of the older houses, there are remains of the ancient acropolis, and fifteen minutes' walk below the town you can swim off a rocky peninsula.

At the southern end of the island, around 4 km from Apollonia, is the growing resort of **Plati Gialos**; you can camp on the large sandy beach here though it can get extremely windy. Taking the path out from Apollonia you'll pass, early on, the beautiful empty monastery of Piyes and (half an hour on) Agios Andreas, offering tremendous views over the islands of Siros, Paros, Ios, Folegandros and Sikinos. Even better is the hike to **Vathi**, again around 2½ hrs from Apollonia but reached by turning right, off the Plati Gialos path, at a white house 2 km beyond Ag. Andreas; en route you pass another exceptional Sifniot monastery, Taxiarchis. Vathi itself is possibly the most attractive place on the island to stay, a fishing and pottery village on the shore of a stunning, funnel-shaped bay. There are rooms to let, two summer *tavernas* and people camp back from the beach. If you've just arrived on the island you can come here directly by boat from Kamares, they leave three times a day in season and since notices are only in Greek attract few tourists. An alternative hike back to Apollonia winds up to the ridge of the Profitis Ilias monastery, with even greater views than Agios Andreas.

Less populous – and adjacent – beaches are at **Faros** and **Apokoftos**, both with good cheap *tavernas* back from their coves. Close to Apokoftos, alone on a rocky sea-washed spit, is the disestablished Hrisiopigi monastery whose cells are sometimes rented out in summer.

From **Plati Gialos** there are seasonal caiques to the island of **Paros** – an immensely useful link.

MILOS AND KIMOLOS

MILOS has always enjoyed prosperity from its strange geology; Minoan settlers were drawn by the obsidian rock, and other products of its volcanic soil made the island important in the ancient world. Today the quarrying brings in a steady revenue, but has left deep scars on the landscape: a large electricity plant adds to the industrial air as you arrive. But the rocks can also be beautiful – on the left of the bay as the boat enters, two rocks, the Arkoudes, rear up like wrestling bears; off the north coast, and accessible only by boat, the Glaronissia (Seagull Isles) are shaped like massed organ pipes, and there are more weird formations on the south coast at Kleftiko. Inland too you frequently come across the strange, often beautiful, volcanic rocks.

ADAMAS, the cramped little port, was founded by Cretan refugees. Today a huge blank wall overshadows the quay: hotels are above it and to the left; to the right you can sit in the shady square watching the island go by. Most of the accommodation is here and it's the point of departure by bus, taxi, boat or bike. Along the sea-front the tourist office has information about boat trips and sells maps of Milos. Buses go in three directions, to Plaka, Pollonia and Zefiria.

Zefiria lies among olive groves below the bare hills at the far end of Milos Bay and used to be the capital until an epidemic drove out the population. Much of the old town is still deserted, though some life has returned, especially to the *taverna* opposite the church. South of here the rest of the island, dominated by Mount Profitis Ilias, is off the bus route and only touched by tourism around **Emborios** where there are beaches, tavernas, and in summer a regular boat to Adamas. The countryside beyond is there to be explored – on foot.

Most tourists stay in the north, but even here they tend to stick together, and there is little problem dodging the crowds. **PLAKA** is the capital of the island, the most pleasant of a horseshoe of villages though again without *rooms*. A stairway above it leads up to the old Venetian Kastro, its roofs peculiarly sloped to channel precious rain water into cisterns. Back in town there are two small museums – an archaeological one with Neolithic pottery from the Filakopi site, and (rather more interesting) the Folklore Museum, displaying a whole range of items from Milotian life. Below Plaka, **Klema** occupies the site of an ancient Greek town whose population was massacred by the Athenians in 416 BC. The road down passes the modern entrance to early Christian catacombs – their corridors lined with tombs and some remains of inscriptions and frescoes. Up the valley by the ruins of the city walls a path leads to the place where the Venus de Milo was found – it was given to the French Consul for safekeeping from the Turks and hasn't been seen here since. Further along a small Roman amphitheatre faces out to sea.

East at **Filakopi** the remains of three prehistoric cities lie at the edge of a small cliff; the site was important archaeologically, but it hasn't been maintained and means little unless you're an expert. Over the hill the road drops down into **POLLONIA**, a popular fishing village with a shady beach, fish *tavernas* and rooms to rent. A caique runs from here to *KIMOLOS*, connecting with the bus – the boat can be hard to find, so ask at the pier.

Of the three islets off the coast of Milos, *ANDIMILOS* is home to a rare species of chamois and *POLIEGOS* has more ordinary goats, but only **KIMOLOS** has any human habitation. Like Milos, it has profitable rocks and used to export chalk until its supply was exhausted. Nowadays it is a source of fuller's earth, and the fine dust of this stone is a familiar sight on the island. Rugged and barren in the interior, there is some green land on the south coast, and this is where the small population is concentrated.

Whether you arrive by ferry or by caique from Pollonia, you'll dock at the hamlet of **Psathi**; around the bay there are a few old windmills, brilliant white **CHORA** hangs on the edge above them, a 15-minute walk up. You'll find most of the island's accommodation here – and indeed it seems a surprisingly large town, a maze of tortuous lanes making it difficult at first to get your bearings. There are only a few cafés and *tavernas*, a handful of rooms and a post office.

Another *taverna* and a few rooms can be found at the village of Alyki on the south coast: there's a long if rather coarse stretch of sand here, and beyond the headland a smaller more secluded beach which is better for camping.

There is another road leading north-east from Chora to a fair beach at the village of **Klima** and beyond that to the radioactive springs at **Prasa**, a route taking in impressive views across the straits to Poliegos and several shady peaceful beaches where you could camp out. Innumerable goat tracks invite exploration of the rest of the island, and towards the west coast is **Palaiokastro** where the ruins of an imposing Venetian *kastro* stake around the church of Christos, oldest on the island.

ANDROS

Andros, the second largest of the Cyclades and the northernmost, is sparsely populated but prosperous; its green valleys have attracted scores of Athenian holiday villas whose red-tiled roofs and white walls stand out among the pine forests. These have robbed many of the villages of life and atmosphere – turning them into scattered settlements with no nucleus, especially in the north – but on the positive side the permanent population is distinctly hospitable. Andriotes traditionally work on ships and many are only too happy to practise their English on you.

The main port is at **GAVRION**, not a very pretty town but all right as a base with a small beach, several rooms and *tavernas*. Most people, however, head 8 km down-coast to **BATSI**, a fast-developing resort with a rash of hotels and discos above its fine natural harbour. From either of them there's easy walking access to some beautiful inland villages – **Arni**, especially, if you're at Batsi. The most rewarding walk is to a well-preserved 60 ft Hellenistic tower at Agios Petri, 5 km from Gavrion or 9 km from Batsi.

An efficient bus service, whose drivers signal to each other with their revolving lights, links this north coast with **CHORA**, or **ANDROS** town, the capital and much the most attractive place on the island. Set on a rocky spur, cutting across a huge bay, much of the town is paved in marble – cut from the active local quarries. Buildings around the bus station are grand C19th affairs and the squares with their plane trees are equally elegant. From the square right at the end of town you pass through an archway and down to the windswept Plateia Riva, its statue of the unknown sailor waving out to sea. Beyond him lies the C13th *Kastro*, precariously joined to the mainland by a narrow-arched bridge. The few hotels in town are a little expensive – try the Aigli (opposite the big church on the main walkway) or ask around for rooms. Sometimes there's a seasonal campsite, and people also sleep on the sands of the south beach below, exposed and none too inviting.

Hiking from Andros the natural target is **Menites**, a village just up the valley that may have been the location of a Temple of Dionysos said to turn water into wine: water flows continuously from the rocks. Nearby are the ruins of medieval **Messaria**, with the deserted Byzantine church of Agios Taxiarchis below, and an hour into the hills to the south is the **Panchranto** monastery, still defended by massive walls but occupied these days by just three monks. **Korthi**, beyond and on the main bus route, is a friendly but nondescript town set on a large sandy bay at the southeast corner of the island; it has a hotel and a few rooms. Ruined castles guard the hills to the north.

TINOS

Tinos is famous throughout the Greek Orthodox world for a miraculous healing icon discovered in 1822. The Panagia Evangelistria, which towers over **TINOS** town, was erected on the spot where it was found and has become a leading centre of pilgrimage. In the church the icon is surrounded by a dazzling mass of gold and silver offerings, while below it is the crypt and a mausoleum for people killed on a Greek ship torpedoed in the harbour. Museums around the courtyard display more objects donated by worshippers. The peak times of pilgrimage are 25 March and 15 August, when queues of the faithful stretch from the church down to the harbour. At these times there is no chance of finding a room.

Two main roads lead down to the port; one is lined with stalls selling icons and candles (wrapped in red paper) while on the other is a museum with some fine amphorae and torsoes of Roman emperors. The town itself could really be anywhere in southern Europe: some old parts have survived but large modern hotels line the seafront and the beaches to the west are crowded. Outside the periods of pilgrimage rooms are plentiful (try the Hotel Eleana) but you may prefer to head for the beaches east of town (**Porto**, 8 km east, is about the best) or to some of the smaller villages inland. Dotting the countryside are hundreds of delightfully patterned dovecots built by the Venetians: periodically flocks of white doves clatter up and wheel around, bright against the drab scenery. A good bus service operates from the quayside and the KTEL office opposite has timetables.

Exobourgo, the hill which dominates southern Tinos, is stooked by the ruins of a Venetian castle which defied the Turks long after the rest of Greece had fallen. Eventually it was abandoned and destroyed by the Turks, but you can still see a fountain and three churches inside the walls. To the south-east there are some charming villages, especially **Thio Choria** and **Trianthros**, but the best place to scale Exobourgo from is **Xinara** on the northern slopes (buses to Pirgos and Kalloni pass close by). Below, a luscious valley stretches down to the villages of **Komi** and **Kalloni** and there's a sandy beach where you can sleep at **Kolimpidria**, half an hour's walk beyond the latter.

Along the west coast a road connects villages high above the sea where you can rent rooms in summer, though it can be a long walk down to the beach. **Agios Nikolaos** is one of the few places with rooms right by the beach, but it's becoming overdeveloped. **Pirgos**, the largest village in the region, is the birthplace of several famous Tiniote artists and now houses a school of fine arts: it is really very attractive, and a popular place to visit in summer. The broad main street curves down into a square shaded by old plane trees where shops sell the work of local artists. Some of the best is on display in the museum near the bus stop. The old port of **Panormos**, 3 km below, has a very short beach and functional cement harbour: not exactly picturesque but it has rooms and a *taverna*.

SIROS

Don't be put off by first impressions of Siros. From the ferry it looks grimly industrial, but away from the port things improve fast. The town rises from the sea on two hills: on the taller one to the left is the intricate medieval quarter **Ano Siros**, with a clutch of catholic churches below the Cathedral of St George. It takes an hour to walk up on Odos Omiron, passing the Orthodox and Catholic cemeteries on the way – the former full of grand ship-owners' mausoleums, the latter with more modest monuments and French and Italian inscriptions.

The modern town, **ERMOUPOLIS**, was founded during the War of Independence by refugees from Psara and Chios and became Greece's chief port in the C19th. Piraeus has left it an age behind, but it is still the largest town in the Cyclades, and their capital. Between the harbour and Agios Nikolaos, the fine Orthodox church to the north, you can still stroll amidst its rather faded splendour. The Apollon Theatre, now derelict, is a copy of La Scala in Milan and once presented a regular Italian opera season. The quayside is still busy, though nowadays dealing more with tourists than ships as a major crossover point on the ferryboat-loops. Down here is the bus station, along with the tourist police and several bike rental places. Between them are shops selling the *Loukoumia* (Turkish Delight) for which the island is famed. Rooms are fairly plentiful but not always too enticing: *Yanni's Guesthouse* has had good reports.

The long, central Plateia Miaoulis is named after an admiral of the revolution whose statue stands there; in the evenings the population parades around its shaded *kafeneia*. Up the stairs to the left of the Town Hall is the small Archaeological Museum (open weekdays except Tuesday 9–3.30, Sundays 10–2) with three rooms of finds from Siros, Paros and Amorgos, and to the left of the clock tower more stairs climb Vrontathi (the second of the two hills) to Anastasis, the church of the resurrection. There are good views from here over Tinos and Mykonos.

North of Ermoupolis the island is barren and high, with few villages. There are no real roads, so any exploration has to be done on foot. By contrast the land to the south has more greenery on its low-lying hills and a popular coastline for summer houses. Thanks to these, although there are good beaches around the coast at **Vari**, **Megas Gialos**, **Dellagrazia** and **Finikas**, there are real villages at none of them, and camping tends to be frowned on. **GALISSAS** is far better. It has a shop, which the others lack, and many people sleep on the beach – one of the island's best; there are caves too. Inland, in villages like **Chroussa**, there are exotic villas built by ship-owners, but little else to savour.

MYKONOS

Originally visited only as a stop on the way to ancient Delos, Mykonos has become easily the most popular of the Cyclades and its archetypal postcard-image. An incredible 600,000 tourists are reputed to pass through each year, but if you don't mind the crowds the capital is still one of the most beautiful of all island towns, its immaculately whitewashed houses concealing hundreds of little churches, shrines and chapels. The labyrinthine backstreets were designed to confuse pirates and they remain effective, everyone gets lost. Unspoilt it isn't, but the island does offer good nude beaches, picturesque windmills, a large gay community and as much nightlife as most major cities.

Rooms in **MYKONOS** town tend to be expensive (as does everything else on this island), but if you can find one, a private room here is likely to be cheaper than staying in a hotel on the beach. Otherwise there is an official campsite at **Paradise Beach**, and every beach on the island has some sort of *taverna* on it. There are occasional purges but usually the local police allow you to sleep out anywhere, even on the beach in Mykonos town itself; the only problem is persuading a bar to keep your baggage, there's no official place. At **Plati Gialos**, **Megali Ammos** and **San Stefanos** there are also a fair number of rooms to rent. A frequent bus service from the windmills to the south of town, or small boats from the harbour every morning, connect Mykonos with almost the whole of the coastline. Other buses cross the island to Ano Mera from outside the Leto Hotel, or you can hire a motorbike. The Folk Museum, by the harbour to the right of the tourist police, has a larger collection of bric-à-brac than most – it includes a vast four-poster bed – while the Archae-ological Museum to the north of town has pottery from Delos, but nothing of exceptional interest. Much more worth visiting is the church of Paraportiani, four chapels joined into one beautiful church on the site of the old *Kastro*.

Mykonos, though, is really about nightlife and hanging about on the beaches. By caique, bus or 45 mins walk **Plati Gialos** is the first you come to south-east of the town and the straightest on the island. **Paradise Beach** and **Super Paradise**, 15 mins and 30 mins walk further on, are both totally nude, and the latter exclusively gay (and male).

ANO MERA, inland to the east, is the only other real village on the island: it has a large concrete hotel and a number of rooms to rent as well as being home to the Tourliani monastery. From here it is an easy walk to **Panormos Bay** and the ruined medieval castle of Darga. In the other direction there's a beach at **Kalafati**, with the islet of Tragonissi just offshore.

DELOS

The caique to Delos leaves Mykonos at 9.00am and returns at 12.30, without loud warning, which gives you three hours on the island. If you really want to see the whole of the large and complex site or have the chance to browse around it at leisure without the crowds, it is worth staying the night in the campsite behind the museum. The boat ride is expensive, and there's no point doing it more often than you have to. Take your own food and drink with you too, as the Tourist Pavilion is a rip-off.

Delos' ancient fame was due to the fact that Leto gave birth to the divine twins Artemis and Apollo on the island, although its fine harbour and central position did nothing to hamper development. When the Ionians colonised the island around 1000 BC it was already a place of cult and by the C7th BC had become the commercial and religious centre of the Amphictionic League. Unfortunately Delos also came to the atten-tion of Athens, which sought to increase its prestige by controlling the island; the Delian Confederacy, founded after the Persian Wars to protect the Aegean cities, developed into an Athenian empire, and Athenian officials took over the Sanctuary of Apollo itself for a while. Athenian attempts to 'purify' the island started with a decree that no one could die or give birth on Delos – the sick and the pregnant were taken to the islet of Rheneia – and culminated in the simple expedient of banishing what remained of the native population. Little affected, Delos reached its peak in the C3rd and C2nd BC after being declared a free port by its Roman overlords. In the end, though, its undefended wealth brought ruin. First Mithridates (88 BC), then Athenodorus (69 BC) plundered the treasures, and the island never recovered. By the C3rd AD Athens could not even sell it, and every passing seafarer for centuries stopped to collect a few prizes.

The remains, though skeletal and swarming now with lizards, give some idea of the past grandeur of the sacred isle. Only the main sites are marked (even then not well) so that some sort of guide is well worth having. Maps are sold on the caique. The ancient town lies on the west coast in a flat, at times marshy, area which rises in the south to **Mount Kythnos**. From the summit – an easy walk – there is a magnificent view of almost the entire Cyclades.

You land with the Sacred Harbour on your left, the Commercial Harbour on your right, straight ahead is the Agora of the Competalists which has offerings to Hermes in the middle (a round and a square base). The **Sacred Way** leads north from the far left corner: it used to be lined with statues and the grandiose monuments of rival kings. Along it you reach three marble steps which lead into the **SANCTUARY OF APOLLO**. The forest of offerings which covered this entire area – for huge amounts were lavished on the god – has been stripped by plunderers. On your left is the Stoa of the Naxians, while against the north wall of the House of the Naxians to the right there stood a huge statue of Apollo. In 417 BC the Athenian general Nicias led a procession of priests across a bridge of boats from Rheneia to dedicate a bronze palm tree: when it was later blown over it took the statue with it. Three **Temples of Apollo** stand in a row to the right along the Sacred Way: the Delian Temple, that of the Athenians and the Porinos Naos, the earliest of them. To the east towards the museum you pass the **Sanctuary of Dionysos** with its marble phalli on tall pillars.

The best finds from the site are in Athens, but the **MUSEUM** (if it's open) still justifies a visit. Next door to it is the Tourist Pavilion. To the north is the **SACRED LAKE** where Leto gave birth clinging to a palm tree. It has lost both its water and its swans, but a modern wall marks where they used to be. Guarding it are the superb **Lions**, their lean bodies masterfully executed. Of the original nine, three have disappeared and one adorns the Arsenal at Venice. Don't try to ride the remaining five, as the guards get apoplectic. On the other side of the lake is the City Wall built, in 69 BC, too late to protect the treasures. The houses to the north have some mosaics.

Set out in the other direction from The Agora of the Competalists and you enter the residential area, known as the **THEATRE QUARTER**. Many of the walls and roads remain but there is none of the domestic detail that makes somewhere like Pompeii so fascinating. Some colour is added by the mosaics; one in the House of the Trident, better ones in the **House of the Mask**. The finest on Delos is here, a vigorous portrayal of Dionysos riding on a panther's back.

PAROS

Paros has some of the finest sandy beaches in the Cyclades, but to visit it for these alone, as increasing crowds seem to do every summer, is to miss much. Gently furled around a single mountain, Paros is, in a quiet, not immediately dramatic way, one of the most beautiful islands of the group. Fortunately it is also large enough to avoid being completely taken over by tourists though in peak season it's now touch and go.

PAROIKIA, the principal town where the boats dock, sets the tone for the rest of the island – the line of old Cycladic houses broken by the occasional Venetian building and a couple of windmills. The waterfront and the outreaches of the town close to the beach have yielded to tourist purposes, but the maze of houses, designed to keep out wind and pirates alike, is little touched by developments. The town has one of the most architecturally interesting churches in the Aegean – the **Ekatonapyliani**, or 'Church of One Hundred Doors'. The original building was overseen in the C6th by Isidore of Miletus but work was carried out by his pupil Ignatius. It was so beautiful on completion that the master, consumed with jealousy, is said to have grappled with his apprentice on the rooftop, flinging both to their deaths. They can be found today kneeling at the column bases across the courtyard; master tugging at his beard in repentance, pupil clutching a broken head. Restored at intervals ever since, the church was substantially altered after a severe earthquake in the C8th, but its essentially Byzantine aspect remains. Enclosed by a great wall to protect its icons from pirates, it is in fact three churches interlocking with one another. Behind Ekatontapyliani stands the Archaeological Museum: its prize exhibit, a piece of the Parian Chronicle, lies rather insignificantly on the floor.

Paroikia is a pleasant enough town to stay in, though overcrowded in midsummer, and there are numerous cheap hotels and rooms to choose from. The windmill where the boats dock doubles up as the tourist police office and the bus stop – the bus timetable is outside as is a list of all the hotels on the island. The official campsite is at **Livadia Beach**, a few hundred yards north of town, but it's not recommended. Low-lying and marshy, it often gets completely waterlogged. There are some good fish restaurants along this stretch of beach – and a cheap *psistaria*, *To Limanaki* – but the best places to eat are away from the tourist section, like *Athinios* in the centre of the old part of town. Similarly the better beaches are some way down the coast – small boats run regularly, or you can hire bicycles for which the island's beetling hills are ideal.

Buses cross the island along three main routes: to Naoussa, to Lefkes and Marpissa, and to Pounda. If you're heading for the beach it's best to get a bus to **Piso Livadhi**: an attractive village, it has a beach a few hundred yards down at Logaras and a multitude of rooms to rent. A short walk into the hills above brings you to two of Paros' finest villages – **Marpissa** and **Marmari** – whilst a couple of hours down the road the beautiful and tiny town of LEFKES (once the island's Chora) lies tucked into a fold in the island's central mountain. Out of season there's no problem camping at any of the beaches on the coast south of Piso Livadi, but in summer it's more diplomatic to stay at one of the beaches a few kilometres down – **Pounda**, **Mezadha** or the notorious and usually lively **Tzirdakia** or **Golden Beach**; there are a couple of good *tavernas* and a small hotel at the latter. **Dryos**, further down the coast, has been spoilt by rich Athenians' villas and has turned into a major resort; campers, anyway, are unlikely to be welcome there. For a little more seclusion head the other way from Piso Livadi – a dirt track from Marmari leads in about 20 minutes to Molos Beach and others to the north. After about an hour's walk you reach **Ambelas**, a hamlet with a pleasant beach and *taverna* from where a road completes the circuit to Naoussa.

NAOUSSA is the most attractive town on Paros, a little fishing port where, impervious to the tourists, fishermen tenderise squids by thrashing them against the walls or mend huge nets spread about the harbour. Entered through an arched gateway, the town is a sparkling labyrinth of winding, narrow alleys and simple Cycladic houses. Near its church an excellent *ouzeri* serves *souma*, the local raki, with delicious fish-based *mezedhes*; there are some fine restaurants, too, and slightly cheaper rooms than at Paroikia. Ten minutes' walk east of town is a small beach where you can camp, and half an hour further round you come to the more popular **Kolimbithres** (basins) where a small *taverna* stands on one of the island's best beaches, backed by weird, wind-sculpted rock formations.

Five kilometres along the inland road from Paroikia to Pounda a track leads off to the left to the **Valley of the Butterflies**. Organised excursions from Paroikia take you on a mule ride through the valley, but it's cheaper to take the bus run each day by the tourist office at 5.30pm. The valley, known in Greek as *petaloudhes* is fenced and closed each day from 1pm–4pm. In July and August especially it really does swarm with migratory moths.

From Pounda, boats shuttle across the narrow strait to the island of **ANTIPAROS**: it can also be reached from Paroikia in about 40 minutes. The island's great cave is still its chief attraction, although electric light and cement steps have taken away much of its mystery and grandeur. In these eerie chambers the eccentric Marquis de Nointel celebrated Christmas Mass in 1673 while 500 bemused but well paid Parians looked on:

at the exact moment of midnight explosives were detonated at the entrance to emphasise the enormity of the event. It's a stoney 30 min. hike from the island's port and village – time not really allowed by the excursion-boats.

Antiparos has just one small village, but there's a campsite 10 mins walk away to the north – a pleasant spot on the island's best beach with washing facilities and a small café.

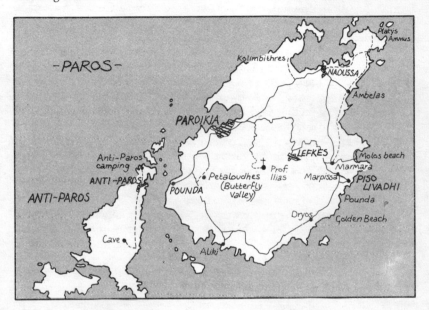

NAXOS

Naxos is the largest of the Cyclades, and with its green and mountainous interior it has a very different feel to many of its neighbours. Less immediately welcoming than, say, Paros, it is very beautiful, none the less, and with fine sandy beaches gets better the longer you stay.

Protecting the harbour on the north, a long causeway connects **NAXOS** town with the islet where legend has it that Theseus abandoned Ariadne on his way home from Crete. The huge stone lintel of a Temple of Apollo (never completed) still stands there. Most of the town's life is down by the harbour or in the streets just behind it, and despite the inroads made elsewhere by tourism this crowded front has changed hearteningly little. In one shop you can sample *kitron*, the island's lemon liqueur; another – upstairs – sells a selection of second-hand books in English. Down on the quay some of the *ouzeris* serve grilled octopus as *mezedhes* with their drinks. Narrow streets behind the harbour lead up eventually to the Kastro from which Marco Sanudo and his successors ruled over the Cyclades for the Venetians. Their Catholic descendants still live in the old houses, many of them with their ancient coat of arms above the crumbling doorway.

For the most part it is a quiet town, though there are a couple of discos, and there is rarely any problem about getting a room. You can sleep hidden from sight among the dunes on the long town beach at **Agios Georgios** where there are several tavernas and a windsurfing rental, but the beaches further out are more pleasant. **Agia Anna** is a short bus ride and its rooms and meals somewhat cheaper. **Plaka**, further on, is outstanding – its 5 km of sand looping round to a headland where you eventually reach **Kastraki** with the remains of a Mycenaean fortress and, an hour's walk inland, the Byzantine castle of T'apaliru. One word of warning, though: the plains behind all of these beaches are swampy and it's worth buying a few *fidhakia* mosquito coils before striking out.

Inland from Naxos town the road to Filoti rises from the coastal plain to a ring of villages littered with historic remains, chief among them **Sangri**. At the far end of the gorgeous Tragea valley, **Filoti**, the largest town in the region, lies on the slopes of Mount Sas (Zeus). This has rooms to rent in summer and its olive groves below make great walking country: among them you stumble across any number of Byzantine churches (invariably locked) and the ruins of fortified Venetian mansions. Look out for the once splendid Pirgos Francopoulos near **Chalki**: in the village itself are two Byzantine churches with frescoes. An hour's hike along goat tracks and over walls leads to the ruins of **Apano Kastro** – a stiff climb at the end but well rewarded by the views from the Venetian castle. The monastery **Panagia Drosani** is an even longer walk, but also worth while.

North of Filoti 2 or 3 buses a day continue to Apollon (48 km from Naxos, 30 from Filoti) along a road which zig-zags through a series of high villages. In **Apiranthos** the stone houses are unpainted, giving the village a dismal air – its port far below at **Multsuna** has a beach and several *tavernas*. **APOLLON** is more popular, a pleasant fishing village with rooms and *tavernas* near the beach. In the marble quarries nearby a gargantuan ancient statue (*kouros*) of Apollo lies unfinished. Two more of these *kouri* can be found at **Melanes**, inland on the bus route to Kinidaros. Much smaller than the one at Apollon – they're a mere 15 feet tall – these statues are far more finely detailed.

MINOR ISLES: KOUFONISSI, SCHINOUSSA, IRAKLIA AND DONOUSSA

In the stretch of the Aegean between Naxos and Amorgos there is a chain

of six small islands – neglected by tourists, by guidebooks and by the majority of Greeks, few of whom have ever heard of them. **Keros** (ancient Karos) is an important archaeological site but has no permanent population and **Kato Koufonissi** is inhabited only by goatherds. The other four islands, however, **Iraklia**, **Schinoussa**, **Ano Koufonissi** and **Donoussa**, are all inhabited, linked by ferry and can be visited. They have few facilities – no mains electricity, scarce water, few provisions in the shop(s), limited choice of food at the restaurant(s), no post office and no organised method of changing money – but this, of course, is most of the reason why you're going. Some knowledge of Greek, at least a phrasebook, is going to be necessary and you should be prepared to be regarded as a distinct curiosity. This said, though, if you're looking for peace and solitude – what the Greeks call *isychia* – you should be able to find it.
. . .

ANO KOUFONISSI (or just Koufonissi) is much the least primitive and, unlike the rest, is beginning to get a few Greek holidaymakers and some seasonal travellers. As it's also the smallest of the group – you can walk round it in an energetic morning – *isychia*, at least in July and August, may be on the way out. There is a new hotel in the solitary village and a number of rooms to rent, notably at the main *taverna*, the Alfroessa. On the east coast, back from a long sandy stretch of beach, there's another seasonal *taverna*. Camping hereabouts presents no problems except that you may have to walk some way for fresh water.

SCHINOUSSA, a short hop to the west, is probably the quietest of all Cycladic islands with a winter population of 85 and hardly any more through the summer. **Myrsini**, its tiny harbour hamlet, has a simple restaurant but the main settlement is at **Chora**, concealed on arrival but less than a mile's walk up the hill. Here, there are two sparse-stocked shops and two similarly endowed *tavernas*, one of which has a few rooms to let. Otherwise it's down to camping at the coarse grey beach (others in the group are fine and yellow) ten minutes below Chora on the south-west coast. Sitting or swimming here you can gaze out and reflect on the tourist-merged islands around – Paros, Naxos, Amorgos and Ios are all visible; a strange sensation.

IRAKLIA at the south-western end of the chain, and **DONOUSSA**, slightly isolated to the north, fall somewhere between the previous two – not as equipped for visitors as Koufonissi nor so primitive as Schinoussa. They are also a little larger and more mountainous, land for a good day's walking. **Donoussa**'s harbour village is its main settlement, and on **Iraklia** the old Chora, an hour's walk up in the hills, is now giving way to its very attractive harbour, Agios Georgios, set in a fertile valley at the head of a deep inlet. The Iraklia beach, Livadi, lies just off the road between the harbour and Chora and is pretty much ideal for camping.

Twice a week in summer one of the Piraeus **ferries** (usually the legendary *Miaoulis* or *Elli!*) calls at each of the islands and a local caique, the *Marianna*, makes the trip around three times a week between Koufonissi, Iraklia and Schinoussa and Naxos and Amorgos. Donoussa has the worst connections as the *Marianna* only calls once a week and the ferries to and from Piraeus always seem to turn up at 4 o'clock in the morning.

AMORGOS

Like Karpathos in the Dodecanese, Amorgos is virtually two islands: roads are so poor that by far the easiest way of getting between Katapola in the south and Egiali in the north is by ferry – they all call at both. Unlike Karpathos the island is often very crowded – with Germans particularly. It has a post office but as yet no bank.

KATAPOLA, the chief port, has rooms and pensions – the best among them *Dimitri's* in the old townhall – but most new arrivals end up sleeping in the fields or on the surrounding beach. Two statues stare it out across the bay: by Erato, muse of love poetry, there are good rocks to dive off. Steps lead up the hill from the harbour to the remains of the ancient city of **Minoa**, but the view is more interesting than what little can be made out of the ruins.

Chora is 40 mins walk away along numerous mule tracks, or there's a shambling old Dodge schoolbus. High up on the far side of the island, a line of windmills stretches out beyond its perfect Cycladic houses to the edge of precipitous cliffs. In summer it is so crowded that people sleep in the streets and the two restaurants are permanently packed, but off season it's still a tremendous place. As ever, a Venetian castle surveys the island from its summit above the town.

Near the bus stop, a path leads steeply down and round the cliffs to the left. Suddenly the monastery **Hosoviotissa** is before you, its vast wall shining out white below the towering orange cliffs. Only three monks occupy the fifty rooms now, but you can still see the C11th icon for which the monastery was founded along with a stack of other treasures; call between 8am–2pm.

In the other direction from Chora you get to the beach at Agia Anna, but for beauty and a bit more seclusion, the countryside and beaches to the south are recommended. A truck leaves Katapola for **Arkesini** daily, but you can walk it in two hours – the ancient town is near the coast at modern Kastri, and there are remains of tombs, walls and houses. Nearby **Agios Triada** has a well preserved pre-classical fort, known locally as **Pirgos**.

EGIALI, the northern port, is a good five hours' walk from Chora. It is beautiful deserted terrain, but going by boat is a lot easier. In summer the ferry services are augmented by regular caiques. Smaller than Katapola, Egiali has a more attractive beach and a genial atmosphere, though again there is no shortage of people there to appreciate it. Nearby are the Tholaria, vaulted tombs which date from Roman times.

IOS

No other island is quite like Ios, or attracts the same vast crowds of young people. The beach is almost as packed with sleeping bags at night as it is with naked bodies by day, and nightlife in the village is long and loud. But crowded as it is, the island hasn't been commercialised in the same way as Mykonos – mainly because none of the visitors (a remarkable proportion of them Irish) have much money. You're either going to decide that Ios is the island paradise you have always been looking for and stay for weeks, as many people do, or hate it and take the next boat out, an equally common reaction.

Almost all the visitors stay in the triangle delineated by the port, Gialos, Ios Town above it and the beach at Milopota Bay. It's a small area, and you soon get to know your way around: two buses constantly shuttle between the three places – you should never wait more than 15 minutes. There is accommodation in all three places, but most of the cheap rooms are in **IOS**, a 20 minute walk up the mountain behind the port. The old white village is becoming overwhelmed by the number of tourists, but it still has a certain charm and some of the windmills on the hill behind are actually in working order. Every evening the streets throb to music from hordes of competing discos and clubs: they're all free to get into, but drinks are expensive. There are plenty of places to eat too, but the *tavernas* in **GIALOS** are more authentically Greek, and you can occasionally escape western culture and hear Greek music down here. The port is also home to the Tourist Information centre, to a small beach, and to the worst of three campsites. The other two are at **MILOPOTA**, the better of them right at the beginning of the beach – anyone can use their showers for a small price.

Despite occasional raids – the police have been known to turn very nasty here – hundreds of people sleep on the beach every night. If there's safety in numbers, you should be all right. A much worse problem is the water shortage, which has dire effects above all on local toilets. Things get particularly grim in Gialos, but even in the *tavernas* on the beach only the desperate and the foolish dare venture out the back. In the village, where there's much more choice, you may find a toilet which flushes, although officially water is too scarce to be used for so frivolous a purpose.

From Gialos boats run at about 9 every morning to **Manganari Bay**, where there is a beach and an upmarket hotel, and to **Psathis Bay**, another popular beach. A 3–4-hour walk across the island will take you to the infinitely preferable **Agios Theodotis Bay**. Nearby is a monastery and a ruined castle, while on the superb beach are the remains of huts which used to be part of a beach club complex and now make excellent places to sleep. So far it's little visited and totally undeveloped, so take provisions.

SIKINOS

Sikinos has so small a population that the mule ride or walk up from the port to the village has not yet been replaced by the usual bus. And with no dramatic characteristics, nor any nightlife to speak of, few foreigners seem to make the short trip over here from neighbouring Ios or well connected Paros, Naxos and Thira.

Yet walking up from the little harbour of **Allopronia**, with its *tavernas*, handful of rooms and sandy beach, the scenery turns out more beautiful than the desolate first impression suggests. **CHORA** itself is a really charming place, quite untouched by tourism though with generally enough rooms to go round. A ruined monastery, Zoodochos Pigi ('spring of life', a frequent name on the Cyclades), crowns the rock above and there are some good basic *tavernas*.

Round the coast you come upon some peaceful, though waterless, beaches while inland are the remains of a Roman temple and, in the extreme north, of an ancient castle. In antiquity the quality of Sikinos wine was widely praised but the local retsina would hardly deserve much of a reputation now.

As well as the regular ferries there are local caiques to Ios and Folegandros. There is no bank.

FOLEGANDROS

The cliffs of Folegandros rise in places over 1000 ft sheer from the sea, a deterrent to tourists as they always were to pirates. It is traditionally an island of political exile, and was used as such in recent decades, but life in the high barren interior has been eased over the last few years by the arrival of electricity and the construction of a road from the harbour to Chora. There are still relatively few visitors and an equivalent dearth of rooms – since ferries mostly roll in around 9.30pm you'll do best to resign yourself to camping, at least for the first night.

Karavostassis, the harbour, is a popular base, its *tavernas* and much-sought rooms a short walk from the beach. A little further round, in the next bay, is the village of **Livadi** and the island's official campsite (sporadically supplied with water); the beach here is fine and shaded, the three *tavernas* mediocre.

The island's real character and appeal is in the **CHORA**, 45 mins walk or a quick bus ride from the port at the far edge of a plateau above the coast. In the town's two plateias villagers meet under the plane trees to collect their water, and in the evening sit passing the time in the *kafeneia*. To the right the houses back on to soaring cliffs – site of the medieval **kastro**, now marked by a square of two-storey houses. The addition of doors and stairways to the outside wall masks its real nature and you get a better feel of the place by walking round inside.

There is a hotel in the **kastro** and a guest house on the far side of town as well as a few rooms in private houses. The post office is here too, Folegandros being another island without a bank. Just above the town, past the cemetery, a zig-zag track with views down to both coastlines leads to the beautiful church of Panagia; beyond it is **Hrissospilia**, a cave with stalactites, but you'll need a guide or close instructions to find it.

The best beach on the island is at **Vathi**, on the opposite coast to the harbour but under an hour's walk (north-west and left down to the sea) from Chora. There are a few other small settlements further round, all in good hiking countryside.

THIRA (SANTORINI)

As the ferryboat manoeuvres into the great caldera of Santorini, the land seems to rise up and clamp around it. Gaunt, sheer cliffs loom hundreds of feet above, nothing grows or grazes to soften the view and the only colours are the reddish-brown, black and grey pumice layers embedded in the cliff face. The landscape tells of a history so dramatic and turbulent that legend hangs as fact upon it. From as early as 3000 BC the island developed as a sophisticated outpost of Minoan civilisation until, around 1450 BC, came catastrophe – the volcano-island erupted, its heart sank below the sea, and earthquakes reverberated across the Aegean. Thira was destroyed and with it, it is believed, toppled the great Minoan civilisations on Crete. It is this point of the island's history that has become linked with legends of Atlantis, the 'Happy Isles Submerged by Sea'. Plato insisted that the legend was true and Solon dated the catastrophe to 9000 years before his time: if you're willing to accept a mistake and knock off the final 0, a highly plausible date.

Evidence of the Minoan outpost was found at **Akrotiri**, a village buried under banks of volcanic ash on the south-west horn of the island. Tunnels through the ash uncovered structures, two and three storeys high, first damaged by earthquake then buried by eruption. Lavish frescoes adorned the walls, and Cretan pottery was found stored in a chamber. Professor Marinatos – the excavator and now an island hero – was killed by a collapsing wall and is buried on the site. Akrotiri (open 9–1.30 and 4–6) can be reached by bus from Phira or Perissa. The frescoes are currently exhibited in Athens, but there are plans to bring them back when a new museum is built.

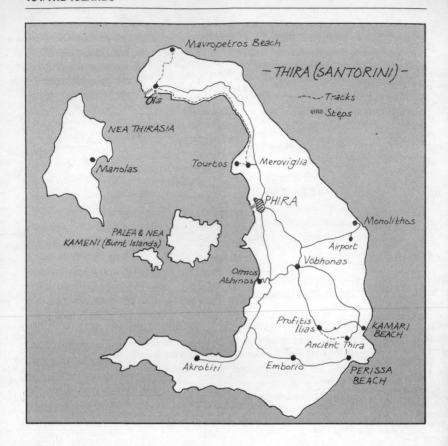

Boats dock at either **Skala Phira** or the tiny somewhat grim port of **Ormos Athinios**, occasionally also at **Oia** in the north. Buses, astonishingly crammed, connect Athinios with the island capital Phira and, less frequently, with the main beaches at Kamari and Perissa: take whatever's going, it's a hefty walk. Docking at Skala Phira you have the traditional route above you – 680 mule-spattered steps to the Chora, or Phira as it's usually known.

Half rebuilt after an earthquake in 1956, **PHIRA** still lurches manically on the cliff edge. Though besieged by hordes of day trippers from the cruise-boats it is an attractive place, if notably more pricey than other Cyclades. Rooms are often tricky to find, even out of season (when the police allow only hotels to stay open). Take any reasonable offer, including places just outside the town, and if you want one of the best rooms, a few steps down the cliffside, reserve a place for the first space going. At the north end of town there's a youth hostel, often full to the gills and oppressively airless, but none too bad if you take one of the cheaper mattresses on the roof.

There are bus services from Thira to most points on the island, worth avoiding if you can afford to rent a bike or moped (from either here, Kamari or Perissa), and boat trips are also routed for the burnt **volcanic islets** and the little visited islet-village of Thirassia. If you can get together a group of people go down early to the port and bargain for your own boat; wear footwear that stands up to the sharp lava surface. And, finally, in Phira there's a very respectable **Archaeological Museum** with a curious collection of erotic Dionysiac figures.

OIA, in the north-west of the island, was once a major fishing port of the Aegean but has declined in the wake of depression, wars, earthquakes and depleted fish. Partly destroyed in the 1956 quake, it presents a curious mix of pristine white rebuilding and ramshackle ruins clinging to the cliff face – by any standards one of the most beautiful and dramatic towns of the Cyclades. It is also much the calmest place on the island though if you want to stay rooms aren't too easy to come by. The NTOG has restored some of the old houses as guest-hostels, all on the pricey side, and the only real alternative is Pension Lauda, a small friendly troglodytic place. Below the town steps switchback hundreds of metres to two small harbours – **Ammoudi**, for the fishermen, and **Armeni** where the ferries occasionally dock. Off the cement platform at Ammoudi you can swim amidst a sea of floating pumice and snorkel amongst shoals of giant fish. At Armeni a single *taverna* specialises in grilled octopus lunches. Beware the currents around the church-islet of Agios Nikolaos.

It is 12 km from Phira to Oia, easy enough by bus but infinitely more satisfying if you walk the stretch from **Meroviglio** – along a tremendous footpath on the lip of the caldera. Nearby Meroviglio, too, is the old Venetian citadel of **Tourlos** on Cape Skaros.

Beaches on Santorini are surprising – long black stretches of volcanic sand which get blisteringly hot in the afternoon sun. **Perissa**, less commercial and more attractively situated than **Kamari**, has the island's campsite but the beach extends so far that there is little problem if you want to find your own tamarisk tree to sleep beneath. There are rooms to rent and seafront *tavernas* at both, but Perissa has the finest restaurant on the island: the Hotel Christi, set back a little way down the beach. The two villages are divided by a jutting headland, Mesa Vouno, on which stood **ancient Thira**. Taxis go up from Kamari, but they're expensive – the best route is on foot from Perissa following a dwindling track up past the hillside chapel. Though they are impressively large, most of the ruins are difficult to place. The view from the theatre, however, is awesome – beyond the stage a sheer drop to the sea: when it was discovered in the 1890s the uniformed band from Phira trooped all the way up to give a concert.

Inland along the same mountain spine and accessible, alas, by tourbus is the monastery of Mount **Profitis Ilias**, now sharing its spiritual refuge with a NATO station whose pylons it will hopefully outlive. Normally Greek monasteries will only show visitors their Katholikon, or main chapel building, but here you're free to wander about the old workshops and cells of the monks, too. They're open from 8–1 and 2.30–6 and have been converted to house a fascinating folklore museum of the old monastic crafts – from winemaking to leatherwork. The easiest approach is probably taking the Perissa/Kamari-Phira bus as far as the village of Pirgos, half an hour's walk below. From near the entrance to the monastery an old footpath heads across the ridge in about 40 mins to ancient Thira.

Thira's volcanic soil is highly fertile, and every piece seems terraced and cultivated. Wheat, small sweet tomatoes, pistachios and grapes are the main crops, all still harvested and planted by hand. The island's *visanto* and *nichteri* wines are a little sweet for most tastes but are among the finest produced in the Cyclades.

ANAFI

An hour's ride to the east of Thira, Anafi is the end of the line for most of the ferries which call there – and another excellent refuge from mid-season crowds. Once or twice a week there'll be a boat going on to Crete or some of the Dodecanese so it can prove a useful halting post, too.

It is a small, rather harsh island with a population of just under 300, almost all of whom live on the south coast. Here, the harbour village has two tavernas, two shops and a handful of houses whilst **CHORA** perches on a conical hill immediately above. The cliffs are too steep for a proper road and the mule track can take nothing more than a motorbike but in any case there are no cars on the island since there is nowhere for them to go. Exposed and very windy indeed when the Meltemi is blowing, Chora has a few rooms to let but only one *taverna* and surprisingly few *kafeneia*. It is one of those villages where the men sit inside rather than out to drink their coffee and play backgammon and at first the place seems a somewhat forbidding ghost town. This impression is slowly dispelled, particularly if you've some knowledge of Greek, as the people of Anafi are really very hospitable. There may not be a wide choice of food in the *tavernas* but the few tiny shops have fresh fruit at the right time of year, there's a good bakery and also a post office. No one should starve, despite ominous warnings in some guides who haven't visited the place!

The harbour, with its tavernas serving fresh fish and little crabs, is the best place to be in the evenings, though if you're staying in Chora there's a stiff climb back – torch essential unless it's a full moon.

There is a beach with another taverna at **Klisidi,** a short walk along the cliffs to the east of the harbour, and further along (in the south-east corner of the island) is the monastery of **Panagia Kalamiotissa,** built on the site of an ancient temple of Apollo and incorporating part of its masonry. In the mountainous north of the island you come upon a ruined Venetian castle whilst numerous tracks lead from Chora into the interior; most seem not to lead anywhere in particular but it's all good walking country. The island is extremely dry, however, and outside the main villages you'll need to take water with you on any hikes.

TRAVEL DETAILS

Most islands in the Cyclades are served by boats from Piraeus, but there are also ferries which start from **Lavrio** (for Kea and Kithnos) and **Rafina** (for Andros, Tinos, Mykonos, Syros, Paros and Naxos). Both are easily reached by bus from Athens. The most complicated and least reliable of the ships – the *SS Kyklades* – has been left out to simplify these lists. Its route is Piraeus (starting Saturday evening), Milos, Folegandros, Thira, Anafi, Agios Nikolaos and Sitia (Crete), Kassos, Karpathos, Chalki, Rhodes (Monday morning), Kos, Kalimnos, Leros, Ikaria, Samos, Chios, Mytilini (Lesvos), Limnos and Kavala on the northern mainland. Then it turns round and goes back through all of them, getting back to Piraeus on Friday: BUT, it is frequently as much as two days late and sometimes doesn't show up at all so isn't for those on tight schedules.

KEA Daily to Lavrio (2½ hrs), once a week to Kithnos.

KITHNOS Five a week to Piraeus (4 hrs). Four to Serifos, Sifnos, Milos. Four or five weekly to Lavrio.

SERIFOS AND SIFNOS Daily to Piraeus (5 hrs) and each other. Four a week to Kithnos and Milos, three to Ios and Thira.

MILOS Daily to Piraeus (5½ hrs). Four a week to Sifnos (2 hrs), Serifos, Kithnos; three to Ios and Thira. Twice weekly to Iraklion (Crete – 8 hrs), Siros and Folegandros. Daily flight to Athens.

KIMOLOS Daily to Pollonia (Milos). Twice a week to Sifnos, Serifos, Kithnos, Piraeus (6 hrs).

ANDROS Daily to Rafina (3 hrs) and Tinos (2 hrs). Three a week to Mykonos and Syros.

TINOS Daily to Piraeus (5 hrs), Rafina (4 hrs), Andros, Siros and Mykonos. Twice weekly to Paros.

SIROS Daily to Piraeus (4½ hrs), Tinos (1 hr), Mykonos (2 hrs), Naxos and Paros. Four times a week to Iraklion (Crete), Thira, Andros and Rafina. Twice to Folegandros and Sikinos.

MYKONOS Daily to Piraeus (5½ hrs), Tinos (1 hr) and Siros (2 hrs). Three times a week to Rafina (5 hrs), and Andros. Daily caique to Delos. Flights daily

to Athens and three times a week to Rhodes.

DELOS Daily caique to Mykonos.

PAROS Daily to Piraeus (7 hrs), Naxos, Ios, Thira, Siros; twice weekly to Tinos, once to Samos. Seasonal caiques to Antiparos and to Sifnos and Naxos. Daily flights to Athens.

NAXOS Daily to Piraeus (8 hrs), Paros (1 hr), Siros, Ios, Thira; less often to Iraklion, Schinoussa, Koufonissi, Donoussa and Amorgos. Seasonal caiques to Paros.

KOUFONISSI, SCHINOUSSA, IRAKLIA AND DONOUSSA Twice a week to Piraeus, Naxos and each other; seasonal caique to Naxos, see text.

AMORGOS Daily to Naxos (4 hrs). Twice weekly to Piraeus (11 hrs), Astipalea, Simi and Rhodes (9 hrs). Once to Rafina (10 hrs), Tinos, Paros, Kos, Kalimnos, Tilos and Nissiros.

IOS Daily to Piraeus (10 hrs), Paros (5 hrs), Naxos (3 hrs), Siros (1 hr) and Thira (2 hrs). Four weekly to Iraklion (Crete). Small boats to Sikinos and Folegandros daily, Anafi less often. Three a week to Milos, Serifos and Sifnos.

SIKINOS Daily to Ios and Folegandros, frequently to Thira. Once a week to Siros and Piraeus (10½ hrs).

FOLEGANDROS Daily to Ios (45 min) and Sikinos. Several weekly to Thira, two to Piraeus (12 hrs) and Siros.

THIRA Daily to Piraeus (10–12 hrs), Paros, Ios and Naxos. Four a week to Iraklion (Crete – 5 hrs). Frequently by small boat to Anafi, Sikinos and Folegandros. Agios Nikolaos and Sitia (Crete), Karpathos, Kassos, Halki and Rhodes all once every week. Flights daily to Athens.

ANAFI Twice a week to Thira (2 hrs) and Piraeus (18 hrs). Once to Ios, Agios Nikolaos (Crete – 4 hrs), Karpathos and Rhodes.

'FLYING DOLPHIN' HYDROFOILS During the summer hydrofoils connect SYROS, NAXOS, PAROS, MYKONOS, TINOS and IOS several times a day. They are about twice as expensive as the ferries, but more than twice as fast.

Chapter six
CRETE

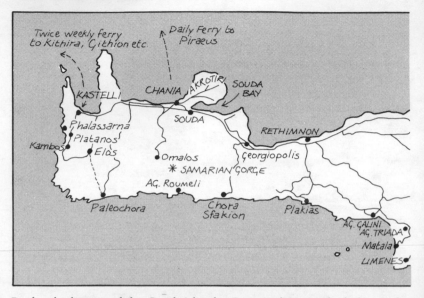

By far the largest of the Greek islands, Crete is distinguished also as the home of Europe's earliest civilisation. It was only at the beginning of this century that the legends of King Minos, and of a Cretan society which ruled the Greek world in prehistory, were confirmed by excavations at Knossos and Phaestos. Yet the **Minoans** had a remarkably advanced society, at the centre of a maritime trading empire, as early as 2000 BC. The artworks produced on Crete at this time are unsurpassed anywhere in the ancient world and it seems clear, wandering through the Minoan palaces and towns, that life on Crete in those days was good. Their peaceful culture survived at least three major natural disasters. Each time the palaces were destroyed, but they were rebuilt on an even grander scale. It is only after the last destruction – probably the result of a massive eruption of Thira (Santorini) and subsequent tidal waves and earthquakes – that significant numbers of weapons begin to appear in the ruins. This, together with the appearance of the Greek language, is taken to mean that Mycenaean Greeks had taken control of the island. Nevertheless for nearly 500 years, by far the longest period of peace the island has seen, Crete was home to a civilisation well ahead of its time.

The Minoans of Crete came originally from Asia Minor; at their height they maintained strong links with Egypt and with the people of Asia Minor, and this position as a meeting point between east and west has played a major role in Crete's subsequent history. Control of the island passed from Greeks to Romans to Saracens, through the Byzantine Empire to Venice, and finally Turkey for 200 years. During the Second

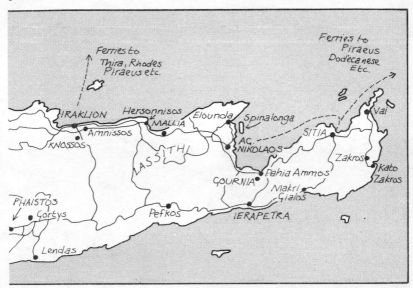

World War the island was occupied by the Germans, and gained the dubious distinction of being the first place to be successfully invaded by parachute. Each one of these diverse rulers have left some mark on Crete.

Today, with a flourishing agricultural economy, Crete is one of the few islands which could probably support itself without tourists. Nevertheless tourism is heavily promoted. The north-east coast in particular is over-developed and, though there are parts of the south and west coasts which have not been spoilt, they are getting harder and harder to find. By contrast, the high mountains of the interior are still barely touched, and one of the best things to do on Crete is to hire a vespa and explore the remote villages round the coast which are only a few kilometres off the beaten track.

Every part of Crete has its loyal devotees and it's hard to pick out highlights – but on the whole if you want to get away from it all you should head west, towards **Chania** and smaller less well connected places along the coast like **Falassarna** or **Paleohora**. It is in this part of the island, too, that the White Mountains rise, and below them the famous **Samarian Gorge**. Whatever you do though the first main incentive is to get as far away from **Iraklion** (Heraklion) as quickly as possible – having paid the obligatory, and rewarding, visit to nearby **Knossos**. The other great Minoan sites are in a tight concentration around the centre of the south coast – at **Phaistos, Agia Triada** and **Gortys** – but there are palaces too around the north-east coast at **Mallia, Gournia** and **Zakros**. For many people, unexpected highlights also turn out to be Crete's Venetian forts – dominant at Rethimnon, above all, but found in various stages of ruin around most of the island.

As the southernmost of all Greek islands Crete has by far the longest summers and you can get a decent tan here right into October and swim pretty much through the year. Its agricultural importance, and the several annual harvests, also make it the most promising (if also the most sought) location for finding **casual work**. The cucumber and pickling factories around Ierapetra have proved winter lifelines for many long-term Greek travellers. The one seasonal blight is the *Meltemi*, which blows harder here and more continuously than anywhere else in Greece: just one of the reasons for avoiding an **August** visit.

IRAKLION, KNOSSOS AND THE EAST

IRAKLION

Most visitors to Crete arrive in **Iraklion**, but it's not a beautiful city, or one where you'll want to stay longer than it takes to get your bearings and visit the museum and nearby Knossos.

The **Archaeological Museum** (open 9am–3pm; 10am–2pm Sun) is in the city's main square, Plateia Eleftheria, directly opposite the offices of the NTOG. Almost every important prehistoric and Minoan find on Crete is included in this fabulous, if bewilderingly large, collection. The museum tends to be crowded – especially when a guided tour stampedes through – but it's worth taking time over; the Hall of the Frescoes, where fragments of the wall paintings from Knossos and other sites have been intricately pieced together, is especially wonderful.

Massive Venetian **walls**, in places up to 45 feet thick, still encircle the old city, but though their fabric has been painstakingly restored, access is virtually impossible. It is possible – just – to walk on top of them from St Anthony's bastion over the sea in the west as far as the tomb of Nikos Kazantzakis, Cretan author of *Zorba the Greek*. Its inscription reads: 'I

Cretan tourist offices stock free maps of the island with townplans of Iraklion, Chania and Rethimnon believe in nothing, I hope for nothing, I am free.' At the weekend Iraklians gather here to pay their respects and get a free view of the football ground below.

In the early evening, especially on Sundays, the city bursts into colourful life as the entire population turns out to parade in their finery: respectable citizens in Plateia Eleftheria, modern youth in Venizelou Square. These two, both crowded with cafés and restaurants, and the streets between them, are the heart of tourist life – and expensive. Much better **places to eat** are in the streets surrounding the market on Odos 1866, while cheaper **accommodation** can be found near the Chania Gate at the bottom of Kalokairinou Street, or around the *youth hostel* on Handakos, below Venizelou Square. The park between the harbour and the east-bound bus station is also crowded most nights – if you're really hard up it's a doubly good place to sleep as local farmers in need of labour come round recruiting in the morning, especially at harvest time. The no. 2 **bus for Knossos** sets off from down here, picking up passengers in Venizelou Square on its way to the site.

Buses for all points to the east leave from the new station by the harbour; south to Ano Vianos, Mirthos and Arvi from just outside the walls at Evans Gate; south-west to Phaistos, Matala, Lendas and Agia Galini from outside Chania Gate; and west to Rethymnon and Chania from the waterfront to the left of the harbour and the Venetian fort. Next to this last is the **Historical Museum**, with a collection of folk costumes and local memorabilia. If for nothing else, you should visit it for the beautifully nonsensical English labelling. **Shipping agencies** are on Odos 25 Augostou, which runs up from the inner harbour to Venizelou Square; Creta Tours have good **free maps** as well as running coach trips to every conceivable part of Crete and cruises to the Pyramids.

KNOSSOS (Weekdays 8–7, Suns – when it's free – 10–2)

As soon as you enter the **palace** through the West Court, the ancient ceremonial entrance, it is clear how the legends of the labyrinth grew up around it. Even with a detailed plan, it's almost impossible to find your way around the site with any success. Knossos was liberally 'restored' by Sir Arthur Evans, who discovered and excavated it at the turn of the century, and these restorations have been the source of furious controversy among archaeologists ever since. It has become clear that much of Evans's upper level – the Piano Nobile – is pure conjecture. Even so, his guess as to what the palace might have looked like is certainly as good as anyone else's could be, and it makes the other sites much more interesting if you have seen Knossos first. Without the restorations, it would be almost impossible to imagine the grandeur of the palace or to see the ceremonial stairways, strange top-heavy pillars and gaily painted walls which distinguish the site.

The superb **royal apartments** around the central staircase and the imposing Throne Room are not guesswork, and they are among the finest of the rooms at Knossos. Look out, too, for the drainage system – guides to the site never fail to point out these clay pipes as proof of the advanced state of Minoan civilisation, but you can't help wondering how they worked on a hill which has no natural water supply. The **Royal Road** on the east side used to run all the way to Phaistos, and on the far side of the ravine is the Caravanserai where ancient travellers would rest and water their animals. There's no lack of watering holes for modern travellers either, and **rooms** at the site are considerably cheaper than they would be in Iraklion. Staying here is one way to get to the site before the crowds.

EAST: AMNISSOS AND THE PLATEAU LASSITHI

East of Iraklion the startling pace of tourist development in Crete can be seen clearly. The merest hint of a beach is an excuse to build at least one hotel, and these are outnumbered by the concrete shells of rivals-to-be. It's hard to find a room in this monument to the package tour, and expensive if you do. **Amnissos** (no. 1 bus from Plateia Eleftheria) is one of the better beaches easily accessible from the city. Little remains to indicate that it once flourished as a port for Knossos – nowadays the long stretch of sand is strewn with tourists and litter – but for a day out from Iraklion it's not bad. The *taverna* is friendly, a campsite offers basic facilities, and no one will object if you sleep on the beach.

As a general rule, the further you go, the better things get: when the road veers inland for an all-too-brief while, the real Crete – olive groves and stark mountains – reveals itself. Beyond the NATO base at Gournes is the turning for the **Plateau Lassithi**. Scores of coach tours drive up here daily to view the thousands of white cloth-sailed windmills which irrigate the high plain. They make two stops, at Kroustellania Monastery in Tzermiadon, and at Psichro for the Diktean Cave, mythical birthplace of Zeus. Although there are disappointingly few working windmills left – a short walk out of any village will reveal that most are rusting on the ground – the trip is worth making; it would be for the drive up alone. Stay in one of the villages for a night or two: when the tourists have left, real life returns. **Tzermiadon**, the local capital, **Aglos Georgios** and **Psichro** all have places to stay. The path up to the **Diktean cave** leads from Psichro and, whatever you're told, you don't have to have a guide if you don't want one, though you will need some form of illumination. On the other hand it is not expensive for a small group to be taken down, and much more interesting. It takes a Cretan imagination to pick out Rhea and the baby Zeus from the other stalactites and stalagmites. The plateau is at its best in midsummer, but in the autumn the trees are weighed down with fruit which no one seems to want to pick. You can fill your pockets with apples and pears safe in the knowledge that they'll only rot if you don't.

Buses run to Psichro from both Iraklion and Neapolis. The latter is an even more mountainous road, coiling through a succession of passes guarded by lines of ruined windmills.

MALLIA AND NEAPOLIS

Back on the coast the road passes the ancient city of **Hersonissos**, now an established tourist trap, before it reaches **MALLIA**. The long sandy beach here can get very crowded, but there are dunes at the end where you can sleep out and two campsites. One is just off the beach, the other at the youth hostel about 15 mins walk inland. The cheapest rooms are also around the hostel. The Minoan Palace (open sunrise to sunset except Sundays; free) is 40 mins walk east of the town on the main road. Any bus will stop, or hire a bike for a couple of hours – it's a pleasant, flat ride. Mallia is much less imposing than either Knossos or Phaistos, but in some ways it surpasses both. For a start, it's much less visited and you can wander among the remains in relative peace. While no reconstruction has been attempted, the palace was never reoccupied after its second destruction, so the ground plan is virtually intact. If you've been to Knossos it's easy to envisage this seaside palace in its days of glory. From this site came the famous gold pendant of two bees (which can be seen in the museum or on any postcard stand), allegedly part of a horde which was plundered and can now be found in the British Museum. The beautiful leopard's head axe, also in the museum at Iraklion, was another of the treasures found here. To the south and east of the palace digs are still going on as an apparently sizeable town comes slowly to light.

The road continues towards **NEAPOLIS**, soon beginning a spectacular climb into the mountains. Set in a high valley, Neapolis is a market town little touched by tourism. There is one hotel, a modern church and a tiny museum which rarely opens, but will usually do so on request. Beyond the town it is about 20 minutes before the bus suddenly emerges high above the Gulf of Mirabello and Agios Nikolaos, now the island's biggest resort.

AGIOS NIKOLAOS, ELOUNDA AND SPINALONGA

AGIOS NIKOLAOS is set around a supposedly bottomless lake, now connected to the sea to form an inner harbour. It is beautifully picturesque, and exploits it to the full. The lake and harbour are surrounded by restaurants and bars, all charging well above the odds. By the lake also is the tourist police office and an aviary from which most of the birds seem to have been liberated. Although it is marked on most maps, there is no longer a youth hostel in Agios Nikolaos. Instead many of the cheaper **pensions** offer mattresses on the roof – the Pension Regina on Odos Koritsas for one, and others near it. The stony beach is by the bus station, but you'd need a strong masochistic streak to sleep on it; far better, really, to head straight out to the little sandy coves at **Istro** (12 km) or **Pahia Ammos**, just beyond the fascinating site of **Gournia**.

The riviera set hang out along the coast road to the west. Hotels here come with bungalows, pools, private beaches and five-star cuisine, while between them are cocktail bars – all soft lighting and tinkling pianos – and upmarket discos. **ELOUNDA** is about 8 km out along this road. Buses run regularly but if you feel like hiring a moped it is a spectacular ride with impeccable views over a Gulf dotted with islands and moored supertankers. Check the brakes first. Just before the village a track (signed) leads across the causeway to the 'sunken city' of **Olous**. There are restored windmills, Venetian salt pans and a well preserved dolphin mosaic, but of the sunken city itself no sign beyond a couple of walls in about two feet of water.

From Elounda, caiques run to the fortress rock of **SPINALONGA**. As a bastion of the Venetian defence, this tiny islet withstood the Turkish invaders for 45 years after the mainland had fallen. In more recent years it served as a leper colony. As you watch the boat which brought you disappear to pick up another load, an unnervingly real sense of the desolation of those years descends over the place. **Plaka** used to be the colony's supply centre: now it is a haven from the crowds with a small pebble beach and a couple of ramshackle *tavernas*. There are boat trips daily from Agios Nikolaos to Olous, Elounda and Spinalonga, usually taking in at least one other island along the way.

GOURNIA

The most completely preserved Minoan town, **GOURNIA** slumps in the saddle between two low peaks – its narrow alleys and stairways inter-secting a throng of one-roomed houses centred on a main square and the house of the local ruler. Although less impressive than the great palaces, the site is compelling in its revelations about the lives of the people ruled from Knossos. Its desolation today – you are likely to be alone save for a sleeping guard – only heightens the contrast with what must have been a cramped and raucous community three and a half thousand years ago.

It is tempting to cross the road here and take one of the paths through the thyme to the sea and a swim. Don't – this seemingly innocent little bay acts as a magnet for every piece of floating detritus dumped off

Crete's north coast. There is a clean beach, and pleasant rooms to rent, in the next valley at **Pahia Ammos**, about 20 mins walk.

This is the narrowest part of the island, and from here a road cuts across the isthmus to Ierapetra in the south. In the north, though, the route on towards Sitia is one of the most dramatic in Crete. Carved into cliffs and mountainsides, the road teeters above the coast before plunging inland at Kavousi. Nearer Sitia the familiar olive groves are interspersed with vineyards, and in late summer the grapes, laid to dry in the fields and on rooftops, make an extraordinary sight in the varying stages of their slow change from green to gold to brown.

ROUND THE EAST: SITIA, VAI BEACH AND ZAKROS

The port and main town for the relatively unexploited eastern edge of Crete, **SITIA** is a pleasant if unremarkable place with a plethora of waterfront restaurants and a long sandy beach. There are also plenty of cheap pensions and rooms, a youth hostel on the outskirts and rarely any problem about sleeping on the beach though it is worth going a little way out of town to avoid any danger of being moved on. The lazy local lifestyle is little affected even by the thousands of visitors in peak season. The rusting hulk of a tanker sits just off shore, providing endless fun for snorkellers, and in the town there is a folklore museum which is well worth visiting.

Beyond the beach, the Vai road climbs above a rocky, unexceptional coastline before reaching a fork to the **Monastery of Toplou**. The monastery's forbidding exterior reflects a history of resistance to invaders, but doesn't prepare you for the gorgeous flower-decked cloister within. The blue-robed monks keep out of the way as far as possible, but their cells and refectory are left discreetly on view. In the church is one of the masterpieces of Cretan art, the C18th icon 'Lord Thou Art Great'. Reproductions are sold here at vast expense.

Vai Beach is famous for its palm trees, and the sudden appearance of the grove is indeed an exotic shock. Lying on the fine sand in the early morning, the dream of Caribbean islands is hard to dismiss. During the day, though, the beach fills as buses pour in in numbers which you begin to think are hardly justified by a few palm trees. As everywhere, notices warn that 'Camping is forbidden by law': they make convenient points to anchor guy ropes. If you do sleep here, watch your belongings – this seems to be the one place on Crete which has crime on any scale. By day you can find solitude by climbing the rocks or swimming to one of the smaller beaches which surround Vai. **Itanos**, 20 mins walk north by an obvious trail, has a couple of tiny beaches and some modest Minoan ruins.

The Minoan palace and town of **ZAKROS** lie around the coast to the south. There is a hotel and several tavernas where the bus drops you, but the palace is actually at Kato Zakros, an 8-km hike down a rough road to the sea. The walk is along an impressive gorge, but it's a lot easier to come with a tour or to hitch the last bit. The eastern end of Crete is slowly sinking, and the west rising, so although the site is some way from the sea, parts of it, including the queen's quarters, are often marshy and waterlogged. Among the remains of narrow streets and small houses higher up you can keep your feet dry and get an excellent view down over the central court and royal apartments. The village of **Kato Zakros** is little more than a collection of *tavernas*, some of which rent out rooms, around a peaceful beach.

IERAPETRA AND THE SOUTH-EAST COAST

From Sitia the route south is a cross-country big dipper ride until it hits the south coast at **MAKRI GIALOS**. This little fishing village has one of the best beaches at this end of Crete. Its fine sand shelves so gently that you start to think you are going to walk the 200 miles to Africa. At present there are a few rooms to rent, but a clutch of deserted restaurants and the shell of a hotel warn of imminent development, so hurry. There is little reason to stop between here and Ierapetra; the few beaches are rocky, the coastal plain submerged under hordes of polythene-covered greenhouses.

IERAPETRA is a drab concrete town and a supply centre for the region's farmers. *Tavernas* along the tree-lined front are pleasant enough, though, and the beach stretches for a couple of miles to the east, its furthest extremities rarely visited. Unfortunately the best swimming is right in the town, the most crowded section. The town has been a port since Roman times, but of its past only the Venetian fort guarding the harbour and a crumbling minaret remain. What little else has been salvaged is in the one-room museum near the post office. Ierepetra's **youth hostel** is about 10 mins walk away from the town, towards Makri Gialos; it can be a useful first source of information about work, though don't be put off by the warden himself.

CENTRAL CRETE

RETHIMNON AND THE COAST TO CHANIA

Most people prefer Chania, but for me **RETHIMNON** is the most beautiful of Crete's major towns. A wide sandy beach and palm-lined promenade front a labyrinthine tangle of Venetian and Turkish houses. And in the streets some of the old men still dress majestically in high boots, baggy trousers (*vrakes*) and black head scarves. Dominating everything is the superbly preserved fortress built by the Venetians after a series of pirate raids had devastated the town.

When you get off the bus, walk down the hill; the tourist information office is to the right down the first main street, the beach and most of the hotels straight ahead and to the left. If you can't find a room, Rethimnon's *youth hostel* (Palou 7: just off Arkadhio, the main shopping street) is a passable alternative, or there are campsites a short way out of town in either direction. With the beach right in the centre of town, the police tend to clamp down on unofficial campers at night and on topless bathers by day. Some of the nicest parts of town are away from the beach in the streets behind the harbour. The small museum is here, as well as the mosque – climb the minaret for some excellent views over the town and surrounding countryside. At ground level local craftsmen sit in front of their workshops plying their trades and talking. In the same area you can also eat better and cheaper than in the tourist *tavernas* which line the waterfront. Nearby the old Arimonti fountain is the *I Gaspari* bakery – with that rare godsend in Greece, fresh brown bread. Motorbike and *moped rental* seems a little cheaper in Rethimnon than elsewhere, a proliferation of outlets in the centre of town giving you the bargaining edge.

Inland and a short bus journey from Rethimnon lies the **monastery of Arkadi**, which played a major role in the 1866 rising against the Turks and is something of a national Cretan shrine. Monks and rebels besieged here, seeing their position was hopeless, torched a powder magazine and took several hundred Turkish attackers with them. You can peer into the roofless vault and wander about the rest of the well-restored monastery grounds, including a startling C16th Venetian rococo basilica. Impressively sited in the foothills of Mount Ida, it's a rewarding morning's excursion.

Leaving Rethimnon to the west the road takes a brief glance at the hills before descending to the coast where it runs alongside sandy **beach** for perhaps 7 km, well worth walking out to if you're staying in town since Rethimnon's beach can get pretty churned up in season. An occasional hotel and a campsite offer accommodation, but much the best base is **GEORGIOPOLIS**. The beach here is cleaner, wider and further from the road, and the village is charming; quiet but far from dead. There are several houses which offer rooms and a few hotels. Within walking distance inland is **Kournas**, Crete's only lake, set deep in a bowl of hills and almost constantly changing colour. At the village of **Mouri**, here, you can also find rooms.

Beyond Georgiopolis the main road heads inland, cutting off a large spur of the coast. It thus misses some spectacular views over the sapphire Bay of Souda, several quiet beaches and the setting for the film of *Zorba the Greek*. **Kokkino Chorio**, the film location, and nearby **Plakas** are indeed postcard-picturesque (more so from a distance), but **Kefalas**, inland, outdoes both of them. On the exposed north coast there are beaches at **Almirida** and **Kalives**, and off the road between them. With luck you can find a room in Almirida, but the much bigger town of Kalives goes about its agricultural business without the least concession to tourism.

THE SOUTH COAST: PLAKIAS AND AGIA GALINI

Crossing from Rethimnon to the south of the island you hit a grand stretch of coast, much of it undeveloped until quite recently and still very much a gathering point for beach-sleeping travellers.

SFAKIA, at the west end of this coast road, is the usual terminal for hikers completing the Samarian Gorge – with regular boats round the coast to and from Agia Roumeli. It's consequently quite an expensive and not very welcoming place, and for a room or beach you should jump straight on the first bus going to Plakias. Plenty of opportunities present themselves en route, one of the most memorable at **Frangokastello**, a crumbling Venetian attempt to bring law and order to a district which went on to defy both Turks and Germans. Its square, crenellated fort, isolated a few kilometres before a chiselled wall of mountains, looks like it's been spirited out of the High Atlas or Tibet. And speaking of spirits, the place is said to be haunted by ghosts of Greek rebels massacred nearby in 1829. Every May these *drossolites* (dewy ones) march at dawn across the coastal plain and disappear into the sea near the fort. The rest of the time Frangokastello is tranquil enough: a *taverna*, rooms, piped spring water and an excellent beach make it a logical stopping point.

Slightly further on – and little bothered by tourism or modern life – are the attractive villages of **Skaloti** and **Rodhakino**, each with basic lodging and food.

The best beaches, however, are around **PLAKIAS**, itself now something of a boom town – half-finished buildings seem to outnumber completed ones – but not yet overcrowded. There is a campsite and no shortage of rooms or of space for sleeping bags on the beach. If you're planning to stay more than a day or two, **MIRTHIOS**, in the hills behind Plakias, is considerably cheaper, and locals there still outnumber the tourists.·The Plakias bus will drop you at the junction, less than 5 mins walk into the village. There is a popular youth hostel around whose taverna local social life revolves. It takes twenty minutes to walk down to the beach at Plakias, but if you're prepared to walk for an hour or more there are several empty, isolated stretches of sand to be found – ask directions in the hostel. Another outing is to the old ruined **monastery of Agios Ioannis** at Preveli, about four hours' walk.

AGIA GALINI, Crete's number one picturesque fishing village, is the next stop round the coast, although to get there you have to go halfway back to Rethimnon. It's so picturesque that you can't see it for the tour buses, hotel billboards and English package tourists. The beach is small and rocky, and apart from some excellent restaurants there seems little reason to come here unless you miss crowds. The exception is from November to April when most people have left and the mild climate makes it an ideal place to spend the winter. A lot of long-term travellers, Australians especially, do just that, so it's a good place to find work packing tomatoes or polishing cucumbers. Cheapest place to stay, if they have space, is the blue-signed rooms opposite the Hotel Moderno.

The plain east of here is probably the ugliest place anywhere in Crete, and Timpakes the drabbest town. The earth is hidden under acres of polythene greenhouses and burgeoning concrete sprawl, but this is the way to **Phaistos** and back to Iraklion, so grin and bear it.

MORE PALACES: PHAISTOS, AGIA TRIADA AND GORTYS

Despite its magnificent setting overlooking the Plain of Messara, the palace at **PHAISTOS** somehow lacks the grandeur of Knossos or Mallia. Much of the site is fenced off, and except in the huge central court it is almost impossible to get any sense of the place as it was – its plan is almost as complex as Knossos, with none of the reconstruction to help the imagination. It's interesting to speculate why the palace was built halfway up a hill rather than on the plain below; not for defence certainly. Psychological superiority over the peasants or reasons of health are both possible, but it seems quite likely that it was the view – Mount Ida to the north and the huge plain with Mount Dikte beyond it to the east – which finally swayed the decision.

What is immediately striking, however, are the strong similarities with the other palaces: the same huge rows of storage jars; the great courtyard with its monumental stairway; the theatre area. Unique to Phaestos is the third courtyard, in the centre of which are the remains of a furnace used for metalworking – this eastern corner of the palace, indeed, seems to have been home to a number of craftsmen including potters and carpenters. Strangely, though, Phaestos was much less ornately decorated than Knossos – there is no evidence of any of the dramatic Minoan wall paintings.

By contrast, some of the finest artworks in the museum at Iraklion came from **Agia Triada** less than a hour's walk away. No one is quite sure what this site is, but the most common theory is that it was some kind of royal summer villa; smaller than the palaces, but if anything even more lavishly appointed and beautifully situated. A paved road, which now divides the villa from the other houses on the site, led down to the sea. There's a Venetian church here too, worth visiting in its own right for the remains of Christian frescoes.

From Phaestos buses run west to Agia Galini, south to Matala and east towards Iraklion via **Gortys**. Tours invariably visit both sites at the same time. At its zenith, Gortys was capital of the Roman province which took in not only Crete but also much of North Africa. There had been settlement here from the earliest times, but today's scattered remains – the site has never been systematically excavated – are almost entirely of this Roman city. At the entrance to the site is the ruined church of Agios Titos – the saint who converted Crete and was also its first bishop. Beyond it is the Odeion which houses the most important discovery on the site, the Greek law code. About 30 feet by 10 and written in Boustrophedon – the lines read in opposite directions like the furrows of an ox-plough – it is reputedly the largest Greek inscription ever found. The laws it sets out clearly reflect a strictly hierarchical society – five witnesses were needed to convict a free man, only one for a slave; raping a free man or woman carried a fine of 100 staters, a serf only 5.

All three of these sites are open all day throughout the summer, with free admission on Sundays.

The ancient city's ports were at **Matala** and **Limenes** both of them popular resorts nowadays. Matala is famed for the caves cut into the cliffs above its beautiful beach. These ancient tombs used to be almost permanently inhabited by a sizeable commune, but nowadays the town tries to present a respectable image and the cliffs are cleared in the evening. People still sleep on the beach, though, or in the adjacent campsite. The last ten years have seen the arrival of new crowds and the development of hotels, discos and restaurants to service them – early afternoon, when the tour buses pull in for their swimming stop, sees the beach get packed to overflowing; at other times it's quite bearable. You could save money, and get a little more peace, by staying at **Pitsidia** a few miles inland. **Limenes**, too, is less developed than Matala, but it's also much less attractive.

Lendas, further east around the coast, is one of the least spoilt of the fishing villages in this part of the south, though it has recently been 'discovered' and pulls fairly considerable summer crowds. Two buses a day run here from Iraklion, via Gortys. There are rooms, a rocky beach and a souvenir shop which will change your money.

CHANIA AND THE WEST

CHANIA

CHANIA, Crete's capital, is for the most part a modern city. As a tourist you might never know it, though. Surrounding the small outer harbour is a wonderful jumble of half-derelict Venetian streets which survived the wartime bombardments, and it is here that life for the visitor is concentrated. Many of the old houses have restaurants downstairs and rent **rooms** with a wonderful decayed elegance above. Some of the cheapest are right on the outer harbour, and nearby is the NTOG in the bizarre, domed Mosque of the Janissaries. A not very central **youth hostel** has opened recently at Drakonlanou 33. Also in the Venetian quarter are the archaeological and naval museums, what little remains of the old city walls and parts of the medieval boathouses – the arches around the inner harbour. Chania's leather goods are arguably the finest and certainly the cheapest in Crete. On Odos Skrydaloph you can watch them being made while dining off the local delicacy – pigs' balls (or *testicules de porc* for those raised on haute cuisine). If you're not tempted the covered market is close by, with excellent fresh fruit, vegetables, cheeses and honey. **Buses** to the port at SOUDA run from the main street outside, all others from the main bus terminal behind Plateia 1866.

As the traditional cultural centre of Crete, Chania can also be a good place to catch local **music**: try some of the places along Akti Tobazi, the street flanking the east harbour. Jazz (recorded) is played each night at *Fangoto*, around the corner from the *naval* museum at the far end of the quay.

The beach stretches out to the west of town for quite a way. At the near end there are showers, but the beach is cleaner and less crowded further out – also more diplomatic if you plan to sleep out. A short bus ride away there are better beaches at **Glaros** and **Agia Marina**.

THE SAMARIAN GORGE

From Chania the **GORGE OF SAMARIA** can be visited as a day trip or part of a longer excursion. At over 16 km it's Europe's longest gorge and is startlingly beautiful – at its best in spring. Buses leave Chania for the top at 5.15am and at 9am, as well as 1pm. It's well worth catching the early one to avoid the full heat of the day while walking down. You will not be alone: there are often as many as three coachloads setting off before dawn for the nailbiting climb into the White Mountains. As you approach Omalos the sky begins to lighten but it's probably a mercy not to have seen the drop beside the road. You could avoid the early start by staying at **Omalos,** but since the village is some way from the start of the trail and the buses arrive as the sun rises it is almost impossible to steal a march. The tourist pavilion at the top is expensive (even to sleep on the floor) and a night under the stars a very cold experience.

At the *Xyloskalon,* or wooden staircase, which marks the start of the trail, the crowds disgorging from the buses quickly disperse as keen hikers march purposefully down while others dally over breakfast, contemplating the sunrise for hours. At an average pace with regular stops the walk down takes about five hours – the upward trek considerably longer. The path is rough: solid shoes vital. Small churches dot the route, and the ruined village of **Samaria** lies about halfway down. At the narrowest point one can almost touch both tortured rock faces at once, and, looking up, see them rising sheer for almost a thousand feet. The park round here is the only mainland refuge of the Cretan wild goat, the Kri-Kri – but don't expect to see one. On the way down there is plenty of water from springs and streams, but nothing to eat. When you finally get down, the village of **Agia Roumeli** is derelict until eventually the beach, and a cluster of *tavernas* with rooms to rent. If you want to get back to Chania buy your boat tickets now, especially if you want an afternoon on the beach: the last boat tends to sell out first. Similarly grab a seat on the bus at **Chora Sfakio** (where the boats dock) as soon as possible. If you're staying on the south coast, both villages have pebble beaches and there's little to choose between them, though Chora Sfakio is bigger. Halfway between the two is **Loutra,** with deserted beaches along the coast to the east. Boats also go west from Roumeli to **Sougia** and **Paleohora.**

AROUND CHANIA: THE AKROTIRI AND RODOPOU PENINSULAS

Just north of Chania the **AKROTIRI** peninsula loops round to protect the Bay of Souda – a US military base and missile testing area which the Greek socialists have pledged (but so far failed) to remove. As irony has it the peninsula's northern coastline is fast developing into a luxury suburb – the beach of Chorafakia, long popular with jaded Chanians, is surrounded by villas and apartments. **Stavros,** further out, has not yet suffered and its beach is quieter and prettier, although sporadically crowded with off-duty NATO personnel. You can rent rooms here, and there are two *tavernas.* Inland are the monasteries of **Agia Triada** and **Gouvernetou.** The former is much more accessible and has a beautiful C17th church inside its pink and ochre cloister; it's also one of the few Cretan monasteries which still seem to be thriving.

The coast to the west of Chania was the scene of most of the fighting during the German invasion in 1941. As you leave town an aggressive diving eagle commemorates the German parachutists, and at **Maleme** there is a big cemetery. There are also beaches, and considerable tourist development, along much of it. At **Agia Marina** there's a sandy beach, and an island off shore said to be a sea monster petrified by Zeus before it could swallow Crete. From the west, its mouth still gapes open. Between **Platanias** and **Kolimbari** is an almost unbroken strand, by no means all sandy, but deserted for long stretches between villages. The road here runs through groves of bamboo and oranges; bamboo windbreaks protect the ripening oranges from the Meltemi. At Kolimbari the road to Kastelli cuts across the base of another mountainous peninsula, **RODOPOU**. Just off the main road is the monastery **Gonias**, with a view most luxury hotels would envy. Every monk in Crete can tell tales of his proud ancestry of resistance to invaders, but here the Turkish cannon balls are still lodged in the walls to prove it, a relic they are far more proud of than any of the icons.

KASTELLI AND THE WESTERN TIP

Apart from being Crete's most westerly town, and the end of the main road, **KASTELLI** (or **KISSAMOS**, as it's also known) has little to recommend it. Its beach is rocky and dirty – although showers make it popular with newly arrived campers – and the town is largely dull and modern. It does, however, have a twice-weekly boat to the island of Kithira, continuing to Githion and Monemvassia in the Peloponnese before eventually reaching Piraeus. Currently this leaves every Tuesday and Friday (at least through the summer) but since there's every reason not to hang around Kastelli you'd be wise to check first. Call E. D. Ksirouhakes (22-337), the local boat agent in Kastelli, or ask at Nanadakis Travel on Halidon Street in Chania.

To the west of Kastelli, in serene contrast, lies some of Crete's loneliest – and to many travellers, finest – coastline. The first place of note on the map is ancient **Falassarna**, city ruins which mean little to the non-specialist although their distance from the sea is further proof that Crete is slowly tilting from west to east. Beaches here are superb, however – wide and sandy with crystal clear water. There are two *tavernas*, one of them with a few rooms, otherwise you have to sleep out: there's not much shade. Nearest shops are in **Platanos**, 5 km up a rough track, which is also the closest you can get by bus. So far this whole western coastline has only been discovered by a few Germans, the road is surfaced only as far as **Sfinari** and there is little in the way of official accommodation. Sfinari has several houses which let rooms, and a quiet pebble beach a little way below the village. **Kambos** is similar, but even less visited. Its beach is a considerable hike down the hill. Beyond them both is the monastery at **Chryssoskalitissa**, hard to get to but well worth the effort for its isolation and beaches; the bus gets as far as VATHI from where the monastery is another hour or two's walk. Four km beyond Chryssoskalitissa the road leads down to the coast opposite the tiny uninhabited island of **Elafonnisi**. It is possible to swim or even wade out to the island with its sandy beaches and rock pools, and the shallow lagoon is warm and crystal clear. There are no facilities here so bring your own food and water if you plan to stay.

If you can find some way of doing it, the circular drive from Kastelli through Platanos and **Elos** is worth the effort for the stunning scenery alone. Along the coast villages cling desperately to the high mountainsides, apparently halted by some miracle in a calamitous seaward slide. Around them olives ripen on the terraced hillsides, the sea glittering far below. Inland the main crop is the chestnut, and the huge old trees shade the village streets. In **Topolia** the church of Agia Sophia is sheltered inside a cave which has been known since Neolithic times. South of Elos a really atrocious road heads through the high mountains towards Paleohora. The bus doesn't come this way, and villagers still stare at the sight of a tourist. A host of small streams cascade beside, under or sometimes across the road.

When the beach at **PALEOHORA** finally appears below it is a welcome sight. The little town is built across the base of a peninsula, its harbour on one side, the beach on the other. Above, on the outcrop, Venetian ramparts stand sentinel. In the evening the main street fills with tables as diners spill out of the restaurants. There is no shortage of places to stay, but the beach is also ideal to camp out on, with showers, trees and acres of sand. A nearby disco and the rock'n'roll bar combine to lull the many campers to sleep. Things are developing fast but it's still in this book one of the nicest places on the island, with beautiful walks up the valley to Voutas (and rare strawberry trees) if you get tired of the beach.

Getting down here by the main road, which is paved, is much easier; the buses from Kastelli and Chania come this way. But although it too has to wind through the White Mountains, it lacks the excitement of the western route. **Kandanos**, at the 58 km mark, has been entirely rebuilt – it was destroyed by the Germans for its fierce resistance to their occupation. The original sign is preserved on the War Memorial: 'Here stood Kandanos, destroyed in retribution for the murder of 25 German soldiers.'

Boats ply regularly along the south coast from Paleohora to **Sougia**, **Agia Roumeli** and beyond. Sougia is never exactly overwhelmed with visitors, and apart from a small beach has remains of the ancient ports of Syia and Lissos. The village church has a Byzantine mosaic floor.

TRAVEL DETAILS

1 Connections

IRAKLION By boat daily with Thira (5 hrs) and Piraeus (12 hrs); four times a wook with Ios, Naxos and Paros, twice with Mykonos, Sifnos and Serifos. Day trips to Thira by ship or hydrofoil every day in season. Weekly ferries to Alexandria (Egypt) and fortnightly to Cyprus, Israel and Brindisi. Daily flights to Athens and Rhodes and regular connections with London.

AGIOS NIKOLAOS AND SITIA By boat twice a week with Piraeus (14 hrs), Thira, Kassos, Karpathos, Halki and Rhodes. Once to Ios, Folegandros, Kos, Kalymnos, Ikaria, Samos, Chios, Mytilini and Kavala.

CHANIA Daily boat to Piraeus (11 hrs) and flight to Athens.

KASTELLI (KISSAMOS) Twice weekly boat to Githion (Peloponnese, 6 hrs), Kithira, Neapolis, Monemvassia and Piraeus. Currently leaves on Tuesdays and Fridays.

2 Main bus routes on the island

Kastelli–Chania (15 daily from 6am–7pm; 1½ hrs); Chania–Rethimnon–Iraklion (11 daily from 6am–7.30pm; 4 hrs total); Iraklion–Agios Nikolaos (over 20 a day; 1½ hrs); Agios Nikolaos–Sitia (hourly 6.30am–7pm; 2 hrs); Iraklion–Ierapetra (hourly 8am–6pm; 2½ hrs); Sitia–Ierapetra (4 daily; 2 hrs); Iraklion–Phaistos (hourly 6.30am–7pm; 2 hrs).

Hitching on Crete is poor, lifts coming mainly from tourist traffic, and if you can afford it this is one island where **renting bicycles, mopeds or motorbikes** makes a lot of difference. There are rental agencies in all the main towns and most of them will give quite reasonable discounts if you're going for two or more days; Rethimnon, last year at least, seemed to have the cheapest places.

Chapter seven
DODECANESE

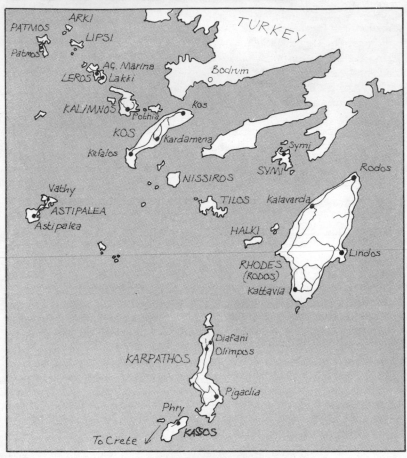

The most distant of the Greek islands, the **Dodecanese** lurk close to the
Turkish coast – some, like Kos and Kastellorizo, almost within hailing
range of the shore. Because of this position, and their remoteness from
Athens, these islands have always had a turbulent history – only being
finally included in the modern Greek state in 1947 after centuries of
occupation by Turks, Crusaders and Italians. Even now the threat – real
or imagined – of invasion from Turkey is very much in evidence: when
you ask about the heavy military presence locals talk always in terms of
'when the Turks come', never 'if'.

Whatever the rigours of the occupations, they have left behind them a wonderful blend of architectural styles and of eastern and western cultures which is the basis of much of the group's attraction. Medieval Rhodes is the most famous, but almost every island has its Classical remains, its Crusaders' castle, and a liberal dose of magnificent public buildings. For this the Italians, who occupied the islands from 1912 to 1945, are largely responsible. In their determination to beautify the islands and turn them into a showplace for fascism they undertook excavations and reconstruction on a massive scale; and if historical accuracy was sometimes sacrificed in the interests of style, only the expert is likely to complain.

Larger islands in the group are connected almost daily with each other, and none are hard to reach. Rhodes is the clear centre of the Dodecanese, and has services to Turkey, Israel, Syria and Cyprus as well as connections with Crete, the north-eastern islands, the Cyclades and the mainland.

PATMOS

Arguably the most beautiful, certainly the best known of the smaller islands in the Dodecanese, the atmosphere of Patmos is unique. It was in a cave here that St John had his revelation (the Bible's Book of Revelation), and unwittingly shaped the island's destiny. The monastery which commemorates him, founded here in 1088, dominates the island both physically – its fortified bulk towering high above anything else – and politically. Though the monks no longer run the island as they did for more than 700 years, their influence is everywhere. It is the presence of the monastery which has both created the tourist industry and stopped the island going the way of Rhodes or Kos: although there are vast numbers of visitors, they have not been allowed to take the island over. There is very little in the way of nightlife, certainly no disco, though the spiritual atmosphere has been added to in recent years by the presence of an I Ching community – eventually thrown out by the monks. It's impossible to describe, but equally impossible not to feel, the air of mysticism which pervades the island.

In **SKALA** the boat docks almost directly opposite the police station; bus and boat timetables are posted outside, the tourist police are upstairs. There is no lack of hotels, but private rooms here are cheaper and as a rule better. It is not advisable to sleep on the beach in town – for one thing you'll get wet feet – so carry on past it and head for **Meloy Beach** instead. There is a small campsite here and usually quite a community. Just behind the beach are a couple of *tavernas*, good but not so enterprisingly named as the excellent *Gregory's Grill* down at the harbour!

From Skala to **HORA** is a half-hour climb, or you can take the bus. Just over halfway up is the **MONASTERY OF THE APOCALYPSE**, inside which is a cave said to be that where St John heard the voice of God. You will be shown the desk where his disciple wrote it all down, and the rock which John used as a pillow. The **MONASTERY OF ST JOHN** (open 8–12 and 3–6) itself shelters behind its massive defences at the top of the hill. The stout walls have helped preserve a fantastic array of religious treasures dating back to the earliest days of Christianity. Sadly the monks, beset by a constant flow of tourists prying into their lives, are none too good-tempered. If you want to see the more exotic relics it is worth dressing respectably and being on your best behaviour. Outside the walls, Hora is a beautiful little town with some good places to eat and over forty other churches and monasteries. The churches, many of them containing beautiful icons and examples of the local skill in wood carving, are almost all locked, but someone living nearby will have the key. Among the best are the Church of Diassozoussa and the monastery of Zoodochos Pigi.

Patmos, as one local guide proclaims, 'is immense for those who know how to wander in space and time': the rest of us can rely on a bus service which regularly connects Skala with Hora, Kambos and Grikou. Around the coast there are some superb beaches; the best at **Psiliamos**. From Skala it is about two hours' walk, but there's a boat which goes there in the morning and will bring you back at night. **Grikou** is an easy walk down from Hora, a bit further from Skala. The beach is good here too, but much more developed. To the north of the island the bus goes as far as **Kambos**, where there is a good cheap taverna on the beach. Another half hour's walk will take you to **Lambi**, a beach covered in multi-coloured pebbles. In summer there are small boats constantly ferrying people around this northern coast, more expensive than the bus, but not unreasonable.

In many ways, though, the island is better out of season. It can get cold in winter, but there is a hard core of foreigners who live here all year round, so things never entirely close down. Thanks to them, Skala boasts one of the few health food shops in Greece, **Lan Tao**. It's on the road to Kambos, just before the turning for Meloy Beach. Many of the long-term residents rent houses in **Levkes**, a fertile valley just before Kambos with a lonely and sometimes wild beach at its end. If you come to Patmos be warned, you could end up joining them – there are more every year.

LEROS

Thanks to its absence from any major tour operators' lists, Leros is much less visited than its neighbours. Although by no means empty in summer, it's not overcrowded, and locals still genuinely enjoy the presence of visitors. On arrival (invariably at night) the port of **LAKKI** is an extraordinary sight, its waterfront lined with huge art-deco edifices put up by the Italians. Indeed the whole town, distinctly faded at closer quarters, retains a marvellously seedy elegance in its broad streets laid out around little parks and statues. If you really want to savour it, stay at the *Hotel Leros* ('C'), a once grand hotel which has definitely seen better days. It's on the front about ten minutes' walk from the jetty, and the large rooms almost all have balconies overlooking the bay. There is nowhere much cheaper in Lakki, though some places offer more in the way of modern facilities. The beach at **Koulouki**, where there's a *taverna* and you can sleep amongst the trees, is in the other direction when you get off the boat – away from town.

Better beaches can be found in the five other huge bays which distinguish Leros's coastline. The one bus visits every village at least once a day, and shuttles fairly regularly between Lakki and the capital at **Platanos** about an hour's walk away. Bikes and scooters can be hired in Lakki, but **PLATANOS** is a more pleasant and less expensive place to be based for any length of time. Originally built on a low ridge with sea on both sides, and protected by the Byzantine castle above, it has gradually spread in both directions to join up with the fishing villages of **Pandeli** and **Agia Marina**. Between them the three support a cinema, two discos and a surprisingly lively nightlife in the cafes and bars. It should be easy enough to find a room somewhere here. The castle, kept in good repair by a series of defenders, is an easy climb above the town. It has superb panoramic views, but for reasons of state security you're not allowed to take photographs; the place is still used as an observation point.

There's a beach at Pandeli, and a better one, with a taverna, further round the bay to the south. North of **Agia Marina** in the other direction is the more developed resort of **Alinda**, and another long beach. Lined with villas, it's a popular spot with holidaying Greeks. On the way you pass a cemetery for British soldiers killed here in a battle in 1943 – immaculately maintained, it somehow seems horribly out of place. Across the island at **Gournas** is another popular beach. Again you can find places to stay, but most people sleep out around the *tavernas*. Round the coast you can see the extraordinary monastery of **Agios Sideros** on an islet connected to the mainland by a long breakwater.

Nowhere in this central part of the island is really too far to walk if you're reasonably energetic, but **Partheni** in the north and **Xirocambos** to the south are further afield. The former, a tiny hamlet overshadowed by an army base and half-built airstrip, has little to commend it, but five minutes' walk beyond is **Blefouti Bay** – the island's most isolated beach, it has a new taverna. There's more military development on the way to **Xirocambos**, but the place itself is unaffected; you can rent rooms with little difficulty and there are several places to eat and drink.

Of the many islets which surround Leros, **LIPSI** is the largest and the only one with any inhabitants. Caiques make the trip from Agia Marina, and it's also on the route of the ferry *Panormitis*. There's absolutely nothing to do, but you won't find many better places to do nothing; two beaches to sleep on and no shortage of food or drink.

KALIMNOS

Most of the population of Kalimnos lives in or around the port, **POTHIA**, a wealthy but not very beautiful town whose fame comes from its sponge divers. In autumn and winter the town is lively and the bars crowded as the men come home to spend their money. In summer, with the fleet away at work, their place is taken by tourists. Warehouses around the harbour process and sell the sponges all year round. During the Italian occupation houses here were painted blue and white to keep alive the Greek colours and irritate the Italians. The custom is beginning to die out, but there is still plenty of evidence of it; even some of the churches are painted blue.

As far as the visitor is concerned, Pothia is not a big place; hotels, bar, restaurants and shops are all concentrated down by the harbour. The beach, with barely enough room to swing an octopus, is squeezed between the yacht club and the jetty – for real sand you have to cross the island. Just round the coast though, and connected twice daily by bus, is **Vathi**: a narrow valley whose verdant fertility makes a startling contrast with the dried-out greys of the rest of the island. At the end of a long fjord there is a tiny harbour, a couple of cafés and a long finger of dark green orange groves.

Heading the other way from the port, the first stop is **Chorio**, the old capital. Above it are the ruins of one of the fortified settlements to which the islanders retreated from pirate attacks, its churches maintained gleaming white among the crumbling houses. On the coast beyond is a string of little settlements with beaches, all of them too popular for their own good. **Panormos** is the oldest established, with big old hotels and some good restaurants. In **Myrties** and **Massouri** accommodation is mostly in villas or apartments. There are a few cheap rooms, but again more people than justified by the size of the beach. The islet of **Telendos**, with a medieval castle, Roman ruins and two beaches, is just off this shore, a short boat ride from **Myrties**.

The bus goes no further, but you can take a taxi on to **Arginonta** or to **Emporios**, the end of the road. Neither has anywhere to stay, but the beaches are much emptier. Emporios has two good *tavernas* and a selection of tamarisks to sleep under.

KOS

After Rhodes, Kos is easily the most popular island of the Dodecanese, and at first sight there are remarkable similarities between the two. The harbour entrance is guarded by an imposing Crusader castle, the waterfront lined with grandiose Italian public buildings. In the town minarets and palm trees spire above extensive Greek and Roman remains; long sandy beaches lined with hotels surround them. At times, though, Kos still has the small-island charm which Rhodes has irrevocably lost: the people who come here are younger, less tied to their organised trips and air-conditioned hotels. Just three miles away across the channel is the Turkish city of Bodrun, and the island has a sizeable moslem minority.

> The NTOG print a free leaflet – Kos/Rhodes – with maps of both islands and plans of their main towns

The town of **KOS** spreads in all directions from the harbour. Around the front is a line of restaurants and bars, not all of them outrageously expensive, and some cheap but noisy hotels; Hotel Kalimnos one of the better among them. The NTOG and tourist police also have their offices here, worth visiting if you have trouble finding a room, or to pick up free maps and check the bus schedule. If you plan to sleep out, the beach to the right is the better bet – further from the centre and with fewer big hotels, but you can also walk out past the back of the castle to the left. The official campsite is a half-hour walk in this direction.

Apart from the castle, the town's main attraction is its wealth of Hellenistic and Roman remains, many of them only revealed by an earthquake in 1933. The largest single section is the ancient agora, reached from the castle or from the main square by the museum, but the Casa Romana, a palatial Roman house restored by the Italians, and the sections of the ancient town bordered by the odeion and the stadium are more impressive. Both have well preserved fragments of mosaic floors, although the best have been taken to Rhodes. There are so many broken pillars, smashed statues and fragments of relief lying around among the ruins that no one knows what to do with them. The best pieces have been taken inside the castle for safe-keeping where most of them are piled up, unmarked and unnoticed. A couple of pillars have even been pressed into service propping up the branches of Hippocrates' plane tree. This venerable tree has guarded the entrance to the castle for generations, and although not really old enough to have seen the great healer, it does have a fair claim to being one of the oldest trees in Europe.

Hippocrates is justly celebrated on Kos – the star exhibit in the museum is his statue and the Asklepeion (45 mins walk from town) is a major tourist attraction. Treatments described by him and his followers were still in current use as recently as a hundred years ago, and his ideas on medical methods and ethics are still influential. The **Asklepeion**, both a temple to Asklepios and a renowned centre of healing, was actually built after the death of Hippocrates, but it is safe to assume that the methods used and taught here were his. The magnificent setting on a hillside overlooking the Turkish mainland reflects the importance given to the environment by these early doctors: springs still provide the site with a constant supply of clean fresh water. There used to be a rival medical school in the ancient town of Cnidus, on the Anatolian coast to the south of Kos, and undoubtedly there was far more contact between the two societies than you'll find today. The moslem village of **Platanis**, where you can rest on your way up, also recalls days of greater trust between Greeks and Turks. The walk from Kos is a long and tiring one; you might prefer to hire a bike for the trip.

KARDAMENA on the south coast is the island's second large tourist centre. The beach stretches out east and west from the town, lined to the east with ill-concealed concrete bunkers as far as **Tolari** where there is a vast new hotel complex. There are several hotels, but more private houses offering rooms. Local restaurants specialise in some superb fish dishes. On its way to this part of the coast, the bus goes through **Pyli**. Above the modern village, the ruins of the old cower in the shadow of a clifftop castle which would be more at home in Transylvania.

On the other side of the island there are beaches at Mastihari and Tingaki. **Tingaki** is in cycling distance of Kos so it can get crowded, but there are several *tavernas* and not many places to stay which makes it a nice patch of beach to camp on. **Mastihari** is the port for the ugly airport town of **Antimahia**. The beach is smaller and the town more developed than at Tingaki, but there is a daily caique service to **Kalimnos** as well as frequent boats to the islet of **Pserimos**.

The end of the line for buses is **KEFALOS**, which squats on a mesa-like hill looking back over the narrow central plain. Below the town, the beach at **Kamari** used to be the best on the island – one or two rooms, excellent fish and a long beach extending to Agios Stefanos where the ruined Roman basilica overlooks a tiny offshore islet. Sadly the complex of bungalows surrounding a new luxury hotel will soon overrun the whole area. Kefalos is the staging point for hikes into the mountainous south-west peninsula. To the west, beyond the monastery of Agios Theologos, you can find deserted stretches of coastline, but the nearest is about 6 km over very rough roads. Along the way you'll be rewarded with views back over the island, Kalymnos and Leros to the left, Nissiros and the coast of Turkey to the right.

NISSIROS

Volcanic Nissiros is noticeably cooler and greener than its southern neighbours. Unlike them it has proved attractive and wealthy enough to hold on to a good proportion of its population – it stays lively even in winter. Much of the island's income comes from quarrying; off shore towards Kos you can see the isle of Giali, a vast lump of pumice on which the workers live as they slowly chip it away.

MANDRAKI is the port and capital, its tightly packed houses decorated in bright contrasting colours. Whitewashed snakes and ladders adorn the streets. The place looks cheerful, and it is. By the harbour are three new hotels, each with a restaurant. Of these the 'Three Brothers' is the friendliest, but the more basic pensions and *tavernas* in the town are cheaper and livelier. Two ancient castles overlook the town: inside the nearer of them is the Monastery of the Virgin Mary. Its church, hewn out of the rock, has a collection of Byzantine icons, invisible beneath their coatings of hammered silver and gold. Elsewhere in Mandraki is a small historical museum, a backyard full of archaeological finds, and in private houses a folk art gallery and a local history collection.

The beach, such as it is, lies beyond the harbour, but if you're planning to sleep out, **Pali** is greatly preferable. Twenty minutes' walk east, this little fishing village has a better beach, several cafés, a shop and one or two rooms, but little else. Paths continue round the coast to more deserted shores. At the end of the beach is a ruined spa which offers shelter if the wind gets up. On its way out here the road passes **Loutra**, a thermal bath and hotel supplied with naturally heated mineral water from the volcano. It works wonders on rheumatism and arthritis.

It is the volcano which gives Nissiros its special character, and no stay would be complete without a visit. There is a bus which runs when the tourist boats from Kos and Rhodes arrive, or failing this at 8am on Mondays, Wednesdays and Fridays. On the way it passes the island's other two villages, **Emporion** and **Nikia**. It is worth walking at least part of the way: both to see the island and to get to the crater when it's relatively deserted. As the road passes above Pali it crosses a steep, stepped path which leads up to **Emporion** – about two hours from Mandraki. An alarmingly precipitous path plunges down the other side of the village on to the plain, where you can strike out straight across the fields or follow the road to the crater in about an hour. As you approach the sulphurous stench drifts out to meet you, and fields gradually give way to stone and scrub. When there are tourists about there is a café open here.

The crater itself is extraordinary, a Hollywood moonscape of grey, brown and sickly yellow. Its perimeter is pocked with tiny blow holes from which jets of steam pour constantly – crystals of pure sulphur form around them in little tubes and trumpets. The whole floor of the crater seems to steam in fact, and standing in the centre you can hear the huge cauldron bubbling away below. In legend this is the groaning of Polyvotis, a giant crushed here by the Titans under a huge rock torn from Kos. On the eastern side of the crater, below the village of Nikia, pools of boiling water break the surface.

To walk back to Mandraki, follow the road south away from Emporion. It soon ends, but a path leads on straight ahead. Just above is a tiny monastery overlooking the sea. The track, the island's main artery until the road was built, is well maintained and has some superb views. It curves around the outside of the volcano, through a pass and back down towards the capital, passing several ancient churches in varying stages of decay along the way. This section takes another two hours, so on foot the whole circuit from Mandraki to the volcano and back takes at least five hours. You can avoid the least interesting and most arduous part by taking the bus to Emporion or Nikia and walking back. The two villages are remarkably similar, perched high above the central plateau with magnificent views down into the crater and out across the sea. **Nikia** is slightly larger, closer to the crater and, if possible, even more spectacularly situated.

TILOS

The small island of Tilos is one of the least visited of the Dodecanese, although now on the list of day trips from Rhodes and Kos. Why anyone should want to visit for just a few hours is a mystery, for while it's not a bad place to rest up on the beach, there is remarkably little to see or do.

A road (The road), runs the 7 km from **Livadia,** the port, to **Megalo Choric**, the capital and only other significant habitation. When the boat arrives there is usually some sort of vehicle to take passengers and goods between the two, but at other times you either walk or hitch. Since there are only about fifteen vehicles on the island, the latter can be a slow business. Of the two villages, **LIVADIA** is the more ready to deal with tourists but the better beaches are around Megalo Chorio. In the port there are three restaurants, a hotel and several rooms to rent; there are also six bungalows, built from communal village funds, by the beach – if you can get one they're excellent value. The mayor, Stefanos Panayiotakis, has the keys; another of his arduous duties is to switch the water off at night – normally about 8pm. No one will mind if you sleep on the beach, but it's stony and most people prefer the rough ground beyond the bungalows.

Staying in **Megalo Chorio** can be more of a problem. There are two luxurious, modern and very expensive apartments and no one else can let a room until these are full. On the other hand there are small beaches on the north-east of the island and an excellent one at **Eristos** on the west coast – due south of Megalo Chorio, about an hour and a half's walk from Livadia, and helpfully signposted on the road between the two villages. There are two *tavernas* near the beach, one of which, Nausica, is particularly good and has rooms to let. It is actually part of a small farm and often has home-grown produce to supplement the freshly caught fish. Anything fresh is well worth getting on Tilos; most of the island is barren, and even bread has to be imported from Symi or Rhodes. While in summer the restaurants do enough trade to have vegetables shipped in, out of season it can be hard to come by any food at all. If the worse comes to the worst, fishing off the beach is surprisingly productive.

Things to see on Tilos include the one-roomed museum in Megalo Chorio with the usual small island mixture of archaeological finds, local history and C19th kitsch. Above the town is a Venetian castle, and on the way to it remains of Pelasgian walls, 12,000-year-old relics of the earliest known Greeks. Above Livadia is another castle accessible only to rock climbers, but follow the path which looks as if it leads there and you can climb down to a small beach on the west coast, or go further to totally deserted parts of the south of the island. From the higher points there are good views across to Turkey. To the north, off the road, is the hamlet of Mikro Chorio, inhabited until recently but now abandoned to the sheep and goats. In this direction too can be found a cave where the petrified bones of several mammoths were discovered – you'll need a guide to get there and a torch when you do.

SYMI

Symi's great problem, no water, is in many ways also its greatest asset. However much it might want to, the island can't hope to support a luxury hotel. Instead hundreds of people are shipped in daily from Rhodes, relieved of their money and sent back. This arrangement suits both the islanders and the few visitors who stay. Many of the latter are regular customers and come back several times a year or own houses here.

The island's capital consists of **Yialos**, the port, and **Chorio** on the hillside above; collectively known always as **SYMI**. Incredible now, but less than a hundred years ago the town was richer and more populous than Rhodes. Wealth came, despite the barren land, from a fame in ship-building and sponge diving which go back to pre-Classical times.

Vestiges of both remain, but the magnificent C19th mansions are now for the most part roofless and deserted, their windows gaping blankly across the harbour. A few are being restored to be let out to tourists. If you plan to stay any time Symi Tours acts as an agent for most private rooms, but make sure there is water left in the cistern – especially towards the end of the summer. Otherwise there are small hotels and pensions all round the harbour. In the *Pension Klimatares*, the first you reach after getting off the boat, the surrender of the Dodecanese was signed in 1945. Again check you will have water – they never switch it off here, it just runs out.

Tourist life centres on the harbour, the one part of town which still thrives. The best places to eat are down here, particularly *Kyriakos' International Restaurant*, though it can be pricey. Climbing up towards **CHORIO** more and more of the houses are empty, the streets silent. At the top of the hill are the remains of a small castle and another populated enclave. The town's museum holds an assortment of local archaeological finds, traditional costumes, antiques and junk salvaged from better days.

Symi has no big sandy beaches, but you can swim in many of the deep narrow bays which pepper the coastline. There is a small pebbly beach near the harbour, but it's in the shade by early afternoon. Further afield the two most popular are **Pedhi** and **Agia Marina**; at **Pedhi**, about 50 mins walk, there are rooms in the summer. Unless you like total isolation, Pedhi is also the best place to camp or sleep out, although the beach is right in the village. A goat track to the right of the bay leads in about half an hour to a tiny but little known beach, Agios Nikolaos. There are plenty of others to be discovered, either with a small boat or by simply following a path. During the summer boats set out regularly round the coast to beaches and the Monastery of Panormitis. At other times you have to make special arrangements, which can prove expensive. In mid-summer, when temperatures rise over 100, walking is no joke.

The huge monastery of **St Michael Panormitis** is Symi's second big tourist attraction. This local patron saint has been adopted by Greek sailors everywhere, and the church has an impressive array of offerings for a safe passage. Otherwise it caters mainly for the day trippers who stop on their way home to Rhodes – the monks' traditional hospitality takes the form of an expensive hotel and restaurant. There is also a beach. You can get here with a tourist trip, but then you have to stay the night or go back to Rhodes; the walk across the island takes nearly five hours. Better to take a small boat in the morning and avoid the masses, but don't expect too much: the main impression is of the massive amount of concrete which must have gone into the construction.

ASTIPALEA

Both geographically and architecturally Astipalea would be more at home among the Cyclades – the island can be seen quite clearly from Thira and Amorgos, and it looks and feels more like them than its neighbours to the east. In antiquity the island's most famous citizen was Kleomedes, a boxer disqualified from an early Olympic Games for killing his opponent. He came home so enraged that he pulled down the local school, killing all its pupils. Things have calmed down a bit in the intervening 2,000 years and today the capital, **ASTIPALEA**, is a quiet fishing port, its steep streets distinguished by the decorated wooden balconies on the whitewashed houses. Above the village is a Venetian castle and a line of nine battered windmills; by the harbour a long grey sand beach. There are two hotels right on the harbour, but rooms in the village are generally better – the *Hotel de France*, run by a Frenchman, has a genuine French bakery.

Half an hour's walk from the capital is **Livadia**, fertile green valley with a good beach and shady restaurants by the waterfront. You can camp here or rent a room or a bungalow on the beach. **ANALIPSI** is about 12 km in the other direction – a taxi ride or a beautiful walk. There's little except a clean, quiet beach and a small *taverna*, but it's a nice place to sleep under the stars. The road ends at **Vathi**, another sleepy fishing village just south of which is a fortress built during the Italian occupation – Astipalea was the first island they took. From Vathi you can often get back to the capital by boat.

RHODES (RODOS)

It's no accident that Rhodes is among the most visited of Greek islands. Not only is its coast lined with sandy beaches, but much of the capital is a beautiful and remarkably preserved medieval city. Sadly it crawls with tourists – as many as 50,000 a day – throughout the year. For some reason Scandinavians predominate, revelling in the cheap drink: the Post Office has one box for Sweden, one for the rest of Europe, and smorgasbord is as much a local delicacy as moussaka. British package tourists, too, are very much part of the local scene.

RODOS TOWN divides neatly into two: the old walled city, and the new town which has oozed out around it. Throughout, the tourist is king. In the new town especially, the few buildings which aren't hotels are casinos, bars or discos. Around them stretches the beach – standing room only for latecomers – complete with deckchairs, parasols and showers. At the northernmost point stands an uninteresting aquarium and a museum with an extraordinary collection of grotesque freaks of nature (a cyclopean goat; an eight-legged calf) and apparently rotting stuffed fish.

The *old town* is the place to be, and the few reasonably priced places to stay and to eat are within its walls. Just outside them is the market, from where buses set off for the rest of the island, and a little further round the post office, OTE and police station. The NTOG and tourist police are also just beyond the walls, behind the **Palace of the Grand-masters**. From outside, it is the palace above all which draws the eye. Destroyed by earthquakes, it was reconstructed by the Italians as a summer home for Mussolini and Victor Emmanuel III (King of Italy and Albania, Emperor of Ethiopia). The exterior is as authentic as possible, but inside things are on an altogether grander scale: a marble staircase leads up to rooms paved with mosaics from Kos, and the furnishings rival many a grand North European palace. Hidden from view are lifts, central heating and the other essentials of life as a modern dictator.

From here the Street of the Knights leads down to the Crusaders' hospital, now the **Archaeological museum**. Reconstructed almost completely to its original state, it still manages to feel more like Disneyland than a city under siege. In the museum a collection garnered from the whole Dodecanese is capped by the superb Aphrodite of Rhodes – the Marine Venus. The main activity otherwise is to wander the streets admiring the architecture, the milling tourists and the thousands of souvenir shops. Laid on for your entertainment are a nightly *son et lumière* at the Palace, folk dances and twice weekly tours of the walls (the only time you can get on to them, so worth going if you're at all interested). Beyond them it is a short walk to **Mount Smith**, the ancient city's acropolis, where the stadium and theatre have been restored. In Rodini Park (no. 3 bus) there's a **wine festival** every evening from July to September, the entrance fee covers as much as you can drink. Real misers should stay in town where many of the restaurants, especially on Socrates Street and around the museum, hand out free ouzos in an attempt to lure you inside. Stroll past looking hungry – affluent too if possible – and you're likely to be collared. But don't eat there: someone has to pay. Cheaper places are found away from the major tourist traps – try behind the Folk Dance Theatre around Omirou Street and look for locals, or ask; it's incredible how friendly most people have managed to remain.

In the same area you can find the cheaper **places to stay**. At the top end of Pithagoras Street, for example, are *Lia's House* and the Pensions *Rena* and *Athinea*. When the town is full in mid-summer it might be safer to accept a good offer as you get off the boat. Sleeping on the beach or in the parks is actively discouraged and, though it is possible to slip through the net, not greatly advised.

One of the few things cheaper in Rhodes than elsewhere is motorbike hire – partly because it doesn't include insurance – and although the bus service isn't bad this is one way of escaping the worst crowds. The northern half of the island is ruled by tourism, regular buses serve both coasts and crowds from local beach hotels are added to by boat and coach tours from the capital. The most pleasant of the resorts in the north is probably **Haraki**, a small town overlooked by an impressive castle, with good rooms and restaurants. Not much further is **LINDOS**, Rhodes's number two tourist draw. Like Rodos itself, the charm is largely spoilt by the commercialism and the crowds, but there are few places to stay in the town so if you can arrive before the tours when the pebble streets between its immaculately whitewashed houses are empty, it really is a beautiful place. In recent years it has become a popular bolt-hole for tax exiles and ageing rock stars; Pink Floyd fans could be in for a treat. The Byzantine church is liberally covered with C18th frescoes, and several of the older houses are open to the public – entrance is free but they tend to expect you to buy something. On the hill above the town, the ancient acropolis is found inside the castle; a surprisingly happy meeting between two cultures.

Despite crowds the beach at Lindos is one of the finest on the island and there are other superb stretches to either side. **Lardhos Bay**, 10 km south of the village, even has dunes behind its strands and there are intermittent sandy patches all the way down through the uninhabited south-east tip of the island. There, a long sand spit extends out to **Prassonissi** or 'Leak Island'.

The rival attraction on the west coast is **KAMIROS**, which with Lindos and Ialysos was one of the three powers which united to found the modern city of Rodos. Soon eclipsed by the new capital, the town was abandoned and only rediscovered in the last century. As a result it is a particularly well preserved Doric city, doubly worth visiting for its beautiful hillside site. On the beach below Kamiros there are several *tavernas*, and more line the route to the modern fishing port of **Kamiros Skala**, 15 km to the south. From here a caique runs daily to **Halki**.

HALKI is a member of the Dodecanese in its own right, even though most of the population has left. After Rhodes it is marvellously tranquil, the big event of the day is when someone catches a fish. Rooms are cheap, and if you're staying any time you can rent a house for next to nothing. As in Symi, many of the houses are empty – from the bigger ferries which call here on their way to Karpathos the blank, staring windows can be disconcerting. There are two beaches, one sandy but minute, the other larger and pebbly. And, inevitably, there is a medieval castle at the top of the hill.

Inland Rhodes is mountainous and wooded. Few places merit a special visit, although the pine covered slopes of **Mount Profitis Elias** makes beautiful walking country. The road down to Eleoussa passes one of Rhodes's finest Byzantine churches, **Agia Eleoussa**. There is also the

Valley of the Butterflies, which is exactly what its name implies, though it might equally be called the Valley of the Tour Buses.

South of Lindos, Kamiros and Embonas you begin to think you have strayed on to another island – at least until you see the prices. Gone are the smart new roads and luxury hotels, and with them most of the crowds. Gone too are the tourist facilities and most of the transport, though. Only occasional buses run to Katavia along the east coast and as far as Monolithos and Apokakia in the west. The beaches are mainly in the east; often windy, but there are dunes which offer sheltered, if lonely, camping. *Tavernas* grace the better stretches of sand, but there are few places to stay. The main exceptions are **Genadi**, where you can find rooms in the village and fresh springwater on the beach, and **Plimiri**, furthest south, where the restaurant has some very basic beds. The road curves inland to **Katavia** where there are one or two rooms if you ask around. A rough track leads from here to **Prassonisi Cape**, the island's southern extremity.

Beyond Katavia on the west coast is a long wild beach – miles of sand with no habitation at all along an often windswept beach. If you are into 'Camping Sauvage' this is the place to do it, but you'll need transport, or a lot of supplies and a sturdy pair of boots. The first town is at **Apolakia**, some way inland. Modern and unexciting, it has a few pensions. Much the same could be said of **Monolithos**, although here you can climb up to the castle. The road passes another castle at **Kastelli**, just before Kamiros Skala. Ramshackle at close quarters, it is little visited but commands great views over a group of islets towards Halki.

KASTELLORIZO (MEGISTI)

Little more than a mile off the Turkish coast and over seventy from its nearest Greek neighbour (Rhodes), Kastellorizo's official name, Megisti – 'the biggest' – seems more an act of defiance than a statement of fact. It is actually the smallest of the Dodecanese and arriving at night you find its lights quite outnumbered by the Turkish town of Kas across the bay. There were once 15,000 people here but war, earthquake, deportation (of moslems) and economics have wrought a dramatic decline. Today the population has declined to just 180, maintained by the thousands of Sydney emigrants and by subsidies from the Greek government who fear that Turkey would have a legitimate claim if there were any fewer inhabitants.

The population of the island is concentrated in the north – in the harbour town of **KASTELLORIZO** (a Hellenised version of the Italian Castello Rosso) and in the adjacent village of **Mandraki**, divided only by a hill and ruined Crusader castle. Locals would never admit it but there is a strong eastern influence in the architecture of the houses: their red tiled roofs, wooden balconies and long narrow windows are of classic Anatolian design. As in Symi and Halki many of the finer ones are ruined. There is a small local history museum in the old Turkish mosque at the end of the harbour, and the cathedral too is worth visiting. To the west of town a stepped path leads up to Palaiokastro, the site of an ancient Doric foundation. Around it there are tremendous views across to Turkey and over the surrounding islets of the Kastellorizo group. None of them is today inhabited except by lighthouse keepers but it is only a few years since one had an elderly resident who resolutely flew the Greek flag each day in defiance of the Turks across the water.

There is one modern hotel, the *Megisti*, and a few other rooms for rent but the island is neither prepared for – nor gets – more than a handful of casual tourists. Water here has to be collected in tanks during the winter and almost all the food at the quayside tavernas is shipped in from Rhodes, fish being the one main exception. If you swim you'll discover the incredible abundance of multicoloured sea life around these shores and though there is no beach the sea is usually clear and flat as glass, perfect for snorkelling off the rocks and steps. Round the coast by boat is the grotto of **Parasta**, famed for its stalactites and the strange blue light effects inside: it's also inhabited by seals.

The journey to Kastellorizo from Rhodes takes six hours – sometimes more in bad weather – and if you wanted to return to Piraeus as long as thirty-four hours. Not a place to be at the end of a holiday if you're committed to a return flight.

KARPATHOS

Despite a magnificent coastline of cliffs and rocky promontories constantly interrupted by little beaches, Karpathos has succumbed surprisingly little to tourism. Only the two ports, Pigadia and Diafani, are really prepared for a large influx.

PIGADIA, the capital, is now more often known as Karpathos. It curves round one side of Vrontis Bay, a long sickle of sandy beach stretching beyond. Hotels (the *Anesis* is recommended) and *rooms* in the town often get full in mid-summer, but it's a nice beach to sleep on, particularly under the trees by the ruined C5th basilica of Agios Fontini – you can't miss it. When there is space you'll be offered rooms as the boat docks. From Pigadia there are rare buses or expensive taxis to get round the south of the island. You could also hire a moped, but the one place makes full use of its monopoly and you pay through the nose.

About half an hour's walk south, **Ammopi**, with a string of small beaches, is the closest thing on the island to a developed resort. But almost every village has its own paths down to the sea, a harbour and a beach. The best are **Lefkos**, **Agios Nikolaos** and **Arkessa**, all of which have places to stay. Five minutes' south of the latter the relics of ancient **Arkessia** can be found on the promontory, with the mosaic floors of several Byzantine churches. The best of these have been taken to Rhodes while a large section is propped incongruously against the wall of the local school, but what is left in situ, half buried under the sand, is well worth a visit. Just beyond is the beach, with dunes to camp amongst. In the other direction the fishing port of **Finikes** sports another beach and a *taverna*.

The *north of the island*, although now connected by road, continues to exist almost entirely independently of the richer south. There is, for example, no bakery, and on Saturdays the women – often in their traditional dress – bake in communal wood-fired ovens. Every boat which comes to Karpathos calls at both Pigadia and at Diafani in the north; this is far the cheapest way between the two bar walking. Although its popularity is growing, rooms in **Diafani** are still cheap, and life slow. Thick pine forests cover the surrounding slopes and paths lead through the north to Vanada Beach, stony but a good place to sleep among the trees, or south to more isolated, nameless beaches. Other beaches are accessible only by the many small boats, which can take you also to the uninhabited islet of Saria, or through the narrow strait to Tristomo Harbour and the ruins of **Vrykus**, once the island's chief port.

Whatever else you do on Karpathos, a visit to **OLIMPOS** is a must. High in the mountains, the village straggles across two small peaks, the ridges above notched by deserted windmills. Although the road and electricity, together with a growing number of tourists, are swiftly dragging the place into the twentieth century, it hasn't arrived yet. The women here are immediately striking in their magnificent traditional dress and after a while you notice that they also dominate the village – working in the gardens, carrying goods on their shoulders or tending the mountain sheep. Olimpos men nearly all emigrate or work outside the village – many in Rhodes – sending money and returning only at holidays. Unique in Greece the local inheritance rules favour women – houses passing down from mother to daughter upon marriage. Isolated for so long, the villagers also speak a unique dialect, said to maintain traces of its Doric and Phrygian origins. Traditional music is still heard regularly and draws considerable crowds of Greek visitors at festival times. From the village, the west coast and tiny port and beach at **Frysses** are a dizzy drop below.

One can get to Olimpos by costly taxi from the south, or make the spectacular 3–4 hour trek from Spoa. Less strenuous and just as scenic is to stay in Diafani and start the steep walk up early. A path – shorter and greatly preferable to the road – leads up a ravine through the forest. A small stream runs beside most of the way, and there is a spring. At your approach snakes slither into hiding and partridges noisily break cover. It takes nearly two hours, longer with a pack, but you are well rewarded and there are several cheap places to stay when you make it; Pension Anixi, run by a retired member of the local folk-dance troupe, is recommended. As you near the top take the left, lower fork. The other leads on to Mount Avlona and down to Vrykus. From Avlona's summit when it is clear you can see Crete to the east and all the islands north as far as Kos.

KASSOS

Barren and depopulated, Kassos attracts few visitors although it's a regular port of call. What is left of the population cluster together in five villages in the north, under the shadow of Karpathos, leaving most of the island unvisited and inaccessible. The crumbling houses which line the village streets and the disused terraces covering the island recall better days. There is little sign here of the wealth brought into other islands by emigrant workers, nor, since the island has little to offer them, by tourists.

It's just ten minutes' walk from **PHRY**, the capital, to the port at **Emporio**; indeed the furthest village, **Poli**, is only 3 km away. There are two hotels in Phry, neither very cheap, and in summer a few rooms. The island's beach, such as it is, is at **Ammousa** the other side of the little-troubled airstrip. There's a large cave there with impressive stalactites.

Striking inland, especially if you're seeking isolation, is more rewarding. Between **Agia Marina** and **Avrantohori** the route across the island leaves the road heading south. Civilisation swiftly becomes remote in a silence broken only by goat bells: for company flies and an occasional wheeling hawk. Smallholdings and olive groves are still sporadically tended, but no one stays long. After about an hour the Mediterranean appears on the south of the island, a desolate mass of water broken only by the odd ship plying to Cyprus and the Middle East. The higher fork in the way leads to the mountain chapel and monastery of Agios Georgios, while the other drops gradually down to the coast. It emerges finally at **Khelathros Harbour**, a beautiful cove at the end of a cultivated but uninhabited valley. The beach is small but sandy, and the swimming great after the hike. Seabirds of every kind circle the cliffs. With plenty of supplies – hard to come by on Kassos which has little fresh produce – it could be a great place to camp.

DODECANESE CONNECTIONS

To simplify the lists below the **SS PAN-ORMITIS** has been left out. For years this tiny ship has been the only regular lifeline of the smaller islands – it visits them all at least once a week throughout the year. Its timetable is approximately: Monday, leaves Megisti for Rhodes, Symi, Tilos, Nissiros, Kos, Kalimnos, Leros, Lipsi, Patmos, Arki, Agathonissi, Samos, then back through all of them to Rhodes and on to Halki, Karpathos and Kassos. By Thursday morning the ship is back in Rhodes, heads north as far as Kalymnos and back to Megisti again.

PATMOS Six boats a week to Piraeus (10 hrs), Leros (1 hr), Kalimnos (3 hrs), Kos (5 hrs) and Rhodes (8 hrs). In summer tourist boats to Samos daily, Kos twice weekly, Lipsi and Arki less often.

LEROS Six a week to Piraeus (12 hrs) and to Patmos (1 hr). Daily to Kalimnos (1½ hrs), Kos (3½ hrs), Rhodes (7 hrs). Once weekly to Samos, Ikaria, Chios, Mytilini, Limnos, Kavala, Halki, Karpathos, Kassos, Crete, Thira and Folegandros. Daily caique to Lipsi, less often to Kos, Kalimnos and Patmos.

KALIMNOS Daily to Piraeus (14 hrs), Leros (1½ hrs), Patmos (3 hrs), Kos (1½ hrs) and Rhodes (5 hrs). Once a week to Astipalea, Amorgos, Halki, Simi, Karpathos, Kassos, Crete, Thira, Folegandros, Samos, Ikaria, Chios, Mytilini and Kavala. Regular caiques to Mastihari (Kos), Kos, Pserimos and Leros.

KOS Daily to Rhodes (3 hrs), Piraeus (12 hrs upwards), Kalimnos (1½ hrs), and Leros (3½ hrs). Six a week to Patmos (5 hrs). One to Astipalea, Amorgos, Megisti, Halki, Karpathos, Kassos, Crete, Thira, Samos, Ikaria, Chios, Mytilini and Kavala. Irregular connections with Bodrun (Turkey). Tourist boat daily to Kalimnos and Nissiros, less often to Leros, Patmos and Symi. Daily hydrofoil to Rhodes. Flights to Athens daily and to Rhodes in summer — charters from around Europe.

NISSIROS AND TILOS Connected by ferry once a week with each other, Simi, Rhodes (4½ hrs), Astipalea (3 hrs), Amorgos, Piraeus and Megisti. Regular tourist boats to Kos and from Rhodes via Symi. Hydrofoil day trips from Rhodes twice a week in summer.

SYMI Two ferries a week to Rhodes, one to Kos, Kalimnos, Tilos, Nissiros, Megisti, Astipalea, Amorgos and Piraeus. Tourist trips daily to Rhodes, frequently to Kos, Tilos and Nissiros.

ASTIPALEA Two boats a week to Amorgos (3 hrs), Piraeus (10 hrs), Rhodes (7 hrs) and Simi. Once to Kos, Kalimnos, Tilos and Nissiros.

RHODES Daily connections with Piraeus (15–24 hrs), Kos (3 hrs), Kalimnos (5 hrs), Leros (7 hrs), Patmos (8 hrs) and with Marmaria in Turkey. Twice weekly to Symi (1 hr), Halki, Karpathos (7 hrs), Kassos, Crete (13 hrs), Astipalea (7 hrs), Amorgos, Megisti (7 hrs), Thira and Cyprus.

Once a week to Israel, Syria, Tilos, Nissiros, Folegandros, Naxos, Paros, Syros, Samos, Ikaria, Chios, Mytilini and Kavala. Hydrofoil daily to Kos. Twice weekly to Tilos and Nissiros. Tourist boats every day to Symi and Halki, less often to Tilos, Nissiros and Kos.

Daily flights to Athens, Kos and Karpathos. Regularly in summer to Iraklion and to major European destinations.

HALKI Ferries twice a week to Rhodes (1 hr), Karpathos (6 hrs), Kassos, Crete, Thira and Piraeus. Once to Folegandros, Naxos, Paros, Syros, Samos, Ikaria, Chios, Mytilini and Kavala. Daily tourist boat to Rhodes.

KARPATHOS (Pigadia and Diafani) AND KASSOS Twice a week with each other, Rhodes (7 hrs), Halki, Crete (Sitia and Agios Nikolaos, 6 hrs), Thira and Piraeus. Once to Folegandros, Naxos, Paros, Syros, Samos, Ikaria, Chios, Lesvos and Kavala.

Several flights a day from Karpathos to Rhodes.

KASTELLORIZO (MEGISTI) Twice weekly with Rhodes (6–7 hrs), sometimes continuing through half a dozen Dodecanese to Piraeus (32–35 hrs).

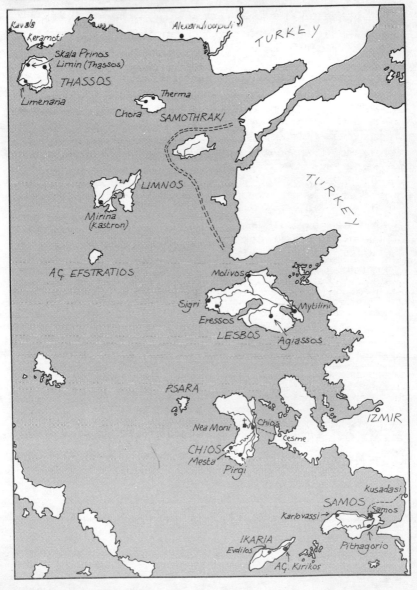

Kavala

Keramoti

Skala Prinos
Limin (Thassos)

THASSOS

Limenaria

Alexandroupoli

TURKEY

Therma

Chora

SAMOTHRAKI

LIMNOS

Mirina
(Kastron)

AG. EFSTRATIOS

TURKEY

Molivos

Sigri

Eressos

Mytilini

LESBOS

Agiassos

PSARA

Nea Moni

Chios

IZMIR

Cesme

CHIOS

Mesta

Pirgi

Kusadasi

SAMOS

Karlovassi

Samos

IKARIA

Evdilos

Pithagorio

AG. Kirikos

Scattered off the border waters of Asia Minor and north-east Greece, these seven islands are a somewhat arbitrary group. Indeed Thassos and Samothraki are both virtually isolated and best taken in with an exploration of the northern mainland. Their only island-hopping link is the port of Kavala, from where two weekly ferries leave for Limnos, Lesvos and a handful of the Dodecanese. **Thassos,** one of the cheapest accessible islands just two hours off-coast, has a varied appeal of sandy beaches, mountainous forest and minor archaeological sites. It is an excellent escape from the barrenness of Thrace and a satisfying introduction to the country if you're coming in from Istanbul. **Samothraki,** ancient Samothrace, has drama in its appearance and one of the most important island-sites but if you're looking to combine this with more laid-back holiday action there are few opportunities.

The five other islands are from this standpoint more conventional and they also form something of a unity – colonised anciently by the Ionian Greeks, and now, within spitting distance of modern Turkey, highly sensitive military points. Oddly **Samos,** which seems to have least going for it, is easily the most popular. Much better bets, and beaches, are on neighbouring **Ikaria** and on **Chios,** the most interesting island of the group with its mastic-rich medieval villages.

Samos, Chios and Lesvos each offer summer ferry connections to the **Turkish coast,** all ridiculously expensive for the distances involved but convenient and attractive points of entry. If your targets are the impressive ancient Greek sites at Ephesus, Miletus and Didyma it's feasible to make a good circuit of Anatolian Turkey, returning via Bodrum to the island of Kos, or from Marmaris to Rhodes.

EASTERN ISLES: OFF ASIA MINOR

SAMOS

Samos is separated from Turkey by just 3 km of water and logically it has the most regular ferry service: from Pithagoreio, its western port, to the town of Kusadassi. Though mountainous it is a richly fertile island and its wine has been famed for centuries, Byron, notably impressed, immortalising it in the chorus of 'The Isles of Greece', 'Dash down yon cup of Samian wine . . .'; the stuff to go for nowadays is Samiana, a non-resinated inexpensive white. But this acknowledged it doesn't seem a very compelling island. Far and away the most popular of the group, with direct charter flights to several European cities, its few sandy beaches have long been discovered. The Scandinavians are here in force, so too are the Germans.

VATHI, or **Samos Town**, is the main port and island capital – modern and uninteresting for the most part and, as far as tourists go, taken over by brusque Greeks in search of quick profit. Only the suburb of **Ano Vathi**, a clump of Turkish-style houses stacked on a hill to the south of the port, retains its indigenous life and architecture, both of which you can feel and see better elsewhere. However there are some relatively cheap rooms going and (next to the town hall) a worthwhile archaeological museum with finds from the Sanctuary of Hera, of which more later. Around the waterfront restaurants you may be able to change money and get good advice from travellers returning from Turkey; most of the boats actually leave from Pithagoreio but ticket agencies here run connecting buses.

Although Vathi Bay is large it is poor for swimming. Most people crowd on to **Gangou Beach**, a negligible strip of sand 1 km north-east along the harbour road. To get away from the crowds take the bus south to the deep sheltered bays and beaches of **Psili Ammos** (9 km) or **Possidion** (13 km), or head west towards the island's third port of Karlovassi. There are plenty of good roads on Samos and if you've got the money it's worth renting a moped for the day to check out where you might want to base yourself. Otherwise the bus service to Karlovassi is quite reasonable and you can reach some good points along the way.

A dozen kilometres in this direction, for example, is **KOKKARI**, a large fishing village built half on a spit and with a really excellent long pebble beach. It's definitely *the* place to stay on the island and a lot of people know it. However, if you want some action this is all to the good – and you should be able to find a room with a little persistence. The best must be the grey house near *Pension Alkyon*, run by the Hadjinikolau's. Most travellers make do with the slightly exposed unofficial campsite on the beach just east of town. For an equally good beach, and some isolation, head 40 mins walk west of Kokkari to **Tzamadou** (pronounced as in 'Kubla Khan'), a good spot for camping with a fresh water spring on the hillside above, or to **Agios Konstantinos**, a quiet fishing village a few kilometres on. Inland, there's a beautiful hour and a half's hike to **Vrondiani monastery**, the oldest on the island (1566) and maintained by just one monk. To get there take the dirt road next to Disco Kilimantzaro, follow the right turn to Vourliotes village and from there you'll see the trail marked by red dots on the rocks.

KARLOVASSI itself is a sprawl of a town, actually 2 km east of its port (where some, not all, of the Ikaria/Piraeus ferries dock). It was planned to be the centre of a Samos leather industry but the idea failed, leaving the town run down and pretty lifeless. On the positive side, though, there are some fair beaches in easy distance — in fact the only ones on the island which are actually substantial and sandy. The closest, if you've just arrived on a ferry, is 1 km west of the port, equipped with a reasonable *taverna* and a disco; buses and also the road terminate at its far end but you can walk on round forest paths to smaller coves. Alternatively, pick up a bus from the town across to the south coast beaches of **Ormos Marathokambos** (17 km: Ormos, the port, is 5 km beyond and below the main upper town), **Votsolakia** (19 km) and **Psili Ammos** (21 km). The first two have *tavernas* and a few rooms; Psili Ammos is a terrific beach but lonely, exposed and without fresh water so bring all supplies.

PITHAGOREIO, renamed in 1955 to honour its native mathematician, was the ancient capital of the island when, under the tyrant Polycrates (*c.* 540–522 BC), Samos was a major imperial power. Today it's a drab, dusty town in the shadow of the international airport and, somewhat inexplicably, a major tourist resort. In summer you've little chance of a room so if you decide to stay it's down to a rudimentary campsite in a field behind the town: run by a man called Stelios, a character everyone seems to know. There are beaches on both sides of town, the larger and better one to the west.

Traces of **ancient Pithagoreio** are much touted in Samos brochures but fade rapidly as you approach. The most important site ought to be the **SANCTUARY OF HERA** (8 km north of town, off the airport road), whose principal temple was, after the Olympeion in Athens, the largest ever built in the Greek world and one of the Seven Ancient Wonders. Its single reconstructed column, amid a scattered complex of sanctuary buildings, does it little justice. Much more interesting, if it hasn't been permanently sealed up, is the **EUPALINOS TUNNEL**, an aqueduct bored through the mountain just north of the town. Its centre has collapsed but it should be possible to explore a considerable part of its 900 metre length: you will, though, need a torch. To get there take the main Vathi road out of town: after a little way a track bears off left past scant remains of a theatre and splits in two — keep left.

IKARIA AND FOURNI

Mountainous and wooded, Ikaria lies just west of Samos — much less visited but connected by virtually all the Samos–Piraeus ferries. Its name is supposed to derive from the unexpected visitation of Ikarus, who fell to the sea just off-coast after melting the wax bindings of his wings, and (as any local will patiently explain) the island is itself clearly wing-shaped.

For years the place's main attraction has been a number of hot radio-active springs, some reputed to cure rheumatism and arthritis though others so potent they've long been considered a danger. There are hotels for the afflicted at **Therma** and the island's tiny port and capital of **Agios Kirikos**, on the south coast, but most travellers head straight out around the island to Evdilos.

EVDILOS, which is also a port of call for many ferries, is the largest village on Ikaria and a thoroughly agreeable place. There's an 'E' class hotel, a fair number of rooms to let and to either side pine forests slope down to the sea. Just outside to the west is **Kambos**, where there's a small museum and the ruins of a Byzantine palace, and you can walk out to some coves for swimming.

The beaches, however, are at **Armenistis**, right at the end of the bus route in the north-west corner of the island. This village is beginning to get popular – there are rooms to let and usually quite a number of campers behind the two 300 metre sandy beaches, 5–10 mins walk outside. Four or five *tavernas* have now gone into business. A word of warning, though, on the life and morals of Ikaria – which you've got to appreciate is an island more used to Greek rheumatics than to surf-seeking backpackers. Nude bathing, above all, is very heavily frowned upon.

Along the coast from Armenistis are the hamlets of **Ayios Liskaris**, a church built on a tiny islet (by a returned Canadian villager) just off its coast, and **Yas** (an hour's walk) with a solitary *taverna* on a small strip of beach. Striking inland you can walk to the *Rahes* ('ridges') villages of **Agios Dimitrios**, **Agios Polikarpos** and **Hristos**, and over to the spectacularly-sited and isolated **Karkinagri**, built on so steep a slope that its main communication with the rest of the island is by boat, many of the ferries stopping off-coast here to pick people up.

From the *Rahes* villages you can gaze down across the strait to Samos, dotted with a number of small islets. The only one that's inhabited is **FOURNI**, a beautiful looking place which you can reach by boat from Agios Kirikos. This is a regular local service, not a tourist excursion, and if you go you'll need to camp the night and take some provisions: there's only one boat a day and it goes straight back.

CHIOS

'Craggy Chios', as Homer describes his (probable) birthplace, is one of the most varied and interesting of Greek islands: a land with an eventful history and a strong sense of place. It has always been relatively prosperous, through its export of mastic (of which more later) and sailors, and it remains so today – the base of several exceptionally rich shipping dynasties. In consequence it hasn't made much effort to cultivate tourism and despite some fascinating villages, an important Byzantine monument and a healthy smattering of beaches, it is still remarkably little visited.

CHORA or **Chios Town**, probably has a lot to do with this for your initial reaction is to stay on the ferry. It is an unusually large island town – in the worst tradition of modern Greek planning – with a bustling commercial centre full of towering concrete office blocks. However, though there's nothing picturesque, it's a lively place with a shambling old bazaar district, some excellent and authentic *tavernas* and a regular evening *volta*, or promenade, along the waterfront. Right at the centre of Chios it is also the nexus of every road: an inevitable but useful point of exploration for the two very distinct southern and northern halves of the island. Buses run to most of the villages, all from the central plateia, though services to the north are very sparse and if you can find any form of transport to rent it's well worth the money.

Hotels are mostly grouped around the harbour: Inn Acropolis, on the quay near the market, is good value, Hotel Rodhon, behind Café Sport on Plateion Street, an okay second choice. If you're after a beach take the local bus (*astiko*, again from the main plateia) to **Karfas** (6 km), a long sweep of dust-like sand with just a 'D' class hotel, some rooms to let and a few *tavernas*: it's not very developed though crowded at weekends. Back in town, round the harbour area, **eating** can become a serious business. *Ta Dhelina* (near the prominent *Acropolis*) is cheap and has very good seafood – so too, at the opposite end of the waterfront by the port police, is *Ta Batsanakia*. More expensive but high quality is *To Mouragio*, halfway between the two, whilst for tremendous yoghourts (like the Mytilinas) there are great milk shops behind the Inn Acropolis.

The **bazaar** in Chora sprawls behind the old mosque on the main plateia, and if you're into old Greek music hover about and listen to some of the tunes from the ancient children's electric hobby horses – amazing, long-disappeared stuff. If you've time to fill in wander out, too, to the old Turkish quarter within the decaying walls of a **Genoese fort**, unusually some way inland. As on Samos, Lesvos and Limnos the Turks only relinquished control of the island in 1912 – and in 1822 committed here one of the worst massacres of the War of Independence, killing 30,000 Chiotes and enslaving some 45,000 others.

The Monastery of **NEA MONI**, founded by the Byzantine emperor Constantine Monomachos IX in 1049, is probably the most beautiful and important medieval building on any of the Greek islands. Its mosaics rank with those of Dafni and Ossios Loukas as among the finest artistic expressions of their age and its setting, high in the mountains west of Chora, is no less memorable. There's a direct bus only on Sunday mornings for the main mass – other times you have to take the local bus as far as Karyes (5 km) and walk the last 6 km. Once a powerful and independent community of 600 monks, the monastery, with its giant refectory and vaulted water cisterns, is now maintained by just five nuns: all are in their 80s and they close the buildings from around midday until 4 or 5pm. For a really good day's hiking you can go on beyond Nea Moni to the extraordinary medieval village of **Anavatos** (11 km; 22 km from Chora), its empty tan buildings almost indistinguishable from the 300 metre bluff on which they're built. As with many of the northern villages it is virtually deserted, a population of twelve remaining to grow pistachio nuts and a little other produce. One of the derelict buildings is being converted to a guesthouse but until this opens you'll either have to sleep out, or hitch at least one way back to Nea Moni if you want to make it back to Chora the same day.

Easier of access are the old mastic-producing towns of **southern Chios**, the only region of Greece where lentisk trees grow from whose resin comes the mastic, a jelly-bean-like chewing gum which became a major addiction at the C18th-19th Turkish Ottoman court. Today these *Mastikochoria* settlements survive mainly from apricots and tangerines but some mastic is still made, an odd acquired taste whether you chew it or drink the local spirit. The towns themselves are also quite unique – the only part of the island spared by the Turks in 1822 – and at the first opportunity you should jump on a bus to Pirgi or Mesta. **Pirgi**, 24 km from Chora, is probably the liveliest and most beautiful of the villages, its houses elaborately fashioned in *sgraffito*, the Italian device of cutting geometric patterns into the plaster and painting them in. Stone arches, an anti-earthquake device, span its streets – forming narrow corridors between the round-roofed buildings – and only at the church (itself boasting fine C12th frescoes) and main plateia do the blind alleys open out. A handful of rooms are available to let, there are some *tavernas* and, if you adopt this as a base, there's a beach 7 km away at **Kato Fana** (a sandy bay with the ruins of a temple of Apollo: go 1 km on the Mesta road and then take the dirt road down) and another, perhaps the best on Chios, at **Komi** (4 km walk down from Kalamoti, village on the main bus route).

Mesta, further on from Pirgi, has a more sombre feel in its stone buildings and cool shaded alleyways. The NTOG are restoring some of the buildings here as 'traditional guesthouses' but others remain in real use, animals housed in windowless ground-floor rooms, the family above. There are rooms to let here too and a good café-*taverna* on the plateia. Beaches nearby can be reached by goat trail (ask the way to Apothiki) or by following the coast around from Mesta's drab concrete port of **Passa Limani**, from where there are ferries most days to Rafina on the Athens mainland.

For a straight seaside village on this side of the island head for **Emborio**, a small fishing community with an excellent taverna 5 km from Pirgi. Its beach, Mavra Volia, is of fine dark sand, 5 mins walk on your right (facing the sea) along the front – follow the track along a shoulder of rock and past a smaller beach.

The villages of **northern Chios** never recovered from the Turkish massacre and many are completely deserted – making bus services accordingly sparse. They are also entirely different in character to the south, cubist hilltop clusters amid a dry deforested landscape more reminiscent of the Cyclades. **Volissos** was once the most important, its old stone houses wrapped beneath the hilltop Genoese fort. Most of the present population, however, live in newer buildings around the plateia. Since the bus comes this way only once a day you'll need to reckon on staying; there are a couple of rooms at the nearby harbour of **Limnia**, or Skala Volissos, and a good long sand and pebble beach 1 km south at Hori.

Kardamilia, in the north-east, is one of several villages that lays claim to Homer and is traditionally regarded as his birthplace: today, though, he'd probably find it somewhat drab-dark. At **Vrondados**, just to the north of Chora, the poet seems to have lived and taught – and you're naturally shown his lectern, strangely remodelled into part of a Classical shrine. Whatever, it's still worth a visit – if only for the little harbour and pebble beach.

There are beaches and *tavernas*, too on both Chios's satellite isles, **PSARA** and **INOUSSES**. Inoussa, just offshore, has daily caiques and tourists but Psara, with four services a week, is still fairly basic.

LESVOS

Lesvos, third largest of the islands (after Crete and Evia), was the birthplace of Sappho, Aesop and – more recently – the primitive artist Theophilos. But these artistic associations notwithstanding, it is neither a particularly interesting nor beautiful island. Additionally, unless you can afford to rent a car (nobody yet hires bikes or mopeds), you're likely to find the distances involved frustrate plans of exploring. Few villages particularly reward lengthy bus journeys.

MITILINI, the port and capital, spreads around two broad bays divided by a rocky promontory and once again a Genoese castle, built with a fair sprinkling of ancient blocks and columns. Everything of interest or relevance to tourists is grouped around the main harbour, the further bay is purely the industrial part of town. Rooms are usually a problem and perhaps it is best to head straight out. There's little to detain you – although it's worth staying long enough to wander round the castle (a sensitive military point, so no photos), and the bazaar (parallel to the harbour) with its junk stalls at the far end. There are two bus stations: nearby villages are served by the one in the middle of the harbour, all further destinations by that at the far end (away from the castle).

A few small resorts have grown in the south of the island (at **Kratigos**, **Plomari** and **Vrissa**) but none are especially compelling. More noteworthy is **Agiassos** (20 km from Mitilini), a beautiful inland village at the foot of Mount Olympos; its traditional houses with thick wooden verandahs wind along narrow cobbled streets, an effect that's only partially stifled by the summer crowds. There are rooms if you want to stay.

Way to the north of the island is **MITHIMNA** (known also as **Molivos**; 62 km from Mitilini), much the best and most attractive base for this region. Its cluster of sturdy red-roofed houses mount the slopes between an equally picturesque harbour and Genoese castle. There are plenty of rooms to let (and a Tourist Office, by the bus stop, to help you find them), a thriving nightlife and in mid-season drama performances in the castle. The town beach gets very crowded but this is remedied by excellent beaches at **Eftalou** (5–6 km north) and **Petra** (4 km south) – both have *tavernas* and at Petra there are a few rooms to let in the village.

Buses to the north-west coast are infrequent so it needs a special effort to get to **SIGRI**, famed for its 'petrified forest' – created by the actions of volcanic ash and waters. The trees, which are rarely more than stark trunks, are hard to find and sadly the best collection is that amassed on a small patio by the kiosk in the village. There is an excellent beach, however, and again a castle above the harbour (this time Turkish). A dozen kilometres to the south is **Eressos** whose ancient city (part of the Acropolis remains on the hilltop) was reputedly the home of Sappho; on the coast. Three kilometres below is **Skala Eressos** one of the best beaches on an island not famous for them and a fast-growing resort. Rooms are now often tricky to find but people camp by the beach – a small community of women usually among them, paying homage. Don't expect any great scene, though: most people holidaying on Lesvos are Athenian families.

LIMNOS

Limnos is a very straightforward Greek island which despite an airport and creeping lines of asphalt roads makes few concessions to tourism. Its landscape is flat and parched (in summer the water often has to be switched off in the evenings) and though there are some decent sandy beaches scattered around the coastline there are few means of getting to them. Buses tend to leave **Mirina** (the main town and port) early and often don't return the same day, and there are no bikes to rent.

The few tourists, swelled by a strong military presence, stay mainly in **MIRINA** (known locally as **Kastron**) on the west coast. It's a relatively pretty town with a fair sprinkling of old Turkish and Thracian houses, backing on to the ever-present Genoese-Turkish castle (free admission and worth the climb). There are a couple of small hotels but you're likely to be met off the boat with the offer of a room. For the best *taverna* simply follow the armed forces! To the north of the harbour is a good sandy beach but also a luxury bungalow complex so it's probably unwise to camp there. Isolated beaches and camping, however, are easy enough to find along the hilly and barren coastline south of Mirina; one of the best (with rolling breakers) is just before the village of Thanos. Further afield, in the great natural harbour of Moudros Bay, which cuts deep into the centre of the island, there are small resorts at **Tsimantria** and **Nea Koutalis**.

Indications of the most advanced Neolithic civilisation in the Aegean have been found at **Poliochni** on the east coast of the island. Its town walls (*c.* 2000 BC), interrupted by towers and gates, still stand in parts to some 16 feet. The Italian excavations of the 1930s uncovered four layers of settlement, ranging from a fourth-millennium BC city (pre-Troy) to an early and late Minoan and Mycenaean culture. But these are hard to make out and the site is still harder to reach.

THE NORTHERN ISLANDS

THASSOS

Just 5 km from the mainland, Thassos has long been a popular resort for northern Greeks, and in recent years has been attracting considerable numbers of foreign tourists. Without being spectacular it is a very beautiful island – its almost circular interior covered in gentle slopes of pine, olive and chestnut, rising to a mountainous backbone and down to a line of good sandy beaches. Whilst it's by no means 'unspoilt', tourists are spread over six or seven fair-sized villages as well as the two main towns so enclaves of bars and discos haven't swamped the ordinary Greek life.

THASSOS TOWN, or **Limin** as it's also known, is the island capital and main centre of life though not the main port, Kavala ferries usually stopping downcoast at Ormos Prinou. It's beachless and gets overcrowded in midseason but is none the less worth some of your time – a good-looking graceful sort of place, climbing back into the hills from a classically pretty fishing harbour, and with substantial remains of its ancient city dotted about and above the streets. *Rooms* are reasonably plentiful though in summer you'll need to take whatever's offered to you on arrival; alternatively there's a campsite just back from the sea, though for a longer-term base you might as well head out to a proper beach. In the town itself there are only a couple of small concrete strips, for which you pay admission – as at the much touted and very popular **Makriam-**

mos. For a day's swimming you'll do a lot better getting out to the east coast, if at all possible on a bicycle.

Ancient Thassos abounded in mineral wealth, controlled goldmines on the Thracian mainland and had two safe harbours: assets which ensured prosperity through Classical, Macedonian and Roman rule. The ruins scattered about the modern town – Limin, incidentally, means 'the harbour' – show traces from each phase of this development. The main excavated area is the *agora*, entered from beside the town *museum*, a little way back from the modern harbour. It's fenced but rarely locked and, taking advantage of this, best seen towards dusk when a calm, always slightly misty air seems to descend. Prominent are two Roman stoas but you can also make out shops, monuments, passageways and sanctuaries from the remodelled Classical city. And at the far end of the site (away from the sea) a C5th BC paved passageway leads through to an elaborate Sanctuary of Artemis, a good stretch of Roman road and a few seats of the odeion.

Above the town, roughly in line with the smaller fishing harbour, steps spiral up to a Hellenistic *theatre*, fabulously positioned above a broad sweep of sea and used for performances of *ancient drama* every Saturday between late July and mid August; tickets can be bought in advance from the town's tourist office, or the NTOG in Kavala. Beyond the theatre a path winds on to a Genoese fort, built with numerous stones from the ancient acropolis. From here you can follow the circuit of *walls* to a high terrace supporting the foundations of a Temple of Apollo and onwards to a small rock-hewn Sanctuary of Pan. Below it a precarious C6th BC 'secret stairway' descends to the far circuit of walls and back into town. It's a satisfying circuit which gives you a good idea of the structure and extent of a Classical city.

The villages along to Limenaria on the island's west coast are quite frequently served by bus but only two a day complete the whole circuit, so along the east you need to start early and plan if you intend to return. This, however, is the more attractive side of the island. Around 5 km out of Thassos town, on a mountainous ledge above the bay of Potamia, is **Panagia**, one of the prettiest of the island villages. Its old Macedonian houses, with their rough slate roofs, are built along winding paths opening on to a shaded plateia and a couple of *Kafeneia*. From here a road leads down in 4 km to **Chrisi Amoudia** ('Golden Beach') where there's a magnificent sweep of sand, a campsite and *taverna*: probably the best beach base. At the far side of this same bay you reach the more developed **Chrisi Akti**, a series of sand and pebble strips fronted by a dozen or so shops, restaurants and small hotels (most of them block booked in season).

Moving round to the west coast you reach **LIMENARIA**, the island's second town, built to house German mining executives brought in by the

Turks at the turn of this century. Their mansions give the town a distinctive character but this apart it's a rather ordinary tourist resort. You can, however, sleep on the beach to the right of town and at **Pefkari** (3 km east) is the best beach on the island, now with a campsite and *tavernas*. Another campsite, small scale and un-plasticy, is at **Dkala Rachoni**, near the drab little port of Ormos Prinou, but despite the standard no camping signs it's an island where you seem able to pitch a tent discreetly almost anywhere.

Few people get to exploring the interior of Thassos but there are worthwhile hikes up several hill villages. If you walk up to Theologos, however, don't be misled by a dotted line on the NTOG map into thinking you can go down to Kinira or Potamia. This particular indicated trail stops abruptly at the edge of an unscalable 300 metre cliff!

SAMOTHRAKI (SAMOTHRACE)

Second only to Thira, Samothraki is the most dramatic of all the Greek islands. Rising abruptly from the sea in a dark mass of granite, it culminates in Mount Fengari at over 5,000 feet. Seafarers have always been guided by its imposing outline, and in legend its summit provided a vantage point for Poseidon to watch over the siege of Troy. The forbidding coastline provides no natural harbour, and landing is still very much subject to the vagaries of the wind. Yet despite the difficulties, pilgrims journeyed to the island for over a thousand years to visit the *Sanctuary of the Great Gods* and to be initiated into its mysteries. The Sanctuary and its exciting natural setting is still the outstanding attraction of the island which, too remote for most tourists, also combines an earthy simplicity with its natural grandeur.

Boats dock at the little port of **Kamariotissa** where there are a few *tavernas*, some *rooms* to let and a small pebbly beach where you could unofficially and uncomfortably camp. Buses run fairly regularly in season along the north coast to Palaeopolis (the site of the Sanctuary) and inland to **CHORA**, the only village of any size, built high in the hills below the ruins of a Byzantine fort. Here too there are *rooms* (Samothraki has only one hotel, the expensive Xenia by the site), along with a tiny bank, a post office and two or three restaurants. It's the obvious place to stay.

The road to **Palaeopolis** follows the line of a river which divides, not far from Kamariotissa, into three arms; in a stony ravine between two of them lie the remains of the **SANCTUARY OF THE GREAT GODS**. Here, from the late Bronze Age to the last years of the Roman occupation, were performed the mysteries and sacrifices of the cult of the Kaberoi. It was the spiritual centre of the Northern Aegean, and its importance in the ancient world was comparable (although certainly secondary) to that of the Mysteries of Elefsis.

The religion of the Great Gods was centred upon a hierarchy of ancient Thracian fertility figures: the Great Mother, her subordinate male Kadmilos and the potent and ominous twin demons, the Kaberoi. When Greek colonists arrived (traditionally from Samos in about 700 BC) they simply assimilated the resident deities with their own – the Great Mother became Demeter, her consort Hermes, and the Kaberoi were fused interchangeably with the Dioskouroi. On the nucleus of a sacred precinct they made the beginnings of what is now the Sanctuary.

The mysteries of the cult were never explicitly recorded, for ancient writers feared to incur the wrath of the Kaberoi, but it has been established that two levels of initiation were involved. Incredibly both ceremonies, in direct contrast to the elitism of Elefsis, were open to all comers – including women and slaves. The lower level may, as is speculated at Elefsis, have involved a ritual simulation of the life, death and rebirth cycle – whatever, we know that it ended with joyous feasting and can conjecture, since so many clay torches have been found, that it took place at night by their light. The higher level of initiation carried the unusual requirement of a moral standard (the connection of theology with morality – so strong in Judaeo-Christian tradition – was rarely made at all by the early Greeks). This second level involved a full confession, followed by absolution and baptism in bull's blood.

The site (open weekdays 9–3.30, Sundays 10–4.30) is clearly labelled, simple to follow and strongly evocative of its proud past. It's a good idea to visit the *Museum* first where typical sections of the buildings have been reconstructed and arranged with friezes and statues to give you a fuller idea of their original scale. An excellent guide by Karl Lehmann – the American excavator of the site – is on sale.

The first building you come to is the **Anaktoron**, dating in this form from Roman times. The Hall of Initiation for the first level of the mysteries, its inner sanctum was marked by a warning stele (now in the museum) and at the south-east corner you can make out the libation pit. Next to it is the *Arsinoeion*, the largest circular building known in Greece. Within its rotunda are the walls of a double precinct (fourth century BC) where a rock altar, the earliest preserved ruin on the site, has been uncovered. A little further on on the same side of the path you come to the *Temenos*, a rectangular precinct open to the sky where the feasting probably took place and, edging its rear corner, the conspicuous *Hieron*. Five columns and an architrave of the façade of this large Doric edifice which hosted the higher level of initiation have been re-erected; dating in part from the C4th BC, it was heavily restored in Roman times. Its stone steps have been replaced by modern blocks but the Roman benches for spectators remain in situ, along with the sacred stones where confession was heard.

To the right of the path you can just make out the outline of the

Theatre, and above it on a ridge is the *Nike Fountain*, famous for the exquisitely sculpted marble centrepiece – the *Winged Victory of Samothrace* – which once stood breasting the wind at the prow of a marble ship: it was discovered in 1863 by the French and carried off to the Louvre. Further along the ridge opposite the rotunda is an elaborate medieval fortification made entirely of antique material. Finally, on the hill across the river, stands a monumental gateway dedicated to the Great Gods by Ptolemy II – many of its blocks lie scattered across the ravine.

If you have energy and a full day to spare it is possible to climb **Mount Fengari** (or Mount Saos as it's also known) for a startling view that does indeed, on a clear day, stretch to the plains of Troy in the east and to the Holy Mountain of Athos in the west. The paths are indistinct so get good instructions or better still a guide in Chora before you set out.

The handful of other villages on Samothraki are mostly tiny, desolate and none too easy of access; in season, and when the weather is good, caiques sometimes run trips from Kamariotissa to **Ammos** the only sandy beach on the island. Isolated in the south-east, this is a terrific strand – 800 metres long and very broad – but it's 6 hours' walk from the nearest village (Dafnai) so bring water and provisions if you plan to stay. The one other place you can get to is **Therma**, 14 km by road east of the port or a shorter walk from Chora. It has hot springs, as its name suggests, with an enclosed pool for each sex but no electricity or development. After soaking out you can swim off the pebbly shore nearby or spend a day hiking in the streams and fruit trees above the village. A few *rooms* are available and there's a campsite 2 km out. From Therma a much easier trail leads in three hours to the summit of Mount Fengari.

TRAVEL DETAILS

Again, to simplify the lists that follow we've excluded two vital boats. These are the **SS KYKLADES** (which, every week, connects Ikaria, Samos, Chios, Lesvos and Limnos with Kavala, Piraeus and many islands in the Cyclades and Dodecanese – see the travel details for the Cyclades) and the **SS SKOPELOS** which runs from Kavala (Wednesday midday) to Samothraki, back to Kavala (Wednesday night) and straight on to Limnos, Lesvos and Agios Efstratios before returning along the same route.

SAMOS AND IKARIA Daily to Piraeus (12 hrs), twice a week to Paros. Weekly from Samos to nearly all the islands in the Dodecanese (on the SS *Panormitis*). Also daily in season to Kusadassi and Ephesus (Turkey). *Flights* from Samos daily to Athens and frequently to many other European cities.

CHIOS Daily to Piraeus (10 hrs), and to Lesvos (4 hrs). Five days a week to Rafina (from Mesta). Twice weekly to Psara.

Weekly to Thessaloniki. Most days in season to Cesme (Ancient Cyrene, Turkey). Daily *flights* to Athens.

LESVOS Daily to Piraeus (14 hrs), and to Chios (4 hrs). Weekly to Thessaloniki. Most days in season to Ayvalik (Ancient Aeolis, Turkey). Daily *flights* to Athens.

LIMNOS Additional to the SS *Kyklades* and SS *Skopelos* only a weekly boat *from* Agios Konstantinos (10½ hrs) via Skiathos and Skopelos (5 hrs) and to/ from Kimi (9 hrs) for connections to Skyros. *Flights* most days to Athens.

THASSOS From Limin/Thassos town daily to Kavala (1½ hrs) and seven times daily to Keramoti (45 mins; bus in 20 mins to Kavala). Also from Ormos Prinou seven times daily to Kavala (1 hr).

SAMOTHRAKI Twice daily ferries in season from Alexandroupoli (2½ hrs), dropping to five a week out of season.

Chapter nine
SPORADES AND EVIA

The three northern Sporades – **Skiathos, Skopelos** and **Alonissos** – are archetypal holiday islands: they have good beaches, transparent waters, thick pine forests, and Skiathos excluded, are far from overrun by tourists. None have any prominent historic sites, nor indeed much history until the Middle Ages, and there's absolutely no pressure to do things cultural. Scattered (as their name suggests: sporadic) just off coast and head to tail with each other they're a very easy group to island-hop and well connected by bus and ferry with Athens (via Agios Konstantinos or Kimi) and with Volos.

Skyros, the fourth Sporade, is slightly isolated from the others, barer too in scenery, but with much the most character – retaining its traditional culture and brilliant white architecture. It's only beginning to get developed and frequented, and for an uncommercialised island within 6–7 hrs reach of Athens is hard to beat. The one slight drawback is onward connections, all of which must be made via the mainland port of Kimi.

The huge island of **Evia** (or Euboea) runs alongside the mainland for over 150 km and is in fact linked by a bridge at its capital, Halkis. Perhaps because it lacks any real island feel or identity it is explored by few foreign tourists. Athenians, in contrast, come here in a big way, unbothered by such scruples and attracted to half a dozen or so major resorts.

SKIATHOS

Vague warnings have already been mooted on the overdevelopment of Skiathos but if you've time to spare, or an overt taste for fellow travellers, there's no reason not to break your journey here, at least for a few hours. The main disadvantage to the place – that all the population lives in just one town, making everywhere else simply and explicitly a tourist resort – can even be turned to your benefit. Not all of the island is host to concrete pockets of villas and a little walking gives due reward. Camping, though, even in out of the way spots, is actively discouraged: summer turns the dry pine needles to tinder, a problem you have to be sensitive of on each of the Sporades.

SKIATHOS TOWN, where the boat docks, looks great from a distance though as you approach its commercial surrender becomes all too apparent. The castle promotes a disco and the old quarter stands overwhelmed by a haze of hotels, restaurants and – be warned – 'English-style pubs'. There are at least some fair *tavernas*, particularly Philippas at Kapodistriou 14 where you'll sometimes catch real Greek dancing to. Hotels in summer will all be full, though paying a little over the odds you'll probably find a *room*. Failing this there's an official campsite at Koulos, half way down the island's only road, around 6 km by frequent local bus.

An hour's walk out of town is the eighteenth century **Monastery of Evangelismos** (open 8am–12 and 5–7pm; strict hours), the only one still inhabited on the island. Here in 1827 the Greek flag was hoisted for the first time ever and, among other heroes of the War of Independence, Kolokotronis pledged his oath to fight for freedom. It is exceptionally beautiful – even beyond the grandeur of isolation you find in all Greek monasteries. To reach it walk out of the centre of town on the road to the airport; a dirt track is signposted just before the road forks. Alternatively, about 200 metres before this there's a quicker and more attractive donkey path; it begins beside a little roadside altar with a conspicuous corrugated roof – keep right all the way up. Beyond Evangelismos a track continues to the disused monastery of Kharalambos and, within a couple of hours, you can cross the island completely to the old ruined capital of **Kastro**, built on a windswept headland and connected to the mainland only by a narrow rock arch. Among the old houses are four chapels, two with fine frescoes, and there's a sheltered sandy bay close by. Some tourist agencies schedule boat excursions out here but as often as not you should have the place to yourself.

The real business of Skiathos, however, is beaches. There are reputed to be over 60 of them on the island, though those on the north-west coast aren't easily accessible unless you pay for a caique ride since much of the interior is mountainous and forested. The bus, however, runs down the 12 km strip of road every hour from around 9am–10pm (returning on the half hour) and from strategic points along the way you can reach a good number. The best are towards the end. **Koukounaries**, the very last stop, is worth at least one visit despite its popularity: a majestic bay of clear, slowly shelving water backed by cool acres of pines. And for more seclusion you only have to walk from here round the headland to a series of small sandy coves – among them **Banana Beach** (3rd round), trendiest of the island's nudist beaches and touted as such in the *Spartacus Gay Guide*. If you want somewhere quieter get off the bus a couple of stops before Koukonaries at the turning to **Agia Elenis** – 2½ km walk through the trees on the north coast of the island, with a seasonal *taverna*.

SKOPELOS

More rugged and better cultivated than Skiathos, Skopelos is also infinitely more attractive. Not that its beaches are any better, nor its pine forests thicker, but it does manage to maintain a character totally independent of tourism. Glossa and Skopelos, its two main towns, are in addition among the prettiest in the Sporades, clambering uphill along paved steps, their houses distinguished by Venetian-style balconies and roofs of softening grey slate.

Most boats call at both ends of the island, stopping first at the small port of **Loutraki** with a thin pebble beach, a couple of hotels and a few rooms to let. High above it looms **GLOSSA**, a sizeable and quite beautiful town, totally Greek but with a very few rooms to let, *kafeneia* and a *taverna*. An hour's walk from Glossa, across to the east coast, will bring you to a beach the locals call **Perivoli**. It's not signposted, nor much known, but is maintained on behalf of Glossa council by two aged but active cousins – Stelios and Diamantis Karvelis. Amazing characters and great company, they've fixed up home-made swings and even fixed a spring from the water seeping out of the cliff.

If you stay on the ferry – and this is probably the best plan – you reach **SKOPELOS TOWN**, clustered into the corner slopes of a huge, almost circular bay. Hotels here too are few, and mainly tucked away on the far side of the bay, but in the main body of the town there are dozens of *rooms* to let: take up one of the offers when you land, most are otherwise unadvertised. With the town's disco also banished to the hotel-enclave, nightlife centres exclusively on open-air eating (a fair choice) and on the dozen or so local bars – among them a fine jazz club, 'O Platonos', slightly more expensive but with the sounds (rare in greece) of Parker, Coltrane and Jarrett.

Within the town, spread below the oddly whitewashed ruins of a Venetian *kastro*, are an enormous number of churches – 123 reputedly, though some are small enough to be mistaken for houses – and perched on the slopes opposite the harbour are three monasteries, Evangelismos (in view of the town), Metamorphosis and Prodromos. **Metamorphosis** was left and locked in 1980 but the other two can be visited by both women and men: they're open 8am–12 and 4–6pm, dress respectfully. A road leads behind the hotels to **Evangelismos** (an hour's walk) and from there it's an extra half-hour's scramble over mule tracks to **Prodromos**,

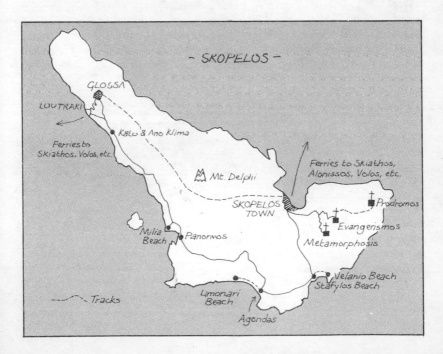

the furthest and most beautiful of the three. Ignore the new road which goes part way: it's longer and takes away most of the beauty of the walk.

Three or four buses a day cover the island's one road, between Skopelos and Loutraki, stopping at the side tracks to all the main beaches and villages. **Stafylos Beach**, 4 km out of town, is the closest: small and rocky with one *taverna*, renting rooms, and a very prominent no camping sign. To pitch a tent, though, you can just walk 5 mins round the coast to **Velanio** whose pines and surf always draw a small in-the-know summer community.

Further round the coast, the beachless fishing harbour of **Agnondas** (with a combination rooms/restaurant) is the start of a 15-minute trail to **Limnonari Beach**, 100 metres of fine sheltered sand and again a single seasonal *rooms*. No *tavernas* and water, though, and camping would be a bit cramped. A much more promising base, if you're after isolation and happy to walk out to a beach, is **Panormos**, a pleasant little village with both *rooms* and *tavernas*. Its beach is gravelly and uninviting but at nearby **Milia** there's a tremendous 2 km sweep of tiny pebbles beneath a terrace of pines, languidly facing the islet of Dasia. There's no *taverna* as yet, just a couple of houses. **Kato** and **Ano Klima**, on towards Glossa, both have rooms and tavernas but neither has a particularly enticing beach.

Marc Dubin, endlessly hiking his way around the islands, reports that there's a 20 km, five hour, **trail** over the ridge of the island from Skopelos Town to Glossa by way of the Vathia forest on the slopes of Mount Delfi. To set out from Skopelos town you'll find the beginning of the trail between the little church and fountain behind the orange walled cemetery at the top of Anapavseos street.

ALONISSOS

The most remote of this island group, I found Alonissos an initial disappointment. Its main village, Chora, was severely damaged by an earthquake in 1965, forcing the islanders to move down to the port of **PATITIRI** and its adjoining village of **Votsi**. The result is a rather sad sprawl of concrete, flat-roofed houses, its monotony broken only by the seafront cafés and by the fact that here at least the old women still genuinely wear their traditional blue and white costumes. This is where most people stay – and it'll probably be your main base since *rooms* are plentiful, much more so (and distinctly cheaper) than on Skopelos or Skiathos. The drab little town beach, and the NTOG-touted pebbly strips at **Marpounta**, are a let-down after the other islands. But don't let initial appearances discourage you: the north of the island is really very fine and there are beaches, mainly small sheltered coves, as isolated and beautiful as any you could hope for . . .

How to get there depends on your money and mood. Easiest is to take one of the caique rides offered at the harbour, check a few places and return next day with provisions for camping out a while. If you can spare £5, though, extra freedom can be bought by hiring a moped and braving the (pretty dreadful) circuit of dirt tracks. Or of course you can walk – distances are not great. Best targets are **Agios Dimitrios** (about halfway down the east coast), and **Kopelousako** or **Gerakis** in the extreme north of the island: there are rudimentary maps sold in Patitiri, worth a quick scan before setting out.

Less ambitiously, you could just head for the old town of **Chora** – only an hour's walk from Patitiri and now reinhabited by a couple of dozen island families, two of whom run *tavernas* and a shop. They've been joined in recent summers by a considerable settlement of Germans who have been buying up and renovating the (water-less) houses in traditional style. It's an atmospheric place – although still shifting uneasily between identities – and if you're not daunted by the new population can be an excellent place to camp. A 20-minute walk, down the hill, leads to a good cove-beach known as **Giala**.

It's possible to visit the neighbouring satellite-isles of **Peristera**, and **Panagia Kyra** by occasional caique from Patitiri. If anyone does we'd welcome accounts for the next edition.

SKYROS

Despite its closeness to Athens (6–7 hrs by bus and ferry), Skyros remains a very traditional and individual island – its ways of life perhaps slowed from change by many of the younger islanders going off to work in the city, leaving a quite contented kind of gerontocracy! It has definitely been discovered over the past four or five years but remains very much a place for people after 'the real Greece', or maybe more accurately 'the disappearing Greece'. Nobody seems to be after flash discos and tourist bars, and few have yet sprung up. There is, however, a psychotherapeutic centre for anyone who feels Skyros alone isn't enough to 'rethink the form and direction of their lives'. (For details of this, *The Skyros Centre*, write to Dina Glouberman, 1 Fawley Road, London, NW6.

Originally Skyros is said to have been two islands but now they are connected by a low-lying neck of land which is host to the only real road on the island – running from Linaria, the port, to Skyros Town, the capital. The towns are about 10 km apart and there is a bus service which connects with the ferries and is thus somewhat infrequent. **LINARIA** is a little village of small-time fishermen, built around a sheltered harbour. There are rooms to let if you want them but the island is off the beaten track and there seems to be no problem about sleeping on the beaches. Try walking north along the road to Skyros Town until you come to a long beach with a *taverna*. Alternatively, a longer walk south along a dirt road takes you to a large bay called **Kalamitsa**; here there is a long sandy beach and, again, a solitary *taverna* (which is reasonably priced and sells fish caught that morning).

SKYROS TOWN is built on the landward side of a high rock which rises precipitously from the sea. From its summit King Lykomedes is reputed to have pushed Theseus to his death; certainly it was the ancient acropolis and traces of Classical walls can be made out amidst the ruins of the Venetian *kastro*. Just within the walls, and dominating everything, is the crumbling C10th monastery of Agios Georgios, its walls partly incorporated into a later Venetian *kastro*. Perhaps equally striking, and splendidly incongruous, is the Memorial to Rupert Brooke – a nude bronze statue of 'Immortal Poetry', half-way down the hill. Brooke, who never visited the island, has become something of a local hero – miscast perhaps as a surrogate Byron; he was buried on Skyros in 1915, having died of septicaemia in a French hospital ship off the coast. (His grave is at a bay called **Tris Boukes**, miles out of the way in the south of the island; it can be visited by caique from Skyros.)

The capital is built in Cycladic style with brilliant white cubist houses stacked upon the hillside – it's a beautiful place. There are several hotels and plenty of rooms to let in private houses. Once again the latter are preferable: they're often exceptionally furnished, the islanders being re-nowned for their wood carving, copperware and a curious addiction to collecting plates. It's a traditional island in dress, too, most of the old men wearing the floating, baggy blue trousers as a matter of course and still more the unique Skyrian sandals with their thick rectangular soles and dense mass of leather thongs.

On the seaward side of the town's rock is a disco, amateur in the best Greek fashion, and below it a long beach of fine golden sand stretches for over a kilometre, reaching the straggly fishing hamlet of **Magazi** (rooms, *taverna*) at its far end. Just by the disco on the cliff is an excellent *taverna*, serving home-made rosé retsina straight from the barrel, and there's a semi-organised *campsite* nearby, behind the Hotel Xenia.

Behind the beach is a great fertile plain, an intense contrast to the rest of this mountainous island; don't be alarmed if the bus to Linaria first takes a detour across it, this is normal practice. Other parts of the island are remote and difficult to reach without committed walking – not aided by the studiously inaccurate local maps! Still, you can hire mopeds in Skyros Town and take to chance on the dirt tracks. There is a beach with a couple of *tavernas* at **Lallari**, immediately south of Skyros, and **Astitsa** on the west coast is still quiet and peaceful despite rumours of develop-ment plans (it usually has a seasonal *taverna* but don't rely on it being open). The walk to Astitsa takes a little over 3 hrs, going through a fertile valley between the mountains outside Skyros town.

If you can possibly coincide, Skyros has some particularly lively and individual festivals. The pre-Lenten **carnival** here is among the most outrageous in Greece – including a paganistic 'Dance of the Goat' performed by masked revellers, among them the Yeros (old man), Frango (Catholic), Korella (a transvestite) and a Pan figure dressed in a goatskin. The other big annual event is a **ponyrace** held along the town beach on 15 August; Skyros has a unique native breed, thought perhaps to be the diminutive horses depicted in the Parthenon frieze.

EVIA (EUBOEA)

The second largest island (after Crete), Evia often seems more like an extension of the mainland. At Halkis the connecting bridge has only a 70-metre channel to span, and there are ferry crossings at no less than six points along its length; additionally, the north of the island is closer to Volos than to the south, and the south likewise to Athens.

Nevertheless Evia is an island and in places a very beautiful one. The north, a rolling fertile countryside, is the most popular among Greeks, who value its greenery, its beaches and the mineral waters at Loutra Edipsou. The east coast is barren, rocky and largely inaccessible; but the west, right down to Karistos, is much gentler and has probably the most of interest to beach-seeking travellers. All the transport systems are biased towards this side of the island.

HALKIS (or Halkida), the island capital, is by far the largest town on Evia; heavily industrial, with its shipyard, railway sidings and cement works, it seems every bit an appendage to the mainland. It is a dire place apart from its old Turkish quarter (known as '**Kastro**' – where there are remains of the old fortress, an arcaded aqueduct, a mosque and the basilican church of Agia Paraskevi, an odd structure converted by the Crusaders in the C14th into a Gothic cathedral) and its **waterfront** – which overlooks the Euripos, the narrow channel whose strange currents have baffled scientists for centuries. Here one can stand on the bridge which spans the narrowest point and watch the water swirling by like a river; every few hours the current changes and the tide also reverses. Aristotle in despairing bewilderment is reputed to have thrown himself into the waters. *O Zoes* restaurant, 50 metres to the right of the bridge, serves cheap sustaining oven food and grilled octopus. The octopus, however, is about the only reason to linger: there's a good bus service from Halkis, serving most parts of the island.

KARISTOS, in the extreme south, is a small fishing port; quiet and unspoilt by tourism, it has a very good beach (to the right of town as you face the sea) and some fine reasonably priced restaurants. The main road from Karistos climbs up the high backbone of southern Evia – the seaside resorts of **Marmari** and **Nea Stira** (both, like Karistos, served by ferry from Rafina) lie far below it on the west coast at the end of branch roads; neither are particularly memorable. Further along the main road the ancient city of **Dystos** lies by the shore of a marshy lake 4 km south of the modern town of Krieza; the site is about 1 km to the west of the road along a farm track. There are remains of C5th BC houses and walls whilst on the Acropolis is a Venetian fortress.

At Lepoura, beyond Krieza, the road forks. The right-hand branch heads east across some of the most peaceful and beautiful countryside in Greece. **KIMI** is at the end of this road. It stands on a ridge high above the sea and its port, **Paralia Kimi**, is about 4 km away down below; town and port are connected by bus. The town is quite nice but the port nothing much in itself – useful only for its connections to the Sporades. Rooms in Kimi town are expensive if you're waiting overnight for a ferry, and (despite its name) there is no beach to sleep on at Paralia Kimi; there are, however, thick woods between the two.

The left-hand branch from Lepoura takes you down to the west coast and the towns of Eretria and Halkis. The road hugs this stretch of coast but not to your advantage as it is a drab disappointing shoreline – the seaside town of **Amarinthos** is a case in point. Curiously, similar scenery around Eretria – a few kilometres on – has attracted the package tour companies. **ERETRIA** is more notable for its ancient site, much of which lies under the modern town. Visible remains are dotted around the centre of town (most conspicuously an *agora* and a *Temple of Apollo*) but more interesting are the excavations in the north-west corner, behind the small museum. Here the *theatre* has been uncovered and from its orchestra steps descend to an underground vault used for sudden appearances and disappearances; beyond are the ruins of a *gymnasium* and *sanctuary*.

The main road north from Halkis crosses flat farmland for a few kilometres, after which it climbs steeply among forested hills. The village of **Prokopi** lies beyond the summit in a valley enclosed by the rich and beautiful woods which are one of its claims to fame; the others are a castle on a precipitous rock and the church of St John of Russia, whose relics are kept there. At **Strofilia** it's possible to take a left fork to **Limni** on the west coast, a small resort (*rooms*) with shingle beaches curving gently around its bay. Most of the traffic from the south bears right at **Strofilia** along the road which works its way around the north coast before looping down to Loutra Edipsou. The coastal road direct from Limni to Loutra Edipsou is dangerous and carries little transport.

Pefki is a seaside resort which gets crowded with Greek tourists in the summer; it has a very long beach and numerous tavernas. At **Orei** the beach is small but it's still essentially a fishing village (though with two cheap hotels). **Loutra Edipsou** attracts older, unhealthy Greeks (*104* hotels of them) who come to bathe at the spas which have been famous since antiquity. Better to cross over to the mainland at **Agiakambos**, a few kilometres back — the cheapest and quickest ferry link in the north of the island.

TRAVEL DETAILS

Skiathos, Skopelos and Alonissos

From Agios Konstantinos Daily to Skiathos (3¼ hrs) and Skopelos (5½ hrs); continuing directly to Alonissos (6 hrs) once a week. (NB Heavily reduced service out of season.)

From Kimi Five times a week (not currently on Thursdays and Saturdays) to Alonissos (2¾ hrs) and Skopelos (3½ hrs); continuing directly to Skiathos (5½ hrs) once a week. Weekly connection to Limnos.

From Volos Two or three boats a day to Skiathos (3 hrs) and Skopelos (4½ hrs); one boat virtually every day to Alonissos (5 hrs). (NB This is much the best service out of season and it's also the cheapest.) In season there are 'Flying Dolphin' hydrofoils to Skiathos and Skopelos — quicker but considerably more expensive.

Skiathos–Skopelos Several times a day (1½–2¼ hrs).

Skopelos–Alonissos Every day in season, nearly every day out (½ hr). Most days you can get a boat from Skopelos or Alonissos to Skyros (via Kimi), and vice versa. Flights daily between Skiathos and Athens.

Skyros

Skyros is served only by ferries from **Kimi**, currently operated by two different companies. The Anemoessa (The Boat of the Skyrian People) runs every day, usually at around 5.30 or 6pm. To connect with this you'll have to take a bus from Athens (Liossion 260) at around 1 pm, a 4 hour journey which in midseason you should certainly buy tickets for in advance (though ferry tickets can be bought quite easily in Kimi: they very rarely sell out). The other ferry, due to the success of the Skyrian People's boat, now runs only three or four times a week — confusingly, often at around the same time of day (5.30–6pm). Its advantage is that you can buy combined boat and bus tickets in advance from the Alkyon Tours agency at Akademias 98, Athens; Akademias is right in the centre of the city, parallel to Stadiou. Either ferry from Kimi to Linaria takes just under 2 hrs.

Evia

By bus from Athens to Halkis every half hour (takes 1½ hrs; leaves from Liossion 260). Good bus service from Halkis to most points on Evia.

Trains, 19 daily to Halkis from Athens (Larissis station); takes 1½ hrs.

By ferry from Rafina–Karistos (3 daily; 2 hrs), Rafina–Marmari (3 daily; 1¼ hrs), Rafina (Agia Marina)–Nea Stira (8 daily; 50 mins), Oropos–Eretria (every hour from 6am–11pm; 25 mins), Arkitsa–Edipsos (12 daily; 50 mins), and Glifa–Agiokambos (every 2 hrs from 6am–8pm; 30 mins).

Buses to **Rafina** (every ½ hr; 1 hr) and to **Oropos** from Mavromateon Street, Athens; to **Arkitsa** and **Glifa** from the Liossion terminal.

SALAMIS

Piraeus
(Ferries
and
Hydrofoils)

AEGINA

Aegina

Ag. Marina

Temple
of
Aphaia

ANGISTRI

Moni

Perdika

PELOPONNESE
(ARGOLID)

Methana

POROS

Kalavria

Poros

Galatas

Ermioni

Hydra

DOKOS

HYDRA
(Idra)

Portoheli

Vrello

Dapias

AG. Anargyroi

SPETSES

Only an hour or three's ferry-ride from Athens and often hardly an olive's throw from the mainland, perhaps the most surprising aspect of the Argo-Saronic islands is their different and distinct identities. Less surprising is their massive popularity, with Aegina especially becoming something of an Athenian suburb at weekends. All in fact have a highly developed seasonal nightlife and, however you live, you'll be paying a fair percentage above normal costs.

Classic sandy beaches are not an Argo-Saronic feature though on pine-cloaked **Spetses**, much the most attractive of the group, there are some excellent small coves. **Hydra** is now ludicrously expensive and pretentiously chic but it does have a strikingly beautiful port and some attractive walks. **Aegina** has one of the finest ancient temples in all Greece: well worth a day trip if you've time to spare in Athens. There's not too much to be said, though, for **Poros** and absolutely nothing for **Salamis** – officially part of the group but essentially an extension of the mainland Elefsina pollution.

Aegina 253, Poros 254, Hydra 255, Spetses 257.

AEGINA (EYINA)

Aegina is so close to Athens – and so popular an escape – that you might expect it to be little different from the capital. This isn't the case: like other islanders the Aigenetans make a living from fishing and from agriculture – particularly pistachio nuts, for which the island is rightfully renowned. And, more important, it's far enough from the Piraeus to avoid major pollution both of sea and air.

Most ferries go to **AEGINA TOWN**, the capital, though in summer a few also call at AGIA MARINA, handier if you've come here just to visit the Temple of Aphaia. The capital, unashamedly geared towards tourism, is a pleasant enough place with some grand old buildings from the time when it served as the temporary capital of Greece in the wake of the War of Independence (1826–8). It was also the island's ancient city and the remains of a Temple of Aphrodite (with one solitary column standing) can be seen near the quay; finds from here and from the Temple of Aphaia (including a reconstruction of the pediment) are displayed in the Museum, next to the Cathedral at the far end of town. There are few cheap hotels in the town but some reasonable priced *rooms* can be found away from the waterfront.

The **TEMPLE OF APHAIA**, the island's great site, lies at the other end of Aegina – visually complex, with a superimposed array of columns and lintels, it seems almost like an Escher drawing. Among the most complete ancient buildings in Greece, it is Doric in style and probably dates from around the C6th BC. Less than two centuries ago its pediments were intact and virtually perfect, depicting two battles at Troy, but they were 'bought' from the Turks by Ludwig of Bavaria and remain in Munich. The dedication is unusual – Aphaia, a Cretan nymph who had fled from the lust of King Minos, was worshipped almost exclusively on Aegina.

To get to the temple from Aegina Town you can go by bus or, the best approach, by hired bicycle. Take the road out along the north coast to the village of Souvala (5 km), where you can make a 3 km each-way detour to the island's old capital, **Palaeochora** – ruined and deserted behind the village and monastery of Agios Nektarios. The town was built here in the C9th as protection against piracy and only abandoned in 1826, after independence from the Turks. A dozen or two of the reputed 365 churches and monasteries remain in recognisable state but nothing of the town itself: when the islanders left, they simply dismantled their houses and moved them to modern Aegina. The temple is well signposted to the right of the coast road 6 km after the Palaeochora turning, its approach road lined with pines resin-tapped for the excellent Aegina retsina.

AGIA MARINA, 13 km from Aegina Town, lies on the far side of the Aphaia Temple ridge. A major resort, its beach is so crowded with Athenians that it is only really worth coming here for the ferries. Rooms and restaurants are both pricey, though scores of backpackers brave the insect life to camp in the olive groves behind the beach: not a great prospect. Beyond the town the road continues south for a little distance but it's impossible to complete a circuit of the island: you must either return the way you came or cut through the centre across a long valley.

For such a popular island, Aegina is curiously short of attractive swimming spots. The best opportunities are to be had if you head towards Perdika on the south-west coast, a slightly quieter region. Halfway along at Marathon a road climbs inland to Mount Oros with Aegina's third temple, dedicated to Zeus, on its summit. **PERDIKA** itself, 20 mins by bus from Aegina Town, is a fishing village with overpriced fish and a small beach but it is certainly the best place to stay on the island. Everyone camps on the abandoned naval reserve on the side of the bay opposite the village, a series of partly shaded terraces. Alternatively, there are caiques from here across to **Moni Islet** where there's an official NTOG campsite, a seasonal *taverna* and tremendous skin diving.

ANGISTIRI, the other of Aegina's satellite isles, is accessible by caique from the capital. It has a village, a couple of small beaches and a dozen (mostly 'D' class) hotels.

POROS

Separated from the mainland by a 400 metre strait, Poros (literally 'the passageway') hardly constitutes an island. Nor does it have too much else going for it: beaches are few and poor, and package holiday companies here in a big way. There are no hotels below 'C' class and ostentatious signs stress that camping is forbidden; nor is there an official campsite so intentions seem clear.

Perhaps the most interesting feature of the island is its topography. It is in fact two islands, Sferia and Kalavria, separated from each other by a shallow engineered canal. Ferries drop you at **POROS**, the only town, which rises steeply on all sides of the tiny volcanic peninsula of **Sferia**. The harbour, though heavily swamped by tourist shops, could be an attractive place to stop over out of season except that then the local police allow no private *rooms* to be let. Other times you might find a place near the clock tower.

Most of the hotels are to be found on **Kalavria**, the main body of the island, a short walk across the canal; they stretch for some 2 km on either side, a strangely ill-placed concentration. The main bay here – **Neorion** – is host to a waterski and windsurfing school but its waters are positively dirty. **Askeli Bay**, to the right of the canal walking over to Kalavria, is clearer but has little in the way of beaches. The best is **Kanali**, near the beginning, which usually charges admission: a reflection both of Poros's commercialism and scarcity of sands.

At the end of the stretch of road around Askeli is the **Monastery of Zoodochos Pigi** (a little under 4 km), a simple C18th establishment whose monks have fled the tourists, leaving just a caretaker to collect admission charges. It's a nice spot though with a couple of *tavernas* under the plane trees nearby, and, striking across from here to the far side of the island through pines and olives you can feel quite free of the plastic and concrete of the new developments. A few columns of a C6th BC Temple of Poseidon can add direction to your wanderings, 5 km up in the hills but sadly it's also been connected by a road, leading up from behind the Hotel Silene on the right of the canal causeway.

More rewarding escapes and excursions are best made on the mainland. You can hire a bicycle, cross over to the village and beach of **Galatas** and head east to the immense lemon groves of **Lemonodassos**, some 30,000 trees and an inspiringly positioned *taverna*, or go west to the gorge of **Trizini**, site of ancient Troizen, birthplace of Theseus. And from Galatas it's no more than a day's excursion to the magnificent theatre at **Epidavros**. By this point however you'll probably have left the island for good – the Peloponnese being less than ½ km distant.

HYDRA

The town of **HYDRA** (or **Idra** as it is pronounced and often spelt), its tiers of Venetian mansions climbing from a perfect horseshoe harbour, is a very beautiful spectacle. Thousands of others think so too and from Easter until September it's packed to the gills. The front becomes one long outdoor café, the hotels are full and the discos flourish. Even beyond Mykonos it is now the most exclusive and expensive resort in Greece. Once a fashionable artists' colony – discovered in the 1960s as people restored the grand old houses – it has taken the old money-raddled path into a haunt of the rich and posing and is not unfairly described as 'the Greek St Tropez'. But this acknowledged I'd still recommend a quick visit if you can get here some time outside peak season.

The town's dozens of **mansions** were mostly built in the C18th, on the accumulated wealth of a remarkable merchant fleet of 160 ships who traded as far afield as America and during the Napoleonic Wars broke the British blockade to sell corn to France. Fortunes were made and the island also enjoyed a special relationship with the Turkish Porte, governing itself, paying no tax, but providing sailors for the Sultan's navy. Waves of immigrants arrived here – persecuted minorities from all over the Greek mainland – and by the 1820s the town's population stood at nearly 25,000; an incredible figure when you reflect that today it is under 3,000. With the War of Independence, Hydriot merchants provided most of the ships for the Greek forces – and inevitably most of the commanders. Their houses are still the great buildings of the town: *Tsombados's* is now a naval training school, *Tombazis's* the school of fine arts.

Yet more distinctive, however, is the fact that there are no motor vehicles of any kind on the island – no roads either, for Hydra is mountainous and its interior accessible only by foot or donkey. The practical result of this is that most of the visiting tourists don't venture outside the town and with a little hill walking you can find yourself in a quite different kind of island. In any case a good proportion of people stay on Hydra only a few hours, enough time for a cocktail and to browse among the opulent waterfront boutiques before piling back into their Aegean cruise ships.

Following the streets of Hydra upwards and inland you reach a path which winds up the mountain to the **Monastery of Profitis Ilias** (Prophet Elijah) and the **Convent of Agia Efpraxia**. Beautifully situated, they are about an hour's walk; the nuns at the convent (the lower of the two) offer hand-woven fabrics for sale. Further, and to the left if you face away from the town, is the **Monastery of Agia Triada**, occupied by a few monks (no women admitted); from here a path descends to Mandraki, a further half hour's walk. Actually Hydra is scattered with hundreds of churches – once again reputedly 365 – and the most important is to be found in the town. This is **Panagia Mitropoleos**, built in a courtyard near the entrance to the port (1774).

The only sandy beach is at **Mandraki**, 1½ km east of the town along a concrete track. On the other side a coastal path round the corner of the harbour leads to a rocky and popular stretch – just before the little fishing village of **Kameini**. **Kastello**, another rocky beach with the ruins of a castle, is just on from here and beyond it **Vlicho** has a good *taverna*. Quite some way further (walkable but easier by boat from the town) is the pine-backed **Molos Bay** and lastly, on either side of the point, the bays of **Bisti** and **Agios Nikolaos**, both of which offer good swimming. The south coast, if you're really energetic and solitude-seeking, is dotted with coves.

Prices on Hydra are high and *accommodation* literally unavailable in high summer and at Easter. *Camping* is frowned upon but you can get away with it.

SPETSES (SPETSAI)

Spetses, the island where John Fowles once lived (and used, thinly disguised as Phraxos, as the setting for *The Magus*), is very green and very small. If you're energetic you could walk the whole way round it in a day. Whatever, you can easily wander off *'away from its inhabited corner [where Spetses is] truly haunted ... its pine forests uncanny'*. Sheltered pebble bays teeming with fish are scattered along much of the coastline and a number of trails link them with the dirt track round the perimeter of the island.

SPETSES, or **Dapia**, the port and town is less immediately striking than Hydra or even Poros but has more charm than either. Pebble mosaiced courtyards and streets sprawl between massive 200-year-old mansions whose architecture is quite distinct from the Peloponnesian styles across the straits, and horse-drawn cabs connect the various quarters of town, spread out along the waterfront. Almost everyone stays here and all kinds of **accommodation** are available – from a massive old Edwardian hotel by the harbour to simple rooms in people's houses. If you can get one, the best *rooms* are in a grand old house behind the Sotiro Anargiro mansion, just uphill from the cannon-studded main harbour: illustrious quarters and not too expensive. For *camping*, head out to the shade of tamarisks behind Lampara Beach, 700 metres north-west of the dock – this seems to be tolerated if somewhat exposed. **Food and drink** can be pricey and if your money's tight you'll probably need to hunt around. Among cheaper places are *Taverna Haralambos* (on Baltiza inlet, by the smaller harbour) and *Restaurant Zammas* (500 metres north from the main harbour). Locals seem to drink around the corner from the main harbour in a *kafeneion* opposite the fish market and hopeful cats.

In town the local **museum**, housed in a magnificent family mansion, is well worth a visit. It has a display of relics from the War of Independence, including the bones of the Spetsiote admiral-heroine Luscarina Bouboulina. Just outside the town, Fowles aficionados will notice Anagyrios

College, a curious Greek recreation of an English public school where Fowles taught.

Although most vehicles are banned on Spetses the restrictions aren't as severe as for Hydra. There are certain official exceptions (including the municipal bus and, rather sadly, mopeds for hire to tourists) and there is a road which encircles the island. Three other tracks branch off from the road (at Dapias, at Vrello and at a point 1 km south of Agios Anargyroi) to meet in the centre of the island at the church of Profitis Ilias – a rewarding walk with a majestic 360-degree view over Spetses, Hydra and the mainland, and a well with bucket for the thirsty.

Heading north and anti-clockwise round the coast from Dapias the road is concreted until the houses run out after 1 km or so; thereafter it is a dirt track which winds through pine trees and around inlets. The forest stretches from the central hills right down to the shore and it makes for a beautiful coastline with little coves and rocky promontories all shaded by trees. **Vrello** is one of the first places you come to – set in a wooded valley known locally as 'Paradise'. It is a fairly apt description except that many of the beaches (including Vrello's) become polluted every year by tourists' rubbish. However, the entire coastline is dotted with coves (claimed to be particularly safe swimming for children) and in a few places there are small *tavernas* – at **Agios Georgios**, for instance, 2 km on from Vrello.

Working your way round to the west coast, you reach **Agia Paraskevi** with its small church and beach and then the larger and more developed **Agios Anagyrios**. Here there is a small town consisting mainly of holiday homes, a popular location with a taverna on the beach (overpriced but enjoying a monopoly) and a daily boat from Dapias. There's also a cave nearby which is said once to have led to the Profitis Ilias monastery before the tunnel was sealed by an earthquake; it is known as Berkeris's Cave after an incident when the islanders hid there from the Turks. The road and coves continue after Agios Anagyrios though often at some distance from each other. The pines thin out, too, but now your attention is caught by the wooded islet of **Spetsopoula**, privately owned by Stavros Niarchos, the Greek shipping millionaire. Someone with a wicked sense of humour has placed the Spetses rubbish dump opposite it. At this point the dirt track becomes a tarmac road and takes you down to **Agia Marina** – which is basically the swinging end of Dapias, with a beach, disco and *tavernas*.

TRAVEL DETAILS

1 Ordinary ferryboats

From the Central Harbour at **Piraeus**: at least hourly to Aegina (1½ hrs); 6 daily to Poros (2¼–3½ hrs); 2 or 3 times daily to Hydra (2½–4½ hrs) and to Spetses (3½–5½ hrs). About five connections daily between Aegina and Poros, and two between Poros–Hydra and Hydra–Spetses.

Most of the ferries stop on the mainland at Methana (between Aegina and Poros) and Ermioni (between Hydra and Spetses); it is possible to board them here from the Peloponnese (or vice versa). Some continue from Spetses to Portoheli. There are also very frequent boats between Poros and Galatas (10 mins).

NB Some boats are designated *Express* and are about 50 per cent quicker than the ordinary ferries; they are, however, the same price. There are more ferries at weekends and less out of season (although the service remains good); they leave Piraeus most frequently between 7 and 9am. Do not buy a return ticket as it saves no money and limits you to one specific boat.

2 'Flying Dolphin' hydrofoils

Hourly from the Central Harbour at Piraeus to **Aegina** only (6am–7pm; takes 40 mins).

All hydrofoils going beyond Aegina leave from the **Zea Marina**: 5 times daily to Poros (1 hr 05–1 hr 25) and Hydra (1 hr 20–2 hrs); 8 times daily to Spetses (2–3 hrs). All these times depend upon the stops en route.

Aegina is connected with the other three islands twice a day; Poros, Hydra and Spetses with each other 3–5 times a day. Hydrofoils, also, often stop at Methana and Ermioni and all of those to Spetses continue to Portoheli (10 mins more). This is a junction of the hydrofoil route – there are usually two a day onwards to Nafplio (and vice versa; 1½ hrs) and two others to Monemvassia (1½–2½ hrs). One of the Monemvassia hydrofoils continues (every day except Sunday) to the island of Kithira.

NB Once again services are heavily reduced out of season (but all the routes still run). Hydrofoils are usually twice as fast and twice as expensive as ordinary boats – although to Aegina the price is little different. If you book a return ticket 12hrs in advance you can make a considerable saving. Details and tickets available from local agents and in Athens, amongst others, from Thomas Cook (Kar. Servias 2, Sintagma; 2nd floor).

Chapter eleven
IONIAN

Trailing down the west coast, these six islands are both cultural and geographical intermediaries between Italy and Greece. The Homeric realm of Odysseus, here alone of all modern Greek territory the Turks never held sway. Instead after the fall of Byzantium possession passed to the Venetians and the islands became a keystone in that city state's maritime empire from 1386 until its collapse in 1797. Most of the population must have remained immune to the establishment of Italian as the official language and the arrival of Roman Catholicism, but Venetian influence remains evident and beautiful (despite a series of earthquakes) in the characteristic island towns. On Corfu it is also mixed with that of the British, who imposed a military 'protectorate' over the Ionian at the close of the Napoleonic Wars before eventually ceding to Greece in 1864. All this notwithstanding there is no question of the islanders' essential Greekness; the poet Solomos, author of the National Anthem, hailed from Zakinthos and the first Greek president, Capodistrias, from Corfu.

Tourism has hit Corfu in a big way – so much, in fact, that it's the only island known to locals and foreigners by different names. In Greek it's **Kerkira**, a land you can still find surprisingly unspoilt outside midsummer and the main resorts; though right out of season beware – rain pours down in intense sporadic torrents here and throughout the group from November until early March. None of the other five islands have had anything like Corfu's scale of development, although it does seem to be beginning on parts of **Zakinthos**, and each have diverse enough traditions and landscapes to keep island-hopping interesting if you decide to see them all in one go.

Kithira, isolated at the foot of the Peloponnese, officially belongs to the Ionian group but since it's easiest reached from Githion or Neapoli it's covered with them in Chapter 2.

CORFU (KERKIRA)

The seductive beauty of Corfu has been a source of inspiration for generations. Shakespeare took the island as his setting for *The Tempest*, Lawrence Durrell paid him tribute by naming *his* book about the island *Prospero's Cell*, and Edward Lear enthused that it made him 'grow

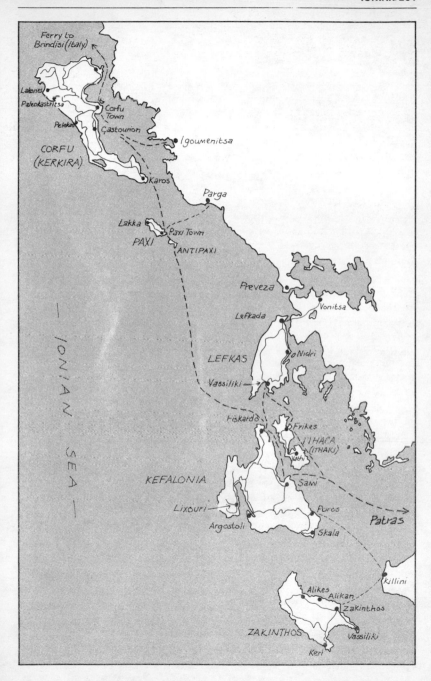

Ferry to
Brindisi (Italy)

Lakones
Paleokastritsa
Peleka
CORFU
(KERKIRA)
Corfu
Town
Castourion
Igoumenitsa
Karos
Parga
Lakka
Paxi Town
PAXI
ANTIPAXI
Preveza
Vonitsa
Lefkada
LEFKAS
Nidri
Vassiliki
Fiskardo
Frikes
ITHACA
(ITHAKI)
Vathi
Sami
KEFALONIA
Lixouri
Argostoli
Poros
Skala
Patras
IONIAN SEA
Killini
Alikes
Alikan
Zakinthos
ZAKINTHOS
Vassiliki
Keri

younger every hour'. Henry Miller, totally in his element, became euphoric, lying for hours in the sun 'doing nothing, thinking of nothing'.

It is still possible to feel this way. Corfu's natural appeal, the shapes and the scents of its lemon and orange trees, its figs, cypresses and olives: all of this remains an experience. But at a price – it now has more package hotels than any other Greek island, more holiday villas, and a whole coast has been virtually ruined. Miller's Corfu, meanwhile, is getting more and more difficult to find.

You realise all this the moment you step ashore at the principal port of **KERKIRA** (or **Corfu Town**), bunched in between two hilltop forts – christened 'old' (*palea*) and 'new' (*nea*) to help the tourist differentiate, though both were actually built by the Venetians in the C16th. Beyond, the alley-like streets are crammed through the summer with holidaymakers converging to 'buy something Greek' from the myriad of tourist shops catering for just that purpose.

This accepted and anticipated, Kerkira is essentially an extremely elegant town. Evelyn Waugh found it reminded him of Brighton and the parallel is definitely on – adding some exceptional Venetian churches and a huge and beautiful square, the Spianada, where the Corfiotes play cricket. (This is one of two main British legacies, the other being ginger beer, or *tsintsi birra* as it's called.) There's a tourist office right in the centre of town, on Dessila Street, where you can pick up free maps of the town and island and information on *rooms* to let in private houses, the likeliest form of summer accommodation. If you arrive fairly early in the day you could also check out the cheaper town hotels – best of all *Hotel Kriti*, right in the heart of town at Nikoforos 43, or the slightly pricier *Hotel New York* opposite the Igoumenitsa ferry dock. Corfu's two youth hostels are both miles out in the interior of the island and, without transport, pretty useless bases. If you're just waiting for an early morning ferry, it's possible to grab a few hours' sleep in the square opposite the Igoumenitsa ferry dock. Among *tavernas* – which need considerable scrutiny if you want anything both cheap and Greek – there's a good no-name place at Solomou 20, below the Hotel Kriti, and *I Klimataria*, behind the Igoumenitsa ferry dock at P.N. Theotiki 19, can be recommended. A functional *souvlaki psistaria* is at Ag. Panton 44, just off Voulgareo street.

Four km walk out of town, and probably one of Greece's five most popular excursions, is the postcard-picturesque 'Mouse Island', or Pondikonisi, capped by a small monastery and joined to the mainland at **Kanoni** by a skinny causeway. If you've had 24 hours in Kerkira Town, though, you'll probably feel it's well time enough. There are two **bus terminals** out: one for numbered routes through the centre of the island on Plateia San Rocco, the other for more remote destinations on Plateia Solomou, just below the Nea Frourio (new fort). **Mopeds** are also for hire here, and at most other main resorts, and are a useful means of working out at which beach you want to base yourself; be more than usually cautious however as an incredible number of people have accidents on the gravel and potholed tracks.

The coast road which stretches for about 15 km to either side of Kerkira Town – roughly from **Kassiopi** in the north to **Messongi** in the south – has been remorselessly developed and really you might as well forget it; you certainly won't be able to camp anywhere along it other than the official sites at (from north to south) **Pirgi, Ipsos, Dassia, Dafnila, Kondokali** and **Messongi**. Kassipi, Dassia and Benitses in particular are beginning to resemble miniature Benidorms.

So, sadly, is **Paleokastritsa** on the west coast; in this case with understandable reason for it is in the loveliest part of the island with a fine sandy beach in a perfect natural harbour between two headlands. This topography has led it to be identified with Homer's 'Scheria', where Odysseus was washed ashore and escorted by Nausicaa to the palace of her father Alcinous, King of the Phaeacians.

The coastline above Paleokastritsa, however, offers much more hope. Some of the roads are still poor and major developers are yet to move in. A few kilometres outside Paleokastritsa is **Lakones** and beneath it (about 2 km walk) a marvellous cove with a huge sandy beach, sometimes known as 'Agios Georgios'; it has three or four good *tavernas* and a handful of rooms. (From Kerkira the best bus to take here is to **Makrades** – which is slightly closer.) From this cove, or from Lakones, you can follow a mule-path round the headland to a spectacular view from the C13th Byzantine castle of **Angelokastro**. There are other good coves and sandy beaches (oddly, the developed east coast is mostly pebbly) all around the coast on this corner of the island. If you've the money, hire a moped for a day in Paleokasritsa and hunt out the possibilities. If not, then you might try the bays of **Afionas**, or **Peroulades** (near Sidari), both connected by occasional bus or caique from Paleokastritsa. **Sidari**, once a popular campers' hangout, is now fully commercialised, though there are some good beaches east of it towards **Roda**, itself also recently taken over by big hotels.

Below **Paleokastritsa** development is pretty concentrated due to the proximity of Kerkira Town. **Ermones** and **Glyfada** are excellent beaches but also very popular resorts; **Agios Gordis** will probably go the same way but at present it's all right. **Pelekas** is weird. Every evening in season a special bus leaves Kerkira to bring tourists out here to watch the sun go down, in an atmosphere reminiscent of the Hollywood screen. The rest of the time Pelekas, with a reputation for 'free living', struggles uneasily on as Corfu's 'hippy beach' where nude sunbathing becomes obligatory ritual rather than natural or spontaneous and occasionally the police turn up to play their own games. The village does, however, have several cheap rooms. To get there take bus 11 from the San Rocco terminal.

South of **Agios Gordis** there are relatively isolated, unspoilt places on the west coast but you're hampered by an absence of good roads (and therefore buses). Quite a number of the beaches, however, have *tavernas* on them during the summer and they're by no means a bad choice, although perhaps lacking some of the north's scenic beauty. **Agios Georgios** (half way down), **Asprokavos** and, around the point, **Kavos** and **Potami** are all supposed to be quite good.

The island's patron saint is **St Spiridion**, after whom about half the male population are called Spiros; four times a year, to the accompaniment of much celebration and feasting, the saint's relics are solemnly paraded through the streets of the town (on Palm Sunday and the following Saturday, the 11 August, and the first Sunday in November). Each of these days commemorates a miraculous deliverance of the island credited to the saint – twice from plague in the C17th, from famine in the C16th and from the Turks in the C18th.

Lastly, and on a more mundane level, there is an incredible monument to bad taste near the village of **Gastourion** (8 km from Kerkira): this is the 'Achillion' Palace, built in a unique blend of Teutonic and neo-classical styles in 1890 by Elisabeth, Empress of Austria. Henry Miller reckoned it 'the worst piece of gimcrackery' that he'd ever laid eyes upon and thought it 'would make an excellent museum for surrealistic art'; it is, in fact, now a casino, though you can just visit the grounds.

PAXI

There are daily ferries in season from both Corfu (Kerkira Town) and from Parga on the Epirote mainland to the tiny island of Paxi. To board one of them, however, there's now a system where you must book accommodation in advance for a minimum of two days. This is easily done, since a man stands by the boat letting out slightly overpriced rooms, but the intent of the measure, actively to discourage camping, should be heeded. You can understand the islanders' concern, for Paxi is too small (just 8 km from end to end) and its olive groves too precious to risk an invasion of campers. Nevertheless, it is a very friendly and charming place – the initial red tape gives a quite falsely offputting impression.

Most people stay in, or around, the main harbour and village of **GAIOS**, whose pastel-coloured houses are clumped around a little creek formed by the rocky islet of 'Kastro' (on which, predictably, stands a ruined Venetian castle). A fair number of cruise ships call in here during the day, filling the *tavernas* and *kafeneions*, but by evening most tourists have disappeared and it takes on a good genuine atmosphere. There's a sandy beach close by and another of sorts is at **Lakka**, Paxi's second harbour and village, connected by the island's single road; elsewhere a network of tracks lead to other diminutive villages and pebbly coves. But the best beaches, and wine, are to be found on the yet smaller neighbouring islet of **ANTIPAXI**, reached by caique from Gaios; here, if you stay, you'll probably have to camp – and no one's likely to be too bothered.

LEFKADA (LEFKAS)

Lefkada is an oddity. Connected to the mainland by a long causeway and 20-metre chain ferry you hardly feel you're on an island. In fact historically it isn't – a canal was cut by Corinthian colonists in 540 BC and has been renewed (after silting up) at various points since. Strategically it was important and, approaching the causeway, you pass a series of fortresses, climaxing in the C13th Frankish castle of Santa Maura – which gave name to the whole island during the Venetian occupation. It is today the least commercialised of the Ionian group, with a workaday unselfconscious charm, lively summer festivals and terrific strong local retsina.

The main town, also called **LEFKADA**, creeps up and around a shallow lagoon opposite the castle. Badly hit by an earthquake in 1948 its houses have been rebuilt in an extraordinary style – their upper stories constructed from hardboard and corrugated iron to lay as little stress as possible upon the foundations. From the old town only a few stone Venetian churches remain but these, too, have bizarre appendages, their bell-towers rising upon little more than elegant scaffolding. There are three cheap hotels in the town ('Averof', 'Patrae' and 'Byzantion') and a good bus service to the attractive coastal villages of Nidri, Vliho and Vassiliki – none of them overfrequented by tourists; the station is at the far end of the long main street.

Nidri, which you reach first on the island's main road (down the east coast), is beautifully sited opposite a string of islets (Mandouri, Sparti, Skorpios and Meganissi); caiques will take you to all of them, although you can't go ashore on Skorpios which is owned by the Onassis family. At Nidri itself there's a fair beach, a few rooms to let and some wooded coves nearby. The German archaeologist, Wilhelm Dorpfield, believed this to be the site of Odysseus' capital and did indeed find Bronze Age tombs in the plain; his theory that the island of Lefkada was in fact ancient Ithaca was popular in the middle of this century but in recent years has fallen into disfavour. **Vliho**, in a deep and virtually landlocked bay 5 km beyond (16 km from Lefkada Town), has much the same character as Nidri; just west of it is **Dessimi Beach** with an organised campsite. There's another small campsite at **Poros**, the next village and beach, a couple of kilometres off the main road.

Eventually the road curls round to **Vassiliki** (40 km from Lefkada), again set back at the mouth of a deep bay and probably the most attractive of the island's little resort villages, with rooms to let and some restaurants. From Vassiliki you can go by caique (or, with some effort, you could walk) to the white cliffs of Cape Lefkados which drop abruptly into the sea, 200 feet below. Byron's Childe Harold sailed past the point, '*saw the evening star above, Leucadia's far projecting rock of woe: And hail'd the last resort of fruitless love*'; the fruitless love refers to Sappho who, in accord with the ancient legend that you could cure yourself of unrequited love by leaping into the waters, leapt – and died. Many others had lived, for the act (known as *katapontismos*) was regularly performed as some kind of trial by the Priests of Apollo, the ruins of whose temple lie close by. In Roman times it was turned into a fashionable folly as youths leapt with feathers and even live birds attached to them, before being picked up by waiting boats.

ITHAKI (ITHACA)

Rugged Ithaca, Odysseus' capital, has no substantial archaeological traces but it feels right: 'the long hill paths, the quiet bays, the beetling rocks . . . yet narrow though it may be, it is very far from poor', all could be noted down today. And despite the romance of its name – and its proximity to Corfu – there's still very little tourist development to spoil the place. There are no real beaches either but there is good walking country, a handful of small fishing villages and a few rocky coves to swim from. Come in a spirit of excitement and you're unlikely to be disappointed.

Ferries from Patras, Kefalonia or Corfu land at the main port and capital of **VATHI**, or **Ithaki**, at the heart of a deep bay which seems to close completely about it. In size it is hardly more than a village, its Venetian-style houses faithfully rebuilt after the terrible 1953 earthquake, and there's a very friendly local feel. Dozens of yachts and cruise ships stop off here for a couple of hours but none too many people actually stay and rooms remain fairly easy to come by, camping on the outskirts tolerated. Small boats shuttle tourists round from the harbour to a series of little concreted swimming platforms but they're a little overfunctional for most tastes. Far better to spend your time walking out to a couple of nearby sites imaginatively identified with Homeric locations, or if you want to swim and rest up to head off and out to the north of the island.

Trails to the 'Odysseus sites' are signed from Vathi and either makes an easy morning's hike across some beautiful country. Both locations refer to scenes in Book XIII of *The Odyssey*: our hero's concealed home-coming. The **Arethousa spring**, 1½ hrs walk south of Vathi, is down to a trickle in summer, but interestingly positioned: above is a crag known locally as 'Korax' (the raven), exactly as described by Homer in the meeting between Odysseus and his swineherd Eumaeus. Below it you can climb down to a couple of good pebble bays, and a little further along the same track you come to Perapigadia hamlet, opposite a tiny islet. Equally tentative, yet quite compelling, is the **Grotto of the Nymphs**, a large cavern about 1 km south-west of Vathi where local knowledge suggests Odysseus, on the advice of Athena, hid his treasure. It was certainly known anciently and seems to have once been used as a place of worship. If its attribution is correct, or at least how Homer imagined things, the Bay of Dexia (just west of Vathi) would be where the Phaecians put in to deposit the sleeping Odysseus and which he failed to recognise as his homeland. Slightly further on, atop a rocky peak, are the ruins of the ancient city of Alkaklomenai – excavated by Schliemann, who quite erroneously declared it the **Castle of Odysseus**, a site it's at least 500 years too late to be. Walking across the very narrow shoulder of the island here you can get down to the pebbly bay of **Pisaetos**, 7 km in all from Vathi and probably the best swimming around this southern half of the island.

There's a rough road down from Vathi through the northern half of Ithaki to the villages of Stavros, Frikes and Kioni and occasional buses take off along it. For Frikes and Kioni, though, there's a regular (at least once daily) caique – a great ride round the rocky east coast; it is cheap and used by travellers and locals alike to get back to Vathi for the Corfu–Patras ferries.

Stavros, near the base of the arid island mountain (Korifi, or Nisiti: a readoption of its old Homeric name), is a fair-sized village with a couple of restaurants, some rooms and a small beach 15 mins walk outside where people camp. Nearby a few Mycenaean remains have been found and this is currently the archaeologists' favourite site for Polis Bay, the main harbour of ancient Ithaca. One km north of Stavros further Mycenaean remains have also been found amid the ruins of a Venetian fort; this, known as Pelikata hill, could perhaps be the site of Odysseus' palace and capital. About an hour's walk beyond Stavros is another bay and the village of **Frikes**, smaller but with a couple of *tavernas* and a pebbly strip of beach. Slightly further on, at the end of the road, you wind round to the village of **Kioni**, probably the best base on the island though its few rooms seem to be block-booked through the summer by an English company. There's some good swimming here, clearer of Ithaki's usual sea urchins, near the end of the trail at Agias Elias just outside the village.

KEFALONIA (CEPHALLONIA)

Kefalonia is the largest of the Ionian islands but probably the least inviting. Virtually all of its towns and villages were levelled in the 1953 earthquake and it can't compare in natural beauty with either Corfu or Zakinthos. Additionally, if you want to travel around the island rather than just stay in one resort you're likely to find it a frustrating exercise unless you have your own transport; distances are considerable and the bus service very poor. That said, don't be completely put off – there are some attractive parts and none too many tourists to share them with; there's also, as with most of the islands in this group, a good local wine, called Rombolla.

Most boats dock at the rather dismal port and town of **SAMI**, built at the entrance to the Ithaca Channel, more or less on the site of Ancient Same (capital of the island in Homeric times, when it was part of Ithaca's maritime kingdom). There are some scant remains of Mycenaean and Classical walls on the hills above the town but of more interest are two notable caves in the area. The first, about 2 km to the left of Sami (facing the sea) near the village of **Vlahana**, is **Melissani** – a remarkable blue-tinged underwater cavern, well worth a visit. You're taken by boat into an inner lake-grotto; its waters, extraordinarily, emerge from an underground fault which leads the whole way under the island to a point near Argostoli, the *katovothrai*, where the sea gushes endlessly into a subterranean tunnel (this has been traced by using coloured dye) and was once harnessed to drive mills. The other cave, **Drogharati**, is more conventional; a huge stalagmitic chamber, sometimes used for concerts due to its marvellous acoustics, ½ km off to the right of the main Argostoli road about 4 km out of Sami.

Just before the Drogharati Cave there's a turning to the left to **Poros**, a small resort with a good beach, rooms to let and some fine restaurants; it's probably the best place to stay on the island. There are only two hotels so camping is probably all right if you're discreet. The dark mass of Mount Ainos, densely wooded with a unique variety of fir tree, towers behind Poros and gives a certain grandeur to the region. A number of rough roads traverse its base to other beaches and villages – **Skala** is becoming a small resort. At the village of **Markopoulo**, a few kilometres on (towards Argostoli), a strange phenomenon occurs around 15 August (the 'Assumption of the Virgin' – one of the main Orthodox holidays) as small, harmless snakes mysteriously converge upon the village church to be grasped rapturously to the bosoms of the faithful. Some distance further on the Argostoli road you reach the village of **Kastro** (8 km from Argostoli), which occupies the site of **San Giorgio**, the medieval and Venetian capital of Kefalonia. The old town once held a population of 15,000 but it was destroyed by an earthquake in the C17th; substantial ruins of its castle, churches and houses can be seen on a hill above the modern village.

ARGOSTOLI itself is a large and thriving town, marvellously situated on a deep bay within another bay. But, totally rebuilt after the earthquake, it's not really an appealing place. Rooms here are scarce though you can camp unofficially north of town. Ferries regularly cross the larger, outer bay to the town of **Lixouri**, opposite, on a rocky and isolated peninsula.

North of Argostoli a poor road (occasional bus) leads to **ASSOS**, a highly picturesque fishing village which before long will be debased to a mere tourist resort; at present it's the island's liveliest base, on a sheltered headland crowned by a Venetian castle. There's a good sandy beach a little to the south of the village. **Fiskardo**, about a dozen kilometres further north, stands at the extremity of the island; a tiny village of elegant Venetian-style houses, it alone survived the earthquake without damage. There's a restaurant and *taverna* there and reasonable swimming nearby and occasional caiques to Stavros on Ithaca. In season some of the larger ferryboats (to Lefkada and even to Corfu and Patras) also call in.

ZAKINTHOS (ZANTE)

Zakinthos, once exceeding Kerkira in architectural distinction, was hit hardest by the 1953 catastrophe and the island's grand old capital completely destroyed. Today, though some of its beautiful Venetian churches have been restored, it's a rather sad town and the attraction for travellers lies more in the thick vineyards, orchards and olive groves of the interior and some really excellent beaches scattered about the coast. Greek tourists descend on the island in considerable numbers through August, and the resort of Langanas has now become a major development, but it's still a much recommended island – and, under two hours and 300 drx from Killini on the Peloponnesian mainland, well worth some of your time.

ZAKINTHOS, or **Zante** (the old Venetian form), also gives name to the island's main port and town. Rebuilt on the old plan it has bravely tried to recreate some of the style of this former 'Venice of the East' but quake-reinforced concrete can only do so much. The most tangible hints of former glory are to be found in Plateia Solomou, the grand and spacious main square. At its north waterfront corner stands the beautiful soft stone C15th church of Agios Nikolaos; whilst paintings and icons salvaged from here and other island churches are displayed in the imposing **Neo-Byzantine Museum** by the town hall. The collection is exceptional for in the C17th–18th Zante became the centre of an Ionian School of painting, given impetus by Cretan refugees unable to practise under Turkish rule. The square itself is named after the island's famous poet Dionysos Solomos, who was responsible for introducing demotic Greek (the language of the people) as a literary idiom. A small museum is dedicated to him in the nearby Plateia Agios Markos (2 blocks up), worth a look if only to see photographs of the town taken prior to the earthquake.

Rooms and hotels in Zante are reasonably priced and not hard to come by: someone will probably meet you off the ferry. Restaurants, however, are all quite expensive, for good value stick to the *souvlaki* grills, especially the one at Vassileos Konstantinos 24, halfway up the main arcaded market street. There's no great swimming in the town itself, only a rather drab pay *beach*, and you'll do better heading out to Vassiliki or Ormos Alikan – the bus station is a block back from the waterfront (in line with the Fina station), or there are bikes to rent, ideal for this island. If you've an evening to fill, the town's massive Venetian *kastro* (an hour's walk) commands tremendous views – right down to Pilos and north to Messolongi – and en route is the suburb-village of **Bohali**, a natural balcony over the harbour, with a number of popular though pricey *tavernas*.

The best beaches on Zakinthos are south-east of Zante Town at the already mentioned Langanas and below **Vassiliki** which in marked contrast to the massed hotels down-coast is still really quite away from it all. Vassiliki itself is a modest village with a few rooms to let – poised below are a series of small wooded bays and long sweeps of sand. Two of these, Porto Roma and Gerakas, are well signposted but there are other possibilities if you want solitude and are happy to walk out to it. Campers congregate under the trees at the smallish **Porto Roma** beach, a good place with rooms and a seasonal *taverna*. But for lazing around and

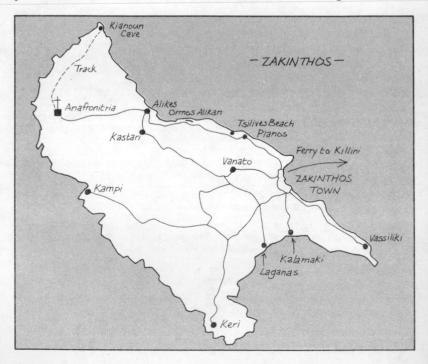

swimming **Gerakas** is definitely the better beach – a magnificent, isolated golden strand. You can't however sleep on it since, as at Langanas, it's a breeding ground for sea turtles. **Keri**, the other side of Langanas, retains some of its old Venetian houses and, more curiously, natural pitch springs commented on by both Pliny and Herodotus and still used for caulking ships. There's a fair beach beneath the village, with half a dozen *tavernas* and *kafeneia*.

Heading in the other direction from Zante you skirt a luxuriantly fertile plain of olive and orange groves, currant vines, wild flowers and sporadic punctuations of tumulus-like hills. **Tsilivi**, 4 km out, is the closest beach worthy of the name but, gravelly and exposed, it is utterly outshone by **Ormos Alikan** (about 12 km from Zante Town) – a huge, gently sloping expanse of sand washed by good breakers. At its northern end Alikan becomes the village of **Alikes**, a growing resort where there are mopeds and rooms to rent, restaurants and a few small hotels. From here also caiques plie to **Kianoun Cave** at the far tip of the island, one of the more realistically named of the many 'Blue Caves' in Greece. **Kastari**, the island's second largest community, lies just inland of Alikes and beyond it a road leads in 8 km to the **Monastery of Anafronitria** which withstood the earthquake remarkably well; it is maintained by a few nuns who will show you the frescoed Katholikon, a medieval tower and – reputedly – the cell of St Dionysos, patron saint of Zakynthos.

All the Ionian islands produce good *wines* but for me Zakinthos has the distinct edge – an enduring, powerful liquor. The island is also the home of *cantadhes*, an old-world style of trio singing accompanied by guitars and mandolins. The *tavernas* at Bohali are the most likely places to hear them.

TRAVEL DETAILS

There are two boats of invaluable aid if you're island-hopping within this group. These are the SS **Ionis** (which sails every two days from June–September from Brindisi–Patras and vice versa; stopping at Corfu (8 hrs), Paxi (10 hrs), Ithaki (13½ hrs) and Kefalonia (14¾ hrs), reaching Patras after 18 hrs total) and the SS **Kefallinia** (which sails once a week from Patras to Sami and Fiskardo on Kefalonia and then to Paxi and Corfu; returning the same route). Neither of these are included in the travel details below.

Corfu (Kerkira) and Paxi
Ferries every 2 hrs from Igoumenitsa–Kerkira (and vice versa; takes 2 hrs). At least one daily between Patras–Kerkira

(10 hrs); usually many more. In season two motor boats daily between Kerkira and Paxi (2½ hrs), and a varying number between Paxi and Parga (on the mainland).

Additionally, many of the main ferry-boats from Italy to Greece (especially those from Brindisi) call at Corfu on the way; if you want to take advantage of this get it written on your ticket.

Several flights daily between Corfu and Athens (45 mins) and numerous other European capitals, particularly London.

Lefkada
Four buses daily to and from Athens (7 hrs); also regularly from Igoumenitsa, Arta and Patras. Four or five boats a

week, in season, from Nidri and Vassiliki to Kefalonia and Ithaki.

Ithaki (Ithaca) and Kefalonia

Daily ferry connection between Patras and Ithaki (5 hrs) via Sami on Kefalonia (3½ hrs). Additional ferries most days between Patras and Sami. Also three ferries daily in season (once daily, out) between Poros (east coast of Kefalonia) and Killini (Peloponnese). Caiques, in season, from Fiskardo (Kefalonia) to Stavros (Ithaca) and Nidri (Lefkas).

Daily flight connection (4 times a week out of season) between Argostoli (Kefalonia) and Athens (45 mins).

Zakinthos (Zante)

Three to six ferries a day (one, out of season; 2 hrs), between Zakinthos and Killini (Peloponnese); thence to Kefalonia. Also expensive speedboats (operated by Alkyonis) daily in season (sporadic, out) between Zakinthos and Patras.

Buses from Athens

Inclusive bus and ferry tickets are available from Athens to Kerkira (11 hrs), Kefalonia (8 hrs) and Zakinthos (7 hrs); all from the Kifissou 100 Terminal. You can also buy combined bus and ferry tickets from Patras to Zakinthos.

Part four
CONTEXTS

LANGUAGE . . . AND A FEW PHRASES

Greeks are such intensive travellers, sailors and emigrants that you'll find someone who speaks English in almost any village – as often as not in a broad Melbourne or New York accent. Add to this the multilingual Greeks who work in the tourist resorts and it soon becomes clear why so many visitors come back having learnt only half a dozen restaurant words between them. You certainly can get by this way, even travelling quite out of the way routes, but it's not especially satisfying. Greek must be one of the world's richest and most beautiful languages and even a small attempt to speak it will pay immense dividends – breaking down barriers and changing

the way you're treated from the new all-staring breed of *touristas* to that of the traditional *xenos*, a word which means both stranger, traveller and guest . . .

The Alphabot

Despite initial appearances the Greek alphabet is fairly easily mastered, and if you're using public transport it'll save a lot of asking and most likely some bad mistakes! When reading Greek bear in mind above all that it is a consistent language in the way that it sounds each of the vowels and syllables in a word – thus 'λενε', for instance, is pronounced 'lenneh' rather than 'lean'.

A	α	'a' as in cat
B	β	'v' as in vet
Γ	γ	guttural 'g' sound; except before an 'e' or 'i' sound – when it becomes hard like a 'y'
Δ	δ	'th' sound as in *th*en
E	ε	'e' as in Lennon
Z	ζ	'z' sound
H	η	like the 'i' in b*i*n
Θ	θ	'th' as in *th*eme
I	ι	between the 'i' in b*i*n and the 'ee' in b*ee*n
K	κ	'k' sound
Λ	λ	'l' sound
M	μ	'm' sound
N	ν	'n' sound
Ξ	ξ	'ks' sound
O	ο	like the 'o' in n*o*t
Π	π	'p' sound
P	ρ	'r' sound
Σ	σ(ς)	's' sound
T	τ	't' sound
Y	υ	like the 'i' in b*i*n
Φ	φ	'f' sound
X	χ	'ch' as in lo*ch*
Ψ	ψ	'ps' as in li*ps*
Ω	ω	between the 'o' in *o*pen and in b*o*ttle

COMBINATIONS OF LETTERS (DIPHTHONGS)

AI	αι	'e' as in Lennon
AY	αυ	'av' or 'af' sound
EI	ει	} both, again like the 'i' in b*i*n
OI	οι	
EU	ευ	'ev' or 'ef' sound
OU	ου	'oo' sound as in f*oo*d
ΓΓ	γγ	'ng' sound (as in 'ΑΓΓΛIΑ' – 'Anglia', or England)
ΓK	γκ	'g' sound at beginning of a word; 'ng' if in middle
ΜΠ	μπ	'b' sound (as in 'ΜΠΑΡ' – 'Bar')
NT	ντ	'd' sound at beginning of a word; 'nd' (as in 'pende', 5) if in middle
ΤΣ	τσ	'ts' sound

Language and Phrases

First of all, a confusion: there are two kinds of Greek – *dhemotiki* (popular or spoken Greek) and *katharevousa* (the formal written language). This means not just different spellings but often different words for the same thing – thus a bakery is called a *fournos* (its *dhemotiki* form) but written on signs in the *katharevousa* as *artopoleion*. Under the colonels' junta there was a crazy attempt to impose the old 'pure' *katharevousa* on everything from school texts to chocolate bars but nowadays only official documents, signs and a couple of the right-wing newspapers are still printed in it. The words and phrases below are all in their spoken demotic forms: but, supremely important, you must **stress** the accented letters or sounds – otherwise you may be saying the right word in a way which is quite unintelligible or might even mean something else entirely!

Basics and greetings

yes	né
no	óhi
okay	endáxi
please	parakaló
thank you	efkharistó
many thanks	efkharistó polí
thanks very much indeed	efkharistó pára polí
it's nothing	típota
excuse me	signómi
certainly	málista
hello, or goodbye	yássou (yássas is plural/formal)
pleased to meet you	hero polí
see you	tha sas dho
goodbye	adío
good day	kaliméra
good evening	kalispéra
good night	kaliníkhta (this is said only when leaving)
good luck	kalí tíhi
good journey	kaló taksídi
today	símera
yesterday	kthés
tomorrow	ávrio
day after tomorrow	methávrio
water	neró
bread	psomí

Asking for things

Have you . . .?	éhete. . .?
is there . . .?	éhi . . .?
I want . . .	thélo . . .
how much?	póso
how many?	pósa
how much does it cost?	póso káni
it's (too) expensive	éene (polí) akrivó
cheap	fthíno
for students	ya fitítes
what time is it?	ti óra ééneh?
what times does it open/close?	ti óra aneéyke/kléenee
now/later	tóra/metá
when?	póte?
never!	poté!

do you have a room?	éhete enna dhomátio?
for one person (two people)	ya énna átomo (thío átoma)
do you have anything . . .	servitére . . .
. . . to eat/drink	. . . fágito/póta
some more . . .	léego akómma . . .
the bill	to logariásmo
can we camp . . .	boróomeh na kataskinósoomoh . . .
. . . here/there	. . . ethó/ekée
great!	oréya!

Directions and hitching

is it . . .?	éeneh . . .?
left/right	aristerá/theksýa
straight on	efthía/éssia
first/second	prótos/théfteros
where is . . .?	poo éeneh . . .?
from where?	ápo poó?
here/there	ethó/ekée
is it far/near?	éeneh makriá/kondá?
wait	periméneteh
up/down	epáno/káto
on foot	meh ta póthia
bus/train	leoforío/tréno
boat	karávia/férrybout
bike/moped	podýlata/mihanáki
station/harbour	stathmós/limáni
ticket	isitírio
bus stop	stássi
what time will it leave?	ti óra tha féeyee?
road/path	dhrómos/monopáti
street/alley	odós/stenó
stairway	skála
junction	stavrodhrómi
where are you going?	poo páss? (or more formally, poo pigéneteh?)
I'm going to . . .	pigéno . . .
stop (let me off)	káneh stássi
where is the road to . . .?	poo éeneh o dhrórnos ya . . .?
where are you from?	ápo poo éesteh?
I am from . . .	éemeh ápo . . .
what's your name?	pos légesteh?
I'm . . . (name)	légomeh . . . (name)
girlfriend/boyfriend	kopélla/filósmo
what do you do (job)?	ti thóollia káneteh?
what's it called in Greek?	pos toh léneh sta Ellenika?
I don't understand	then katalavéno

Places and things

ancient ruins	arhaiótites
bakery	fóurnos
bank	trápeza
beach	paralía/ammoudhiá
cave	spília
centre	kéndro
chemist's	farmakio
church	eklísia

doctor	yatrós
hospital	nosokomío
hotel	ksenothohío
monastery	monastíri
petrol station	benzinathíko
police	astinomía
post office	takidhromío
(letter/stamp	grámma/grámmatóssíma
sea	thálassa
spring	piyí
square	platéia
toilet	tooaléta
village	horió
youth hostel	ksenothohio neótitos

Numbers and the time

1	énna/mía	11	éntheka	70	evthomínda
2	thío	12	thótheka	80	ogthónda
3	tría	13	théka tría	90	ennehnínda
4	téssera	14	théka téssera	100	ekató
5	pénde	20	ékossi	150	ekaton penínda
6	éksi	21	ékossi énna	200	thiakóssia
7	eptá	30	triánda	300	triakóssia
8	octó	40	saránda	400	tetrakóssia
9	ennéha	50	penínda	500	pendakóssia
10	théka	60	eksínda	1000	hília

what time is it?	ti óra éeneh?
at – o'clock	stís – óres
it's – o'clock	éeneh – óres
half hour	misí óra
quarter hour	énna tetárto
how many minutes?	pósa leptá?

Greeks' Greek

orísteh?	can I help you?
seegár, seegár	take your time
élla!	come!
pos ísteh	how are you (formal)
ti kánes?	how's it going?
kalá . . .	fine . . .
. . . kai esées?	. . . and you?
étsi k'étsi	so so (can also have gay connotations)
kalóstane!	welcome
hére/hérete	hello (slightly formal greeting)
sto kaló	go with God (formal parting)
po, po, po!	what have we here!
ópa!	look out!
ámeh . . .	go on (yeah . . .)
paídhia	guys (as in 'endáxi paídhia?' – okay guys?)
aléetes	bum (a derogatory term: what some Greeks think of campers)
mastóura	drunk

Greeks, of course, also speak extremely fluently with their hands, and faces. One piece of **sign language** which may initially confuse you is the habit of jerking the chin up sharply, or even just raising the eyebrows or eyes – this means 'no'. 'Yes' is indicated by a very slow downward angling of the head. A general waggling of the head, especially from shopkeepers, enquires 'what do you want?'

For **food and menu** vocabularies see the 'Eating and Drinking' section in BASICS (p. 9).

Books

British **teach yourself** Greek books are far from brilliant, and seem designed to push you towards proper lessons: *Colloquial Greek* (RKP £2.95) is as good as any. Best of the American tomes is *Manual of Modern Greek* by A Farmakides (Montreal, McGill, 1979) but it's expensive. For a very basic 'how to say it' course the BBC's *Greek Language and People* (BBC, 1983, £7.95) is admirably clear. The best Greek–English **dictionaries** are published by RKP (£5.95) and Collins (pocket dictionary, £3.50).

Much the best **phrasebook** I've come across is *Greek Travelmate* (Drew £1), a positively un-useless selection!

THE HISTORICAL FRAMEWORK

This history is intended to do little more than bring a certain perspective to your travel.

Other than the solitary discovery of a fossilised Neanderthal skull near Salonika, the earliest evidence of human settlement in Greece is to be found at Nea Nikomedia, near Veria (c. 6000 BC), where traces of large, rectangular houses are still visible to the visitor's eye. It seems that man originally came to this land in the eastern Mediterranean in fits and starts, predominantly from Anatolia. People settled in essentially peaceful farming communities, made pottery and worshipped Earth goddesses, symbols of fertility embodied in the clay, female statuettes which are still found on the sites of old settlements. A simple way of life, which in turn had to bow before the unavoidable demands of progress, the necessity to tap the land's resources for profit and to compete and exchange in trade.

Difficult as the time scale is to visualise, you must try to imagine the years between the 20th and 11th centuries BC as a time of fluctuating regional dominance based at first upon sea power, with vast royal palaces serving as centres of administration. Particularly important were those at Knossos in Crete, and Mycenae, Tiryns and Argos in the Peloponnese. Crete monopolised the eastern Mediterranean trade routes for a time latterly called the **Minoan Age**, the palace at Knossos surviving two earthquakes and a massive volcanic eruption on the island of Thira (Santorini), at some undefinable point between 1500 and 1450 BC. The most obvious examples of Minoan culture can be seen in frescoes, in jewellery and in pottery, the distinctive red and white design on a dark background marking the peak period of Minoan achievement. Most museums seem to be very well stocked. When Knossos eventually succumbed to disaster, natural or otherwise, around 1400 BC, it was the flourishing centre of **Mycenae** that adopted the leading role, it in turn giving its name to a new 'age'.

This is a period rich in enchanting fables: Mycenae boasts Perseus, son of Zeus, as its mythological founder, while the construction of the masonry at the palace of Tiryns is attributed to the immense and one-eyed Cyclops. One ruler of Mycenae, Atreus, is supposed to have hated his brother Thyestes so much that he offered him his own children to eat. Thyestes in turn cursed Atreus and his children, one of whom was Agamemnon, who obligingly fulfilled the terms of the curse by getting murdered by his wife Clytemnestra and her lover. The tombs of the two miscreants can still be seen at Mycenae, in the area between the Lion Gate and the main road.

Just as the fables reflected the prevalence of violence as a means of revenge, war had now become a fact of life, initiated and irritated by trade rivalry and exemplified in the fortifications which were built around the various palaces.

The Greece of these years was by no means a united nation; the country was divided into what were in effect a series of splinter groups, owing to the peculiar physical conditions which gave each area access to both mountains and pasture. Settlements flourished according to their proximity to the sea and the fertility of their land; most were self-sufficient, specialising in the production of particular items for trade. Olives, for example, were associated with the region of Attica of which Athens was head, marble with Melos.

The jigsaw-like states had also to cope with and assimilate the periodic influx of 'barbarians'. The **Dorians** brought their less refined version of the Greek language from the northern borders and had a devastating influence. They infiltrated the Peloponnese, Rhodes, Kos, Knidos and part of Crete during the C11th BC, flattening the palaces at Pylos, Mycenae and Tiryns en route. By thereby paralysing that vital sea power they ushered in a so-called Dark Age, or period of enforced introspection of which nothing much is known. The Dorians sought to develop their traditions within the city of Sparta; happily for the future of Greece they had kept their hands off Athens.

This was the period of the Greek **city-state** (*polis*), and people busied themselves in the intrigues of government, and took part in community activities of both industry and leisure. Colonial ventures increased, as did commercial dealings, and the consequent rise in the import trade was gradually to give rise to a new class of manufacturers. The city-state was the life of the people who dwelt within it and each state retained both independence and distinctive style, with the result that the sporadic attempts to unite in a league against the enemy without were always pragmatic and temporary. To give a couple of examples:

The society of the town of Sparta was based very much on Dorian military traditions, accentuated by the need to defend the exposed and fertile land on which it stood. Rather than build intricate fortifications, the people of Sparta relied upon an intrinsic military prowess; one imagines a rather stolid society, bent on the pursuit of heroic ideals and adhering staunchly to the state law. Males were subjected to military instruction between the ages of seven and thirty. Weak babies were known periodically to 'disappear'. Girls too had to perform athletic feats of sprinting and wrestling, and even dwellings were more like barracks than houses, which to some extent accounts for the lack of remains in Sparta today.

Athens, the fulcrum of the state of Attica, was dynamic and exciting in contrast. Home of the administrations of Solon and Pericles, the dramatic talents of Sophocles and Aristophanes, the oratory of Thucydides and Demosthenes and the philosophical power of Socrates and Plato, it made up in cultural achievement what it lacked in Spartan virtue. Yet Sparta did not deserve all the military glory. The Athens of the C4th and C5th BC, the so-called **Classical Period** in Greek history, is the Athens which played the major part in repelling the armies of the Persian king Darius at Marathon (490 BC) and Salamis (480 BC), campaigns recorded later by Aeschylus in *The Persians*.

It is also the Athens which gave rise to a tradition of democracy, or *demokratia*, literally meaning 'control of the people', although at this stage 'the people' did not include either women or slaves. Each city-state had its *acropolis*, or high town, where religious activity was focused. In Athens there were three organs of government: the Areopagus, composed of the city elders, had a steadily decreasing authority and ended up dealing solely with murder cases. Then there was the Council of 500 men, elected annually by ballot to prepare the business of the Assembly and to attend to matters of urgency. The Assembly gave every free man a political voice; it had sole responsibility for law-making and provided an essential arena for the discussion of important issues. Rule was therefore by amateurs, a genuine council of citizens.

Bound up in the city-state were inevitable power struggles in which Athens and Sparta above all contended for supremacy – a process which eventually culminated in the Peloponnesian Wars of 431–404 BC. It was nevertheless a period of intense creativity, particularly in Athens whose actions and pretentions were fast becoming imperial in all but name. Here the Parthenon was constructed, the tragedies of Sophocles performed, and the philosophies of Socrates and Plato expounded. Religion at this stage was polytheistic, ordering all under the aegis of Zeus. In the country-side the proliferation of names and of sanctuary finds suggests a preference for the slightly more mundane Demeter and Dionysus.

After the **Peloponnesian Wars** the city-state ceased to function so effectively – in part due to drained resources and political apathy, but to a greater degree through the increasingly commercial, complex and specialised pressures on everyday life. Trade was expanding and Athens, for example, was exporting wine, oil and manufactured goods, getting corn in return from the Black Sea and from Egypt. The amount of time each man had to devote to the affairs of government decreased and a position in political life became a professional job rather than a natural assumption. Democracy, in a word, had changed. In philosophy there was a shift from the idealists and mystics of the C6th and C5th BC to the cynics, stoics and Epicureans – followers, respectively of Diogenes, Zeno and Epicurus.

The most important development in the decline of the city-states was meanwhile taking place outside their sphere in the kingdom of **Macedonia**. Here Philip II (359–336) was forging a strong military and unitary force, extending his territories into Thrace and finally establishing control over Athens and southern Greece. Alexander the Great, in an extraordinarily brief but glorious eleven-year reign, extended his father's gains into Persia and Egypt and parts of modern India and Afghanistan. This unwieldy empire splintered almost immediately upon his death in 323, to be divided into the three Macedonian dynasties of **Hellenistic** Greece: the Antigonids in Macedonia, the Seleucids in Syria and Persia, and in Egypt the Ptolemies. Each were in turn conquered and absorbed by the new Roman Empire – the Ptolemies last of all under their queen Cleopatra.

Mainland Greece was subdued over some seventy years of campaigns, from 215–146, but **Rome**, having annexed Macedonia, allowed considerable autonomy to the old divisions of the city-states. Greek remained the official language of the eastern Mediterranean and its traditions and culture co-existed fairly peacefully over the next three centuries. In central Greece both Athens and Corinth remained important cities but the emphasis was shifting north – particularly along the new Via Egnatia, a military and civil road engineered between Rome and Byzantium via the port of Brundisium (modern Brindisi).

This was a process given even greater impetus, and finality, by the decline of the Roman Empire and its subdivision between eastern and western emperors. In the year AD 330 the Emperor Constantine moved his capital to the Greek city of Byzantium and here emerged Constantinople, the 'new Rome' and spiritual and political centre of the **Byzantine Empire**. Whilst the last western Roman Emperor was deposed by barbarian Goths in 476, this oriental portion was to be the dominant Mediterranean power for some 800 years and only in 1453 did it finally collapse.

Christianity had been tolerated under Constantine and by the end of the C4th was the official state religion – its liturgies (still in use in the Greek Orthodox Church), creed and New Testament all written in Greek. A distinction has to be drawn here, though, between Greek as a language and culture and as a concept. The Byzantine Empire styled itself Roman, or 'Romeos', rather than Hellenic and moved to eradicate all remaining symbols of pagan Greece. The Delphic Oracle was forcibly closed and the Olympic Games discontinued.

The C7th saw Constantinople besieged by Persians, and later Arabs but the Empire survived, losing only Egypt – the least 'Greek' of its territories. Through the C9th and early C10th it underwent an archetypal 'golden age', both in culture (the church of Ossios Loukas is among the architectural achievements) and in confidence and security. Tied up in the Orthodox Byzantine faith was a sense of spiritual superiority and in Constantinople the Emperors now saw a 'new Jerusalem' for their 'chosen people'. It was the beginning of a diplomatic and ecclesiastical conflict with the west which was to have disastrous consequences over the next six centuries. In the meantime the eastern and western patriarchs mutually excommunicated each other.

Through the C7th to C11th Byzantine Greece, certainly in the south, became something of a provincial backwater. Administration was absurdly top-heavy and imperial taxation led to semi-autonomous provinces ruled by military generals – their lands acquired from the bankrupted peasants. This alienation generated among the poor in itself provided a force for change, with a floating populace ready to turn towards or co-operate with the empire's enemies if terms were an improvement. Meanwhile tribal groups moved down from Central Europe and were absorbed with little difficulty: the nomadic Vlachs from Romania eventually settled in the Pindus Mountains, and later immigrants from Albania repopulated the islands of Spetses, Hydra, Andros, Evia and parts of Attica.

From the early years of the C11th, however, less welcome and assimable western forces began to appear. The Normans landed first, in 1085, and returned again with papal sanction a decade later on their way to liberate Jerusalem. Nothing of this, though, was to compare with the **Third Crusade** of 1204, when Venetians, Franks and Genoese turned their armies directly on Byzantium and sacked and occupied Constantinople. These Latin princes and their followers, intent on new lands and kingdoms, settled in to divide up the best part of the empire. All of Byzantium that remained were four small peripheral kingdoms or despotates – the most powerful in Nikaea in Asia Minor, less significant ones at Trebizond on the Black Sea, and (in present-day Greece) in Epirus and around Mistra in the Peloponnese.

There followed two extraordinarily involved centuries of manipulation and struggle between Franks and Venetians, Genoese, Catalans and Turks. Byzantine Nikaea recovered the city of Constantinople in 1261 but with it little of its former territory and power. Instead the focus of Byzantium shifted to the Morea, or Peloponnese, where the autonomous Despotate of **Mistra** eventually succeeded in wresting all of the peninsula from Frankish hands. At the same time it underwent an intense cultural renaissance, strongly evoked in the churches and the shells of the cities remaining today at Mistra and Monemvassia. Within a generation of driving out the Franks, however, the Byzantine Greeks faced a much stronger threat in the expanding empire of the Ottoman **Turks**. Torn apart by internal struggles between their own ruling dynasties, the Palaeologi

and Kantakouzenes, and unaided by the Catholic west, they were to prove no match. On Tuesday 29 May 1453, a date still solemnly commemorated by the Orthodox Church, Constantinople fell to besieging moslem Turks. Mistra was to follow within seven years – by which time virtually all of the old Byzantine Empire lay under Ottoman domination. Only the Ionian islands, which remained Venetian, and a few scattered and remote enclaves – like the Mani in the Peloponnese, Sfakia in Crete and Souli in Epirus – were able to resist the Turkish advance.

Under the 'Dark Ages' of **Ottoman rule** the lands of present-day Greece passed into rural provincialism, taking refuge in the self-protective mode of village life which has only recently been disrupted. Taxes and discipline, sporadically backed up by the genocide of dissenting communities, were inflicted from the Turkish Porte but estates passed into the hands of local chieftains who often had considerable independence. Greek identity meanwhile was preserved essentially through the Orthodox Church which, despite instances of enforced conversion, the Sultan allowed to continue. The monasteries, often secretly, organised schools and became the trustees of Byzantine culture – though this had gone into stagnation from the fall of Constantinople and Mistra, scholars and artists emigrating west and adding impetus to the Renaissance.

As Ottoman administration became more and more decentralised and inefficient individual Greeks rose to local positions of considerable influence and a number of communities achieved a degree of autonomy. The Ambelakia villages in Thessaly, for example, established an industrial co-operative system to export cloth to Europe, paying only direct taxes to the Sultan. And on the Albanian re-populated islands of the Argo-Saronic a Greek merchant fleet came into being in the C18th, permitted to trade throughout the Mediterranean. Greeks, too, were becoming organised overseas in the sizeable expatriate colonies of Central Europe.

Opposition to Turkish rule was becoming widespread in its defiance, exemplified most directly by the Klephtic brigands of the mountains. It was not until the C19th however, that a resistance movement could muster sufficient co-operation to prove a real challenge to the Turks. In 1770 a Russian-backed uprising had been easily and brutally suppressed but fifty years later the position was different. In Epirus the Turks were stretched to subdue Ali Pasha's expansionist campaigns; the French revolution had given impetus to the confidence of 'freedom movements'; and in Odessa Greek intellectuals and merchants had joined together to found a society for Greek independence. It was this group, supported by Klephtic brigand leaders, who were to launch a new insurgence. On 25 March 1821, at the monastery of Kalavrita in the Peloponnese, the Greek banner was raised. **The War of Independence** had begun.

To describe in detail the course of the War of Independence would be to provoke unnecessary confusion, much of it consisting of local and fragmentary guerrilla campaigns. What is important to understand is that Greeks, though essentially fighting for liberation from the Turks, were not fighting as and for a nation. Motives differed enormously: landowners assumed their role was to lead and sought to retain and reinforce their traditional privileges, whilst the peasantry saw the struggle as a means towards land redistribution. Outside, prestige and publicity for the struggle was promoted by the arrival of around a thousand European Philhellenes, almost half of them German – but much the most important Lord Byron, who died at Messolongi in April 1824. Though it was the Greek guerrilla leaders, above all Theodor Kolokotronis, 'the old man of the Morea', who brought about the most significant military victories of the war, the death of Byron had an immensely important effect on public opinion in the west. Aid for the Greek struggle had come neither from Orthodox Russia, nor from the western powers of France and Britain, ravaged from the Napoleonic Wars. But by 1827 these three powers had finally agreed to seek autonomy for certain parts of Greece and sent a combined fleet to put pressure on the Sultan's Egyptian army, then ransacking and massacring in the Peloponnese. Events took over and an accidental naval battle in Navarino Bay resulted in the destruction of the entire Turkish-Egyptian fleet. The following spring Russia itself declared war on the Turks and the Sultan was forced to accept the existence of an autonomous Greece. In 1830 its independence was confirmed by the western powers and borders were drawn. They included, however, just 800,000 of the 6 million Greeks living within the Ottoman empire, and they, for the most part, the poorest lands of the Classical and Byzantine territories – the Peloponnese, the Cyclades and Attica.

Modern Greece

Modern Greece began as a republic, its first president, Capodistrias, concentrating his efforts on building a viable central authority and government in the face of diverse protagonists from the War. Almost inevitably he was assassinated – in 1831, by two chieftains from the Mani – and perhaps equally inevitable the great Western Powers stepped in. They created a monarchy, gave limited aid, and set on the throne a Bavarian prince, **Otho**.

The new king proved an autocratic and insensitive ruler, bringing in fellow Germans to fill official posts and ignoring all claims by the landless peasantry for redistribution of the old estates. In 1862 he was eventually forced from the country by a popular revolt – and the Europeans produced a new prince, this time from Denmark, with Britain ceding the Ionian islands to bolster support. George I, in fact, proved very much more capable: he built the first railways and roads, introduced land reform in the Peloponnese and oversaw the first expansion of the Greek borders. From the very beginning the single and unquestioned motive force of Greek foreign policy was the **Megalo Idea** (great idea) of liberating Greek populations outside the country and incorporating these old lands of Byzantium into the kingdom. In 1878 the rich agricultural plains of Thessaly, along with southern Epirus, were ceded to Greece. Less illustriously, the Greeks failed to achieve *enosis* (union) with Crete by attacking Turkish forces on the mainland, and in the process virtually bankrupted the state.

It was from Crete, however, that the most dominant statesman of modern Greece emerged. **Eleftherios Venizelos**, having led a civilian campaign for his island's liberation, was in 1910 elected as Prime Minister. Two years later he organised an alliance of Balkan powers to fight the **First Balkan War** (1912–13), a campaign that saw the

Turks virtually driven from Europe. With Greek borders extended to include Crete, the north-east Aegean, northern Thessaly, central Epirus and parts of Macedonia, the *Megalo Idea* was approaching reality. At the same time Venizelos proved himself a shrewd manipulator of domestic Greek public opinion – revising the constitution and introducing a series of liberal social reforms.

Division, however, was to appear with the outbreak of the **First World War**. Venizelos urged Greek entry on the British side, seeing in the conflict possibilities for the 'liberation' of Greeks in Thrace and Asia Minor; the new king, Constantine I, married to a sister of the Kaiser, imposed a policy of neutrality. Eventually Venizelos set up a Revolutionary Government in Thessaloniki, and in 1917 Greek troops entered the war to take part in the Macedonian campaign. On its completion – with the capitulation of Bulgaria and Ottoman Turkey – they occupied Thrace, and Venizelos presented at Versailles demands for the predominantly Greek region of Smyrna on the coast of Asia Minor.

It was the beginning of one of the most disastrous episodes in modern Greek history. Venizelos was authorised to move forces into Smyrna in 1919 but, by then allied support had evaporated and in Turkey itself a new nationalist movement was taking power under Mustafa Kemal, or Ataturk as he came to be known. In 1920 Venizelos lost the elections and monarchist factions took over, their aspirations uncontrolled by the Cretan's skill in foreign diplomacy. Greek forces were ordered to advance upon Ankara in an attempt to bring Ataturk to terms: the **Second Balkan War** was launched and swiftly brought to a close as Turkish troops forced the Greeks back to the coast and a hurried evacuation from Smyrna. As they left the Turks moved in and systematically massacred the city's Armenian and most of its Greek populations.

There was now no alternative but for Greece to accept Ataturk's own terms, formalised by treaty in 1923, which ordered the **exchange of ethnic and religious minorities** in each country. Turkey was to accept 390,000 moslems resident on Greek soil. Greece, mobilised continuously for the last decade and with a population of under 5 million, was faced with the resettlement of over 1,300,000 refugees.

Changes, inevitably, were intense and far reaching. The great agricultural estates of Thessaly were finally redistributed, both to Greek tenants and refugee farmers, and huge shanty towns grew into new quarters around Athens, Piraeus and other cities, a spur to the country's almost non-existent industry. Politically, too, reaction was swift. A group of army officers moved in after the retreat from Smyrna, 'invited' Constantine to abdicate and executed five of his ministers. Democracy was restored with the proclamation of a republic – but for much of the next decade changes in government were brought about by factions within the armed forces. Meanwhile, among the urban refugee population, unions were being formed and the Greek Communist Party (KKE) was established. By 1936 it had enough democratic support to hold the balance in parliament: and would have done so had not the army and king decided otherwise.

King George II had been restored by a plebiscite held – and almost certainly manipulated – the previous year, and so presided over an increasingly factionalised parliament. In April 1936 he appointed as prime minister **General John Metaxas**, despite the latter's support from only six elected deputies. Immediately a series of KKE organised strikes broke out and the king, ignoring attempts to form a broad liberal coalition, dissolved parliament without setting a date for new elections. It was a blatantly unconstitutional move and opened the way for five years of ruthless and at times absurd dictatorship.

Metaxas averted a General Strike with military force and proceeded to set up a state very much along fascist models of the age. Left-wing and trade union opponents were imprisoned or forced into exile, a youth movement and secret police set up, and rigid censorship imposed – extending even to passages of Thucydides. It was, however, at least a Greek dictatorship, and though Metaxas was sympathetic to Nazi organisation he completely opposed German or Italian domination. When Mussolini occupied Albania and sent an ultimatum demanding passage for his troops through Greece, Metaxas responded with the one-word answer '*ohi*'. The date, 28 October 1940, marked the entry of Greece into the **Second World War**, and is still celebrated as a National Holiday.

Well prepared – and fighting as a country in a sudden unity of crisis – the Greeks drove Italian forces from the country and in the operation took control of the long coveted, predominantly Greek, north of Epirus. The war soon passed into a new phase, however, and by the end of May 1941 airborne German invasion forces had completed the occupation of both Crete and the mainland. Metaxas had died before their arrival, but King George and his new self-appointed ministers fled into exile in Cairo; few Greeks, of any political persuasion, were sad to see them go.

The **German occupation** of Greece was among the bitterest experiences of the war in Europe: Thessaloniki's Jewish community was massacred, as were whole villages of the Peloponnese and, particularly, Crete. With a quisling government in Athens – and an unpopular, discredited Royalist group in Cairo – the focus of Greek political and military action over the next four years passed entirely to the EAM, or National Liberation Front. By 1942 it was in virtual control of most areas of the country, working with the British on tactical operations, with its own army (ELAS), navy and both civil and secret police forces. On the whole it commanded popular support throughout Greece, a natural structure for the resumption of post-war government: except that its membership were communists, and Churchill and Truman were determined to re-impose King George II.

Even with two years of the war to run it became obvious that there could be no peacable post-liberation option other than an EAM-dominated republic. And accordingly in August 1943 representatives from each of the main resistance movements – including two non-communist groups – flew from a makeshift airstrip in Thessaly to ask for guarantees from the 'government' in Cairo that the king would not return unless a plebiscite had first voted in his favour. Neither the Greek nor British authorities would consider the proposal and the one possibility of averting **civil war** was lost.

EAM returned divided, as perhaps had been the British intention, and a conflict broke out between those who favoured taking peaceful control of any government imposed after liberation, and the hard-line, mainly Macedonian, guerillas who believed such a position could not be allowed to develop. In October 1943, with fears of an imminent British liberation force and takeover, ELAS launched a full-scale attack upon its Greek rivals; by the following February, when a ceasefire was arranged, they had wiped out all but the EDES, a monarchist grouping believed in part to be armed by the Germans. At the same time other forces were at work, with both the British and Americans infiltrating units into Greece in order to prevent the establishment of communist government when the Germans began withdrawing their forces.

In the event, as the Germans began to leave in October 1944, most of the EAM leadership agreed to join a British-sponsored 'official' interim government. It quickly proved an error, however, for with 90 per cent of the countryside under their control the communists were given only one-third representation, the king showed no sign of renouncing his claims, and in November Allied forces ordered ELAS to disarm. On 3 December all façades were dropped: the police fired on a communist demonstration in Athens and fighting broke out between ELAS and British troops. A truce of sorts was negotiated the following spring but in 1947 guerilla activity had again reached the scale of a full civil war.

By this time the Americans, putting into action the cold war Truman doctrine, had taken virtual control of Greece, their first significant post-war experiment in anti-communist intervention. Massive civil and military aid was given to a puppet Greek government with King George II back on the throne and a prime minister whose documents had to be countersigned by the American Mission in order to become valid. In the mountains US 'military advisers' supervised campaigns against ELAS and there were mass arrests, courts martial and imprisonments. Over 3,000 executions were recorded, including a number of Jehovah's Witnesses, 'a sect proved to be under communist domination' according to US Ambassador Grady. In the winter of 1948, with the Yugoslav-Greek border closed after Tito's rift with Stalin, the last ELAS guerillas finally admitted defeat. Atrocities had been committed by both sides, including widescale destruction of monasteries by the left, and it was a demoralised, shattered country which emerged into the modern western world of the 1950s.

It was also, inevitably, an American-dominated state and government, enlisted into the Korean War in 1950 and NATO the following year. The US Embassy in Athens even arranged a new electoral system, which was to ensure victory for the right over the next twelve years of elections. The communist party, obviously, was banned and many of its members went into exile across the borders of eastern Europe; an exile from which some have just been emerging over the last few years.

The American-backed party, which won a decisive victory in 1952, was General Papagos's right-wing 'Greek Rally', taken over after his death (and to some extent liberalised) by **Constantine Karamanlis**. Stability of a kind was certainly found in the 1950s and some economic advances, particularly after the revival of Greece's traditional German markets, but it was also a decade which saw mass depopulation of the villages and migrant work in Australia and western Europe. The main crisis in foreign policy throughout this period was **Cyprus**, scene of a long terrorist campaign against British rule and the sporadic threat of a new Greek-Turkish war. A temporary and unworkable solution was forced on the island by Britain in 1960, granting independence without the possibility of self-determination and union with Greece. Much of the traditional Greek-British goodwill was destroyed by the issue – with Britain seen to be acting with regard only for its two military bases over which it still retains sovereignty.

By 1961, unemployment, the Cyprus issue and the imposition of US nuclear bases on Greek soil were changing the whole political climate: and when Karamanlis was again elected there was strong suspicion of a fraud arranged by the king and army. Strikes became frequent in industry and even agriculture, and King Paul and autocratic fascist-inclined Queen Frederika were openly attacked in parliament and at protest demonstrations. The far right began to grow uneasy about 'communist resurgence' and, losing confidence in their own democratic influence, arranged the assassination of left-wing deputy Gregoris Lambrakis at Thessaloniki in May 1963. (The assassination, and its subsequent cover up, is the subject of Vassily Vassilikos's thriller *Z*, filmed by Costa Gavras.) It was against this volatile background that Karamanlis **resigned**, lost the elections and left the country.

The new government – the first controlled outside the Greek right since 1935 – was formed by **George Papandreou**'s Centre Union party, and had a decisive majority of nearly fifty seats. It was to last, however, for under two years as conservative forces rallied to thwart its progress. In this the two chief protagonists were the army officers and the new king, 23-year-old **Constantine II**, who was their constitutional Commander in Chief. Since so much power in Greece depends on a network of political appointees, Papandreou's most urgent task in order to govern securely and effectively was to reform the armed forces. His first Minister of Defence proved incapable of the task and, whilst he investigated the right-wing plot which was thought to have rigged the 1961 election, 'evidence' was produced of a leftist conspiracy connected with Papandreou's son Andreas (himself a minister in the government). The allegations grew to a crisis and George Papandreou decided to assume the Defence portfolio himself, a move which the king refused to give the necessary sanction. Papandreou resigned, to gain approval at the polls, but the king would not order fresh elections – instead persuading members of the Centre Union to defect and organise a coalition government. Punctuated by strikes, resignations and mass demonstrations, this lasted for a year and a half until new elections were eventually set for 28 May 1967. They failed to take place.

It was a foregone conclusion that Papandreou's party, having moved towards the left in the course of events, would win massive popular support against the discredited coalition partners. And it was equally certain that there would be some sort of anti-democratic action to try and prevent them from taking power. Constantine was said to have briefed senior generals for a *coup d'état*, to take place ten days before the elections, but was himself forestalled by an earlier coup conducted by a group of 'unknown' colonels. It was, in the words of the current prime minister, 'the first successful CIA military putsch on the European continent'.

The **colonels' junta**, in control of the means of power, was sworn in by King Constantine and survived a half-hearted counter coup which he attempted to organise. It was an overtly fascist regime, absurdly styling itself as the true Revival of Greek Orthodoxy against western 'corrupting influences'. All political activity was banned, trade unions were forbidden to meet, the press was so heavily censored that many papers stopped printing, and thousands of 'communists' were arrested, imprisoned and often tortured. Among them were both Papandreous, the composer Mikis Theodorakis (reported as 'unfit to stand trial' after 3 months' custody), and the best known Greek actress, Melina Mercouri, who was stripped of her citizenship. Culturally, the colonels put an end to popular music (closing down most of the Plaka clubs) and inflicted ludicrous censorship on literature and the theatre, including once again a ban on production of the Classical tragedies.

They lasted for seven years, opposed by the Greek people, excluded from the European community, but propped up and given massive aid by US presidents Lyndon Johnson and Nixon. To the Americans and the CIA they were not an unsuitable client state: human rights considerations were unimportant (then as now), orders were placed for sophisticated military technology, and foreign investment on terms highly unfavourable to Greece was open to the multinational companies. It was a fairly routine scenario for the exploitation of an underdeveloped nation.

Opposition, from the beginning, was voiced by exiled Greeks in London, the United States and western Europe, but only in 1973 did demonstrations break out openly in Greece. On 17 November the students of Athens **polytechnic** began an occupation of their buildings. Tanks were brought out on to the streets and eighteen students were shot dead. Martial law was imposed, and the junta chief Colonel Papodopoulos replaced by the even more noxious and reactionary Brigadier Ioannides, head of the Secret Police. The end, however, came within a year as the dictatorship embarked on a disastrous politcal adventure in **Cyprus**: attempting to topple the Makarios government and impose *en-*

osis on the island, they provoked a Turkish invasion, occupation and partition of 40 per cent of the land. The army finally mutinied and Karamanlis was invited to return from Paris to take office. He negotiated a ceasefire (but no solution) in Cyprus, withdrew from NATO and warned that US bases would have to be removed except where they specifically served Greek interest. In November 1974 he was rewarded by a sizeable majority in elections, with a centre and socialist opposition – the latter PASOK, a party newly formed and led by Andreas Papandreou.

New Democracy, the majority government, were in every sense a safe conservative option. But to **Karamanlis**'s enduring credit it oversaw an effective and firm return to democratic stability, even legitimising the KKE communist party which had been outlawed for nearly thirty years. A referendum was held on the monarchy – in which 59 per cent of Greeks rejected the return of Constantine – and Karamanlis instituted in its place a French-style presidency, which post he has himself occupied since 1980. Economically there were limited advances although these were more than offset by inflationary defence spending (the result of renewed tension with Turkey) and hastily negotiated entrance into the EEC.

Still more important, vital reforms in bureaucracy, social welfare and education were not forthcoming; and though the worst figures of the junta were brought to trial the ordinary faces of Greek political life and administration were little changed. By 1981 inflation was hovering around 25 per cent, and it was estimated that tax evasion was depriving the state of one-third of its annual budget. In foreign policy the US bases had remained and it was felt that Greece, back in NATO, was still acting as hardly more than an American satellite state. The return of the traditional right had undoubtedly proved stagnant.

Pasok: The Politics of Change

Allagi. The word means 'change' and was a keyphrase in the election campaign that swept **Andreas Papandreou**'s PASOK party into power on 18 October 1981. The campaign, even by Greek standards, had been passionate – with a real belief among the people that Andreas (as he's universally known) could offer radically different, socialist, solutions where thirty years of right-wing rule had manifestly failed. PASOK, who had built up a web of activists in virtually every town and village in the country, put their alternative policies across in a series of highly effective symbolic posters (ranging in issues from sexual equality to the problems of small businesses) and at their major rallies attracted crowds well in excess of 150,000. The party's green rising sun logo was painted everywhere, carved into hillsides, and the word *socialismo* was on everybody's lips; and by election day only the western media was taken by surprise at the scale of PASOK's victory. They took 174 out of the 300 parliamentary seats, the conservative New Democracy moving into opposition with 113, with KKE-Exoterikou (the Moscow-aligned half of the Greek communist party) returning the other 13 deputies, among them the composer Mikis Theodorakis.

Five years ago – and certainly ten, or twenty – such a break in the Greek political mould would have been unimaginable. And even in 1981 there were fears whether transition to a socialist government could be completed without interference by the military. Although these proved unfounded they were intensely focused for many Greeks when Andreas, in his first move as Prime Minister, announced that he would assume the Defence portfolio, the same position that had been denied his father and had ultimately led to the Colonels.

Broader doubts – as to whether PASOK could pursue their foreign policies without American interference – are, however, fast becoming confirmed. 'That's too bad,' said President Reagan on hearing of PASOK's election and pledge to withdraw from NATO, 'we'll have to see what can be done.' What has been done is all too clear. With the US turning Turkey into their major Near East base and providing massive amounts of military and civil aid to its military junta, the Greeks have had to make concessions to retain their own 'balancing' military aid. The NATO withdrawal has been dropped and an election commitment to remove US bases watered down to an agreement to phase them out by 1990. On a positive front, however, Papandreou has sought international support for a 'nuclear free Balkans' and is attempting to adopt a more non-aligned position in the United Nations.

In Greece itself the honeymoon period of PASOK is now definitely over, with increased unemployment and little progress in the promised 'socialisation' of industry, in education, nor in welfare benefits. They have, however, made more impact in social reforms – and this may well turn out to be Papandreou's most lasting achievement. Civil marriage has been introduced, the voting age lowered, women's rights established in law (see p. 13), the penal system improved and capital punishment abolished. Whether they can go further than this, and really begin to implement radical ideas into the economy and state, will depend to a great degree on the new 'green guards' who have been placed in positions long occupied by what the *Guardian* described as 'the smooth, hard-faced men in dark suits, dark glasses and Mercedes'. In Greek bureaucracy it seems impossible to completely remove the old business of *rousfeti*, or patronage, but in replacing senior diplomats, military officers and civil servants, and in disbanding a staggering 50,000 quangos, there must be some hope of improvement.

There are three **peace movements** in Greece, the most powerful of them, KEDEA (Valaoritu 1, Athens), directly aligned with PASOK. AKE (Non-aligned Peace Movement, Solonos 74) is a small group broadly associated with the Euro-Communists and the Greek left. The long-established Centre for International Détente and Peace (Chalkokondili 4, Athens) is run by the official KKE.

At the time of publication a new 'International Group for Nuclear Disarmament' has just been established in Athens. Organised by a number of British, Scandinavian and Dutch teachers, it welcomes all contact with anyone working or living in, or just passing through, Athens. The group can be contacted on tel. 895 8349 or 252 9846. Meetings are currently held in the AKE offices.

BOOKS

Travel

Patrick Leigh Fermor *Roumeli* (Penguin £2.95); *Mani* (Penguin £2.95). These are not really travelogues: Fermor is more an aficionado of the vanishing minorities, relict communities and disappearing customs of rural Greece. Authoritative scholarship interspersed with strange and hilarious yarns . . . and perhaps the best books anyone has written on any aspect of Greece.

Henry Miller *The Colossus of Maroussi* (Penguin £1.75). Corfu and the soul of Greece in 1939 – and Miller, completely in his element, at his most inspired.

Lawrence Durrell *Prospero's Cell*; *Reflections on a Marine Venus*; *Bitter Lemons* (all Faber & Faber £1.50/£1.75/ £1.75). Concerned respectively with Corfu, Rhodes and the developing crisis on Cyprus in the 1950s.

Peter Levi *Hill of Kronos* (Zenith £2.95). Beautifully observed involvement with Greece: its landscape, monuments and eventually politics as Levi is drawn into resistance to the Colonels.

Robert Byron *The Station* (Duckworth, 1929). Not as polished or brilliant as Byron's classic *Road to Oxiana* but a more than interesting account of his travels on Mount Athos and pioneering interest in Byzantine art and architecture.

James Theodore Bent *The Cyclades, or Life Among Insular Greeks* (Argonaut Press reprint 1966). Originally published in 1881, this remains the best account of island customs and folklore; it's also a highly readable, droll account of a year's travel including a particularly violent Cycladic winter. Difficult to find.

Sheelagh Kanelli *Earth and Water* (Hodder 1965). British-born novelist, whose *Nets* has just been published by Women's Press (£2.50), writes of her experiences as a woman marrying into Greek society.

Elias Kulukundis *Journey to a Greek Island* (Cassell, 1967). In this case Kasos, one of the poorest of the Dodecanese: once again as much sociological study as travelogue and immensely readable.

Nikos Kazantzakis *Travels in Greece* (Cassirer £3.95). Rather pedestrian translation of the Cretan novelist's journey around the Morea's Frankish monuments and his increasing alienation.

Kevin Andrewes (ed.) *Athens Alive* (Hermes Press, Athens). Impressions, experiences and accounts of the city from the C4th AD to 1940. A great book.

Specific Guides

Marc Dubin *Backpacker's Greece* (Bradt £4.95). Slightly pricey but well worth it if you plan to do any serious hikes around Greece. Marc, who is also a contributor to this new edition of the Rough Guide, details fifteen trails from around Sifnos to traverses of the Parnassos, Pindus and Olympus mountains. The guide is also strong on general practical details, literally encompassing all aspects from Greek flora to the dangers of tracer bullets on army ranges!

Tim Salmon *Walkers Guide to Greece* (Cicerone Press £4.95). New guide by another Rough Guide contributor. Very stong on the mainland mountain hikes and including an epic trail from Delphi to Albania.

Stuart Rossiter (ed.) *Blue Guide Greece* (Benn £7.95). The definitive guide to all archaeological sites in Greece, over 700 dense pages and hardly a beach to be found!

Peter Levi (ed.) *Pausanias: The Guide to Greece* (Penguin Classic, 2 vols, £2.50 each). Written and compiled in the second century Ad, this is worth considering if you're extensively touring the classical sites. Functionally edited with notes on all modern identifications of sites.

Evi Melas (ed.) *Temples and Sanctuaries of Ancient Greece: A Companion Guide* (Thames & Hudson £1.95). Worth snatching up if you can find it – seventeen very lucid essays on principal sites, written by archaeologists who have worked on them.

A. R. and Mary Burn *The Living Past of Greece: A Time Traveller's Tour of Historic and Prehistoric Places* (Penguin; remaindered £2.25). Unusual in extent this covers *all* the main sites – Minoan through to Byzantine and Frankish – with good clear plans and lively text.

Lycabettus Regional Guides Published in Athens – and available at Compendium (see below) – these are a series of individual guides gradually taking in all the main islands and regions. Most that I've used have paid their way both in interest and usefulness and those on *Patmos* and *The Mani* can certainly be recommended.

David Talbot Rice *The Appreciation of Byzantine Art* (Oxford University Press £3.75). Not exactly a guide but a useful introduction to the subject.

History: Ancient, Classical and Byzantine

A. R. Burn *Pelican History of Greece* (£2.75). Probably the best general introduction, though for fuller and more interesting analysis on the early and classical periods you'll do better with one or other of the following . . .

M. I. Finley *The World of Odysseus* (Pelican £1.95).

Oswyn Murray *Early Greece* (Fontana £3.50).

J. K. Davies *Democracy and Classical Greece* (Fontana £2.95).

F. W. Walbank *The Hellenistic World* (Fontana £2.95).

Homer *The Odyssey*, *The Iliad* (both translated in Penguin). The Odyssey, beyond reasonable doubt, is the greatest possible companion when you're battling with or resigning yourself to the vagaries of inter-island ferries. *Among* other virtues.

M. I. Finley (ed.) *Portable Greek Historians* (Penguin £3.50). Also well worth travelling with – the best chunks of Herodotus, Thucydides, Xenophon and Polybius.

Steven Runciman *Byzantine Style and Civilisation* (Penguin £3.95). Perhaps the main surprise for most first-time travellers to Greece is the fascination of Byzantine monuments – above all at Mistra; this is the best book to begin extending your interest . . .

Michael Psellus *Fourteen Byzantine Rulers* (Penguin Classic £3.50). . . . and this, once it's extended, is among the most fascinating contemporary sources, detailing the stormy but brilliant period from 976–1078.

Modern Greece: History and Politics

Richard Clogg *A Short History of Modern Greece* (Cambridge University Press 1979, £7.50). By far the best general study – a short and remarkably clear account of Greece since 1454 (where the Pelican History ends) with an emphasis on the events of the last decades.

Andreas Papandreou *Democracy at Gunpoint* (Penguin 1972 – but long out of print). Of interest both for the events it describes – the origin and aftermath of the Colonels' coup of 1967 – and as an insight into Andreas himself, now leader of PASOK and Prime Minister of Greece.

Melina Mercouri *I was Born Greek* (Dell 1973). The title words were Melina's response on being stripped of her Greek citizenship under the Colonels' junta. She's now an MP for Piraeus and Minister of Culture in the PASOK government.

Oriana Falacci *A Man* (Pocket Books £1.95). Again an account of the junta years and the most dramatic and compelling of the lot as Oriana recounts her involvement with Alekos Panagoulis, the anarchist who attempted to assassinate Colonel Papadopoulos in 1968.

Evangelos Averoff *By Fire and Ax.* Listed here by way of 'balance', an account of the Civil War years of 1940–50 (and hatchet job on the activities of EAM-ELAS) by the Richard Nixon of Greece . . . and a man heavily implicated in each of the above books. Meanwhile, talking of Nixon, you might be able to find . . .

Colin Spencer *How the Greeks Captured Mrs Nixon* (Quartet) which is actually a novel – satirical and very sharp – on the farce of the colonels and the CIA's inevitable presence.

Vassilis Vassilikos *Z* (Sphere). Another novel but based very tightly on events – the political assassination of Gregoris Lambrakis in Thessaloniki in 1963. It was filmed by Costa Gavras.

Greek Novels . . .

Nikos Kazantzakis *Zorba the Greek* (£1.95); *The Last Temptation* (£4.50); *Christ Recrucified* (£4.95); *Report to Greco* (£3.95); *The Odyssey: A Modern Sequel*; *The Fratricides* (£3.25); *The Greek Passion* (all published by Faber & Faber/Simon & Schuster). The best known Greek novelist, though still almost exclusively through *Zorba*. *Report to Greco* is possibly his finest.

Stratis Haviaras *When the Tree Sings* (Picador £1.95). After *Zorba* the most internationally successful modern Greek novel – surprisingly so, for Haviaras is more poet than storyteller.

Lawrence Durrell *Pope Joan* (Peter

Owen £6.95). Imaginative adaptation of a C19th novel by Emmanuel Royidis.
Alexandros Papadiamantis *The Murderess* (Writers & Readers £5.95). Turn of the century Skiathiot novelist, in a sense 'the Greek Thomas Hardy'.
Demetrios Vikelas *Loukas Laras* (Doric Publications, London £3.50). Classic C19th novel set mainly on Chios.

. . . and Poets
With two Nobel Laureates in recent years – George Seferis and Odysseus Elytis – modern Greece has an extraordinarily intense and dynamic poetic tradition. Translations of all of the following are excellent: British editions are cited but most are available in the US from Princeton University Press.
Odysseus Elytis *The Axion Esti*; *Selected Poems* (Anvil Press £3.50/£6.95).
Constantine Kavafy *Poems* (Chatto & Windus £3.50).
George Pavlopoulos *The Cellar* (Anvil £1.95): less well known poet from Pirgos in the Peloponnese.
Yannis Ritsos *Selected Poems* (Efsta-thiadis, Athens £3.50); *the* poet of the Greek left.
George Seferis *Collected Poems* (Anvil £5.95).
Angelos Sikelianos *Selected Poems* (Allen & Unwin £3.95).
Modern Greek Poetry (Efstathiadis, Athens £7.50). good collection of translations, predominantly of Seferis and Elytis.

Bookshops
Virtually all books listed here can be obtained in London from the **Hellenic Bookservice** (122 Charing Cross Rd, WC2 – opposite Foyles; 01 836 7071) friendly, knowledgeable, devoted exclusively to Greece and well worth browsing around before you set out. Also worth a look – and rather better for second-hand out of print classics – is **Zeno's Greek Bookshop**, just around the corner from the Hellenic at 6 Denmark Street (01 836 2522). In Athens the best source for English-language books on Greece is **Compendium** at 33 Nikis Street in the Plaka (3226 931).

MUSIC

Music – like most Greek cultural traditions – is a mix of East and West. The older songs, invariably in Eastern-favoured minor keys, often have direct comparisons in Turkey and Iran; and almost all native Greek instruments are descendants, or near duplicates, of ones used throughout the Islamic world. To this Middle Eastern base both Slavs and Italians have added their share, and as a result the repertoire of traditional and more modern Greek pieces is extraordinarily varied. It's not difficult to seek them out – though Greeks listen and dance increasingly to cassettes these days – and you *certainly* shouldn't jump to conclusions after suffering through an evening of endless bouzouki riffs in some plasticy tourist *taverna*.

Crete, Kassos and Karpathos
This arc of southern islands is probably the richest musical area in Greece. The main instrument here is the **lyra**, a three-stringed fiddle directly related to the Turkish *kemence*. They are played not on the shoulder but balanced on the thigh, often with tiny bells attached to the bow, which the musician can jiggle for rhythmical accent. The strings are metal, and since the centre one is just a drone the player improvises only on the outer two – a unique, intriguing sound.

Usually the *lyra* is backed up by one or more **laouta**, identical to the Turkish *oud* and not unlike the medieval lute. These are rarely used to their full potential but a good player will find the harmonics and overtones to a virtuoso *lyra* piece, at the same time coaxing a pleasing, chime-like tone from his instrument. A *laouto* solo is an uncommon treat.

In several places in the southern Aegean – notably traditional Karpathos – a primitive bagpipe, the **askomandra** or **samvouna**, joins the *lyra* and *laouto*. During the colonels' dictatorship the playing of the bagpipe in the Cyclades, further north, was banned lest anyone think the Greeks too culturally primitive! Hopefully, all concerned have recovered from any sense of political inferiority. If you remember Kazantzakis's classic novel, Zorba himself played a **santouri**, or hammer dulcimer, for recreation. Today, accomplished players are few and even in *Kritiki* (Cretan music) it's been relegated to a supporting role; except in a couple of Athens *kentra* you're more likely to see the instruments gathering dust in antique shops.

The Cyclades

On most of the Aegean islands, and particularly the Cyclades, you'll find the *lyra* replaced by a more familiar-looking **violi**, essentially a western violin. The music is lyrical and usually up-tempo. Back-up is again often provided by *laouta*, though they're sometimes replaced or complemented by various reed-wailers: the goat hornpiped **keratas**, or **ciftes** and **duduks** – both basically bagpipes without the bag.

Unlike Crete, where you can often catch the best music in special clubs or *kentra*, Cycladic performances tend to be spontaneous and less specialised. Festivals and saints' days are obviously the most promising times and venues but my most memorable recital happened at 10 am one Sunday morning when a 20 ft caique chugged out of Kimolos harbour with two musicians aboard. They pounded and sawed away on a *laouto* and a *violi*, singing in the key of ouzo as they circled the ferry *Ionion*. The execution may have been a little imperfect but their spirit was wildly applauded by both passengers and crew; after a repeat performance around the *Kimolos* just behind us, the little boat did one more pass and headed for port.

Urban sounds: *rebetika*

Most outsiders equate Greek music with the **bouzouki**, though only a fraction of Greek musicians rely on it. The instrument – derived from the Turkish *saz* and *baglama* – has been played in Greece for at least two centuries, but it was only really propelled into the limelight by refugees from Asia Minor in 1923. These Anatolian Greeks used the *bouzouki* and *santouri* as accompaniment to their **rebetika** (literally 'of the gutter') music.

Their melancholy songs, imported from the backstreets of Smyrna, have often been compared to American blues, and there is similarity in both spirit and circumstance. Original *rebetika* was so blatant in their praise of sex and hashish, and so disparaging of the law and honest labour, that from 1890–1930 even possession of a *bouzouki* was pro-

hibited. The **rebetes** musicians, later blackballed by the Greek recording industry, went underground into a network of proletarian, hash-smoking *tavernas* where they had no need to compromise their lyrics. As an authentic tradition it was effectively destroyed by the 1958 outlawing of hashish (organised incidentally, by the US drug enforcement agency) but *rebetika* was rediscovered in the Athenian boites of the 1960s and can still be heard in a few clubs.

Rebetika are subdivided by dance rhythms, most of which were once the exclusive preserve of a particular guild; the slow, plodding **hasapiko**, for example, of the butchers! My own favourite is the **zeibekiko**, named after a warrior caste of old Anatolia. Responding to its compelling rhythm, a man who may have been sitting quietly with eyes closed will leap from his chair and begin a solo response: a pirouetting, self-caressing improvisation, crouching and lunging as appreciative onlookers dash entire tables of crockery to the floor in tribute to his spirit.

The Peloponnese and central mainland

Most of the folk lyrics of the Peloponnese, central and western Greece hark back to the years of Turkish occupation and to the Independence Movement. In the mountains, the simple instrumental music is even more conservative – shepherds play their **floyeres** (flutes) in ways that can differ little from their pre-Christian ancestors.

The main music is **palea dhimotika**, traditional folk ballads with very basic accompaniment on the *klarino*, or clarinet. *Kythara* (guitar), *violi* and tambourine can also add to the backing. Most of the songs are dance pieces, too, and again each region has its own brand – *Epirotiko* (from Epirus) are among the most popular, slow, expressive and almost stately. Since the songs are strongly associated with national identity it's not surprising that they've been pressed into political service: and if you arrive in the course of an election campaign you'll get a free crash course in folk music, each store-front party HQ blasting out continuous *palea dhimotika* interspersed by political harangues.

Thrace and the north

Thrace and Macedonia were in the hands of the Turks only seventy years ago, so music here – louder and less vocalised than in the south – has an unremitting Oriental feel. The Thracian **kaval**, or end-blown flute, is identical to the Turkish articles; so too is the northern bagpipe, or **gaida**. In Macedonia you'll find the **zourna**, a screechy double-reed oboe similar to the Islamic world's *shenai*. It's much in evidence at local festivals, as is the **daouli**, or deep-toned drum. Dances are fast and hard-stamping.

Ionian islands
Alone of all modern Greek territory, the Ionian islands never saw Turkish occupation and have a predominantly western musical tradition. The indigenous song-form is Italian both in name, **kantadhes**, and instrumentation (guitar, mandolin); it's most often heard these days on Lefkada and Zakinthos.

The New Wave: contemporary composers
Neo Kyma – new wave – music emerged in small Athenian clubs, or boites, during the early 1960s. It was in part a rediscovery of the forms of *rebetika*, in part a move towards the politicised folk movements of France and America: and its young, improvisatory composers strongly identified with the left and the communist movement, some of whose revolutionary songs they revived and adapted. Most of the Athenian boites were closed down during the 1967–74 military junta, and those that survived degenerated into expensive glossy nightclubs. Over the last couple of years, however, there has been a revival – centred on three clubs in Tholou Street in the Plaka. See the Athens section, p. 44, for more details.

Though not directly associated with the Neo Kyma movement, Mikis Theodorakis and Manos Hadzikakis – the two best known modern Greek composers – have much in common with its spirit. **Theodorakis** is undoubtedly the most important musical figure modern Greece has produced – and a committed political presence, too, currently a KKE deputy in parliament. If you've only ever heard Theodorakis's music for the film of *Zorba* check out some of the astonishing settings that he's recorded of poems by Yannis Ritsos.

Records and live artists
Discs available in Britain and the US are denoted*; others are stocked by most large Greek record shops. Listings here are obviously highly selective, and are slanted somewhat towards the arcane and the traditional.

Rebetika

I Rebetiki Istoria 1922–55 (EMI Regal 2J048; 6 vols*). The classic anthology – volume one, especially, has some fantastic Smyrneiki and Anatolian pieces. *Prodhromos Tsaousakis* (Melophone SMEL40*). Great renditions of *rebetika* standards, if occasionally marred by hokey accordion. **Dimitris Mitropanos** *14 Zeibekika* (Phillips 633II52*). Currently very popular in Greece – slick sound, okay compositions. **LIVE** Some of the Athens boites and *kentra* (regional folk clubs) feature *rebetika*; try 'Sousouro' (Tholou 17, Plaka) if you're around between September and Easter. *Kostas Kollias*, who died recently in a car accident, had a more traditional sound than Mitropanos: his work is still often performed.

Traditional

Greek Traditional Music: A Musical Atlas of Greece (EMI Odeon/Unesco*). Don't be put off by the subtitle, this is an excellent anthology – as are all the Unesco projects. *Tragoudhia Kai Hori Tis Sterias* ('Songs and Dances of the Mainland'; Minerva 22008). The finest collection of *palia dhimotika* I've come across. **Kostas Zakinthinos** *Pimenika* (Melophone SMEL22). Evocative shepherd's clarinet. **Aristidhis Moshos** *Solo Santouri* (Studio SD22). **LIVE** Watch for *Vasilis Soukas*, a *klarino* player; *Takis Karnavas*, a vocalist who often performs with Soukas; *Thanasis Kapathlis*, interpreter of *palia dhimotika*.

More contemporary Kritiki and Nisiotiki (island) music

Mihael Polyhronakis *Pali Tha Vgo Na Tragoudho* (Pan-Vox X33SPV16204*). Spine-chilling Cretan singing and accomplished *laouto* solos.

Mana Tevendoyenna (Pan Vox X33SPV16168). Almost as good.
Giorgos Biles *Yasou Kapetanissa* (Aegaion LPEG51*). Unusual blend of mainland and island styles.
LIVE Alekos Polyhronakis is among the best *lyra* players around.

FEATURES

The Vlachs: A Vanishing Race
The Last of Europe's Wandering Shepherds
Unless you are a mountain freak you are not likely to come across a Vlach shepherd in his natural habitat. For the Vlachs' homeland is in the remote fastnesses of the Pindus Mountains in north-western Greece towards the Albanian frontier.

Traditionally the Vlachs were transhumant shepherds, although some have long led a more settled existence in villages, notably Metsovo. They are an ancient, close-knit community with a strong sense of identity, like their rival shepherd clan, the Sarakatsans, whom they despise as 'tent-dwellers' and who, in turn, just as passionately despise them for living in houses. Unlike the Sarakatsans, however, their mother-tongue is not Greek, but Vlach, a Romance language, which even today is full of words that someone with a little knowledge of Latin can easily recognize: 'loop' for wolf, 'mulier' for women, 'pene' for bread. 'When the Italians invaded Greece,' a Vlach told me, 'we could communicate with them easily. Vlach soldiers were often used as interpreters on the Albanian front.'

Their language is Latin-based and akin to Romanian. It used to be thought that the Vlachs were Slavs, descendants of Roman legionaries stationed in the provinces of Illyria and Dacia, who over the centuries had wandered down through the Balkans in search of grazing for their sheep and finally settled in northern Greece, where they had been trapped by the creation of modern frontiers on the disintegration of the Austro-Hungarian and Ottoman empires.

Because of these supposed Slav connections and the old Greek anxieties about the Slavophile separatist tendencies of the peoples of northern Greece, the Vlachs have been objects of suspicion to the modern Greek state. To their chagrin many of their villages with Slav-sounding names were renamed in the 1930s, and the school-children forbidden to use their tongue.

There is, however, a new theory about their origins, which argues that the Greek Vlachs are of Greek descent and have always inhabited these same regions of the Pindus Mountains; that during Roman times the Romans found it convenient to train local people as highway guards for the high passes on the old Roman road, the Via Egnatia, which connected Constantinople with the Adriatic. Thus the Vlachs learned their Latin through their association with the Romans and preserved it because of the isolation of their homeland and the exclusive nature of their pastoral way of life.

Sadly, though probably inevitably, the Vlachs' unique traditions are in danger of extinction today. A young Vlach lawyer in Athens has told me that in his grandfather's day the family had 10,000 sheep, and when they set off on the annual migration from their lowland winter pastures to the mountains, it was like a small army on the march, with two or three complete generations together with all their animals and belongings. Nowadays few flocks number more than 250 ewes, and the annual migration takes place in trucks – though a few veterans still do it on foot. Hundreds of Vlachs have sold their flocks and moved to the town or emigrated: many a sheepfold boasts an ex-Volkswagen factory hand. There are depressingly few young among the remaining shepherds. The hardships of their life are too many and the economic returns too small.

Yet to the outsider this ancient pastoral way of life has the magic of the Homeric age about it. Last summer I had the good fortune to stay at one of the loveliest sheepfolds I have seen. It lies on a grassy plateau at the edge of a vast beech forest at an altitude of nearly 2000 metres within sight of the guard post on the Albanian frontier where the first shots of the Greeks' Second World War were fired at the invading Italians. It consists of five huts, rebuilt each year from beech branches. Behind the huts an icy stream cascades 50 metres into a rocky gulley. Above rises the summit ridge of Mt Grammos, where violets, gentians and saxifrages bloom among the collapsed dugouts where the Greek Communist guerrillas made their last stand in the 1946–9 civil war.

Five families live in these huts. Only one was young enough to have a small child with them. Every summer of their lives they have come to this mountain, mostly to these very huts. Among them they have 2000 sheep, which they divide into two flocks and the men take turns to tend them. At the beginning of the summer the ewes still have plenty of milk and need to be milked three times a day by hand. Each morning a train of ponies winds down through the forest carrying the milk to the cheesemaker, who, like the shepherds, comes every season to set up his cheese plant.

The women see to the domestic work, fetching water, cooking and spinning. The huts are kept spotless, the earth floors swept clean as cement. The cooking is done outdoors, in big copper cauldrons over open fires.

In the evening it gets cool – by September there is often a frost at night – and each hut has a fire burning on the floor. People gather in one hut or the other for a little socialising. You have to sit down, on one of the low beds – made like the rest of the meagre furnishings from beech branches – to avoid being suffocated by the smoke, which collects in the roof of the hut. Apart from the fire, the only light comes from the naked flame of a wick floating in oil.

It is a strange and moving experience to sit in the flickering lamplight listening to the wind and the ceaseless, frantic barking of the sheepdogs scenting wolf in the forest edge, and hear the shepherds tell how one of their number, trapped in Albania by the revolution, had slipped off his sheeps' bells and driven them over the closely guarded ridge that marks the frontier one pitch black night in the 1950s.

'There was a lot of movement across the frontier after the war,' one of them said, 'from both sides. The woods were full of people, you were afraid to go in them. I remember, there was a spring where we watered the sheep, close to the frontier. Many times at night, when I came down for a drink, I would hear voices and creep up behind the rocks and there were strangers there. Who knows what they were doing? One time, just after dawn, a man in a suit carrying a small case came up to me and said he wanted to give himself up to me. He was an Albanian doctor. He'd been out on a call, driving through the woods close to the frontier. The woods are very thick there, and he'd just left the car and waited for night to cross into Greece.'

The shepherds are great talkers and have long and detailed memories. The oral tradition is still very much alive among the older ones. 'Our language has no alphabet, so we have no written history. Our grandparents always told us our history.'

Today all Vlachs speak Greek as well as Vlach – in fact, the children, especially of migrants to the cities, often know very little Vlach. I have noticed too that some older women speak Greek with a distinctly 'foreign' accent, presumably because they have mixed little outside family circles.

One morning I set out with the sheep and climbed to the top of Mt Grammos. I found myself sitting on the edge of a crumbling dugout, surrounded by the rusting reminders of war, talking to a shepherd whose sheep were cropping the coarse grass in the screes some way below. 'I was wounded here in 1949, fighting the guerrillas,' he said. 'They fought like devils. We couldn't shift them from their positions. They had to send for the planes to get them out' – as I could easily imagine: an infantry assault on these heights must be virtually impossible. I could not help thinking of the guerrillas crouched here in these shallow holes, their last toe-hold on Greek soil, pinned down, waiting for the planes to come in at eye level and finish them off, like El Sordo in *For Whom The Bell Tolls*. I wondered what the shepherd felt, leaning there on his crook watching his sheep, their bells the only sound interrupting the silence. 'I had nothing against them,' he said. 'They were my brothers. The great powers set us at each other's throats.'

Three hundred metres to the west and a little lower, we looked down on the Albanian border. Three soldiers were patrolling the Albanian side. As we watched they unslung their rifles and sat down in the sun. Beyond them a flock of Albanian sheep grazed under the eye of their shepherd.

'Those are our people,' my shepherd said. 'Vlachs like us. But they haven't even said a "kali mera" to us in thirty years. They never answer when we call, won't accept a cigarette. They're afraid.' But he told me with some envy that they were government employees on a regular salary and a month's holiday with pay. Their flocks had been nationalized.

Wild Flowers of Greece

People who know only the parched lowlands and seashore of summertime Greece would never guess at the extraordinary profusion of flowers that grace roadside, olive grove, city wasteland and rocky hill in spring. Indeed there are few times in the year when you cannot find something interesting.

It is hard to say quite when spring begins. Very early in the year pink, mauve and crimson anemones begin to bloom in the fields and grassy patches among the scrub. On New Year's Day at Cape Matapan, the most southerly point of continental Europe after Cape Tarifa in Spain, I found the stony ground covered with narcissus, a stout and strongly scented variety with multiple flowerheads, called *tazetta*. And all the prickliest and most uncompromisingly hostile bushes had a delicate feathery blue iris growing out of them, *iris cretica*.

February and March are blossom time. First to flower is the almond tree, followed by the wild pear and the judas tree. The judas puts out its gawdy rose-mauve flowers on bare wood before the heart-shaped leaves have had a chance to break. Legend says it is the tree on which Judas Iscariot hanged himself, and this glorious blossom is the tree's blush of shame. Ancient Olympia abounds in judas trees and is a marvellous sight when they are all in bloom.

Chemicals are not as widely used in agriculture as in more developed countries, so the corn fields fill with tulips and poppies. The olive groves are seas of pink and blue. The roadside verges are thick with grape hyacinths and a green iris known as the Snake's Head or Widow iris, because of the black edging of the flowers. The goat-cropped hillsides are waist-high with clumps of green euphorbia and the tall white flowers of the asphodel, which Edward Lear, the English painter and writer of nonsense verse, irreverently calls assfiddles in the copious notes he used to write in the corners of his drawings.

This is also orchid time, and the orchids are one of the most decorative and curious groups of plants found in Greece. Their varieties range from the sedate and upright Holy Orchid of the eastern Aegean islands to the yellow Pale-Flowered Orchid of the mountains to the cool and luscious-looking *italica* and Monkey Orchid, whose compact flower-heads are made up of what look like dozens of wildly waving little pink, white and mauve arms. Their names bear witness to their extraordinary shapes: Man Orchid, Butterfly Orchid, Lizard Orchid. The oddest of all are the insect-resembling *ophrys*. Many species are common and can be seen in the course of any unambitious springtime walk, provided you are alert, for they are only a few inches high and lurk in the shelter of bushes of thyme and spurge. One of the handsomest is the Mirror of Venus, which holds out a shiny glazed lip like blue enamel, just the thing for the Queen of Love to preen in before setting out in pursuit of her beautiful boy, Adonis. He too has given his name to a flower, a small red poppy-like flower which legend has it sprang from the ground where drops of his blood fell when he was wounded out hunting.

Some spring days are so beautiful they make your heart ache. I remember such a day on the island of Samos. The sea shone. The air was clear and blue. Not a breath of wind stirred the cypresses and poplars. The streams were still running and the moist ground, warmed by the spring sun, was host to a ticking, seething variety of insect life. I found wild gladioli in the fields, numerous orchids and, most rewarding of all, a great clump of a now rare red peony growing close to a spring by the terraced apple orchards on the slopes of Mount Lazarus.

I had two other, non-botanical, surprises that day. One was seeing my first Golden Oriole, which must have popped across from Turkey for the day; it is only a mile or two across the narrow straits. The other was finding a little yellowgreen dragon with black swivelling eyes teetering across the path in front of me. It snarled ferociously and frightened me off when I bent to touch it. It was, I learnt, a chameleon. Samos is its only European home.

Altitude of course has a lot to do with the timing of the seasons. Spring comes later in the mountains. By the end of April the thaw is well under way in central and southern Greece. You find dense carpets of crocus in bloom round the edges of the retreating snow, intermingled with the glossy leaves and royal blue flowers of Alpine Squills and pink *corydalis*. Tight clumps of red and white saxifrage cling to the damp rock. Yellow and lilac violets, hellebores, orchids and the blue Mountain Windflower abound in open spaces in the forest.

The flowers themselves are exquisitely beautiful, but your appreciation of them is greatly enhanced by the magnificence of the setting and the excitement of getting to such remote places. Once, coming down from the frozen summit of Mount Athos, I paused at the edge of the forest to examine the green and maroon bells of a fritillary, and there before my eyes was a scene out of Brueghel. A party of monks rode out of the trees in a jangle of harness and reek of sweat, with the bloody carcass of a wild boar lashed across a mule's saddle and hunting dogs running at their heels. Another time, after a nail-clawing traverse along the side of a deep and gloomy ravine, with one eye anxiously cocked for rocks falling off the crag above my head, I came to the supposed source of the Styx, the ancients' river of the dead, which the dead soul had to cross in order to enter Hades. In a cave behind the 70-metre waterfall that gives birth to the river grows a rare and beautiful columbine, named *Amaliae* after Amalia, Greece's first queen.

By mid-summer, when the rest of the country is sweltering in the heat, spring has just arrived in the high mountains of the north. The weather settles down. Sunlight dapples the forest floor. Tortoises appear. Butterflies bask on the warm rock, Peacocks and Purple Emperors and, high up, the handsome Apollo, whose wide white wings are veined with black and stamped with big red roundels. The mountain meadows, fresh-watered by the winter snow, are loud with the bells of grazing sheep.

Helleborines bloom in the forest shade and thick ranks of Marsh Orchid line the springs and watercourses. If you are lucky your trip will be in time to see what, in my view, is the prince of Greek mountain flowers, the Scarlet Martagon Lily.

On the bare, inhospitable slopes above the trees, there is, paradoxically, an even greater profusion of flowers: gentians of an intense burning blue, the lovely rosy-purple violet, *delphinantha*, cranesbills, alyssums and aubretias and all the familiar plants of English rock gardens, or at least their wild cousins.

In fact the flower season never really ends at all. Even in stifling August you can find the white Sand Lily in flower on the remoter beaches. Come September, the cyclamen appear and all the bewildering variety of autumn crocuses, and before you know where you are, spring is on the way again.

Unfortunately, inaccessibility and scarcity do not guarantee the survival of these plants. Some species have already been driven from their original habitats and others are in danger of extinction. The Greek public is not really aware of the uniqueness of this natural heritage and the rallying cries of ecology and conservation have made no impact yet. The havoc wreaked among the still abundant wild flower population of Mount Parnitha just outside Athens every May Day, a day when Greeks traditionally gather flowers, has to be seen to be believed. At the end of the day the road back to Athens is strewn with discarded posies of wilting orchids and dwarf iris.

The work of cataloguing, protecting and promoting this rich heritage of wild flowers is carried on more or less unaided by the tiny staff of the privately funded Goulandris Natural History Museum in Athens. Anyone interested in the flora, or fauna, of Greece ought to contact them.

The museum has also published two very beautiful books on Greek wild flowers, one by the late Dr C. Goulimis, illustrated with paintings by Niki Goulandris, and the other, more recent, by the Danish botanist Arne Strid, on the flowers of Mount Olympos. Other very useful books are *Flowers of Greece* by Huxley and Taylor, and *Flowers of the Balkans* by Oleg Polunin. The latter describes specific areas of Greece (and other Balkan countries) that are particularly good for flower-hunting.

FLOWERS OF GREECE and THE VLACHS: A VANISHING RACE are both by Tim Salmon; 'Vlachs' was originally printed in *The Athenian*.

FEATURES is a new section of the Rough Guides, where we'll be printing contributors' articles on a broad range of Greek-related subjects. Pieces should be between 1000–1500 words and sent to Mark Ellingham, RKP, 39 Store Street, London WC1, England.

ONWARDS FROM GREECE: SOME NOTES

Historically a crossroads between east and west, Greece is well poised for onwards travel. It was for many years a first/last stop on the India overland route and remains a good place to pick up cheap flight tickets there – see the addresses listed under 'Travel' in the Athens section. Closer to hand its four land borders and innumerable international ferry connections from the port of Piraeus offer hardly less interesting possibilities.

TURKEY is the most obvious target, though for many people the recent military junta (still essentially in control of the country) and abuses of human rights make travel here feel a distinctly ambiguous exercise. On the positive side Turks do express a real desire for western contact and their hospitality, at least among the people of Anatolia (on the western coast), rivals even that of the Greeks. It's a sad fact that more Americans and Britons have seen the film *Midnight Express* than have visited Turkey: this, and lurid tales of hassles in Istanbul, shouldn't be allowed to colour your judgment too much. Accounts of sexual harassment probably should – it's a pretty terrible place for women travelling alone.

Visas are not necessary for British, American and Irish passport holders: though they are for Australians, who can get them routinely at the Turkish consulates in Athens or Thessaloniki. **Inoculations** for typhoid and cholera and tablets for malaria are, however, strongly recommended. It's best to get these before you leave home since the injections are more effective with a booster six weeks after the initial shot. If you do suddenly decide to set off from Greece get the basic inoculations from the IKA Clinic in Athens – it's at the corner of Leof. Alexandhras and Leof. Kifissias (just beyond the Panathenaikos football ground) and makes a nominal charge. Malaria tablets are not easy to obtain in Greece – have them sent out to you.

The cheapest **approach** to Turkey is by coach from Athens or Thessaloniki to Istanbul. In Athens most of the travel offices around Fillelinon Street have offers; hitching this route is also quite feasible and there's a train, the '604 Express'. Alternatively, you can cross over to the western coast of Turkey from the islands of Lesvos, Chios, Samos, Kos and Rhodes. See their respective travel details for ferry frequencies – and bear in mind that they're all heavily reduced (or stop completely) out of season. Best bet for winter travellers is probably the ferry from Rhodes to Marmaris. At all times of year ask widely around – the NTOG tend not to hold, or suggest, details of Turkish boats. For the distances involved all the Greek island-Turkish coast ferries are outrageously expensive – Samos to Kusadassi, for example, is around £16 one way, getting on for double the cost of Samos–Piraeus! And there's also a hidden charge, a £6 entry permit payable if you're staying in Turkey for one or more nights. All this duly reckoned on, you should find costs once you get there quite phenomenally cheap, and the varied ways of life – ranging through Mediterranean and Balkan to Middle Eastern and Central Asian – of enduring interest.

There are at least weekly boats through the year from Piraeus to the port of Alexandria in **EGYPT**. They cost upwards of around £40 for a student ticket and take two days – most sailing via Crete (Heraklion). Alexandria, an atmospheric but crowded resort, is just under 4 hrs from Cairo – only around £3 by train. In season there are also **flights** virtually daily from Athens to Cairo, not much more expensive than the boats if you've got a student card. All **injections** specified above for Turkey should definitely be obtained for travel in Egypt – malaria tablets are essential and hepatitis inoculation a wise precaution. All nationalities need **visas**, which can normally be obtained on arrival but better in advance from the Egyptian consulate in Athens at Zalakosta 1. One important point is that on arrival in Egypt you must purchase 100 Egyptian pounds (around £70) and if you can't you'll be turned straight back. There's an Egyptian Tourist Office in Athens at Amerikis 10, just off Sintagma. An exceptional **guidebook** to the country is *Travolaid Guide to Egypt* by Michael von Haag, widely available in Britain.

From Athens there are also daily flights to **ISRAEL** (Tel Aviv), currently around £55–£65 one way with a student/youth card. **Boats** from Piraeus to Haifa work out about 25 per cent cheaper and have the added advantage of sailing via Cyprus, allowing stopover possibilities if you work things out carefully. Most also call at Kos and Rhodes. Israeli authorities maintain that no **inoculations** are necessary – though typhoid-cholera is certainly still a good idea – and Americans, British and Australians don't need **visas**; Irish, oddly, do but can pick them up routinely on arrival. A *Rough Guide to Israel* is planned for 1985 publication.

CYPRUS, since the 1974 Turkish invasion and occupation of the northern half of the island, has been relatively (and unjustly) ignored by many travellers. It's easily and not too expensively reached by ferry from Piraeus, Kos, Rhodes and Crete; or by flights from Athens and Rhodes. Information and maps are dispensed in Athens by the Cyprus Tourist Office at Fillelinon 10 and at all the (Greek) points of arrival. To stay in the Turkish occupied half you have to go there from Turkey.

Some 90 per cent of Greek visitors who come overland through **YUGOSLAVIA** pass through without getting off the train or coach and get totally the wrong impression. That particular journey *is* notably grim but a more libellous representation of the country would be hard to find.

Even if you've only a couple of days it's worth getting off the main route for an initial look: getting in poses no problem since a full passport acts as a visa and entitles you to stay for up to 30 days, and the main border crossing at Gevalija (90 km from Thessaloniki) puts you within striking distance of two particularly compelling regions. Beyond Skopje and Yugoslav Macedonia is the Albanian-dominated moslem province of **Kosovo**, and heading from here to the sea you come upon **Montenegro** with the best beaches and least tourists on the whole coastline.

Money is *New Dinars*, of which you can (and should) take 1500 into the country: rates are slightly better on the Greek exchange. **Buses** are excellent and go everywhere: avoid trains which are not and do not. Like Greece the cheapest places to stay are private **rooms** in people's houses, which you obtain by going along to the Tourist Biro found in almost any sizeable place. For a really full treatment check out the newly-researched *Rough Guide to Yugoslavia*.

For information on the ferries from Greece to **ITALY** see the 'Getting There' section in BASICS (p. 4). Never buy railway tickets for through travel across Italy when you're in Greece – it works out around 20 per cent extra.

INDEX

HELP US UPDATE

This is the second edition of **The Rough Guide to Greece** and we've considerably expanded it – adding new maps and plans, reams of fresh practical information and even a few 'new' islands unmarked on most maps. Much of the credit for all this rests with travellers who have used the book and sent us accounts, for which we're always really grateful. If you reckon we've got something wrong, or you feel more needs to be said about a particular island or place please let us know. We'll send a free copy of the new edition (or another of the Rough Guides if you prefer) for the best letters. Send them along to Mark Ellingham,

RKP Rough Guides,
39 Store Street,
London WC1E 7DD.